Kierkegaard's Ethic of Love

DIVINE COMMANDS AND MORAL OBLIGATIONS

C. STEPHEN EVANS

OXFORD

UNIVERSITY PRESS

OXFORD

UNIVERSITY PRESS

Great Clarendon Street, Oxford OX2 6DP

Oxford University Press is a department of the University of Oxford.
It furthers the University's objective of excellence in research, scholarship,
and education by publishing worldwide in

Oxford New York

Auckland Bangkok Buenos Aires Cape Town Chennai
Dar es Salaam Delhi Hong Kong Istanbul Karachi Kolkata
Kuala Lumpur Madrid Melbourne Mexico City Mumbai Nairobi
São Paulo Shanghai Taipei Tokyo Toronto

Oxford is a registered trade mark of Oxford University Press
in the UK and in certain other countries

Published in the United States
by Oxford University Press Inc., New York

British Library Cataloguing in Publication Data
Data available

Library of Congress Cataloging in Publication Data
Data available

ISBN 0–19–927217–4

1 3 5 7 9 10 8 6 4 2

Typeset by Kolam Information Services Pvt. Ltd, Pondicherry, India.
Printed in Great Britain
on acid-free paper by
Biddles Ltd., King's Lynn, Norfolk

KIERKEGAARD'S ETHIC OF LOVE

To
Joel and Janis Carpenter,
Good and Loving Friends

PREFACE

In the last thirty years there has been a resurgence of interest in divine command theories of moral obligation. There has also been renewed attention and appreciation for Kierkegaard as an ethical and not merely a religious thinker. Some of those interested in the former, such as Philip Quinn and Robert Adams, have also been interested in the latter. However, there has been no systematic attempt to look at Kierkegaard as a moral philosopher that takes into account contemporary developments in divine command theory. I have tried to remedy this lack in this work. The book is, however, by no means a comprehensive treatment of Kierkegaard as an ethical thinker. Its focus is limited mainly to the area of moral obligations, though it sees such obligations as nested within a broader theory of the good that is not a divine command theory. I centre my attention on the meta-ethical issues concerning the nature and foundation of moral obligation, but it is not possible to separate a discussion of these issues from primary normative questions about our actual moral obligations.

I am convinced that this book will serve at least two audiences: those interested in Kierkegaard studies, and those simply interested in moral philosophy generally. I think that Kierkegaard scholars have not paid sufficient attention to the crucial role the related notions of divine command and divine authority play in Kierkegaard's writings, and I hope this book will make it evident how important these ideas are for Kierkegaard. Secondly, I think many moral philosophers still underestimate the power and attractiveness of a divine command theory of obligation. Those who do will, I hope, be challenged by the version of this view I develop and attribute to Kierkegaard. To make this case I include three chapters where I compare Kierkegaard's view favourably to some contemporary secular alternatives.

I am particularly hopeful that taking Kierkegaard as an exemplar of a divine command theory of moral obligation will make it possible to see such a theory as a viable competitor in a secular, pluralistic society. For, as I argue in the concluding

viii   *Preface*

chapter, no one is more sensitive than Kierkegaard to the dangers of politically privileging any particular religion.

The ideas for this book began in an article I was invited to write for the volume, *Christian Theism and Moral Philosophy*, edited by Michael Beaty, Carlton Fisher, and Mark Nelson. I thank them for prodding me to think about these issues, and also David Solomon, who urged me to develop the article into a book. There are many others to whom I owe a large debt. The National Endowment for the Humanities awarded me a 'Fellowship for College Teachers' which, along with a sabbatical from Calvin College, made possible the completion of the first draft during the year 2000–1. Westmont College invited me to be a Scholar-in-Residence for that year, and I am also grateful for the hospitality of that community and the excellent working and living environment provided. Baylor University provided me with research time for the succeeding year that allowed the book to be refined and polished.

My friend and former colleague John Hare, from whom I have learned a lot about divine command theories of obligation, gave the whole work a careful reading and critique, and as a result it is a much better book than it would otherwise have been. Robert Roberts, who has been a true friend for more years than either of us would care to admit, also read several chapters, and the entire Baylor Philosophy Department discussed one chapter in its colloquium. Finally, my research assistant at Baylor, Mark Tietjen, helped greatly by preparing the Bibliography, hunting down and checking many references, and preparing the index. My heartfelt thanks to all of the above.

C.S.E.

Baylor University
17 February 2003

CONTENTS

1

God and Moral Obligation: Is a Link Possible?

Dostoevsky's *The Brothers Karamazov* is well known for posing the claim that if God did not exist, then 'everything would be permitted'. A great many ordinary religious believers, and quite a few unbelievers, continue to believe in a link between morality and God. They are inclined to think that the existence of objective moral obligations depends in some way on the existence of God. The believers among them hold that both the obligations and God are real, while unbelievers who link morality to God are inclined to think that moral obligations are not truly objective, but rather are subjective or relative, being cultural or personal constructions. We would need God to have genuinely objective moral obligations on such a secular view, but—fortunately or unfortunately—God is not available.

What do I mean when I speak of objective moral obligations? This is by no means a simple question. The first task is to explicate the notion of an obligation, for not all obligations are moral obligations. There are, for example, legal obligations, social obligations, and familial obligations, all of which overlap somewhat with moral obligations. Synonyms for the notion of obligation can of course be given; an obligation is a duty, something that is required of us. It is, however, unlikely that anyone who does not know what an obligation is will be enlightened by such answers. Perhaps it is best to begin with simple examples of obligations that are not necessarily moral in character: By virtue of being best man at a wedding, I am socially obligated to propose a toast in honour of the happy couple. By virtue of being a citizen of the United States, I am legally obligated to file an income tax return.

Such obligations often overlap with moral obligations but not always. We can easily imagine legal and social obligations that are in fact immoral in character. Consider, for example, the situation in which I live in a racist society and I am legally obligated to discriminate against members of a minority group. In such a case my legal and moral obligations do not coincide.

I believe that there are two characteristics that help to distinguish moral obligations from other kinds: being overriding and being objective in character. One of the characteristics of moral obligations is that they are generally in some way overriding and final. If I am morally obligated to treat members of a minority group with fairness and respect, then this obligation will override any legal obligation to behave differently. To say of moral obligations that they are objective is just to say that they are the kind of thing individuals—and even whole societies—can be right or wrong about. They do not depend on the contingent beliefs, actions, customs, or emotions of particular individuals or groups.

A third characteristic often associated with moral obligations is universality. We often think of moral obligations as holding for all societies and times in ways that could not be true for obligations generated by particular social relations. I believe that many of our moral obligations are indeed universal in this way, and it is for this reason that we associate morality with universality. Though I want to allow that there might also be particular obligations that are binding only on certain individuals and groups, an important group of moral obligations hold for all people. Universality is also associated with morality when one considers the scope of moral obligation. I do not have moral obligations merely to my family, friends, and fellow citizens; rather I have moral obligations to all people.

Here are some other examples of such moral obligations: I am morally obligated to come and help my neighbour Joe move his belongings on Saturday morning when I have promised him that I would do so. As a parent I am morally obligated actively to care for my children by doing what I can to see that they are properly fed, housed, educated, and so on. I am morally obligated not to take a piece of jewellery from a store without paying for it. In general, concrete moral obligations are duties to perform or refrain from performing specific actions or series of actions, or to acquire certain characteristics. It is important that we have duties that pertain not only to actions but to those character traits we call virtues. However, for the sake of conciseness, I shall in what follows speak only about duties that pertain to actions.

To say that such obligations are objective is simply to say that it is possible for humans to be mistaken about them. We can believe ourselves to be obligated or feel obligated when we are not. We can be obligated without any awareness that this is the case. 'Objectivity' in this sense is quite compatible with a recognition that obligations are typically matters of subjective concern, the kinds of things that tend to move us when we are aware of their reality, and which we typically notice by way of emotions.

Obligations are by no means the whole of morality. Moral theory must treat such things as a positive concern for goods of many types as well as the development of those moral traits usually designated virtues. In due course I will consider the relation of moral obligations to some of the other dimensions of the ethical life, since there are important connections between obligations and such topics as the good, for example. Nonetheless, moral obligations are themselves a significant aspect of morality; parents usually work hard to see that their children develop an understanding of their moral duties and a concern for fulfilling them. It is safe to say that our understanding of morality would be fundamentally transformed if we came to believe that there were no such things as moral duties. If moral duties do depend on God in some significant way, this is not a trivial matter.

There are several ways that God and moral duties might be linked. The most fundamental way is ontological: God might be responsible for the existence or reality of moral obligations. This ontological relationship could be conceived in various ways: as one of identity, causal dependence, or supervenience, for example. It is this kind of link that is the main focus of this work. However, it is important to see even at the outset that such an ontological connection could be related to other kinds of links between God and morality. If moral obligations depend on God, for example, this might have epistemological consequences that could run in various directions.

One might, for instance, claim that a person must know something about moral obligations in order properly to know

God, or at least that knowing about such moral obligations provides one way of coming to know God. Alternatively, one might claim that a person must know God in some way in order to know something about moral obligations. (The latter claim might be more plausible for some subclass of moral obligations that is linked directly with God, such as an obligation to have an attitude of gratitude to one's creator.) There are various ways this could be construed. The religious believer does not have to defend the implausible claim that people who do not know about God do not understand moral obligation at all. Rather, one might hold that a person who does not know about God might know a lot about moral obligations without realizing that at the deepest level those obligations depend on or even consist in a relation to God. Such a person might have some understanding of moral obligation but not realize precisely what the nature of moral obligation is, just as a scientifically uneducated person might recognize and know what water is without realizing that water is H_2O.

Moral duties and religious faith could also be linked psychologically or motivationally. For example, faith in God (or gratitude or some other attitude) might provide a reason for striving to fulfil one's moral duties. Such a thesis is sometimes put negatively, as a claim that without a divine giver of rewards and punishments, there would be less motivation for moral action. My own view is that a positive version of this claim is more plausible: it seems likely that faith in God provides a kind of motivation for moral action that is not available to unbelievers. There is no reason to think that such motivations consist solely or even mainly of desires for rewards and fears of punishments, though this is not to say that rewards and punishments do not have a role to play.

Though the idea that God and moral obligation are linked has popular appeal, it is rejected by the great majority of philosophers today, and I shall explore the reasons for the lack of philosophical appeal in due course, along with a look at alternative, secular perspectives on 'the foundations of ethics' problem.[1] Neverthe-

---

[1] Throughout this book I shall treat 'ethics' and 'morality' as synonyms, though I realize some philosophers make various distinctions between the two.

less, religious views of the foundations of ethics are once again receiving serious consideration. Robert Adams and Philip Quinn have recently defended plausible versions of the metaphysical linkage claim by defending a 'divine command theory' of moral obligation, a type of theory widely regarded as discredited only a few years ago.[2] This kind of meta-ethical theory entails a direct link between God's reality and this aspect of morality, and Adams argues that part of the strength of a divine command theory is that it gives a plausible view as to how humans are motivated to live morally.

More recently, Adams has developed a magisterial theistic 'framework for ethics' in his book *Finite and Infinite Goods*, which will be discussed at several points in what follows. This book argues that ethics must centre on the Good, conceived as infinite and transcendent, which turns out to be identical with a personal God. Finite goods are good because of their resemblance to God. Within this broadly Platonistic framework of the Good, Adams reworks and expands his divine command theory of moral obligation. On such a theory, ethics as a whole is linked to God, with a special tie between moral obligations and divine commands.

On several fronts then, contemporary philosophy seems open to reconsidering the case for a theistic basis for ethics. I intend in this book to develop, examine, and evaluate an account of how moral obligation depends on God that is derived from the writings of Søren Kierkegaard. A tremendous amount has been written on Kierkegaard's view of God. A good deal has been written about Kierkegaard's views on ethics and 'the ethical'. Not much attention has been given, however, to Kierkegaard's meta-ethical views, his understanding of the

---

[2] See Philip Quinn's ground-breaking work, *Divine Commands and Moral Requirements* (Oxford: Oxford University Press, 1979), and also his article 'The Primacy of God's Will in Christian Ethics', in *Christian Theism and Moral Philosophy*, ed. Michael Beaty, Carlton Fisher, and Mark Nelson (Macon, Ga.: Mercer University Press, 1998). Also see his 'Divine Command Theory' in *The Blackwell Guide to Ethical Theory*, ed. Hugh La Follette (Oxford: Blackwell, 2000), 53–73; and 'Recent Revival of Divine Command Ethics', in *Philosophy and Phenomenological Research*, 50, suppl. (Fall 1990), 345–65, as well as Robert Adams' two articles on divine commands and moral obligations in *The Virtue of Faith and Other Essays* (Oxford: Oxford University Press, 1987).

foundations of ethics. I believe that Kierkegaard holds an interesting version of the view that moral obligations depend on God, a view that deserves thoughtful consideration. In making this claim I do not mean to imply that Kierkegaard gives an extended, explicit philosophical account of such matters. His purposes are not primarily theoretical or philosophical. However, I shall argue that Kierkegaard's writings do contain an account of the nature of moral obligations, an account which is sometimes stated explicitly and sometimes is only implicit in the text. As one might expect, it will not be possible to develop Kierkegaard's meta-ethical position without extended treatment of his normative ethical views as well.

WHY KIERKEGAARD?

Why take Kierkegaard as a discussion partner in such an enterprise? One might begin by noting that Kierkegaard has himself been a significant influence on both Philip Quinn and Robert Adams, particularly Quinn.[3] If Kierkegaard has been a significant influence on two of the philosophers who have done

---

[3] Philip Quinn's works that make reference to Kierkegaard include 'Moral Obligation, Religious Demand, and Practical Conflict', in *Rationality, Religious Belief, and Moral Commitment*, ed. Robert Audi and William Wainwright (Ithaca, NY: Cornell University Press, 1986); 'The Primacy of God's Will in Christian Ethics'; 'Kierkegaard's Christian Ethics', in *The Cambridge Companion to Kierkegaard*, ed. Alastair Hannay and Gordon Marino (Cambridge: Cambridge University Press, 1998). The last paper overlaps substantially with 'The Divine Command Ethics in Kierkegaard's *Works of Love*', in *Faith, Freedom and Rationality*, ed. Jeff Jordan and Daniel Howard-Snyder (Lanham, Md.: Rowman and Littlefield, 1996). Also worth mentioning is a short response, 'Unity and Disunity, Harmony and Discord: A Response to Lillegard and Davenport', in *Kierkegaard after MacIntyre*, ed. John J. Davenport and Anthony Rudd (Chicago: Open Court Publishing Co., 2001). Adams also has shown an interest in Kierkegaard's thought unusual for a contemporary analytic philosopher, and though he is more critical of Kierkegaard than Quinn, he clearly has appreciation for many of Kierkegaard's special themes. See his essays 'Kierkegaard's Arguments Against Objective Reasoning in Religion', and 'The Leap of Faith', both reprinted in *The Virtue of Faith and Other Essays*, and his extensive engagement with Kierkegaard in chs. 12 and 13 of *Finite and Infinite Goods* (Oxford: Oxford University Press, 1999).

the most to develop a contemporary ethical theory that roots obligations in God, then perhaps Kierkegaard is worth considering in his own right.

A second reason that I believe Kierkegaard's views on this issue are worth serious consideration comes from reflection on contemporary pluralistic societies. A major drawback to a religiously based ethic is fear that such an ethic would be sectarian at best, and at worst would positively encourage the kind of strife and division that one might think it is the business of morality to constrain. Certainly, this worry was one of the factors that lay behind the Enlightenment project of grounding morality in reason rather than any particular religious tradition or alleged revelation, a project that Alastair MacIntyre has well described in *After Virtue*, even though MacIntyre believes the project failed. One might think that any attempt to ground an ethical theory in religion necessarily gives that religion, or religion in general, some kind of privileged position in society, and that such a privileged position is incompatible with a genuinely pluralistic, democratic society.

It is hard to name a religious thinker more sensitive to the dangers of giving a religion a privileged position in society than Kierkegaard. His writings as a whole constitute a long, sustained protest against 'Christendom', which is a society in which the nation-state and Christian faith are identified or put into close alliance, whether that be done officially and formally or merely through cultural practices and assumptions. Kierkegaard protests loudly against Christendom, not in the name of some secular, liberal ideal, but in the name of Christianity. As he sees it, when Christianity becomes an official, established religion, it is necessarily prostituted and falsified. So when Kierkegaard argues, as he does in his book *Works of Love*, that ethics must be grounded in the commands of a particular religious tradition found in the New Testament, he does not do so with the aim of giving Christianity any kind of official or unofficial privileged position in society. If Kierkegaard is successful, he provides an intriguing model as to how those whose highest moral allegiance is rooted in religious faith might participate in a pluralistic society without compromising their convictions, but also without asking that religious faith be given any privileged or hegemonic position.

However, the ultimate justification for looking at Kierkegaard's views on the subject must come from the results of
doing so. My conviction that Kierkegaard has something significant to say on these issues can only be defended by actually
showing that his thoughts are insightful, timely and relevant.
This requires not only that we look at what Kierkegaard said,
but also that we put Kierkegaard into conversation with some
leading contemporary thinkers.

DIVINE COMMAND THEORIES AND HUMAN
NATURE THEORIES

I began by calling attention to the recent revival of
divine command theories of moral obligation. I shall try to
show that Kierkegaard's account falls within this tradition.
However, the type of meta-ethical theory that directly
links God with moral obligation is not the only way that religious faith might be linked with moral obligations. The Thom-
istic tradition, inspired by Aristotle, sees ethics for humans as
linked to the happiness to be found through the actualization of
human potentiality. On ethical views inspired by Thomism,
God is the foundation for ethics by virtue of his creating
human beings with particular potentialities, including the potential to enjoy a relation with God. Moral obligations are
genuine, and are even understood by Aquinas as divine commands, but those commands must be understood in relation to
God's purposes in creation and the potential goods there to be
realized. Such a teleological account of how God provides a
ground for moral obligation might be termed a 'human nature
theory'.

Divine command and religiously based human nature theories have often been seen as rivals. By looking at their characteristic strengths and weaknesses, a dilemma can be posed for the
idea of a religiously grounded ethic, based on a variation on a
question posed in Plato's *Euthyphro*. Are particular actions
morally right because God commands them, or does God command those actions because they are morally right? A divine
command theorist might wish to say that the former is the case,
and if so, it appears that moral obligations do indeed depend on
God. However, such a view appears to make moral duties

arbitrary. Would murder, theft, and lying become moral duties if God commanded such actions to be performed?

The religious ethicist might want to say then that God has reasons for commanding us to perform certain actions; perhaps God commands the actions because they are morally right. A human nature theory can say, for example, that right actions are those which fulfil the good potential present in the natural order. It is these characteristics that make the actions right, and since God recognizes their rightness, he commands them. However, in this case, it is not so obvious that moral duties depend on God. One might think that the actions would still possess the right-making characteristics they possess, whatever those might be, even if God did not command them. A secular thinker may argue that the goods that underlie the duties are present whether God has created them or not. A religious person may put a particular gloss or spin on the ethical life, but the reality of moral obligations would not change if God did not exist. Hence, if moral duties do depend on God they are arbitrary. If they are not arbitrary, they do not depend on God. Neither alternative is attractive to a theist.

I shall attempt to show in this book that the above line of thought is wrong-headed. I shall follow the lead of Robert Adams and John Hare in arguing that a divine command theory of morality does not have to see moral obligations as pointless or arbitrary.[4] Rather God's commands are rooted in God's broader teleological vision of the good. This account will bring morality into connection with human nature and what fulfils human nature. To that degree this version of a divine command theory is closer than one might think to a human nature theory. God's commands can be understood as fitting our human nature and as being directed to our happiness. This divine command theory, however, differs from a human nature theory in claiming that moral obligations do not follow directly from human nature alone. On such a view morality fits our human nature, but one cannot deduce our moral duties simply from a knowledge of human nature. In the next section I shall

---

[4] See ibid. 252 ff., and John Hare, *God's Call: Moral Realism, God's Commands, and Human Autonomy* (Grand Rapids, Mich.: Wm. B. Eerdmans Publishing Co., 65, 73–75.

try to show in more detail the role divine commands can play when they are connected to a teleological account. As we shall see, some of the insights of a traditional human nature theory can be appropriated by a divine command account. I shall begin with an account of how religious thinkers have developed human nature theories, and then see how much of this account can be preserved within a divine command view.

HUMAN HAPPINESS AND OBEDIENCE TO GOD

Many influential ethical theories derive from Aristotle, the father of the type of theory I have termed a 'human nature' theory.[5] Aristotle developed the classical account of morality in which it is linked to the actualization of certain potential qualities inherent in human nature. To be happy and generally to flourish human beings must seek to develop those qualities that are distinctive of their nature; certain ways of acting and certain kinds of social arrangements foster this actualization of our humanness and are good. On this kind of view, our moral duties stem from the goods that certain acts and practices make possible. People have moral obligations because they have good reasons to act in ways that lead to human flourishing.

There are of course a broad range of theories that fit within this general type. Obviously, Aristotle himself was not a Christian thinker, and one prominent option in contemporary ethical theory is a return to a naturalistic version of an Aristotelian ethic, the kind of position represented by the work of Martha Nussbaum.[6] Philip Quinn has rightly called attention to the tensions between the Aristotelian picture of the ethical life and the religious stance embedded in the New Testament, remarking that 'Aristotle's optimistic paganism and the grim realities of the Christian drama of sin and salvation are worlds

---

[5] This section draws heavily on my article 'A Kierkegaardian View of the Foundations of Morality' in *Christian Theism and Moral Philosophy*, 63–76.

[6] See Martha Nussbaum, 'Aristotle on Human Nature and the Foundation of Ethics', in *World, Mind, and Ethics: Essays on the Ethical Philosophy of Bernard Williams*, ed. J. E. J. Altham and Ross Harrison (New York: Cambridge University Press, 1995), 86–131.

apart.'[7] Nevertheless, it is not hard to understand the position
of those who have followed Thomas Aquinas in developing
modified versions of the Aristotelian approach that do fit into
a Christian framework. Some evidence for the affinity between
Aristotelian and Christian positions (and the difficulties that
face contemporary secular versions of the Aristotelian position)
can be seen in the apparent correlation between the decline of
religious faith and the increase in 'postmodern' views that are
suspicious of any claims about a universal human nature.[8] Contemporary thinkers who do not believe in a God who created
human beings with a particular idea of what they should be
seem to have difficulty believing there is such a thing as a
human nature that transcends the relativities of history and
culture.

Christian versions of a human nature theory must of course
see our nature as grounded in God's creative intentions. In
creating human beings God gave them a particular nature,
with a distinctive set of potentialities, because he willed them
to become particular kinds of creatures. So human nature theories by no means ignore the divine will.

Such a human nature account of moral obligation can allow
divine commands to play a significant role, as is illustrated by
Thomas Aquinas.[9] In fact, it is arguable that obligations per se
are present in Aquinas in a way that is not true for Aristotle,
precisely because Aquinas sees moral obligations as commanded by God. Without a God who is the source of moral
laws, it is arguable that what we now call moral obligations
would only be 'actions that are good to do', but would not
strictly be obligations. There is a difference between recognizing an action as one that is productive of goodness and recognizing an action as obligatory in a stricter sense. There is

[7] Quinn, 'The Primacy of God's Will', 282.

[8] Though there are counter-trends as well. Evolutionary ethics and sociobiology have produced a new interest in the idea of human nature. See the
discussion of evolutionary ethics in Chapter 10 of this work.

[9] See, for example, the role Aquinas gives to the divine will as that to which
the human will must conform in order to be good. *Summa Theologica of St.
Thomas Aquinas*, trans. by Fathers of the English Dominican Province (Westminster, Md.: Christian Classics, 1948), complete in 5 vols., ii (pt. I–II, Q. 19,
A. 10), 678–9.

therefore a sense in which even Aquinas' human nature theory can be seen as a type of divine command theory. However, for Aquinas, the commands of God, at least according to one prominent school of interpretation, seem to follow for the most part directly from the character of the human nature God has created.[10] A divine command theory in a stronger sense will see divine moral obligations as rooted in a free act of the divine will, an act that is not directly entailed by a judgement of the divine intellect as to what is good in light of human nature. What I wish to do is show how such a stronger theory can be developed that is rooted in views characteristic of a human nature theory, thus narrowing the gap between the two types of view.

To see how a divine command account in this stronger sense can be developed, one must pay close attention to the relational character of human life.[11] One of the central features of human beings that will be emphasized in any plausible version of a human nature theory will be the social character of human life. Human persons were not created as or intended to be solitary individuals. They can only flourish and achieve happiness by relationships with others.

Furthermore, it is very plausible that some kinds of relationships are more consistent with our nature than others in that they tend to be fulfilling and conducive to human happiness and flourishing. For example, I would argue that families, at least when families are functioning in a healthy manner, are social arrangements that embody such relationships. Other things

---

[10] Such commentators as Henry Veatch and Anthony Lisska affirm that this is Aquinas' view. However, other distinguished interpreters, such as John Finnis, disagree. See Henry Veatch, *Aristotle: A Contemporary Appreciation* (Bloomington, Ind.: Indiana University Press, 1974); Anthony Lisska, *Aquinas's Theory of Natural Law* (Oxford: Oxford University Press, 1996), 199; John Finnis, *Natural Law and Natural Rights* (Oxford: Oxford University Press, 1980), 33ff. I am indebted to John Hare, both for pointing out this nuance in Aquinas interpretation, and for suggesting the references.

[11] The argument that follows parallels the one developed by Robert Adams in 'Divine Commands and the Social Nature of Obligation', that appeared in *Christian Theism and Moral Philosophy* along with my own 'A Kierkegaardian View of the Foundations of Morality'. However, I did not have the opportunity to read the Adams essay before it appeared with my own, though I am greatly indebted to his earlier work on the divine command theory.

being equal, life is better when it is lived in the context of a good family. Human beings are generally happier when they themselves have the opportunity to become parents and grandparents, and enjoy close ties with other relatives.

Robert Adams has argued that social relations of this type carry with them obligations.[12] To say this is not to say that the obligations are necessarily moral in character. I have already noted that not all obligations are moral obligations, since one can be legally obliged to do something which in itself may be morally forbidden. The point is that social relations are in fact partly constituted by systems of obligation, even though these obligations may be 'pre-moral' in character, to use Adams' term.[13] People who become parents have an obligation to nourish and care for their children. Most people will agree that children also have obligations to respect and show gratitude to parents who have cared for them in this way, and such obligations are an essential part of the relationships between parents and children. So even ethical theories that link morality with human happiness in a teleological way, presuming a particular view of human nature, will also very naturally link certain kinds of social relationships with obligations of a sort. A religious version of such a theory might interpret those social relations as part of God's intentions in creation. Thus, most Jews and Christians have interpreted the family as a divinely ordained institution, though of course there have been many disagreements over the specific form families should take.

What does this have to do with divine commands? So far it appears that I have developed an account of obligations that are rooted in social relations with no mention of divine commands. Here we need to recall that God, as he has traditionally been understood in Judaism, Christianity, and Islam, is himself a person, and that genuinely social relations are possible with him. Within Christianity, for example, it has generally been taught that such a relation is the highest good that is possible for a human person. It follows very plausibly from this that a need for such a relationship is a constituent of human nature.

---

[12] In addition to the previously cited essay, this relational account of obligation is also found in *Finite and Infinite Goods*, 241–8.
[13] Ibid. 243.

To quote Augustine, 'For thou has made us for Thyself and our hearts are restless till they rest in Thee.'[14] If this is true, then a social relationship with God has a vital importance if humans are to flourish as they are intended to flourish.

It is plausible that this particular social relation, like others, would carry with it specific obligations. In a human family, children owe loving parents respect and gratitude, and, at least while they are young children being supported by their parents, obedience with respect to most things a parent might ask. (Though we would not necessarily think an older child should obey an immoral command.) It is important to note in the analogy that having such duties is consistent with the parents wishing to have their children gain increasing autonomy and thus make many decisions for themselves as they mature.

It is no accident that many religious traditions have conceived of God as like a loving parent. If theism is true, creatures owe their very existence to a being whom they understand to be a just and loving Creator, and it would seem reasonable to conclude that such creatures owe to God respect and gratitude of a particular sort, as well as a duty to obey the commands the Creator might issue to them. (This is also compatible of course with assuming that the Creator might want them to make many decisions on their own, including the decision as to whether freely to comply with his commands.) One might say that a response of love and gratitude to the Creator is fitting and proper in light of human nature and its ends, and that this response gives human individuals a reason to obey God's commands.

These commands might include some that direct humans to live in ways that lead to their flourishing by living in accord with their nature. It would not be surprising that God would issue such commands since his creative intentions are already embedded in that human nature. Clearly such divine commands directed at our good would not be arbitrary. With regard to this kind of case, many of our obligations could be looked at in various ways and might be said to have multiple foundations. One might see such principles as 'good principles of action'

[14] St Augustine, *Confessions*, tr. F. J. Sheed (Cambridge, Mass.: Hackett Publishing Co., 1993), 3.

since they contribute to human happiness, and thus people would have some reason to act on them even if God did not command them. Some of these principles might also have the status of duties of some sort (though not necessarily fully moral duties) because they stem from social relations with humans that give rise to obligations (assuming we accept the claim that social relations as such can give rise to obligations). However, at least some of these principles might owe their status as *obligations* to the fact that they are divine commands, and thus following them is a duty one owes one's Creator, and some of these might not be duties at all if God did not command them.

Perhaps, and this is what a full-fledged divine command theory of moral obligation will claim, *all* truly moral obligations owe their status as moral duties to the fact that God commands them. Though some of our moral duties would be obligations of some kind without God, they would not be part of a system of obligations that has the characteristics we think moral obligations have: chiefly objectivity and overridingness.[15] Actions that would be obligatory in some sense even if God did not command them, because they are essential to social relationships in which we participate, take on a special character when commanded by God, a character that is rightly signalled by designating the obligations as moral obligations.

[15] Some would add universalizability to these two characteristics. While I do want to hold that many important moral obligations are universalizable, and by virtue of this fact it is true that the realm of moral duty applies to everyone, I do not wish to claim that each and every duty is universalizable. As will become apparent from what follows, I hold that there are 'individual essences' and that some duties are uniquely directed to the individuals who have the duties. Even these duties have a kind of universality in that everyone is subject to them; individuality is one of the universal characteristics humans share. We might say that it holds universally that human beings are subject to individual obligations rooted in their unique essences. However, it would be misleading to call such individualized obligations 'universalizable' since they do not apply to any other human beings by virtue of relevant similarities. One might say that the duties are still universalizable, but since the individual essences are unique the relevant similarities are never present, but this move seems to me to generate a picayune sense of 'universality'. I claim in Chapter 5 that there may also be some moral duties that apply to particular groups as well as individuals, since God may issue commands to such entities as families and communities.

Do divine commands do enough work on this view? It might appear that at least some of these commands simply reinforce what would be obligatory anyway. After all, I began from the premise that some social relations involve obligations, and if those relations exist, then one would think the obligations hold, whether or not they are commanded by God. This does imply that even without God, social relations would be the ground of obligations of some type. However, those obligations would not necessarily have the character that we presently attribute to moral obligations. In particular, it seems doubtful to me that obligations grounded in family relationships or friendships would have the absolute character of moral duties. I have already noted that Robert Adams describes such socially grounded obligations as 'pre-moral' and this description seems fitting.[16] I shall later try to show (particularly in Chapters 10 to 12) the plausibility of the claim that it is characteristic of genuinely moral duties that they are not only overriding, but objective in character, and part of a system of obligations that extends to all other human beings.[17] Obligations that are grounded merely in particular social relations to other humans would not have this character.

However, one might argue that the teleological character of divine commands on the view I am presenting undermines the need for the principles to be commanded. On such a view doesn't God just command what it would be good to do anyway? I do not think so. It is a plus for the theory that God's commands are directed towards what is good, and thus are not arbitrary in character. However, it does not appear that the concept of obligation is identical to the concept of that which it is 'good to do'. Many acts are good in this sense without being obligatory. This can be clearly seen in the case of super-ogatory acts. It might be good, even saintly, for me to give a kidney to benefit a stranger, but it is not an act I am obliged to do. It seems quite coherent to claim that a divine command

---

[16] See Adams, *Finite and Infinite Goods*, 243 ff.

[17] In speaking of this system of obligations that extends to all people, I do not mean to claim that there could not be some obligations that apply to particular individuals and groups. This is possible so long as the latter kind of obligations are related in the right kind of way to duties that apply to everyone.

could give an act that was good to do the additional character of being an obligation of a certain sort.

Such divine commands would not necessarily simply 're-inforce' what it would be best to do anyway. For there might be several alternative principles equally good, and a divine command could give one of these principles an obligatory status it would otherwise not have relative to those alternatives. On such a view, moral obligations would 'fit' our human nature, and God's commands would not be arbitrary. However, the obligatoriness of the acts would not stem from that human nature alone, because there are alternative actions, equally conducive to human happiness and fitting to human nature, God could have commanded.

Besides this, God might very well command humans to live in certain ways rather than others even when there is no intrinsic link between those ways we are commanded to live and our happiness. Perhaps, for example, God commands certain things as a test of our loyalty and devotion to him. Part of the process by which our loyalty and devotion is developed might include such testing. One might say that in such a case our happiness is still an end, since following such commands and thereby passing the tests would deepen the relation to God that is itself the source of our deepest happiness. However, the link to our happiness would in that case depend on the fact that these principles are commanded and would not precede the command as a ground.

The link between divine commands and human happiness does not imply that one's specific motive in obeying God is to further one's own happiness. It is true that the relation to God is one that leads to human flourishing inasmuch as God has created us to enjoy this relationship, and thus that we have good reasons to deepen our relation to God by following his commands. Nevertheless this does not imply that such behaviour must be seen solely as self-interested, much less selfish. A child may realize that respect and obedience to parents will contribute in the long run to his or her happiness, but nevertheless particular acts of obedience to the parents may still be motivated by such emotions as respect and gratitude. In a similar way, a human creature of God may understand that his or her happiness will be furthered in the long run by obedience to

God, but still may be motivated to perform specific actions out of love and gratitude towards God, rather than some self-serving motive.

KIERKEGAARD AND THE ETHICAL TASK

The task of interpreting Kierkegaard's writings is a daunting one. The individual works are themselves complex and richly literary, including an unusual mix of poetic images and philosophical analyses and arguments. The number of significant works is also quite large and varied; sometimes it seems difficult to believe they were all authored by the same human being. Furthermore, many of the works are attributed to pseudonyms, poetic creations of Kierkegaard who seem to possess their own perspectives and characteristics. Besides these difficulties, there are of course reasons to doubt that Kierkegaard himself had much interest in developing a view that is recognizable as a philosophical 'theory'. It is therefore no easy matter to develop and defend a philosophical account of anything as 'Kierkegaard's'. I shall therefore devote a substantial part of the following chapters to an account of how the view I wish to defend in this book is situated in Kierkegaard's writings. I will try to show that though Kierkegaard's own interests and concerns are not primarily philosophical, he does, along the way so to speak, sometimes explicitly and sometimes implicitly present views on morality that can usefully be the subject of philosophical attention.

Nevertheless, before we get too immersed in such methodological and textual questions, and the arguments that Kierkegaard does hold a certain view, it seems good to give a preliminary sketch of what that view is. In the remainder of this chapter I shall draw freely on a number of works of Kierkegaard, both pseudonymous and non-pseudonymous, and leave to one side the interpretive questions raised by these texts in their relation to each other. The view that I will expound is, I believe, the view that best represents the perspective found in the most important, mature writings of Kierkegaard, but I ask the reader who may be initially inclined to doubt this to suspend judgement, at least for now. I grant to such a reader that this view is probably not the only account of the ethical and the relation between God and the ethical to be found in that authorship as a whole. If anyone thinks in the end that the view I shall expound is not Kierkegaard's, that will not for me be all that significant. It is enough for me that it is a powerful position that can be found in Kierkegaard's writings, and thus it can be called 'Kierkegaardian' whether or not someone recognizes it as Kierkegaard's own view. The question of the adequacy of this 'Kierkegaardian' view is much more important to me than the question of whether it is to be attributed to Kierkegaard.

But what is the view? I have thus far attempted to sketch a divine command theory of ethics that can incorporate some of the insights of a human nature theory of moral obligation. On this view we are creatures made by God for fellowship with God, and our deepest happiness depends on such a relation, one that requires love and gratitude to God on our part. The relation with God, like other social relations, generates obligations. In this case the obligations to obey God's commands are of a character to merit the description 'moral'. I believe that this is the right perspective from which to view Kierkegaard's ethics. We find in the Kierkegaardian corpus various characterizations of what we might call the supreme task of human life, and a variety of positions have been attributed to Kierkegaard, depending on which book is emphasized. In *Concluding Unscientific Postscript* the pseudonymous author Johannes Climacus tells us that it is 'every individual's task to become a whole person'.[18] Such a 'self-actualization' perspective clearly seems Aristotelian in spirit. The task of becoming a whole person is fleshed out in a proper Aristotelian way with reference to capacities that are both universally human and distinctive in the way that humans exemplify them; to become a self one must develop the capacities for thought, imagination, and emotion.[19]

On the other hand, *Fear and Trembling*, which may be Kierkegaard's most widely read book, seems to breathe different air. Although I will argue (in Chapter 3) that it is a mistake to regard this book as the definitive one for understanding Kierkegaard's

[18] Søren Kierkegaard, *Concluding Unscientific Postscript*, ed. and trans. by Howard V. Hong and Edna H. Hong (Princeton: Princeton University Press, 1992), 346.
[19] Ibid. 346.

ethical views, many authors have attributed to Kierkegaard views drawn from the musings of Johannes de Silentio, the pseudonymous author of this book, who discusses at length God's command to Abraham to sacrifice his son Isaac.[20] This Johannes extols Abraham's willingness to obey God in this respect as a model of faithful action.

In *Fear and Trembling* Abraham's act is characterized as one that cannot be ethically understood. It involves a 'teleological suspension of the ethical' and it is one that Abraham cannot explain or justify to his peers.[21] Abraham is not a tragic hero, the 'beloved son of ethics', who sacrifices one ethical good for a higher ethical good.[22] Rather, Abraham's act is one justified by faith, which is a distinct sphere from that of ethics.

However, this denial that Abraham's act can be understood as ethical seems to presuppose a particular conception of ethics. In *Fear and Trembling* the ethical seems to comprise those duties that can be understood and accepted in the context of human social institutions, relying solely on human reason as it is embedded in human language and society.[23] A divine command given to a specific individual cannot be regarded as 'ethical' on such a view and cannot give rise to what we call a moral duty. Abraham's act may be a religious duty but it is not an ethical duty.

If, however, we have a different conception of the ethical, then *Fear and Trembling* would seem to lead to a different judgement on the relation between Abraham's act of faith and moral duty. Suppose one defines an ethical duty as a person's overriding duty, that which is an actual duty when all things have been considered. Since *Fear and Trembling* seems to

---

[20] I will explain in Chapter 3 why I believe it is a mistake to make *Fear and Trembling* the definitive work to understand Kierkegaard's views of the ethical.

[21] Søren Kierkegaard, *Fear and Trembling*, ed. and trans. by Howard V. Hong and Edna H. Hong (Princeton: Princeton University Press, 1983), 54–67.

[22] Ibid. 13.

[23] Merold Westphal has a fine discussion of *Fear and Trembling* that makes it clear that the book's intended target is not Kantian ethics, but the Hegelian ethics in which the 'universal' is concretely embedded in society. See Westphal, 'Abraham and Hegel', in *Kierkegaard's Critique of Reason and Society* (Macon, Ga.: Mercer University Press, 1987), 76–7.

approve of and admire Abraham's act and sees this religious duty as in some sense higher than his human social obligations and therefore as overriding them, then on this revised concept of the ethical, Abraham's act would qualify as ethical. The view embodied in the book then would seem to be a form of a divine command theory of ethics. This is in fact how *Fear and Trembling* has often been read, even though this contradicts the book's own semantic usage, according to which religious duties transcend 'the ethical'.

If one takes a human nature theory and a divine command theory of ethics as rivals, then the Aristotelian ethical view expressed in *Concluding Unscientific Postscript* appears to be in tension with that of *Fear and Trembling*, read as expressing a divine command theory. However, if we recognize the way in which a divine command theory can build on and incorporate the insights of a human nature theory, as explained in the last section, the tension disappears.

To see how Kierkegaard combines a divine command theory with a teleological view of human nature, we must recognize that for Kierkegaard the potential self we must strive to actualize is a self that was created for a relationship with God. Self-actualization is impossible without a relationship with God, and such relationships are in turn only possible through faith. Someone who has faith in God, that is, someone such as Abraham who wholly trusts in God's love and goodness, will surely have a reason to obey God's commands. A true God-relation (and thus a true self) is impossible without this obedience.

Nor do we have to think that the commands God makes are divorced from our human need to actualize our true selves, for what God asks from us is precisely to become the self he intends us to become. The coincidence of the task of becoming yourself and achieving a God-relationship is expressed in *Fear and Trembling* quite clearly when Johannes de Silentio asks what Abraham's motive is for being willing to sacrifice Isaac: 'Why, then, does Abraham do it? For God's sake and—the two are wholly identical—for his own sake.'[24]

I shall argue that what is true for Johannes de Silentio is true for Kierkegaard on this point: becoming yourself and achieving

[24] Kierkegaard, *Fear and Trembling*, 59.

a relationship with God are not two distinct and therefore potentially rival tasks, but the same task characterized in different ways. The self that I must strive to become is a self that is constituted by a God-relationship. Hence I cannot truly be myself apart from God. However, when I attempt to relate myself to God I find that I am called by him to be the finite self God created me to be. This is captured very nicely in the formula for authentic selfhood given by the pseudonym Anti-Climacus in *The Sickness Unto Death*: 'In relating itself to itself and in willing to be itself, the self rests transparently in the power that established it.'[25]

Kierkegaard's conception of the self as a spiritually and morally qualified being helps him to import a Kantian dimension to what seems formally to be an Aristotelian framework. For example, in *Concluding Unscientific Postscript* it is often said in a Kantian manner that the truly ethical individual does not care about results, but only about whether the individual has willed to do what is right in a pure manner.[26] My ethical task is the Aristotelian one of becoming myself, but when I fully understand the nature of myself, I will see that this involves coming to care about performing moral duties simply because I want to do what is right, since my nature is such that I can only be myself when I care deeply about moral goodness. And this is quite consistent with the view that those moral duties are in reality divine commands. My own happiness and flourishing cannot be defined purely or even mainly in terms of such natural goods as health and prosperity, but ultimately must be measured by my own moral and spiritual development, and such development is inextricably linked to my relation with God and my obedience to him.

---

[25] Søren Kierkegaard, *The Sickness Unto Death*, ed. and trans. by Howard V. Hong and Edna H. Hong (Princeton: Princeton University Press, 1980), 131. On my interpretation the term 'power' here does and does not refer to God. Ontologically, every self is in fact established by God, and ethically we only become ourselves by a God-relation. However, since God has granted humans freedom, it is possible for humans to attempt to ground themselves in some other 'power', a God-substitute. See my article, 'Who Is the Other in *Sickness Unto Death*? God and Human Relations in the Constitution of the Self', in *Kierkegaard Studies: Yearbook 1997*, ed. Niels Jørgen Cappelørn (Berlin: Walter de Gruyter, 1997).

[26] See, for example, Kierkegaard, *Concluding Unscientific Postscript* 135–6.

'THE INDIVIDUAL'

So far I have characterized Kierkegaard's ethical view as a variation on a human nature theory, with the main difference that human nature is construed with a sharper focus on moral and spiritual qualities, rather than 'merely natural' goods. Contrary to a Sartrean definition of an 'existentialist' as one who denies that there is a universal human essence, Kierkegaard affirms a universal human nature that includes some qualities recognizable as essential. However, as we shall see, it makes a significant difference that the self I must become is one that I am *commanded* to become.

The divine command aspect of Kierkegaard's thought can be clearly seen in what is for him an absolutely fundamental concept: that of 'the individual'. God does not create generic human beings, and he does not command us to become generic human beings. Each one of us is created as a unique individual, and the ethical task is to discover that individual identity: to learn to stand before God *as an individual*. This theme is pervasive in the authorship, but I am particularly fond of an image used in *The Sickness Unto Death*, in which Anti-Climacus says that every person has been given a unique name by God.[27] My task is to become myself by discovering that name, learning just who I am in God's eyes. This 'individualism' should not be taken to mean that humans were intended to be solitary, or that they can be understood apart from their relations. On my reading of Kierkegaard, the self is fundamentally relational; it is not possible for a human being to be a completely autonomous, independent self, since the self is grounded in relations to something that is an 'other'. Rather, the idea is that each human being is different from all others, and among the differences that define each of us are the differences in the relations we have with others.

This individualism does not contradict the claim that there are universal qualities that all humans share. Being unique individuals does not imply that we have nothing in common with our fellow humans. There is such a thing as human nature, and this common human nature gives rise to tasks that are

---

[27] Kierkegaard, *Sickness Unto Death*, 33–4.

shared by all humans. But this common nature does not completely define human persons as individuals. There are differences in the way the universal qualities are exemplified, which in turn give rise to differences in the way each of us must carry out our common human tasks. We may all have the task of becoming kind, but we will face different types of difficulties in becoming kind, and we will find that we will exemplify kindness in different ways, owing to our unique abilities and circumstances. Perhaps all persons should develop the characteristic of being generous and concerned about those who are less economically fortunate. For some this might require regular and substantial gifts to the needy, while for others it might require a drastic change in lifestyle, perhaps even divesting themselves of their wealth altogether. Someone who completely lacks material resources will express generosity in yet other ways.

In addition to unique ways of realizing universal qualities, there are unique potentialities that each of us possess as individuals that give rise to the task of developing what Kierkegaard calls differentiating qualities. I may be a gifted poet, musician, mathematician, or athlete, and I must ask how those gifts that are unique to me should be developed and used. God may call me to become a philosopher, or a plumber, and this call will create unique ethical tasks for me.

One might object that ethical responsibilities must be universalizable. I believe that one of the strengths of a divine command conception of moral obligation is that it allows us to see how individual and unique tasks can take on a moral character. However, though such moral tasks are not strictly universalizable, they nevertheless have a kind of universal character. Paradoxically, one of the universal qualities I share with all human beings is uniqueness. One of the ways I resemble all other human beings is by virtue of being different from all other human beings. All of us therefore share the universal task of discovering the implications of that uniqueness.

I believe that what Kierkegaard has in mind by 'becoming an individual before God' is closely related to what some Christian thinkers have discussed through the concept of a *vocation* or *calling*. If we think of a vocation not simply as a calling to a special ministry of the church, or even as a calling to a particular

kind of work or profession generally, but simply as God's call to
a particular person to become what that person should be, then
the concept of vocation can be taken as a fundamental ethical
concept. Each of us is called to become the individual self God
has created us to be, and this calling can be understood as a task
laid on us by divine command. The selves we must become
include a universal human nature which gives rise to universal
human tasks, but these selves are individual both in the sense
that these universal tasks must be carried out in a unique
manner and in the sense that there are genuinely individual
tasks as well. God may then be thought of not only as commanding us to actualize certain human potentialities that are
universally present in human beings, but as commanding individuals to realize those universal possibilities in particular ways
and as commanding them to realize some of the uniquely individual potentialities they possess.

As an omniscient being God is not limited to knowledge of
human nature in general, and he is not limited to the issuance of
'general rules'. God can of course promulgate principles that
are highly specific and detailed in character yet still universal in
the sense that they make no reference to any specific individual
(or place or time). However, if God has truly created human
beings as unique individuals, his commands may also be
directed to individuals as individuals. He knows each individual
as an individual and desires a relation with each person. God's
requirements can then be relative to the particular abilities and
talents God has given to individuals and also to the particular
life situations into which he has placed them. God might ask me
to sacrifice one possibility for the sake of another. Perhaps I
might be called to sacrifice a career as a singer in order to work
as a teacher. Such a requirement might be imposed for several
reasons: to further God's purposes in history, to purify my own
character, to help me acquire some needed virtue, or perhaps
just to deepen my relationship with God and the character of
my devotion to him.

These last ends might justify aspects of my vocation that are
genuinely unique in substance, not merely in the means by
which they realize universal ends. God may call me not only
to achieve universal goods in a unique manner, but might have
specific tasks for me, tasks that will help me realize some unique

quality or ability God intends me to have, or fulfil some unique role that God intends for me.

Some might worry that the notion of an individual calling is a threat to autonomy and individual freedom; certainly versions of such a view that would be inimical to freedom can be imagined. However, for Kierkegaard, freedom is a defining aspect of selfhood, and he thinks that one of the characteristics God calls me to actualize is that of being a responsible chooser, who exemplifies the kind of relative autonomy and freedom that a finite, dependent creature can possess. It is plausible that part of my calling will include demands on God's part that I make some difficult decisions for myself, relying on principles and values that I must personalize, interpret and apply to the particular situation in which I find myself. (We will see in the next section that this kind of creative freedom is particularly necessary for genuine love, the supreme quality that God wishes human persons to develop.) While God may require me to develop certain virtues and live in accordance with certain principles, I must still decide whether freely to fulfil the requirement. Furthermore, in fulfilling the requirements a great deal of room may be left for choices that can be seen as my own highly personal decisions. For example, God may require me to care about a certain principle of justice and work for change, but leave it up to me to decide what kinds of actions directed towards that end will be most effective and consistent with my own particular gifts and situation.

The importance of the idea that God calls us to be individuals is that it keeps in focus the primacy for human beings of the task of relating to God. It reminds us that God is a personal being, and that we can relate to him in a personal way, not merely as the issuer of universal edicts or commands or the creator of universal traits or qualities. God's omniscience is quite capable of conceiving a task for every individual as a unique individual.

Kierkegaard often expresses this idea that every person is intended by God to be such an individual through the concept that Howard and Edna Hong translate as 'primitiveness' (*Primitivitet*). I am not sure there is a better English term for what is meant (though I personally prefer the term 'authenticity'), but the translation can easily be misleading. It does not mean that an individual should necessarily forego modern conveniences or 'return to nature'. Rather, the idea is that there is something within the self that is not merely the creation of society, a set of potentialities given by God that cannot be reduced to fulfilling the social roles handed to one by one's culture. The individual must try to discover this self and become it; God's judgement, not that of human society, is what ultimately matters. *The Sickness Unto Death* expresses this thought very powerfully: 'Every human being is primitively intended to be a self, destined to become himself, and as such every self certainly is angular, but that only means that it is to be ground into shape, not that it is to be ground down smooth, not that it is utterly to abandon being itself out of fear of men, or even simply out of fear of men not to dare to be itself in its more essential contingency (which definitely is not to be ground down smooth).'[28]

An ethic that emphasizes self-actualization is not necessarily egalitarian in character, and it is easy to see why. Since humans seem to differ in potentialities, an ethic that focuses on actualizing such potentialities does not seem friendly towards equality. This is evident from the examples of Nietzsche and Aristotle. Nietzsche, in his call to 'become what you are', is notorious for his hostility towards egalitarian perspectives, whether rooted in socialism or religion. Aristotle frankly affirms that not all humans have the same potentialities to actualize; slaves and women simply are not capable of the highest forms of human life.

Kierkegaard's ethical thinking, however, is noteworthy for its egalitarian demands. For him, no ethical view that does not regard all human beings as capable of achieving 'the highest' can be acceptable.[29] This egalitarian demand is partly satisfied by his emphasis on moral and spiritual qualities. Though humans certainly differ in intellectual and aesthetic talents, it is plausible that every normal person is capable of moral choices and the development of moral character. Moral and spiritual character is a matter of developing what Kierkegaard calls 'the

---

[28] Ibid. 33.

[29] See for example Climacus' claim that 'the ethical is and remains the highest task assigned to every human being'. *Concluding Unscientific Postscript,* 151.

passions' and he believes that in this sphere the cards are dealt equally. The passions are roughly to be understood as emotions or enduring dispositions to emotions that can provide direction for a person's life. Regardless of whether a person is intellectually or artistically gifted, he or she is capable of love and trust.

One may of course disagree with Kierkegaard that the cards are dealt equally even in this sphere. Think, for example, of the person with psychopathic characteristics. However, even if we exclude genuine cases of mental illness and focus on 'normal' people, one might reasonably claim that even in the moral and spiritual spheres there are significant differences in potential. Kierkegaard has a back-up position to save the heart of his position against such an objection. Kierkegaard's individualism, paradoxically again, is present to save equality. Since each person is called by God to become the unique self that person can be, the task is relativized to the ability. Each of us is called to become the person he or she is capable of becoming. The God who issues the requirement is identical with the God who has given the abilities. Everyone is therefore equally capable of forming a God-relation by becoming what God requires. If the self is constituted by such a God-relation, we are all equally capable of selfhood.

LOVE AS THE FOUNDATION OF THE HUMAN SELF

For Kierkegaard there are two passions that are specially crucial in the formation of the self God intends one to be: faith and love. The two are so closely connected that it is perhaps a mistake to separate them. Nevertheless, to the degree that we can distinguish them, it is interesting to ask which of the two is primary. Faith is the passion that lies at the centre of the God-relationship, and hence without faith it is impossible for a human person in the fullest sense to become the self God intends. There is a sense then in which faith is the highest passion. Certainly, Kierkegaard does not believe that it is possible to love other people rightly apart from a God-relationship, and thus faith would seem to be crucial if love is to become actualized in a person's life.

There is another sense, however, in which one can see love as primary, in that love is the quality at which faith aims. Love, we might say, provides faith with a *telos*. God's own nature is essentially love, and God's demand that his human creatures relate to him in faith is one that has as an aim that those creatures better image God by becoming more like him in loving. Thus, Kierkegaard says that a person who succeeds in living life without learning to love has 'forfeited everything'.[30] To echo the words Kierkegaard invents for the Apostle John, 'to love people is the only thing worth living for, and without this love you are not really living.'[31] The self we must become has as its primary characteristic love. The self is primarily shaped by 'the heart', and love is not only something that stems from the heart; it is what *'forms* the heart'.[32]

It is not surprising, then, that Kierkegaard's greatest ethical work, arguably in fact his only work that is primarily ethical in character, is *Works of Love*. This book takes as its major text the command from the New Testament that 'you shall love your neighbour as yourself.'[33] *Works of Love* contains an extended treatment of the concept of 'neighbour-love', which is seen as distinct from and often even opposed to such 'natural' forms of love as erotic love, friendship, and patriotism. This confirms the claim above that the ethic of self-actualization found in Kierkegaard is, unlike those of Aristotle and Nietzsche, one in which the self is thoroughly qualified in moral and spiritual terms. We have, then, a divine command ethic in which the fundamental command is that a person become what God intends. What God intends for each of us is that we become like him in loving. The most fundamental obligation is the obligation to love God. Tightly linked to this love of God is the command to love our fellow human beings as our neighbours. The major focus of *Works of Love* is this second command, but the book contains a sustained argument that this can only be done in the context of loving God.

[30] Søren Kierkegaard, *Works of Love*, ed. and trans. Howard V. Hong and Edna H. Hong (Princeton: Princeton University Press, 1995), 6.

[31] Ibid. 375.

[32] Ibid. 12. Italics are Kierkegaard's.

[33] The words of Jesus are found in Mark 12: 31. Jesus is of course quoting from Leviticus 19: 18, and hence this command is one that belongs to Judaism as much as to Christianity.

The heart of the account given focuses on the following themes. Love is something that is commanded, a claim that seems strange to the poet who glorifies love as something spontaneous and free. The object of this commanded love is, first and foremost, God, but with respect to our fellow humans the object must be 'the neighbour', who is both universal and concrete. I cannot love God unless I love my neighbour and I cannot adequately love my neighbour without loving God. I am not allowed to exclude any person from the category of the neighbour, and yet the neighbour is 'the first person I see'. If I ask how I am to love the neighbour, the answer is that I am to love him or her 'as myself'. Such a view clearly presupposes the existence of a certain kind of self-love, though this does not mean that everyone loves himself or herself rightly. The primary task of love is to seek to help others become themselves, which in turn means that I must seek to help others become more loving. Paradoxically, in helping others to become themselves in this way, I also develop my own self in a way that leads to my ultimate happiness, even though this is not my immediate aim.

Kierkegaard's account of neighbour-love is notable for its lack of casuistry. Though he says that love is 'the fulfilling of the law'[34] there is little attempt in *Works of Love* to work out a list of ethical principles that the loving person must follow. In particular, there is no attempt to spell out a list of actions to be performed or not performed. Such a list would be neither necessary nor sufficient for love, though I do not think this means that love has no concern for principles of action at all. It seems possible for someone to be genuinely loving who gives little thought to any articulated principles; such a person may live in accordance with key ethical principles but is not consciously motivated by devotion to principles as such. It also seems possible for someone consciously to order his or her life on the basis of such principles but to be lacking in genuine love. I believe that this open-endedness, the difficulty we have in codifying genuine love, is partly motivated, on Kierkegaard's view, by God's desire to give full scope to human freedom and creativity. Our task in loving is not simply to measure ourselves

[34] Kierkegaard, *Works of Love*, 91–134.

by a checklist of moral rules, but creatively to seek to determine how love should express itself in a particular situation.

This does not mean that a person can do anything so long as it is motivated by love; we do not have here an earlier version of Joseph Fletcher's 'situation ethics', which interpreted the Christian ethic of love as a relativistic claim that there are no absolute duties.[35] Clearly, if love is to be the fulfilling of the law it must serve the ends that the moral law seeks to realize. This will give determinate content to the way love expresses itself and thus it cannot be 'anything goes'. Nevertheless, there are no algorithmic formulas for what love demands in particular situations, and no substitute for the good judgement of a wise, experienced lover.

Since my primary concerns in this work are meta-ethical, I will pay special attention to the 'commanded' character of love. Why must love be commanded? Can love be commanded at all? However, as noted above, this meta-ethical discussion cannot be separated from normative ethical issues, since Kierkegaard believes that there is a close link between the content of the command and the fact that it is commanded, as well as a link between the content of the self one is commanded to become and the relation to the commander. Ultimately, of the kinds of human love we humans can show to each other, it is only neighbour-love (and love for God) that can be commanded, just as it is only God who has the authority to ground our obligation to love by commanding it.

The above sketch is of course completely introductory in nature and raises many questions that have yet to be considered. Nevertheless, I thought that it would be helpful to have a concrete picture of what I take to be Kierkegaard's version of a divine command ethic in mind, however sketchy that picture might be, before considering the complex interpretive questions raised by Kierkegaard's authorship. In the next chapter I shall begin to look at that authorship as a whole and the various ways it treats the concept of the 'ethical' in an attempt to justify the claim that the view I have begun to develop is the best candidate to fill the role of Kierkegaard's view of the

---

[35] See Joseph Fletcher, *Situation Ethics: The New Morality* (Philadelphia: Westminster Press, 1966).

ethical. I shall first look at the general character of that authorship and try to show that its ironical and humorous literary
character does not make it impossible to develop from it something like an ethical theory. I shall then look at the role of the
ethical within the doctrine of the three 'stages' or 'spheres' of
human existence, with a particular look at an influential interpretation of *Either/Or*.

In Chapter 3 I shall go on to examine the treatment of the
ethical in *Fear and Trembling*, though the primary conclusion
there will be negative: *Fear and Trembling* is not the place to
look for a positive account of Kierkegaard's ethical views. It is
not primarily a book about ethics but a book about faith, though
written by an individual who stands outside the realm of faith
and does not even profess to understand it from the inside.

In Chapter 4 I shall examine the ethic of self-actualization
that is developed by the pseudonym Johannes Climacus in
Concluding Unscientific Postscript. Though Johannes Climacus
is clearly not Kierkegaard, his concerns and views are closer to
Kierkegaard's than are some other pseudonyms, a fact signalled
by Kierkegaard's decision to affix his name to the Climacus
books as 'editor'. Kierkegaard himself calls attention to this
fact in *The Point of View for My Work as an Author* and tells
us that putting his name on the title page was a 'hint' for the
'person concerned about this sort of thing'.[36] We shall see that,
though the ethical thinking of Climacus is not distinctly Christian and is clearly distinct from Kierkegaard's view in certain
respects, it provides a formal structure which can be used to
illuminate what Kierkegaard does say in his own voice in *Works
of Love* and other places. The close connection between *Concluding Unscientific Postscript* and Kierkegaard's own thinking
is shown by a comparison between this work of Climacus and a
book Kierkegaard wrote at almost the same time: *Upbuilding
Discourses in Various Spirits*.

Having completed a selective account of the ethical in the
pseudonymous literature, in Chapters 5 to 9 I shall sketch the
ethical views in *Works of Love*, with a few glances at other
mature works of Kierkegaard. We can see delineated in *Works*

---

[36] Søren Kierkegaard, *The Point of View*, ed. and trans. by Howard V.
Hong and Edna H. Hong (Princeton: Princeton University Press, 1998), 31–2.

of Love, I shall argue, an account of moral duties as rooted in divine commands. The treatment of *Works of Love* will be selective, large sections of the book will not be discussed at all.[37] I will not strictly limit the discussion to the notion of obligation, however, since on the account given, moral obligation is itself rooted in a broader understanding of God as love and love as supremely good.

After giving an account of Kierkegaard's view, I shall in Chapters 10 to 12 compare this account with three influential contemporary secular alternatives: evolutionary naturalism, a social contract theory of morality that I shall call humanistic naturalism, and a frankly relativistic form of naturalism. The concluding chapter will recapitulate the strengths of a divine command theory of morality as developed by Kierkegaard as providing a viable way of understanding the moral life in a pluralistic society, and defend the account against some plausible objections.

---

[37] Many of the sections I do not discuss are given good treatments in Jamie Ferreira, *Love's Grateful Striving* (New York: Oxford University Press, 2001).

2

The Ethical as a 'Stage' of Existence: *Either/Or* and Radical Choice

As might be expected from the great critic of 'systems', Kierkegaard left us no system. One cannot therefore turn to particular books in his authorship with the expectation that here is to be found his epistemology, there his metaphysics, or his ethics, as if these were neatly packaged bits of a comprehensive theory. Some will conclude from this evident fact that it is misguided to expect Kierkegaard to answer any traditional philosophical questions. Those who advance such a view would claim that Kierkegaard's mission did not consist in helping us to understand better the nature of the ethical life or the religious life in any positive way. They do not see Kierkegaard as attempting to help us gain clarity about the nature of the human self, or any such thing. Rather, they see Kierkegaard's writings as designed solely to continually call into question all the answers we give to such questions; to ironically and humorously pull apart the 'systems' we humans build.

Such a view certainly captures one pole of Kierkegaard's thought. Kierkegaard relentlessly hammers on the theme of what we might call the vital importance of negativity. In the words of the pseudonym Johannes Climacus in *Concluding Unscientific Postscript*, the 'negative is the distinctive mark' of the positive; the existing thinker, particularly the religious existing thinker, cannot simply move through the negative and leave it behind in a higher 'positivity'.[1] The life of the existing, subjective thinker is 'continuously just as negative as positive'.[2] This means, for example, that a religious individual never reaches a point where he or she can leave repentance behind. It also means, I think, that the ethical and religious

---

[1] Kierkegaard, *Concluding Unscientific Postscript*, 524.
[2] Ibid. 85.

convictions we have must never be taken uncritically as absolute and final. We must be open to the possibility that we have misunderstood their meaning and twisted their truth. As unfinished, existing beings, our convictions, like our lives, are always works in progress.

Nevertheless, if we see only negativity in Kierkegaard, we err as well. Kierkegaard's doctoral dissertation on irony is a critique of irony that is absolutized, a critique directed especially at the late German romantics. In the dissertation Kierkegaard defends irony as essential to authentic human life, but argues that irony must be 'mastered' or 'controlled', directed to a higher, positive end. 'As soon as irony is controlled, it makes a movement opposite to that in which uncontrolled irony declares its life. Irony limits, finitizes, and circumscribes and thereby yields truth, actuality, content; . . . .'[3] It has become fashionable to interpret the dissertation not only as about irony but as itself a piece of irony.[4] Such a view, however, seems more trendy than warranted to me, for the dissertation seems chock-full of serious argument.[5]

I realize that in today's academic climate it is risky to claim that anything in Kierkegaard should be taken 'straight'. The proponent of such a claim is always in danger of appearing to be the dull-minded pedant who is incapable of seeing the joke. However, there is no reason to think that Kierkegaard himself thinks the presence of irony is incompatible with positive convictions. His pseudonym Johannes Climacus sees a precise balance between inappropriate seriousness and inappropriate laughter: 'Therefore, it is just as questionable, precisely just as questionable, to be pathos-filled and earnest in the wrong place

---

[3] Kierkegaard, *The Concept of Irony with Continual Reference to Socrates*, ed. and trans. by Howard V. Hong and Edna H. Hong (Princeton: Princeton University Press, 1989), 326.

[4] For an example see Roger Poole, *Kierkegaard: The Indirect Communication* (Charlottesville, Va.: University Press of Virginia, 1993), 44–9.

[5] For a powerful demonstration that the account of irony given in Kierkegaard's dissertation can and should be read straightforwardly and not as itself ironical, see Richard M. Summers, '"Controlled Irony" and the Emergence of the Self in Kierkegaard's Dissertation', in *The Concept of Irony: International Kierkegaard Commentary*, ed. Robert L. Perkins (Macon, Ga.: Mercer University Press, 2001), 289–316.

as it is to laugh in the wrong place.'[6] His polemical target here is the person who cannot laugh at all, but the underlying claim makes it evident that unrelenting humour is just as foolish as universal seriousness.[7]

At the other end of his career, in *The Point of View for My Work as an Author*, Kierkegaard expresses a view of these matters remarkably similar to that found in *The Concept of Irony*. Though he insists on the pervasive role of irony and humour in his authorship, and attempts to explain and justify their presence, he argues that the whole authorship does indeed serve a higher, religious purpose. In *The Point of View* Kierkegaard attempts to say 'what I in truth am as an author, that I am and was a religious author, that my whole authorship pertains to Christianity, . . . '[8] Though his situation in Christendom demanded that he begin with aesthetic writings that constituted a kind of godly deception, the real irony in his authorship is that the irony masks a serious purpose which contemporary readers missed. 'When someday my lover comes, he will readily see that when I was regarded as being the ironic one the irony by no means consisted in what a highly cultured public thought it did . . . He will see that the irony consisted in just this, that in this esthetic author and under this *Erscheinung* [appearance] of worldliness the religious author concealed himself.'[9] The irony in this statement is that among Kierkegaard's 'lovers' today there are many who still wish to think of him solely as ironist, and use this misunderstanding so as to make it possible to evade his religious claims, or else understand the religious life itself in such a way that it does not make any claims on our intellect.

Nor is this balanced perspective on the negative absent from the authorship proper. The emphasis in *Concluding Unscientific Postscript* is certainly on negativity; the polemical targets are the builders of systems who have forgotten what it means to exist as an individual human being. But it is easy to see that the striving

[6] Kierkegaard, *Concluding Unscientific Postscript*, 525.

[7] For a good treatment of Kierkegaard's use of humour and irony, see John Lippitt, *Humor and Irony in Kierkegaard's Thought* (New York: St. Martin's Press, 2000).

[8] Kierkegaard, *The Point of View*, 23.

[9] Ibid. 69–70.

that constitutes human existence must not consist merely in a recognition of constant failure. It is true that we never arrive at the finish line in this life, but existence is also abolished if we never move towards a goal at all. The existing thinker is 'as negative as positive' but this obviously implies that the positive cannot be excluded. 'But the presence of irony does not necessarily mean that the earnestness is excluded. Only assistant professors assume that.'[10]

I think, therefore, that it is not misguided to attempt to see what Kierkegaard has to say about the ethical life and its relation to God. It will be salutory to be reminded that in doing so we are not writing part of the system. Neither what Kierkegaard has said or what I have to say in response to him will be the final word on the subject. However, if we universalize the ironical and humorous in Kierkegaard, the result is, ironically, that he becomes much less interesting. One can only show the pointless character of theorizing so many times before the point becomes boring.

In reality, even Kierkegaard's attack on 'speculative philosophy' is often misunderstood. Kierkegaard does not reject speculation per se, but rather speculation that is detached from existence and that sees itself as 'the system'. He is in fact a great admirer of Greek philosophy and notes the way in which speculation and existence are linked in ancient thought. In any case, thinking about the ethical life is not properly characterized as 'speculation', for such thinking is precisely thinking about existence. I shall therefore proceed by looking at Kierkegaard as a thinker who has something important to say about the ethical life and its relation to God.

INTERPRETING THE PSEUDONYMS

This does not mean, however, that we can afford to ignore the literary character of Kierkegaard's writings. Those who take what we might call the literary approach to Kierkegaard's writings have lately criticized philosophers for ignoring the poetic quality of those writings. Much of Kierkegaard's writings of course are attributed by Kierkegaard himself to his

---

[10] Kierkegaard, *Concluding Unscientific Postscript*, 277 n.

own pseudonymous creations, literary characters with their own perspectives and agendas, which may or may not overlap with Kierkegaard's own. Kierkegaard himself explicitly disclaims the works of the pseudonyms: 'Thus in the pseudonymous works there is not a single word by me. I have no opinion about them except as a third party, no knowledge of their meaning except as a reader, . . .'[11]

Such literary critics of Kierkegaard as Roger Poole thus have a point when they argue that it is a mistake to compile perspectives from various books of Kierkegaard, including the pseudonymous ones, as if the whole constituted the philosophy of Kierkegaard.[12] Certainly such a perspective was common among earlier generations of American Kierkegaard scholars.[13] Poole is apparently unaware, however, that the recognition of the importance of the pseudonyms has now become standard among philosophers and theologians who write about Kierkegaard, most of whom today understand that the views of the pseudonyms must be understood in relation to those pseudonymous characters' own agendas.[14] It has become common practice to honour Kierkegaard's request: 'Therefore, if it should occur to anyone to want to quote a particular passage from the books, it is my wish, my prayer, that he will do me the kindness of citing the respective pseudonymous author's name, not mine.'[15]

Where critics such as Poole err is their implicit assumption that if one takes seriously the literary character of the authorship, this makes it impossible to see in it any overall purpose or

[11] Kierkegaard, 'First and Last Declaration', ibid. 626.

[12] For Poole's complaint against 'blunt reading', see his 'The Unknown Kierkegaard: Twentieth Century Receptions', in *The Cambridge Companion to Kierkegaard*, 48–75, as well as Poole's book, *Kierkegaard: The Indirect Communication*.

[13] Including, I must confess, my own doctoral dissertation, later published as *Subjectivity and Religious Belief* (Grand Rapids, Mich.: Wm. B. Eerdmans Publishing Co., 1978), which has one chapter on Kierkegaard that does not do justice to the pseudonyms.

[14] See, for example, the writings of the authors of such authors as Sylvia Walsh, Jamie Ferreira, David Gouwens, and many others who appear in the *International Kierkegaard Commentary* series. My own books and articles on Kierkegaard could of course also be cited as an example.

[15] Kierkegaard, 'First and Last Declaration', in *Concluding Unscientific Postscript*, 627.

thrust. The best argument in favour of this possibility is that Kierkegaard himself, while stressing the importance of the pseudonyms, still claims that there is such an overall purpose. He describes his task from beginning to end as an attempt to 'reintroduce Christianity into Christendom'. Since Christianity is primarily a way of existing, this required him to explore the meaning of existence, to seek to awaken his contemporaries to the questions of existence. Each pseudonym has his own existential place, as it were, and sees the world from that particular spot. Nevertheless, we can look at them as a whole and get a picture of human existence in its multifariousness. This by no means implies that the pseudonyms' views are equally remote from Kierkegaard's own. None of the pseudonyms can be identified with Kierkegaard; in that sense they are all equally distinct. However, just as would be the case if they were actual and not fictitious characters, their views may be closer to or more distant from his own. To get the picture of human existence that Kierkegaard wishes us to see, however, it is absolutely essential to take the pseudonyms seriously, and I will do my best to honour this principle in this work.

Given the multivocity or polyphony of the authorship, how can we get a sense for Kierkegaard's own purposes and aims, since these can by no means be identified with any or all of the pseudonyms? Well, we could decide to take Kierkegaard's own word for what he was about, as developed in *The Point of View for My Work as an Author*. However, it must be conceded, and Kierkegaard himself stresses this point, that an author is not necessarily his own best interpreter. No avowal can be of value if its claims are not confirmed by the texts themselves. Furthermore, and Kierkegaard admits this as well, the perspective developed in *The Point of View* is a retrospective one, and does not precisely match the understanding Kierkegaard had at the time when he wrote some of the earlier works. Kierkegaard attributes the overall coherent meaning that he sees in the authorship to 'Governance', and does not claim that the authorship was the result of a pre-existent plan that he had.[16]

---

[16] '[W]hat I cannot understand is that I can now understand it [the whole plan of the authorship] and yet by no means dare to say that I understood it so accurately at the beginning.' *The Point of View*, 77.

Nevertheless, many readers, myself included, find the interpretation Kierkegaard gives in *The Point of View* to be confirmed in a powerful way when they read the authorship.

I believe another way of reaching what is substantially the
same point is to take the non-pseudonymous writings of Kierkegaard as a baseline by which to understand Kierkegaard's
own views. After all, Kierkegaard's admonition not to confuse
the views of the pseudonyms with his own can hardly be taken
as a warning against attributing to him the views he puts forward under his own name. In addition to the works published
under his own name, we may also cautiously draw on some of
the entries from Kierkegaard's 'Journals', taking care that we
are using material that reflects his own voice.[17] If we have some
clarity about what Kierkegaard says in his own voice, we may
well get some ideas about how the pseudonyms serve his wider
purposes, giving us insight into where the pseudonyms provide
him with a foil, where they prefigure or seem to be developing
views he personally held.

I am aware that some of the 'postmodern' interpreters of
Kierkegaard fall into the camp of those who have announced
the 'death of the author' and have claimed that 'S. Kierkegaard'
should be seen as simply one more pseudonym, another per-
sona.[18] However, anyone who seriously advances this line of
thought cannot possibly object that the view I propose to develop is not that of the 'real Kierkegaard', since such a reader
denies the possibility that there could be such a thing. So far as I
can see, such a position not only undermines any positive account of Kierkegaard's meaning, but also undercuts any claim
that Kierkegaard's 'real' intentions are solely negative and ironical. If we have no identifiable author, there can be no such
intentions. If someone doubts that there is any such thing as
Kierkegaard's view of ethics (recognizing of course that this

---

[17] Caution in the use of the 'Papirer' is necessary because it seems possible
that some of the entries reflect poetic perspectives Kierkegaard was developing that were not his own. See Henning Fenger, *Kierkegaard: The Myths and
Their Origins: Studies in the Kierkegaardian Papers and Letters*, trans. George
Schoolfield (New Haven: Yale University Press, 1980).

[18] Louis Mackey, for example, makes such a claim in *Points of View:
Readings of Kierkegaard* (Tallahassee, Fla.: Florida State University Press,
1986).

view may have changed over time), he or she is welcome to consider the following account as one inspired by Kierkegaard's writings and simply drop the claim that the view is Kierkegaard's, since, as pointed out in Chapter 1, the truth and soundness of the view is more important than the question of whether or not Kierkegaard held it.

Of course even within Kierkegaard's non-pseudonymous authorship, there is a lack of uniformity. There are clear differences between the early generically religious *Upbuilding Discourses* and the sharply Christian tone of *Judge for Yourself!* and *For Self-Examination*. Yet it seems reasonable to take the later works as providing the decisive, mature view of Kierkegaard, especially insofar as we can see continuity in the changes from the earlier to the later books, and can also see clearly that the later writings articulate the Christian perspective that *The Point of View* affirms to be Kierkegaard's own.

If, however, we are to follow the principle of taking later works as coming from the 'mature' Kierkegaard, what role is to be assigned to the very late writings, the 'attack on Christendom' found in Kierkegaard's newspaper and magazine articles written shortly before his death? Bruce Kirmmse, for one, has argued very persuasively that these writings should be viewed as the culmination of Kierkegaard's whole authorship.[19] Should these writings be taken as definitive in determining 'what Kierkegaard really thought?'

I agree with Kirmmse that there is much in these late writings that must be seen as a logical culmination of themes developed in the earlier authorship. However, I cannot regard these writings as definitive for an understanding of Kierkegaard as a philosopher for several reasons. First of all, Kierkegaard himself thought of these writings more as 'action' than 'literature'. Kierkegaard worried sometimes that his writings were only 'poetry', and that he perhaps had substituted writing about the Christian life for actual obedience. So, although on the whole Kierkegaard understands that literature can be helpful to human beings in stimulating reflection and insight on life, he

---

[19] Bruce Kirmmse, 'On Authority and Revolution: Kierkegaard's Road to Politics', in *Kierkegaard Revisited*, ed. Niels Jørgen Cappelørn and Jon Stewart (New York: Walter de Gruyter, 1997), 254–73.

also knows that a writer is first and foremost a human being. After spending most of his life as a writer, in his latest writings he attempts to step out and do something as a Christian, namely to make a vigorous protest against the ways in which the State Church has falsified New Testament Christianity, although, ironically, his 'action' still takes the form of writing. Because he thought of this peculiar kind of writing as a 'deed' I believe Kierkegaard felt free consciously to exaggerate and use all kinds of polemical and rhetorical devices which aim directly at what might well be called a political end, if Kierkegaard had not so firmly refused any positive political aims and rebuffed any alliance with others opposed to official Christianity. His end seems only to be the negative one of inspiring people publicly to confess that the official Christianity was not the Christianity of the New Testament. These exaggerations and rhetorical and polemical aims make it risky to rely primarily on these writings if we wish to know precisely what Kierkegaard thought was the sober truth about philosophical and theological issues.

Another reason for care in the use of the last writings is one that I advance with some sadness, but I nonetheless feel compelled to state it. There are elements in the attack on Christendom that strike me as misogynistic and some that seem misanthropic.[20] I state this with misgivings, because it is easy for those who wish to evade the legitimate force of Kierkegaard's critique to use these elements as an excuse to dismiss the whole of the attack. And those who see the attack itself as the culmination of the authorship may then argue that the authorship as a whole is deeply flawed by these same elements. Let me discuss the problem of misogyny first.

I cannot deny that Kierkegaard shared in the sexism common to his time. However, I think that even some of his severest feminist critics have noticed that there are interesting and

---

[20] For examples of misogyny in the later writings and journal entries, see *Søren Kierkegaard's Journals and Papers*, ed. and trans. by Howard V. Hong and Edna H. Hong (Bloomington, Ind.: Indiana University Press, 1975), iv. 572–85, and Søren Kierkegaard, *The Moment and Late Writings*, ed. and trans. by Howard V. Hong and Edna H. Hong (Princeton: Princeton University Press, 1998), 163–4. For examples of misanthropy see *Søren Kierkegaard's Journals and Papers*, iv. 526–7; and *The Moment and Late Writings*, 135 ('the human being is a born hypocrite').

complicated ways in which Kierkegaard's writings can be helpful to feminists.[21] Though Kierkegaard certainly held some
traditional and stereotypical views of masculinity and feminin-
ity, he also clearly thought that at the highest levels of spiritual
existence, there is a fundamental equality between men and
women. To become themselves, men must learn and acquire
characteristics that the society of his day stereotypically assigned
to women, such as devotion, and women must acquire the
spiritual courage and freedom the society of his day stereotypically assigned to men. The models that Kierkegaard holds up for
emulation for both men and women are frequently female.[22]
Hence, I would argue that at the deepest level, Kierkegaard's
thought, as expressed in the bulk of his writings, though marred
by sexism, is not misogynistic.

I cannot deny, however, that there are elements in the attack
on Christendom that have at least a misogynistic undertone. I
therefore do not regard the attack as definitive or even representative of Kierkegaard's mature positions. I confess that I
believe that at certain points the attack may reflect, not Kierkegaard's own best thinking, but the damaging effects of years of
loneliness created by the *Corsair* controversy and the illness that
was soon to take his life.

This means that in reading Kierkegaard primacy must be
given to such non-pseudonymous works as *Two Ages* (1846),
Upbuilding Discourses in Various Spirits (1847), *Christian Discourses* (1848), *For Self-Examination* (1851) and *Judge for Yourself!* (written in 1851 but published posthumously in 1876). I
would include in this category the special works attributed to
the pseudonym Anti-Climacus, *The Sickness Unto Death* (1849)
and *Practice in Christianity* (1850), because I agree with the
common view (confirmed by Kierkegaard himself) that this
late pseudonym has a different character and function than the

---

[21] See the essays in Céline Léon and Sylvia Walsh (eds.), *Feminist Interpretations of Søren Kierkegaard*, (University Park, Pa.: Pennsylvania State
University Press, 1997). The essays in this volume vary greatly in their
evaluation of sexism in Kierkegaard, but even the more critical typically
discern redeeming features in Kierkegaard's works.

[22] See Mark Lloyd Taylor's article, 'Practice in Authority: The Apostolic
Women of Søren Kierkegaard's Writings,' in *Anthropology and Authority:
Essays on Søren Kierkegaard.*, ed. Poul Houe (Atlanta, Ga.: Rodopi, 2000).

rest. The earlier pseudonyms, disavowed in the statement quoted above from *Concluding Unscientific Postscript*, all represent viewpoints distinct from Kierkegaard's own and voice views that may or may not be his. Anti-Climacus was invented by Kierkegaard to allow him to say what he wished to say as a Christian, keenly conscious of the gap between the ideals he wanted to express and the actuality of his existence. Anti-Climacus thus does not say things with which Kierkegaard would disagree, though he says many things Kierkegaard sees as directed towards his own failings.

Above all, I believe that anyone wishing to understand Kierkegaard as an ethical thinker must focus on *Works of Love* (1847), which will therefore be the primary text in my attempt to develop Kierkegaard's view of the ethical and its relation to God. *Works of Love* is clearly both Christian in its perspective and aims and has the ethical life as its primary theme. This by no means implies that there is nothing to be learned about the ethical from the pseudonymous works. It does mean, however, that when we decide what in the pseudonymous works represents a view that Kierkegaard himself might endorse, we must appeal primarily to *Works of Love* and other similar non-pseudonymous books. Before turning explicitly to *Works of Love*, it will be helpful to canvass some of the pseudonymous works on 'the ethical', particularly so as to see their limitations as a source for Kierkegaard's ethics. In this chapter I discuss the 'ethical' in relation to the 'stages' or 'spheres' of existence, and deal with a common misinterpretation of Kierkegaard in relation to *Either/ Or*. In the next chapter the focus moves to the pseudonymous *Fear and Trembling*. I shall argue that *Fear and Trembling* does not represent Kierkegaard's own 'voice'. Even more importantly, *Fear and Trembling* is not primarily about ethics at all; it is about faith. In Chapter 4 I will go on to examine the ethic of self-actualization developed in *Concluding Unscientific Postscript* by Johannes Climacus, a book that will provide an illuminating framework for *Works of Love*.

THE ETHICAL AS A 'STAGE' OR 'SPHERE' OF EXISTENCE

Most readers who know anything at all about Kierkegaard know of his famous account of the three stages or spheres of human

existence: the aesthetic, the ethical, and the religious. These
stages or spheres—I will shortly explain why both names are
appropriate—provide a kind of 'map' of the existential possibilities that face human beings as they attempt to understand and
define their lives. Strictly speaking, this view is best developed
by a pseudonym, Johannes Climacus, in *Concluding Unscientific
Postscript*.[23] However, Kierkegaard employs these categories
often enough in his *Journals* and in his non-pseudonymous
works that we can have some confidence that he found them
useful tools in thinking through human existence himself. The
idea of the stages seems also to be a kind of common currency
that we can see as shared by a number of pseudonyms, however
different their own existential stances may be. Such pseudonyms as A from *Either/Or, I* and Judge William from *Either/Or,
II* not only exemplify these categories, but clearly employ them.

How should these stages be understood? I can here present
only a brief and over-simplified account.[24] The aesthetic stage
is the natural life-stance of a child; it is the place where human
existence begins. The aesthete is characterized in various ways:
as someone who lives 'for the moment', as someone who lives
for pleasure, happiness, or satisfaction. The aesthete lives a life
dominated by 'immediacy' in the sense that the purpose of life
seems to be simply to satisfy as many desires as possible.

The above description of the aesthetic life must be qualified
in one important respect. Kierkegaard presents actual aesthetic
lives as falling at some point on a continuum between two

---

[23] The relationship between Kierkegaard and the Johannes Climacus
pseudonym is both close and complex, and will be discussed below. I give
this matter more detailed attention in *Kierkegaard's* Fragments *and* Postscript: *The Religious Philosophy of Johannes Climacus* (Atlantic Highlands,
NJ: Humanities Press, 1983) and *Passionate Reason: Making Sense of Kierkegaard's* Philosophical Fragments (Bloomington, Ind.: Indiana University
Press, 1992).

[24] One reason this account is oversimplified is that there are more than
three stages. The religious stage comes in at least two different forms, religiousness A and religiousness B, the distinctively Christian form of religiousness. In addition to this, Kierkegaard understands 'irony' and 'humour' to be
existential stances that form 'boundary zones' or 'transition spheres' between
the other stages. For a fuller account see ch. 10 of *Kierkegaard's* Fragments
and Postscript. For an excellent account of the role of irony and humour in
Kierkegaard see Lippitt, *Humor and Irony*.

extremes. One extreme is the life of sensuous immediacy sym-
bolized by the mythical (and existentially impossible) figure of
Don Juan in *Either/Or, I*. The other pole is the highly reflective,
intellectual figure of A, who is the author of *Either/Or, I* and may
or may not be identical with the 'reflective seducer' who is the
author of the infamous 'Diary of a Seducer' which concludes the
volume. The reflective aesthete seems to lack immediacy; he has
learned to enjoy life by stepping back from life and taking its
events as raw materials for aesthetic reflection and creation.
Even the story of seduction told in the Diary reflects this ambiguous relation to actuality. Though the author of the Diary
appears to be giving a narrative about actual events, Victor
Eremita, the editor of the book, hints that these events may not
have actually occurred. Victor says that although it seems some
actual events lie at its core, the narrative we have is so poetically
coloured we cannot know what actually transpired.[25] For the
reflective seducer, the sexual experience itself has little importance. The chase has more significance than its culmination, for
what the seducer values is the challenge of the interesting project
of seducing a young woman while at the same time convincing
her that she is the one who is seducing him.

It may appear then that the aesthetic life is not solely 'immediate', since it can take such a highly reflective form. However,
for Kierkegaard intellectual development is not identical with
existential development, and a person can be intellectually sophisticated without personally becoming anything at all. If
reflection is not put at the service of responsible choice, it
becomes a pathway to diversion, not self-development. Even
the most intellectually developed aesthete, therefore, remains
'immediate' in a way. Such a person still lives for the moment
and in the moment, and his life lacks the continuity that Kierkegaard sees as necessary if an individual is to have an
identity.[26]

---

[25] Søren Kierkegaard, *Either/Or* (2 vols.), ed. and trans. by Howard V.
Hong and Edna H. Hong (Princeton: Princeton University Press, 1987). For
examples of the lack of continuity in the aesthete's life, see *I*, 8–10. For the
criticism of this lack of continuity as preventing selfhood see *II*, 159–60, 250.

[26] While it is of course possible for women to be aesthetes in Kierkegaard's
sense, it seems right to use the male pronouns here as Kierkegaard's own
examples of aesthetes are invariably masculine.

As pointed out above, children are naturally aesthetes. It is characteristic of the child to live in the moment; 'I want it' is a powerful argument for a child. The ability to 'defer gratification' does not come easy to us. But there are at least two kinds of reasons why we do defer gratification. Sometimes we discipline our desires because we recognize that by doing so we will be able to satisfy more of them in the long run. Such calculative self-discipline falls within the realm of prudence; it is closely linked to what Kierkegaard terms 'cleverness' or 'shrewdness' (*Klogskab*),[27] and it is entirely compatible with the aesthetic stance. In fact, in *Either/Or, I*, the pseudonym A offers us a theory of 'social prudence'.[28]

Sometimes, however, we choose not to satisfy desires because of deeper reasons. A person's sense of identity is linked to ideals that have some kind of claim on him or her. The kind of person Kierkegaard calls ethical is one who has such ideals. Judge William claims in *Either/Or, II* that there comes a time in a person's life when the individual senses a need to become a self in this higher sense, a time when the 'spirit ripens' so to speak.[29] In the ideal case, the child becomes an adult by learning to ask who she is and finding an answer to this question. The person who has made this transition no longer thinks of herself simply as a series of desires, but as a being with *commitments* to be taken seriously. The fundamental choice is to take choice itself seriously, to seek ideals for which a person can live and die.

Self-development, or what Kierkegaard often calls spiritual development, does not, however, happen automatically. One does not become a self the way one acquires facial hair or wisdom teeth. It is quite possible for the individual who is called to become a self by making the transition to the ethical life to refuse the demand. The refusal is one with consequences; Kierkegaard sees the aesthete as beset by boredom and meaninglessness. The aesthete who is conscious of the nature of his existence will in fact experience despair. Nevertheless, Kierkegaard believes that this refusal is quite common and pervasive in

---

[27] The Hongs usually translate this term as 'sagacity', but I believe Kierkegaard's use is much closer to 'cleverness' than the traditional concept of 'wisdom' used to denote the quality possessed by the sage.

[28] Kierkegaard, 'Rotation of Crops', in *Either/Or, I*, 298.

[29] Kierkegaard, *Either/Or, II*, 188–9.

the Denmark of his day. In *The Sickness Unto Death* the pseudonym Anti-Climacus gives many acute descriptions of the diversions and self-deceptions necessary to keep the aesthetic form of life afloat.

We can therefore think of the aesthetic and ethical stances not merely as stages that one lives through, but as existential spheres which can define a person's life as a whole. They confront each other as rival views of how life should be lived, mutually exclusive existential standpoints.

Though I believe that Kierkegaard puts many telling criticisms of the aesthetic life in the mouths of his ethical pseudonyms, it is clear that the ethical stance represented in *Either/Or, II* and *Stages on Life's Way* is far from Kierkegaard's own. This is evident from the fact that the ethical standpoint is characterized by a defence of a kind of universal duty to marry (though the ethicists grudgingly admit the possibility of 'exceptions' to this rule). At the time these books were written Kierkegaard himself had already decisively rejected married life by breaking his engagement with Regine Olsen, an action that he viewed (at least sometimes) as his religious duty. (Whether or not he was mistaken in so thinking is here irrelevant.)

What is it that might move a person beyond the ethical life as conceived in *Either/Or, II* towards a deeper religious stance? The answer lies in the general neighbourhood of the emotions; it is linked to what Kierkegaard calls 'passions'. On Kierkegaard's view a person is not moved from one life stance to another purely by intellectual insight. The transitions from one sphere to another are not merely 'logical' but 'pathos-filled' transitions.[30] Just as a person may be motivated to move from the aesthetic life to the ethical life by feelings of meaninglessness and despair, so a person may experience emotions which reveal the limits of the ethical life. The emotions that motivate a transition to the religious life arise from an encounter with suffering and, most importantly of all, guilt.

---

[30] See Gregor Malantschuk, *Kierkegaard's Thought*, trans. Howard V. Hong and Edna H. Hong (Princeton: Princeton University Press, 1971), 79–82, for a clear account of the fundamental importance of the distinction between logical and pathos-filled transitions in Kierkegaard.

It is easy to misunderstand the Kierkegaardian distinction between the ethical and religious spheres of existence. Those with a focus on the alleged epistemological problems of religious belief may be tempted to think of the ethical life as one free from risky metaphysical commitments, a kind of humanistic stance that does not require belief in God. Such a view is quite alien to Kierkegaard, however, as are the epistemological worries about the reasonableness of belief in God that have dominated philosophy of religion since the Enlightenment. Kierkegaard's ethicists are invariably devout and pious individuals who believe in God and participate in church life. (For that matter, his aesthetes can be people who believe and go to church as well, but their attitudes toward church are defined by their aesthetic standpoint.) Kierkegaard's ethicists typically see their ethical duties as divine commands, and Kierkegaard does not think this is a mistake on their part. The difference between the ethical and religious spheres therefore has little to do with belief or lack of belief in God. Rather, it has to do with the self-confidence of the ethical persons who are seeking to become themselves, their conviction that the task is one that can be successfully carried off. The religious sphere begins when an individual acquires a sense that the demands of the ethical life are ones that cannot possibly be fulfilled. Such an individual has discovered what John Hare has called 'the moral gap', the yawning chasm between what ethics requires and what human choice can achieve.[31]

Johannes de Silentio describes the situation quite clearly in *Fear and Trembling*: 'An ethics that ignores sin is a completely futile discipline, but if it affirms sin, then it has *eo ipso* exceeded itself.'[32] The ethical life is described as a process in which an individual seeks a relation to God through a commitment to becoming the self God calls one to be. However, within the ethical sphere the demands of God are seen as general rules and not individual callings, and so the relation to God is not individual and personal in character. De Silentio once again characterizes the situation well: 'The ethical is the universal, and as such it is also the divine. Thus it is proper to say that every duty

[31] John Hare, *The Moral Gap: Kantian Ethics and God's Assistance* (Oxford: Oxford University Press, 1996).
[32] Kierkegaard, *Fear and Trembling*, 98–9.

is essentially duty to God, but if no more can be said than this, then it is also said that I actually have no duty to God. The duty becomes duty by being traced to God, but in the duty itself I do not enter into relation to God.'[33]

The religious life begins when a person discovers that the task, which is 'simultaneously to relate oneself absolutely to one's absolute *telos* and relatively to relative ends', is one that has been bungled already.[34] The self is suffocated by relativity, incapable of becoming what it ought to be simply through ethical resolution. For such an individual, the possibility that the ethical sphere does not exhaust life's possibilities is life-saving. He or she longs for the possibility of an individual who 'determines his relation to the universal [the ethical] by his relation to the absolute [God], not his relation to the absolute by his relation to the universal'.[35] Such an individual has a personal relation to God; he takes as his model the biblical Abraham, who was justified not by ethical deeds but by faith, an attitude of personal trust in God. As de Silentio describes faith it is a risky business. It by no means can be equated with the satisfaction of those ethical ideals whose fulfilment we rightly admire, but 'it is one thing to be admired and another to become a guiding star that saves the anguished.'[36]

Since my primary concern at the moment is the place of the ethical within the 'stages', I shall not pursue the religious sphere in much detail, but a few points must be made. In *Concluding Unscientific Postscript* Johannes Climacus makes a fundamental distinction between the Christian form of the religious life that essentially presupposes the historical revelation of God in Jesus Christ (Religiousness B) and the kind of religious life that can in principle be lived without such an historical revelation (Religiousness A). Religiousness A has, as we

---

[33] Ibid. 68. It is not clear that de Silentio (or Kierkegaard himself) clearly sees the distinction between a general rule and a principle that is highly specific (and thus applicable only in specific situations) though still universalizable.

[34] The description of the task is from *Concluding Unscientific Postscript*, 387, and the claim that the task has already been bungled can be found on 525–7.

[35] Kierkegaard, *Fear and Trembling*, 70.

[36] Ibid. 21.

have already seen, as its 'initial expression' the task of achieving 'an absolute relation to the absolute and a relative relation to the relative'.[37] This task seems to grow out of the ethical life when that life is understood most deeply, and it is probably for this reason that this form of religiousness is sometimes described as the 'ethico-religious' life. The person who seriously undertakes the task soon discovers the difficulty of the 'resignation' demanded; we cannot be absolutely committed to the absolute if we are unwilling to relinquish the relative when that is called for by the absolute. The 'essential expression' of the religious life then is a kind of suffering, a dying to immediacy. When we understand how far we are from accomplishing this task, the religious life gets 'decisively' defined as guilt, and it is certainly arguable that a good deal of the concern of the world's religions lies in finding some way to deal with guilt and suffering.

CAN THE SPHERES BE RANKED? A RESPONSE TO MACINTYRE'S READING OF *EITHER/OR*

Ultimately, I wish to argue that the ethical in Kierkegaard is not merely a 'stage' to be left behind or a 'sphere' to be rejected in favour of the religious life. Rather, I want to claim that the ethical is a component of human life when it is lived in its fullest and best form. This view will be justified, I think, if it can be shown that the spheres or stages should be viewed, as I have done in the previous section, as having a ranking or hierarchy. There is a sense in which the ethical life represents an advance over the aesthetic life, and a sense in which the religious life is an advance over the ethical. My primary reason for viewing the stages in this way is that I believe each succeeding stage in some way captures or fulfils the aims of the preceding stage; to use Hegelian language, each stage in some way preserves the 'truth' of the preceding stage.[38] If this is so, then the ethical cannot be

---

[37] This is a paraphrase of the formula Climacus gives in *Concluding Unscientific Postscript*, 387.

[38] Many authors have noticed the quasi-Hegelian character of the stages. One of the best treatments of this theme, one that captures both the Hegelian and anti-Hegelian character of Kierkegaard's view, is found in Merold Westphal, *Becoming a Self: A Reading of Kierkegaard's* Concluding Unscientific Postscript (West Lafayette, Ind.: Purdue University Press, 1996), 20–32.

merely a vanishing element in human existence. Though
the ethical as a distinct stage or sphere may be something the
individual must advance beyond, a transformed version of
the ethical must persist and be incorporated in the highest forms
of human existence. Support for this view can be found in *The
Concept of Anxiety*, where Vigilius Haufniensis, the pseudonymous author, discusses what he calls a 'second ethic', an
ethic that presupposes the dogmatic truths of Christianity.[39]

Such a reading of the stages, and such a claim about the
ethical in Kierkegaard, runs smack against one very influential
interpretation of Kierkegaard. In a book that I find in many
respects insightful and helpful, Alastair MacIntyre claims that
Kierkegaard was the first philosopher to discern the failure of
the 'Enlightenment project' to find a rational foundation for
ethics. For MacIntyre Kant epitomizes this Enlightenment
project, with his attempt to ground morality in universal human
reason, rather than sentiment, tradition, religious authority, or
anything else. MacIntyre claims that 'Kierkegaard and Kant
agree in their conception of morality, but Kierkegaard inherits
that conception together with an understanding that the project
of giving rational vindication of morality has failed.'[40] Kierkegaard's solution to this problem, according to MacIntyre, was
to appeal to the will: 'an act of choice had to be called in to do
the work that reason could not do.'[41]

It is Kierkegaard's *Either/Or* that MacIntyre sees as crucial in
developing this account of the foundations of ethics. *Either/Or*,
in two volumes, is a pseudonymous book with multiple fictional

---

[39] Søren Kierkegaard, *The Concept of Anxiety*, trans. Reidar Thomte
(Princeton: Princeton University Press, 1980), 20, 23.

[40] Alasdair MacIntyre, *After Virtue*, 2nd edn. (Notre Dame, Ind.: University of Notre Dame Press, 1984), 47.

[41] Ibid. 47. It is worth noting that in a later essay, MacIntyre concedes that
his earlier treatment of Kierkegaard had not been sufficiently nuanced, and
that he 'had unjustly assimilated Kierkegaard's position to that of Sartre'.
Despite this concession, however, MacIntyre still insists that his original
claim that Kierkegaard thinks that the transition from the aesthetic to the
ethical occurs by way of a presuppositionless choice is valid. See Davenport
and Rudd (eds.), *Kierkegaard After MacIntyre*, 340–1. This volume contains a
number of excellent essays critical of the MacIntyre thesis, but with regard to
this point I would make special note of the papers by Norman Lillegard and
Edward Mooney.

authors. The first volume includes a variety of writings by a rich, young aesthete, called simply A, including a 'Diary of a Seducer' which A attempts to disown, but which seems likely to have been written by A, according to the editor, Victor Eremita. The second volume is by an older married man, Judge William, and it consists chiefly of two long letters from William to A, in which he argues for the superiority of the ethical life and marriage as its most significant expression. (William also sends A a copy of a sermon from a country pastor in Jutland.) Victor Eremita himself appears to be a disinterested editor who makes no attempt to adjudicate the argument between A and William. As Johannes Climacus, the pseudonymous author of *Concluding Unscientific Postscript* notes, the book contains no resolution; we are not told whether or not A ever mended his ways and got married, or whether William became bored with the ethical life and had an affair.[42]

MacIntyre reads this lack of resolution as a dramatic expression of what he terms the doctrine of 'radical choice'. The concept of a radical choice is simply that of a choice for which no reasons can be given, because it is a choice of what is to count as a reason. In a crucial paragraph, MacIntyre vividly presents the position of the individual making a radical choice between the aesthetic and the ethical:

Suppose that someone confronts the choice between them having as yet embraced neither. He can be offered no *reason* for preferring one to the other. For if a given reason offers support for the ethical way of life ... the person who has not yet embraced either the ethical or the aesthetic still has to choose whether or not to treat the reason as having any force. If it already has force for him, he has already chosen the ethical; which *ex hypothesi* he has not. And so it is also with reasons supportive of the aesthetic. The man who has not yet chosen has still to choose whether to treat them as having force. He still has to choose his first principles, and just because they are *first* principles, prior to any others in the chain of reasoning, no more ultimate reasons can be adduced to support them.[43]

MacIntyre goes on to present a powerful critique of the notion of radical choice. He argues that there is a deep

[42] Kierkegaard, *Concluding Unscientific Postscript*, 254.
[43] MacIntyre, *After Virtue*, 40.

contradiction between the doctrine of choosing a form of life for no reason, and the concept of the ethical as represented in *Either/ Or, II*. The ethical is that which has authority over us, which binds us independently of our desires and wishes. However, a form of life adopted for no reason cannot have this kind of authority. It might be adopted on a whim or caprice, but our awareness that our own arbitrary choice is the basis of the authority is sufficient to undermine the authority, since we realize that we can at any time make a new choice.[44] A radical choice might then be the foundation of an aesthetic life, which recognizes no binding authority, but it could not provide a basis for an ethical life.

This criticism of radical choice is telling. But why should we take it as directed against Kierkegaard? Why should we think that Kierkegaard himself accepts the doctrine of radical choice? The argument MacIntyre presents against radical choice is in fact precisely the same argument presented by Kierkegaard in the voice of his Christian pseudonym Anti-Climacus in *The Sickness Unto Death*.

The Sickness Unto Death is a book about despair, which is understood as a loss of selfhood. One of the forms of despair Anti-Climacus describes is 'the despair of defiance', in which an individual attempts to become his own master, the autonomous author of the self, recognizing no binding authority or transcendent values that might limit the freedom of the self. Such a self, according to Anti-Climacus, has a kind of freedom, but the problem is that in such a self 'there is nothing steadfast'. No commitments that the self makes are really binding; since the sole ground of those commitments is the freedom of the self, 'at any time it can arbitrarily start all over again ...'[45] Such an autonomous self turns out to be no self at all: 'it is easy to see that this absolute ruler is a king without a country, actually ruling over nothing; his position, his sovereignty, is subordinate to the dialectic that rebellion is legitimate at any moment.'[46]

MacIntyre recognizes that his interpretation of *Either/Or* is at variance with Kierkegaard's own interpretation of the work, and that the best Kierkegaard scholars have largely agreed with

---

[44] Ibid. 42.
[45] Kierkegaard, *The Sickness Unto Death*, 69.
[46] Ibid.

Kierkegaard's self-portrait.[47] Since *Either/Or* is pseudonymous, even if MacIntyre were right about *Either/Or* it would not follow that this represents Kierkegaard's own mature view. But is MacIntyre right about *Either/Or*? He claims that Kierkegaard's later self-interpretation is different from the view Kierkegaard had at the time *Either/Or* was written. According to MacIntyre, this later interpretation 'is difficult to sustain' if we take into account 'all the evidence that we have of Kierkegaard's attitudes in and up to the end of 1842'.[48] However, MacIntyre does not cite any of this evidence except to say that 'the text and the pseudonyms of *Enten-Eller* [*Either/Or*] are the best evidence of all.'[49]

However, so far as I can see, the 'text and pseudonyms' of *Either/Or* offer no evidence at all that Kierkegaard wishes to advocate a doctrine of radical choice. Even if the doctrine of radical choice is advocated by the pseudonyms found in the book, we have no reason for thinking that any or all of the pseudonyms represent Kierkegaard's own view at the time, any more than we would think that the characters in a novel necessarily speak for the author of that novel. And in fact only one of the two principal pseudonyms seems to espouse a doctrine of radical choice, and that is the aesthete A. A advocates radical choice, however, not as a basis for ethics, but as a defence against an ethical view of life. He presents his own 'philosophy' of either-or: 'Marry, and you will regret it. Do not marry, and you will also regret it. Marry or do not marry, you will regret it either way.'[50] A argues that the boredom and meaninglessness of existence can only be combated by an arbitrariness in choice that prevents choice from being taken seriously, and allows the individual to 'play shuttlecock with existence'.[51]

Judge William by no means adopts such a view of the ethical life. He attempts to give reasons why the ethical life is superior to the aesthetic life, and those reasons are not, contra MacIntyre,

---

[47] MacIntyre, *After Virtue*, 41. Davenport and Rudd (eds.), *Kierkegaard After MacIntyre* has some excellent critiques of MacIntyre on this point.

[48] MacIntyre, *After Virtue*, 41.

[49] Ibid.

[50] Kierkegaard, *Either/Or, I*, 38.

[51] Ibid. 294.

reasons that presuppose that the individual to whom they are directed has already made a 'radical choice' for the ethical. Rather, William argues that the ethical life is superior to the aesthetic life even on aesthetic grounds. In a long essay on marriage, he defends lifelong monogamous commitment on the grounds that it is a better realization of the needs and wants of romantic love than the casual love affair. It is true that William appeals to the young aesthete to make a fundamental choice, to make what we might call the choice to take choice seriously. Such a fundamental choice is analogous to the 'fundamental resolution' that Kant believes marks the beginning of the ethical life. However, William does not view such a choice as in any way arbitrary. In effect, he argues as follows: 'If you choose the aesthetic life and seek the satisfaction of your desires as your highest end, you will not be satisfied. If you choose the ethical life, you will not only realize the goods of ethical existence, but will satisfy your aesthetic desires as well.'

Is William's argument a good one? It is easy to show, I think, that William's positive view at the time is no more identical with Kierkegaard's own view than is that of A. As Johannes Climacus hints in *Concluding Unscientific Postscript*, the task of reconciling the spontaneity of romantic love and the demands of duty may not be as easy as William thinks.[52] However, this does not mean that William's criticisms of the aesthetic life are not telling and powerful, particularly in the second long essay, in which he argues that a life dominated by momentary desires ultimately leads to boredom and meaninglessness. I am personally inclined to agree with Johannes Climacus' judgement, which is that 'in the second part of *Either/Or* one finds answers to and a rectification of every deviation in the first part.'[53]

It is true that *Either/Or* contains no external 'result'. The Preface does not inform us who wins the argument. The 'plot' does not include an episode in which A goes insane or commits suicide. However, Johannes Climacus is again on target when he informs us that this in no way implies that the two perspectives represented are somehow 'equally valid'.

---

[52] Kierkegaard, *Concluding Unscientific Postscript*, 179–81.
[53] Ibid. 298.

A reader who needs the trustworthiness of a severe lecture or an unfortunate outcome (for example, madness, suicide, poverty, etc.) in order to see that a standpoint is in error still sees nothing and is merely deluding himself; ... Take a character like Johannes the Seducer. The person who needs to have him become insane or shoot himself in order to see that his standpoint is perdition does not actually see it but deludes himself into thinking that he does. ... the person who comprehends it comprehends it as soon as the Seducer opens his mouth; in every word he hears the ruination and the judgment upon him.[54]

I conclude that it is only if we identify with the position of A that we can think that *Either/Or* defends a doctrine of radical choice. And *Either/Or* itself, or at least the second volume, presents powerful arguments against the position of A, arguments that by no means beg the question in favour of the ethical. Perhaps someone will object here that the fact that A himself and aesthetes such as A may be unmoved by the Judge's arguments means that the arguments are not really powerful after all. Of course we do not know whether or not William's arguments had an effect on A. But suppose they did not? Are we to suppose that an argument that fails to convince an individual to make a basic change in her life-stance is not a good argument just because it failed to motivate the individual to change? This supposition would be dubious indeed. It is quite common for human beings to be presented with perfectly good arguments that fail to move them, especially if the arguments impinge on areas of fundamental human concern. It is in fact a proverb that 'a man convinced against his will holdeth the same opinion still.' It is quite possible for a good argument to fail to move an individual for the simple reason that human beings are not purely rational creatures.

It is telling that MacIntyre also claims that the doctrine of radical choice is present in *Philosophical Fragments* as the ground of faith.[55] It is true that *Fragments* argues strongly against evidentialism with respect to faith. The faith in the 'God in time' that is the subject of the book is not seen as something that can be created in a person by any amount of

---

[54] Ibid. 296–7.
[55] MacIntyre, *After Virtue*, 41.

historical evidence. However, MacIntyre here confuses a choice
that is not made on the basis of evidence with the different idea
of a choice that is made arbitrarily and therefore for 'no reason'.
Fragments argues quite clearly, however, that faith is not something that can be created in an individual by an act of will at all.
The thesis of the book is that faith is a new condition that results
from being 'born again'. It is not an arbitrary choice, but
something like a gift: a condition that God creates in the individual when there is a kind of first-person encounter with
God.[56] For the person of faith, faith appears to be anything
but an arbitrary choice. Faith that is not based on evidence may
still have a ground; the ground in this case would be the encounter between God and the individual that leads to faith.[57]

What I think is actually present in Kierkegaard's pseudonymous work is a movement away from Enlightenment conceptions of 'reason' as 'that which would convince any rational
being', or 'that which is impervious to doubt'.[58] Kierkegaard
recognizes that in moral and religious matters (as with most
philosophical issues) one cannot come up with rational arguments that meet such criteria. Rather, he believes that our
ability to grasp moral and religious truths depends in part on
the condition of ourselves. People with healthy moral and religious concerns are able to see truths that people who lack such
concerns cannot see. He is concerned therefore not simply to
'didactically' present and argue the truth, but to help people

[56] For a fuller account of the nature of faith and how it comes to be in the
person according to *Philosophical Fragments* see my *Passionate Reason:
Making Sense of Kierkegaard's* Philosophical Fragments, 119–69.

[57] For a clear discussion of the distinction between evidence and grounds
and its importance for philosophy of religion see Alvin Plantinga, 'Reason and
Belief in God', in *Faith and Rationality*, ed. Alvin Plantinga and Nicholas
Wolterstorff (Notre Dame, Ind.: University of Notre Dame Press, 1983). For
an application of this distinction to Kierkegaard and Plantinga, see my own
'Kierkegaard and Plantinga on Belief in God: Subjectivity as the Ground of
Properly Basic Beliefs', *Faith and Philosophy*, 5/1 (1988).

[58] For an interesting discussion of Kierkegaard's ethics that highlights the
theme of the tension between disengaged and committed thinking, see Anthony Rudd, *Kierkegaard and the Limits of the Ethical* (Oxford: Oxford University Press, 1993). Rudd is in some respects a follower of MacIntyre in his
analysis of the contemporary ethical situation, but he disagrees with MacIntyre's account of the role Kierkegaard plays in relation to modernity. Also see
Rudd's essay in Davenport and Rudd (eds.), *Kierkegaard After MacIntyre*.

become transformed so that they are capable of seeing the truth. Truth is linked to inwardness and subjectivity.[59] But such a post-Enlightenment account of reason is far from a doctrine of radical choice. It actually is close to MacIntyre's own conception of reason as something that is necessarily historically situated.

CONCLUSION: THE ETHICAL AS A TRANSCENDED STAGE

The task of developing an account of Kierkegaard's ethical views is then a complicated one. The term 'ethical' is often used in the authorship to refer to a particular stage or sphere of existence, one that is transcended by the religious life. However, if my argument above is correct, the basis for the ranking of the spheres lies in the ability of the higher spheres to realize the aims of the lower ones. If this is so, then the ethical should reappear within the religious sphere. This is in fact precisely what we shall find, though the term itself is not always found, and that is not surprising, since the word is so heavily used to describe the transcended stage.

There is of course no 'neutral' standpoint from which it can be decided whether or not this characterization of the stages is correct. The person who believes that he or she is doing pretty well at the task of becoming the self he or she ought to be may be deaf to the claims of the religious life that it better realizes the aims of the ethical life than does the ethical sphere itself. So the argument that follows may be one that has more force to someone who recognizes the pervasiveness and seriousness of the problem of guilt in human life. However, every argument begins somewhere, and no argument can be compelling to everyone. The recognition of the situatedness of human thinking about such issues is not a reversion to the doctrine of radical

---

[59] For a strong argument for the claim that emotions enable us to discern moral truths see Robert Roberts, 'Feeling One's Emotions and Knowing One's Self', *Philosophical Studies*, 77 (1995), 319–38. This view is implied by Roberts' basic account of emotion, found in 'What is an Emotion: A Sketch', in *Philosophical Review*, 97 (1988), 183–209. Also see Adams, *Finite and Infinite Goods*, ch. 15, and my article 'The Epistemological Significance of Transformative Religious Experience', *Faith and Philosophy*, 8 2 (1991).

choice. Nor is it a despairing embrace of a kind of 'presupposi-
tionalism' that is simply resigned to ultimate differences that
cannot be discussed or resolved. Questions about the pervasiveness and seriousness of guilt within the ethical can certainly be
discussed and debated, as can the adequacy of religious solu-
tions to the problems. We can look for common ground. We
simply cannot be assured in advance that we will find it.

As promised, I shall turn next to a pseudonymous work in
which the relation between the ethical as a stage and the religious life is made the central focus of discussion: *Fear and
Trembling*. There is much to be learned about both the ethical
and the religious life from this work. However, it is not Kierkegaard's own definitive account of the ethical life. It is a book
about religious faith, not ethics, and it is written from the point
of view of a person who in some ways does not understand the
faith that he writes about.

3

'The Ethical' in *Fear and Trembling*

Kierkegaard would hardly have been surprised that readers are still captivated by *Fear and Trembling*. He said prophetically that after he is dead, '*Fear and Trembling* alone will be enough for an imperishable name as an author. Then it will [be] read, translated into foreign languages as well.'[1]

The success of *Fear and Trembling* is certainly linked to the literary quality of the book. It is as much poetry as philosophy, and any attempt to summarize its contents must inevitably falsify the character of the work as a whole. Nevertheless, the work's treatment of the frightful test to which God put Abraham in demanding that he sacrifice his son Isaac has had a profound influence on discussions of the relation between ethics and religion. Several of the best treatments of the relation of ethics to God, particularly with respect to the question of whether it would be right to obey a command to perform an act that would otherwise be immoral, have used *Fear and Trembling* as their point of departure.[2]

Kierkegaard was of course not the first writer to discuss the Abraham and Isaac story and its implications. There is a long tradition of rabbinical interpretation, and the case was thoroughly discussed by such medieval writers as

---

[1] Kierkegaard, *Journals and Papers*, vi. entry 6491.

[2] I would cite three writers in particular. Gene Outka's essay, 'Religious and Moral Duty: Notes on *Fear and Trembling*', in *Religion and Morality*, ed. Gene Outka and John P. Reeder, Jr. (Garden City, NY: Anchor Books, 1973) is a model of lucidity and care. Philip Quinn has written several essays that employ *Fear and Trembling*, including 'Moral Obligation, Religious Demand, and Practical Conflict'. Finally, Robert Adams devotes an entire chapter in *Finite and Infinite Goods* to a careful, sympathetic treatment of the issues raised by *Fear and Trembling*. I will discuss Adams' view in Chapter 13 and register my dissent from some of his conclusions.

Aquinas.[3] Closer in time to Kierkegaard, both Kant and Hegel
had discussed the case, and both agreed that it would be wrong
for Abraham to sacrifice his son, even if he has received a
command to do so that purports to be from God. Kant's reason
for saying this is primarily epistemological. It is, he believes,
certain that a person ought not to kill his son. However, that an
apparition or voice urging someone to kill his son is really a
revelation from God cannot be known with certainty, and hence
such an alleged revelation should not be obeyed.[4]

Fear and Trembling can indeed be read with profit by one who
wishes to think hard about the relation of moral duties to religion. Moreover, the central question the book is often thought
to raise, whether God could make an otherwise immoral act
obligatory by commanding it, is one that a divine command
theory of moral obligation must face, and I will consider it in
the concluding chapter of this work. However, I want to argue
that *Fear and Trembling* is not the book on which to focus if one
wants to understand Kierkegaard's own views on ethics. Kierkegaard's primary concern in creating the pseudonym Johannes
de Silentio, and through him, *Fear and Trembling*, is not to
develop an ethical theory, but to combat widespread nineteenth-century assumptions about the nature of theology and
its relation to philosophy and to culture. The book is primarily
about the nature of the self and its identity. I shall develop my
argument that *Fear and Trembling* is not about ethics by
defending three theses: (1) The book is primarily about faith,
and the role faith should play in the formation of the self's
identity. The ethical is treated because it is something that can
easily be confused with faith, and this confusion is prevalent in
many nineteenth-century thinkers. (2) The conception of the
ethical the book embodies is not identical with the view of

[3] For a study of Jewish treatments of the problem, see Louis Jacobs, 'The
Problem of the *Akedah* in Jewish Thought,' in *Kierkegaard's* Fear and Trembling: *A Critical Appraisal*, ed. Robert L. Perkins (Tuscaloosa, Ala. University of Alabama Press, 1981), 1–9.
[4] See Immanuel Kant, *The Conflict of the Faculties*, trans. Mary J. Gregor
(Lincoln, Nebr.: University of Nebraska Press, 115 n. The principle underlying this judgement is also explained in *Religion Within the Limits of Reason
Alone*, trans. Theodore M. Greene and Hoyt H. Hudson (New York: Harper
and Row, 1960), 175.

the ethical Kierkegaard develops under his own name, or even with the view of the ethical developed by other pseudonyms closer to Kierkegaard, such as Johannes Climacus. (3) *Fear and Trembling* is a pseudonymous work, and its pseudonymous author, Johannes de Silentio, is most emphatically distinct from Kierkegaard. I will attempt to elaborate on each of these points, taking them in reverse order.

THE ELUSIVENESS OF 'JOHN OF SILENCE'

As noted above, *Fear and Trembling* is a book about faith. It is therefore notable that its pseudonymous author, Johannes de Silentio, on numerous occasions confesses that he is not a person of faith, and affirms that he does not understand faith. Perhaps his 'silence' is a way of stressing that because he lacks faith and lacks an insider's understanding of faith, he necessarily fails to communicate what faith is.

A strong hint in this direction is given by the book's epigraph: 'Was Tarquinius Superbus in seinem Garten mit den Mohnköpfen sprach, verstand der Sohn, aber nicht der Bote. [What Tarquinius Superbus said in the garden by means of the poppies, the son understood but the messenger did not.]'[5] The quotation refers to a story from antiquity in which the son of Tarquinius Superbus had gained control of the city of Gabii, and sent a messenger to his father to inquire as to what he should do. Tarquinius did not trust the messenger and simply walked around his garden, cutting off the tallest poppy flowers. The messenger did not understand this, but when he related the father's actions to the son, the son correctly inferred that he should seek to weaken the city by bringing about the death of its leading citizens.

It seems to me quite plausible that Johannes de Silentio is himself the messenger of the book, and that he communicates something that he himself does not really understand. One may well ask how Johannes can communicate anything about something he does not understand? Perhaps the 'son' who is the intended audience may well learn something indirectly about

---

[5] Kierkegaard, *Fear and Trembling*, 3. Subsequent references to this work in this chapter are denoted by page nos. in parentheses.

faith by coming to see what Johannes does not grasp and why he cannot grasp it, much as readers of P. G. Wodehouse's 'Jeeves' series come to see the truth about various situations amusingly through Bertie Wooster's accounts, even though those accounts frequently are rooted in deep incomprehension on the part of Wooster himself. However, Johannes himself, though he may not know what faith is, may well know a lot about what faith is not, and offer helpful clarifications to block the identification of faith with things with which we are tempted to confuse it. Nor is it impossible for him to have a kind of formal understanding of faith, an 'outsider's' view of the elements or structure of faith, without a clear grasp of what motivates what he calls the 'movements' of faith from the inside.

Confirmation of Johannes' confession that he is not a person of faith can be found in his attitude towards faith. Johannes describes himself repeatedly as someone who does not understand faith, but admires it nevertheless. He affirms that he 'can understand a tragic hero, but cannot understand Abraham, even though in a certain demented sense I admire him more than all others' (p. 57). Kierkegaard himself affirms, however, that in the realm of spirit, admiration is a dubious quality. In *Works of Love* he argues that genuine love for the neighbour is distinguished from the natural love present in paganism precisely by the fact that the ground of these natural loves includes admiration. 'The neighbor, however, has never been presented as an object of admiration.'[6] In *Practice in Christianity*, the person of faith is described as a follower, not an admirer, since admiration can be a psychological substitute for imitation.[7] It is easy to convince myself I must be a fine fellow because of my great admiration for a Mother Teresa; it is hard to live like a Mother Teresa. 'The ethical truth of the matter is just this— that admiration is suspiciously like an evasion.'[8] Kierkegaard would, I think, endorse the claim of Johannes Climacus in *Concluding Unscientific Postscript*: 'What is great with regard to the universal must therefore not be presented as an object for

---

[6] Kierkegaard, *Works of Love*, 54.

[7] Søren Kierkegaard, *Practice in Christianity*, ed. and trans. by Howard V. Hong and Edna H. Hong (Princeton: Princeton University Press, 1991), 237–57.

[8] Kierkegaard, *Journals and Papers*, iv. entry 4454.

admiration, but as a *requirement*.'[9] There is nothing so conducive to sleep, ethically speaking, as admiration.[10]

One may well question whether Kierkegaard is altogether fair
to admiration here. Although admiration may be a substitute
for imitation, can it not also be an inspiration for ethical
striving? Whether that be so or not, the point is that from
Kierkegaard's own viewpoint, there is something suspicious
about someone who admires faith, a suspicion that expresses
itself in self-doubts as Kierkegaard worries that he also might
merely be a 'religious poet' who substitutes praise of faith for
emulation.[11] Johannes de Silentio, however, seems clearly to be
such a poet, who admires what he does not see himself as
capable of achieving.[12]

That the perspective of Kierkegaard does not coincide with
that of his pseudonym can also be seen in the careful way
Kierkegaard comments about *Fear and Trembling* in his *Journals and Papers*. Almost every reader recognizes the autobiographical dimension to *Fear and Trembling*, seeing Regine
Olsen as the 'Isaac' Kierkegaard believed he was called to
sacrifice, or (less commonly) Kierkegaard himself as the Isaac
sacrificed by his own father.[13] This autobiographical dimension
is sometimes present in Kierkegaard's *Journals and Papers*
when he comments on the book. However, when he focuses
on the *views* presented in the book, Kierkegaard's tone changes.
He is generally careful to attribute these views to Johannes, and
in fact often comments as if he were simply a reader and had no
role in the creation of the work.[14]

It is also worth pointing out that the major concepts and
strategies employed in *Fear and Trembling* do not for the most
part reappear in other writings of Kierkegaard, particularly in

[9] Kierkegaard, *Concluding Unscientific Postscript*, 358.
[10] Ibid. 360.
[11] See the evidently autobiographical anxieties expressed in Kierkegaard,
The Sickness Unto Death, 77–9.
[12] See de Silentio's discussion of the relation between the 'poet' and the
'hero' in Kierkegaard, *Fear and Trembling*, 15–16. In many ways de Silentio
appears to be the poet whose task is to eulogize Abraham as a hero of faith.
[13] For the latter view see Gregor Malantschuk, *Kierkegaard's Thought*, 238.
[14] See, for example, entries 3130, 6434, and 6598 in Kierkegaard, *Journals
and Papers*.

the non-pseudonymous works. The imaginative figures of the 'knight of faith' and the 'knight of infinite resignation' play no role when Kierkegaard articulates faith in his own voice. Alastair McKinnon has shown, through his computerized studies of Kierkegaard's texts, that the concept of faith as 'the absurd,' while present in other pseudonymous texts of Kierkegaard, is virtually absent from the non-pseudonymous writings.[15] This is one more clue that the perspective of Johannes de Silentio is the self-confessed perspective of an outsider who lacks faith. It is clearly distinct from the perspective of Kierkegaard himself, though this of course should not be taken to imply that Kierkegaard must be thought to disagree with everything de Silentio affirms.

THE CONCEPT OF THE ETHICAL IN *FEAR AND TREMBLING*

Fear and Trembling attempts to contrast the life of faith with ethical existence. To understand the contrast and its implications, it is crucial to see clearly what conception of the ethical serves as the backdrop for the comparison. What perspective on the ethical do we get from Johannes de Silentio, keeping in mind that this perspective may not be Kierkegaard's own view of the matter, either at the time of writing or later?

Some commentators have thought that the operative conception of the ethical present in *Fear and Trembling* is Kantian. It is true that the ethical is sometimes described in the book in Kantian language: 'The ethical as such is the universal, and as the universal it applies to everyone, which from another angle means that it applies at all times' (p. 54). It is also the case that in other Kierkegaardian works, notably *Upbuilding Discourses in Various Spirits* and *Concluding Unscientific Postscript,* various ethical claims associated with Kant are defended. However, I think there is strong evidence that the concept of the ethical that

[15] McKinnon notes that '[t]he difference between the pseudonymous works and acknowledged works may be seen in the fact that, according to our lists, the words Paradoks and Absurde, together with their variants, appear 238 times in the former but never in the latter.' 'Kierkegaard and His Pseudonyms: a Preliminary Report', in *Kierkegaardiana* (Copenhagen: Munksgaard, 1968), 64–76 (quotation from p. 70).

is present in *Fear and Trembling* is much closer to Hegel than to Kant.

We must begin by noting that the Kantian language of the 'universal' cannot here be decisive, since Hegel uses this language as well.[16] The agreement in language between Kant and Hegel does not of course signify substantive agreement. Kant uses the language of universality to speak of general principles (grounded in one supreme principle) that are valid for all people in all times and places. Hegel, on the other hand, considers this to be an 'abstract' universal, and prefers what he calls the 'concrete' universal, the general will as embodied in the laws and customs of a people. So to determine the significance of the 'universal', we must look at the actual characterizations of what counts as ethical duties and why they are duties. In order to decide the question, a very brief sketch of the difference between Hegelian and Kantian thinking about the ethical will be helpful.

One key difference is that for Kant our fundamental moral duties apply directly to individual human beings as rational agents. The moral law has its ground in pure practical reason. It binds the individual because the individual is a rational being who autonomously lays these obligations on himself.[17] Kant distinguishes sharply between actions that stem from what he terms 'inclination' and actions that stem from reason; true moral worth attaches only to the latter. The individual as an individual is capable of grasping the Categorical Imperative, and, using this imperative as a touchstone, rationally deciding which maxims can be consistently willed as universal laws. Although Kant certainly recognizes that the individual has particular moral duties that are grounded in the social relations in which he finds himself (such as duties to the state and family), by and large the fundamental character of morality rests in reason,

---

[16] The Hongs rightly call attention in an endnote to a passage in *The Philosophy of Right*, a book Kierkegaard owned. See endnote 4, p. 346 in the Hong translation of *Fear and Trembling*.

[17] The full story is considerably more complicated than this. I believe John Hare is correct to argue that Kant's claim that moral duties must be understood as divine commands, with God as the Head of the Kingdom of Ends, is an important part of the story. See ch. 3 of Hare, *God's Call*. However, this aspect of the story can be ignored for the purpose of this contrast with Hegel.

understood as a faculty possessed by the autonomous, historically unembedded individual. Fundamental moral obligations
are universal, and so do not vary from temporal era to era or
between cultures. (Hegel would of course agree that ethics rests
on 'reason' but has a different conception of reason as expressing itself in history.)

In Hegel's dialectic, Kantian morality, like other moments in
the development of Absolute Spirit, has its truth, but it is not
the whole truth. For Hegel, Kant's morality (*Moralität*) rests on
a faulty understanding of individuals as existing independently
of the social relations in which they are involved. Hegel criti-
cizes the categorical imperative as overly formal and ultimately
unable to guide actions by determining particular duties. He
thinks rather that the demands of reason must become concrete
by becoming embodied in social institutions that would make
possible an ethic (*Sittlichkeit*) that could actually guide the lives
of a people. Such an ethic would overcome such dualisms as the
split between reason and inclination and that between the individual and society. The individual satisfies the demands of
reason not by autonomously legislating for himself, but by
recognizing and affirming those demands as they are embedded
in the institutions of the society in which he participates.

There is an historical dimension to Hegel's account of the
ethical life that is largely missing from Kant. The story begins
with social systems, such as the ancient Greek city-state, in
which the individual's identity is given by the social roles and
responsibilities assigned. With such figures as Socrates, reason
begins the process of criticizing the historically contingent features of such societies, a process that culminates in the kind of
individual morality found in Kant. However, Hegel believed
that modern states had achieved or were achieving a social
system in which the demands of reason would no longer be in
opposition to the demands of society, because those societies
were themselves the realization of those demands of reason.[18]

---

[18] Hegel has a somewhat ambivalent attitude toward liberal democracy. His
ideal state is definitely capitalist, and he believes that the people must have a
voice in society, but he supports an hereditary monarchy, and clearly his
communitarian views would not favour the individualism presupposed by
classical liberalism. I am grateful to Merold Westphal for this point and
suggestions about this whole section on the ethics of Hegel and Kant.

Ethical obligations then stem from such concrete social institutions as the family and the state, which is for Hegel the pre-
eminent source of ethical duty.

To summarize, for Kant individuals are subject to moral
duties simply because as human persons they are rational
agents. Moral duties hold not only for all human beings but
for all 'rational agents' who do not have a 'holy will' that
conforms perfectly and spontaneously to the requirements of
duty. For Hegel, however, individuals have the ethical duties
they have by virtue of the concrete social relations in which they
participate.

When we look at what Johannes de Silentio says about the
ethical in light of this contrast, the fundamentally Hegelian
character of his thought is striking. The ethical is most clearly
illustrated by de Silentio in the three 'tragic heroes' he sketches,
the figures of Agamemnon, Jepthah, and Brutus. The tragic
heroes are explicitly designated as representatives of the ethical;
a tragic hero is 'the beloved son of ethics' (p. 113). De Silentio
describes these figures because they bear a superficial resemblance to Abraham, in that each believed himself to have a duty
to bring about the death of his child. Agamemnon must sacrifice
Iphigenia if the Greek fleet is to be allowed to depart successfully on its military mission. Jepthah wins a victory to save his
people, but the victory is contingent on a vow he has made that
requires him to sacrifice his daughter. Brutus' civic duty requires him to order the execution of his sons.

According to de Silentio, none of these figures is really analogous to Abraham, because 'the tragic hero is still within the
ethical. He allows an expression of the ethical to have its *telos* in
a higher expression of the ethical' (p. 58). In each of the three
cases, the ethical duties grounded in the family are trumped by a
higher duty that is grounded in the state or the nation. The case
of Abraham is different, precisely because Abraham did not
participate in any social institution higher than the family. 'It
is not to save a nation, not to uphold the idea of the state that
Abraham does it. . . . There is no higher expression for the
ethical in Abraham's life than that the father shall love the
son' (p. 59).

I think it is clear that the concept of the ethical embedded in
this notion of the tragic hero is not the Kantian one of timeless

duties that persons have because they are autonomous rational beings, but something like the Hegelian notion of the ethical as grounded in the social institutions in which an individual participates. Moreover, there is a striking element of historical relativity to this concept of the ethical. De Silentio portrays the actions of his tragic heroes in putting their children to death as actions that are unambiguously ethically right, actions that any ethical person can understand, justify, and admire. But this is most emphatically untrue if we take as our ethical standard contemporary ethical convictions.

I believe that few contemporary ethicists would approve of the idea of a monarch sacrificing his daughter in order to make possible a military adventure. Nor would many ethicists agree that a rash vow such as Jepthah's would in fact be morally binding. Perhaps only the actions of Brutus would come close to being morally approvable today, for we can understand and endorse the idea that a public official should judge impartially and show no favouritism to his own family, though we might have questions about the harshness of the legal system Brutus administers.

Of course even to raise questions about whether such actions would be approved today is to indulge in anachronism. The descriptions Johannes makes of the actions of Agamemnon and Jepthah clearly presuppose as a given such things as divine oracles. But this makes it still more evident that when de Silentio affirms that these actions are clearly ethical, the relevant ethical standards are not timeless Kantian moral laws, but the actual standards of the societies of the tragic heroes in question.

I believe that this means that the claims de Silentio makes about the relation of the ethical to the religious life must be understood as relative to a particular conception of the ethical. I thus largely agree with Gene Outka's claim that the tension between rational ethical duties and religious duties in *Fear and Trembling* is a tension that may appear differently or could even disappear if one had a different conception of the ethical. '[O]ne may appeal to plausibly rational characterizations of the ethical which call into question Kierkegaard's insistence on a conflict in principle and suggest an excessively stipulative element in the account of the ethical he offers.'[19] I would correct Outka only by

---

[19] Outka, 'Religious and Moral Duty', 205.

insisting that the view of the ethical at issue should be attributed to Johannes de Silentio rather than Kierkegaard, and by noting that, given the influence of Hegel at the time, the concept of the ethical employed is not really properly described as 'stipulative', though it is certainly a debatable one today. This does not mean that there is nothing to learn about the ethical from *Fear and Trembling*, but it does mean that one cannot simply attribute the views of Johannes de Silentio about the ethical to Kierkegaard himself without additional argument.

THE ETHICAL AND 'INFINITE RESIGNATION'

Many commentators have assumed that the contrast between religious duty and ethical duty in *Fear and Trembling* centres around the decision of Abraham to sacrifice Isaac. Certainly, there is much in the book that supports this. If, however, we think of this contrast as one between an ethical action that can be rationally justified and a religious duty that is in some sense 'absurd' and thus rationally unjustifiable there are reasons to doubt that this is the correct way to think about the contrast. Most commentators either have not noticed or else have not properly appreciated the fact that de Silentio argues that there is a sense in which Abraham's willingness to sacrifice Isaac can be understood.[20] What is 'absurd,' and what de Silentio claims not to understand, is not Abraham's willingness to sacrifice Isaac, but rather Abraham's *faith*. This faith does *not* show itself in Abraham's willingness to draw the knife, but in Abraham's ability to receive Isaac back again with joy.

The point is one that de Silentio makes by a contrast between the 'knight of faith' and the figure he calls the 'knight of infinite resignation', a position he appears to identify as his own, at least potentially.[21] The latter figure is a kind of religious hero who

---

[20] An exception is Edward Mooney, in his article 'Getting Isaac Back: Ordeals and Reconciliations in *Fear and Trembling*,' in *Foundations of Kierkegaard's Vision of Community: Religion, Ethics, and Politics in Kierkegaard*, ed. George Connell and C. Stephen Evans (Atlantic Highlands, NJ: Humanities Press, 1992), 71–95. Also see Mooney's book *Knights of Faith and Resignation: Reading Kierkegaard's* Fear and Trembling (Albany NY: SUNY Press, 1991).

[21] The question as to the relation of the knight of infinite resignation to the tragic hero is a difficult one that will be discussed below.

does not relate to God via some particular revelation, as does Abraham, but through a natural human faculty. Infinite resignation is a position that every human being can achieve 'who wills it' and those who lack it are simply lacking in courage (pp. 45, 48). 'The act of resignation does not require faith, for what I gain in resignation is my eternal consciousness. This is a purely philosophical movement that I venture to make when it is demanded and can discipline myself to make' (p. 48). As de Silentio explains this attitude, through this act of resignation a person can gain a kind of God-relationship that empties finite, temporal goods of significance; one gains an 'eternal consciousness' that is 'love for God' (p. 48).

If a knight of infinite resignation is placed in the situation of Abraham, the problem for him is not deciding whether to obey the command. Imagining himself in this situation, Johannes says he would have followed through: 'I would not have been cowardly enough to stay at home, nor would I have dragged and drifted along the road or forgotten the knife in order to cause a delay. I am quite sure that I would have been punctual and all prepared—more than likely I would have arrived too early in order to get it over sooner' (pp. 34–5). The result of all this is an attitude that appears to border on despair: 'Now all is lost, God demands Isaac, I sacrifice him and along with him all my joy— yet God is love and continues to be that for me, for in the world of time God and I cannot talk with each other, we have no language in common' (p. 35).

The knight of faith and the knight of infinite resignation have in common this 'philosophical movement' of resignation. Both have, as it were, given God everything. However, for the knight of faith resignation is only a preliminary movement, something faith presupposes, but which clearly is not identical with faith. What is distinctive about faith is a second movement, in which, having renounced the finite, temporal goods are received again as a joyous gift 'by virtue of the absurd' (p. 40). What de Silentio finds impossible to understand in Abraham is this second movement. He can understand Abraham's willingness to sacrifice Isaac; what is baffling to him is Abraham's ability to receive Isaac back with joy. Johannes could have sacrificed Isaac himself, but he could not have responded to God's gift as Abraham did:

[F]or if I had gotten Isaac again, I would have been in an awkward position. What was the easiest for Abraham would have been difficult for me—once again to be happy in Isaac!—for he who with all the infinity of his soul, . . . has made the infinite movement and cannot do more, he keeps Isaac only with pain. (p. 35)

Infinite resignation cannot enjoy the finite because it has essentially given up the finite world and lives only for eternity. Abraham, however, did not merely 'have faith that God would bless him in a future life but that he would be blessed here in the world' (p. 36).

How should we understand these two positions of faith and infinite resignation? It seems to me that what we have here is a contrast between two different religious stances. Resignation in some sense involves love for God and belief in God's goodness, but it is a love and belief that cannot be translated into temporal concerns, but expresses itself only as an abandonment of such concerns. An 'Abraham' who is a knight of infinite resignation could sacrifice Isaac, if called by God to do so, because such a figure has already sacrificed the finite world and has no expectations about this life. The Abraham who is a model of faith in de Silentio's sense, however, is an Abraham who believes and trusts God in the temporal world. God has promised Abraham that he will be a father of many nations in Isaac. Abraham believes and trusts God, even when it makes no sense to do so from a human, rational perspective. He believes that even though God has asked him to sacrifice Isaac, somehow Isaac will not be sacrificed, or that if he is sacrificed, God will raise Isaac from the dead (p. 36).

Since infinite resignation is supposed to be a 'philosophical' movement that any human can make, it is clear that de Silentio is claiming that there is a human perspective that must be in some sense rational from which a decision to sacrifice Isaac would be understandable. What he cannot grasp is that someone who has heroically achieved such a stance of resignation could in some way receive back that which he has renounced. 'By faith Abraham did not renounce Isaac, but by faith Abraham received Isaac' (p. 49).

The inference I wish to draw from this is not that contemporary readers and thinkers should find nothing problematic in Abraham's willingness to sacrifice Isaac. This is certainly a case whose implications are troubling for advocates of a divine command ethic, and I have already promised a serious treatment in Chapter 13 of the issues the case raises. Rather, it is the fact that *Johannes* professes to find the real problem to lie in getting Isaac back again rather than sacrificing him (at least some of the time) that is striking. Since Johannes clearly links the ethical with human reason, the fact that he finds the action of sacrificing Isaac comprehensible may mean that in some sense it could be 'ethical', though if this is so there must be some sense of the 'ethical' that is distinct from the Hegelian conception in the book. (Whether this is so depends in part on the relation between the tragic hero and the knight of infinite resignation; they appear to be different figures but de Silentio seems to identify them at one point.[22]) This may simply deepen our sense that the concepts of the 'ethical' and 'human reason' that de Silentio seems to accept are problematic, though that is not to say his concepts are indefensible. However, the problematic character of these views adds weight to my claim that de Silentio's perspective on the ethical cannot automatically be credited to Kierkegaard.

FAITH: WHAT IS *FEAR AND TREMBLING* REALLY ABOUT?

In this chapter I have so far given two reasons for denying that *Fear and Trembling* is definitive for understanding Kierkegaard as an ethical thinker. We have seen that Johannes de Silentio is a character with his own perspective that is clearly distinct from Kierkegaard's, and that his views on the ethical are quite distinctive and even problematic. The 'ethical' with which faith is contrasted seems to be a stance that is quite Hegelian, seeing ethical obligations largely as embodied in the historically relative institutions and practices of societies. Furthermore, from the perspective of de Silentio, the 'absurdity' of Abraham's

---

[22] They appear to be different when introduced because the tragic hero makes the sacrifice of one finite good for a higher good (the State), while infinite resignation sacrifices the whole of the finite for the eternal. However, on p. 78, de Silentio describes the tragic hero as an individual who has made 'the infinite movement, and is now secure in the universal', and he seems to equate the tragic hero and the knight of infinite resignation on p. 34.

action lies not in his willingness to sacrifice Isaac, but in his ability to receive Isaac back again with gladness.

One might think that this problematic view of the ethical would be a severe liability in the work. This might be so, if *Fear and Trembling* were primarily designed to illuminate the ethical life. However, this is clearly not the case. The point of the book is not to help us get clearer about ethics, but to help us get clearer about faith. De Silentio appears to think that the gravest danger on this score is the confusion of faith with the ethical life in precisely its Hegelian sense. The error he fears most is that of thinking that a person who is 'nice' or 'good' in a conventional sense, who fulfils the social responsibilities assigned to him or her, therefore possesses faith. This is the attitude of 'Christendom', the attitude that assumes that we all have faith and that faith is something easy, natural, and immediate. If faith is being confused with ethics in the Hegelian sense of *Sittlichkeit*, then it is a merit of the book and not a problem that the ethical is understood in the way that it is.

That this is the main theme of the book can be seen if we look at the 'frame' of the book. Kierkegaard pays close attention to the way his books begin and end, and *Fear and Trembling* is no exception. The main targets of both the Preface and Epilogue are those who think faith is something easy and natural, those who think that if one wants to be special one must 'go further'. Johannes begins with some satirical doubts about universal doubt: 'Every speculative monitor who conscientiously signals the important trends in modern philosophy, every assistant professor, tutor, and student, every rural outsider and tenant incumbent in philosophy is unwilling to stop with doubting everything but goes further' (p. 5). Johannes clearly does not think universal doubt is as easy to accomplish as modern philosophy supposes:

What those ancient Greeks, who after all did know a little about philosophy, assumed to be a task for a whole lifetime, because proficiency in doubting is not acquired in days and weeks, what the old veteran disputant attained, he who had maintained the equilibrium of doubt throughout all the specious arguments, who had intrepidly denied the certainty of the senses and the certainty of thought, who, uncompromising, had defied the anxiety of self-love and the insinuations of fellow feeling—with that everyone begins in our age. (pp. 6–7)

The Preface draws a parallel between this attitude towards doubt and the assumption that faith is something easy: 'In our age, everyone is unwilling to stop with faith but goes further.' However, 'it was different in those ancient days. Faith was then a task for a whole lifetime' (p. 7).

The Epilogue ends the book on precisely the same note: 'Faith is the highest passion in a person. There perhaps are many in every generation who do not come to faith, but no one goes further' (p. 122). The illusion that one can go beyond faith is grounded in the Hegelian view that the human task is grounded in the particular stage of world-history in which one finds himself, particularly in the Hegelian claims that the modern world and the modern state are the completion of the process in which Spirit is actualizing itself, and that this achievement embodies the truths of religion as well as philosophy. Johannes proposes a different view of history in which every generation has the same task and begins at the same point:

> the generation does indeed have the task and has nothing to do with the fact that the previous generation had the same task, unless this particular generation, or the individuals in it, presumptuously assumes the place that belongs to the spirit who rules the world and who has the patience not to become weary. (p. 122)

Johannes sees the combination of Hegelian ethics and Hegelian philosophy of history to be fatal for an understanding of genuine religious faith. If my society is itself the concrete embodiment of the divine, then *Sittlichkeit*, ethical participation in those social institutions by accepting 'my station and its duties', is at the same time true religion.[23] It makes perfectly good sense to think of faith as a common social possession. What is at stake here is precisely the transcendence of the divine. Is the will of God entirely mediated through society, understood by Hegel as embodied most fully in the state? Or is it possible that God might speak directly to an individual human being as an individual, calling that individual to a task that challenges the prevailing cultural norms and values, perhaps demanding that

---

[23] The phrase 'my station and its duties' is of course taken from the title of a famous essay by the English follower of Hegel, F. H. Bradley. The essay can be found in Bradley's *Ethical Studies* (London: Oxford University Press, 1876).

the individual accept the martyrdom from the state that was the fate of both Socrates and Jesus?[24]

It is against this backdrop that the argument of Johannes that Abraham's act cannot be understood in ethical terms must be understood. Three characterizations of the contrast between ethical and religious duties are given, corresponding to the three 'Problemata' Johannes discusses. First, the case of Abraham involves a 'teleological suspension of the ethical'. What is important to note here is that this suspension of the ethical in question is *teleological*, that is, a suspension for the sake of a higher end or goal. The question as to whether there can be such a thing as a teleological suspension of the ethical is then essentially whether there can be an end higher than those posited by *Sittlichkeit*. If 'my station and its duties' is the highest *telos* for a human being, then obviously such a thing is not possible.

The second Problema clarifies what is at stake by characterizing the issue in terms of the relation between 'the absolute' and 'the universal'. The universal is specifically identified with the ethical, and it is clear that the absolute is God. The question posed is whether or not there is such a thing as an absolute duty towards God. The proponent of *Sittlichkeit* may say that all duties are duties toward God, but if God is identified with the social order, then God as a transcendent reality disappears; his reality is exhausted by my social duties: 'God comes to be an invisible vanishing point, an impotent thought' (p. 68). Only if God transcends the social order is a teleological suspension of the ethical possible. An absolute duty to God would then relativize one's ordinary ethical duties. The person of faith is the individual who 'determines his relation to the universal by his relation to the absolute, not his relation to the absolute by his relation to the universal' (p. 70). That is to say, the God-relationship of a person of faith is a real relation that can shape that individual's relations to others. Such a claim makes no sense if

---

[24] It is worth noting here that Socrates, along with Jesus, is a figure that Kierkegaard constantly admires and uses as a model. For an arresting treatment of parallels between these two figures, see Paul Gooch, *Reflections on Jesus and Socrates: Word and Silence* (New Haven: Yale University Press, 1996).

God simply is a personification of the social demands that are embedded in those social relationships.

The third Problema, which concerns whether or not Abraham was ethically justified in not communicating what he intended to do to Sarah, Isaac, and his servant Eliezer, might appear to be different. Johannes argues in this section that Abraham has no choice in the matter: 'Abraham *cannot* speak, because he cannot say that which would explain everything (that is, so it is understandable)' (p. 115). Why is this so? I believe that a Wittgensteinian perspective on language can illuminate the Hegelian picture that Johannes has in mind at this point. Human language is not separable from the social practices in which it is embedded. To learn to speak a language is analogous to learning a game, and in fact language itself can be understood as a complex of 'language games'. Such language games are embedded in social realities; in Wittgenstein's words, 'to imagine a language means to imagine a form of life'.[25]

If we accept this, then the third Problema is one more manifestation of the possibility of something higher than *Sittlichkeit*. What counts as a justification cannot be separated from the social practices of society, for justification is itself a set of social practices embedded in language. If Abraham could explain and justify his actions to others in his society, then in effect he would be conforming to the universal and his actions would be understandable in terms of prevailing social morality. For that morality is linked to and expressed in the linguistic practices of that society. If, on the other hand, Abraham as an individual can have a real relation to God in which God makes demands on him, there is no guarantee that those demands can be explained and justified in ways that his society will understand.

Note again that I am not concerned here with the adequacy of the Hegelian/Wittgensteinian understanding of ethics and language in terms of which the contrast with the religious is drawn. We might well wish to challenge such an understanding, and if we do, we might redraw the issues. Perhaps Abraham's actions are not really unintelligible per se but only unintelligible from a

---

[25] Ludwig Wittgenstein, *Philosophical Investigations*, 3rd. edn., trans. G. E. M. Anscombe (New York: the Macmillan co, 1968), 8e.

particular perspective.[26] Perhaps the linguistic and ethical practices of a given society are not so coherent and unified as to be
able to speak of 'the ethical' in the sense of *Sittlichkeit* at all. But
if we wish to understand Johannes' point about religious duties
and faith, we must look at the issues from his perspective. If
understanding and justification are themselves grounded in the
social practices of a particular culture, then no radical challenge
to those practices that stems from a transcendent authority can
hope to make itself intelligible to that society by appeal to the
standards that are being challenged.[27]

Why should we care about whether such a possibility of
radical challenge to existing values is kept open? Well, we
might worry about the dangers that stem from deifying existing
social and cultural norms. The possibility of a future Socrates
or a Jesus would be precluded by such a deification, because we
would complacently assume that from an ethical perspective we
have arrived. We are at 'the end of history', ethically speaking. I
think that the possibility of this kind of cultural critique is
indeed important to keep alive, and that it is perhaps what
thinkers such as Richard Rorty have in mind when they argue
that we should leave space for new ways of speaking and thinking.[28] Perhaps it is what Heidegger had in mind in his description of the 'poet' who speaks the new words that might provide
the basis for a new 'world' in which to exist.[29] Otherwise, we are
stuck with the world Johannes de Silentio describes as the world
of the 'bourgeois-philistine', the world in which human understanding is reduced to the kind of 'calculative reason' Johannes

---

[26] This is certainly the thrust of the Outka essay mentioned in n. 2 above. I
have made a similar argument myself in 'Faith as the Telos of Morality: A
Reading of *Fear and Trembling*', in Fear and Trembling and Repetition:
International Kierkegaard Commentary, ed. Robert L. Perkins (Macon, Ga.:
Mercer University Press, 1993), 9–27.

[27] Mark Dooley's *The Politics of Exodus: Kierkegaard's Ethics of Responsibility* (New York: Fordham University Press, 2001) gives strong and clear
support to such a claim.

[28] See 'The Contingency of Language', in Richard Rorty, *Contingency,
Irony, and Solidarity* (New York: Cambridge University Press, 1989), 3–22.

[29] See Martin Heidegger, 'The Origin of the Work of Art', in *Martin
Heidegger: Basic Writings*, ed. David Krell (New York: Harper and Row,
1977), 185 ff.

has in mind when he describes this faculty as the 'stockbroker of the finite' (p. 36).

Important as such concerns might be, however, they are not the ground of Johannes' own conviction that Abraham represents a valuable possibility. Johannes has in mind not primarily the dangers to society when society deifies itself (though Kierkegaard himself is by no means unaware of this issue), but the despair that such a social system entails for the individual who is in some way unable to 'fit in', unable to accomplish the 'universal' by assuming 'my station and its duties'. The possibility that Abraham represents is that there is another path to selfhood than cultural conformity. At one point Johannes imagines an Abraham who is an ethical tragic hero courageously choosing suicide rather than obeying God. Such an Abraham 'would have been admired in the world, and his name would never be forgotten; but it is one thing to be admired and another to become the guiding star that saves the anguished' (p. 21). Who are the anguished ones Abraham can save? And how can he save them?

Throughout the book Abraham is represented as a 'righteous man' who has fully accomplished his ethical tasks, fulfilled his ethical duties. How is it that by imagining Abraham as a paragon of the ethical (an assumption by no means supported by the Biblical text, which several times shows Abraham as deceitful[30]), the character of faith as something distinct from the ethical is supposed to be delineated more clearly? The answer, I think, is that if Abraham were not pictured in this ethical way, his faith would have to take the character of *repentance*, an action that would bring him back into relation with the ethical. Given that Abraham is already perfectly ethical, his faith shows itself in an exceptional action that appears to be unethical. Presumably as a person of faith Abraham lives his whole life in faith, including his ethical life. His faith can be dramatically seen, from the outside so to speak, only in an action that cannot be understood ethically. As a person of faith, Abraham has 'an absolute relation to the absolute', and this can be seen most clearly in a case in which the absolute (God) asks him to do

---

[30] See, for example, Genesis 12: 10–20, where Abraham deceives by claiming his wife is his sister.

something that is opposed to the ethical universal. However, at several points Johannes drops hints that there is another type of person for whom the possibility of this type of direct relation to God is very important: not the righteous paragon of the ethical that we see in Abraham, but the person who for some reason finds it impossible to fulfil the ethical.

Several examples are given in Problema III. Johannes gives an extended treatment of the legend of Agnes and the merman, and at one point imagines the merman as a demonic figure, unlike Abraham in his guilt, but who, like Abraham, is a 'single individual . . . higher than the universal' (p. 97). Conceived in this way, despite the differences from Abraham, the kind of direct relationship to God seen in Abraham's life is crucial to the merman as well: 'In other words, when the single individual by his guilt has come outside the universal, he can return only by virtue of having come as the single individual into an absolute relation to the absolute' (p. 98).

Johannes goes on to hint that this is a point of tremendous importance, signalled by the comment that 'here I would like to make a comment that says more than has been said at any point previously' (p. 98). The comment centres on sin and guilt. He explains that '[i]n sin, the single individual is already higher (in the direction of the demonic paradox) than the universal, because it is a contradiction on the part of the universal to want to demand itself from a person who lacks the *conditio sine qua non* [indispensable condition]' (p. 98). In effect, citing the Kantian principle that 'ought implies can', he asserts that the person in the grip of sin is in some way free from or outside the ethical.

Another example of the kind of individual he has in mind is given later in the figure of Shakespeare's Gloucester (Richard III), whose physical deformity and the pity it evokes from others embitter him against ordinary life. According to Johannes, '[n]atures such as Gloucester's cannot be saved by mediating them into an idea of society' (p. 106). He goes so far as to say that ethics 'makes sport' of such people.

For individuals such as the merman and Gloucester, ethics is not a path to salvation, but a path to despair. For people who must come to terms with sin, ethics cannot be the final answer to the problem of selfhood: 'An ethics that ignores sin is a completely futile discipline, but if it affirms sin, then it has *eo ipso* exceeded itself' (pp. 98–9). The same point is repeated in a footnote: 'As soon as sin emerges, ethics founders precisely on repentance, for repentance is the highest ethical expression, but precisely as such it is the deepest ethical self-contradiction' (p. 98 n.).

What does this have to do with Abraham? In one sense, not much, at least for Johannes' Abraham, 'who did not become the single individual by way of sin—on the contrary, he was a righteous man, God's chosen one' (p. 99). Johannes has given us in his Abraham a sketch of what true religious faith would be like in a person who is perfectly ethical. In such an individual, faith can only be seen, or is at least most clearly visible, in an act that 'teleologically suspends' the ethical. The demonic individual is in a different situation. This person would only be in Abraham's situation after he has been able to 'fulfil the universal'.

And just when will that be? It is at this point I think that the pseudonymous character of the work is most strongly evident. If Johannes de Silentio were a Christian believer, he would know and believe in the doctrine of original sin. Kierkegaard himself regularly claims that this doctrine lies at the heart of Christian faith, comparing it to a 'knot' that a sewer must tie at the end to prevent all the thread in a garment from unravelling.[31] According to this doctrine, the Abraham of *Fear and Trembling* is truly a fictional character, for 'all we like sheep have gone astray; we have turned every one to his own way.' The 'exceptional' figures of the merman and Gloucester are not really exceptional; they represent the human condition. All of us are stuck with the problem that John Hare calls the 'moral gap'.[32] Faith for such individuals does not express itself primarily in exceptional situations in which they must go against the ethical, but in a repentance that makes it possible for them to become a coherent self at all. If this is the case, we can understand why Johannes Climacus, in commenting on *Fear and Trembling*, in *Concluding Unscientific Postscript*, says that the 'teleological suspension of the ethical' needs to be given 'an even more definite religious expression'.[33] The relevance and importance of such a 'suspension' is not fully understood until

---

[31] See Kierkegaard, *The Sickness Unto Death*, 93.
[32] See Hare, *The Moral Gap*.
[33] Kierkegaard, *Concluding Unscientific Postscript*, 266–7.

we see that we are, as a result of sin, already 'suspended', in the most terrible way, from the ethical requirement, obligated to achieve the ideal but completely unable to do so.

If that is our situation, if we find ourselves to resemble the merman and Gloucester, then we may truly be among those 'anguished ones' for whom Abraham is the 'guiding star'. For, as we have already seen, Abraham represents the possibility that an individual may determine 'his relation to the universal by his relation to the absolute, not his relation to the absolute by his relation to the universal' (p. 70). In other words, it may be possible for a person to relate to the ethical by means of a direct relation to God, rather than simply relating to God through fulfilling one's social duties.

The tendency of theology from Kant to Hegel, and indeed in nineteenth-century Protestant liberalism as a whole, was to reduce genuine religious faith to ethics. Jesus was viewed more as a profound ethical teacher, less as a divine saviour. Kant himself is explicit that true religious faith is closely linked to the ethical life: '*Whatever, over and above good life-conduct, man fancies he can do to become well-pleasing to God is mere religious illusion and pseudo-service of God.*'[34] It is true that Kant thinks that the religious person may legitimately hope that God has done something to help us overcome the moral gap, but for Kant belief that God has acted in history to make atonement for sin lies outside what is required by reason, morally or religiously.

Fear and Trembling raises troubling and profound questions about the identity of the ethical and the religious, particularly when the 'ethical' is understood in a Hegelian way so that it is concretely embodied in the dominant ideals of a society, what Kierkegaard calls, in a phrase reminiscent of a much-later student radicalism, 'the established order' or 'establishment'. Once we see that the main point of the work is to call into question the identification of faith with ethics, we can see that it is a misunderstanding to view it primarily as a positive account of the ethical life. The conception of the ethical with which faith is contrasted is the conception dominant in Danish society at the time, at least as Kierkegaard perceives it. It is by no

---

[34] Kant, *Religion Within the Limits of Reason Alone*, 158 (emphasis Kant's).

means the account of the ethical life that will appear from within the life of faith. For that account, we must look to someone who speaks from the perspective of faith, not Johannes de Silentio.

4

The Ethical Task as the Human Task

My primary task in this book is to look at the ethical perspective Kierkegaard presents in *Works of Love*. One might think at this point that the task has been deferred too long already. Nevertheless, before plunging into an examination of some of the major themes of *Works of Love*, I believe it is worthwhile to examine the thinking about the ethical life presented in two other works of Kierkegaard: *Concluding Unscientific Postscript* and *Upbuilding Discourses in Various Spirits*, particularly the section from Part 1 that has been published separately in English under the title *Purity of Heart Is to Will One Thing*.

So far we have looked very briefly at *Either/Or* and *Fear and Trembling*, mainly to argue that these are not the works from which to develop an account of Kierkegaard's mature ethical thinking. My analysis of *Concluding Unscientific Postscript* will be of a very different character, with constructive aims. I believe that consideration of themes from this book will provide an illuminating perspective from which to view the claims made in *Works of Love*.

One might object at this point that *Concluding Unscientific Postscript*, like *Either/Or* and *Fear and Trembling*, is a pseudonymous book and that one cannot therefore identify the views of its author Johannes Climacus with those of Kierkegaard. This is true, and what I have to say about the book, far from ignoring its pseudonymous character, partly depends on that character. *Works of Love* is an explicitly Christian book, that takes its starting place in a Biblical text and is introduced by a trinitarian prayer. It is not easy to see how such a book can be introduced into contemporary debates in ethical theory, which for the most part assume a 'secular' point of view. What I wish to do is to use Johannes Climacus, who is not a Christian thinker, as a kind of bridge between *Works of Love* and philosophical debates about ethics.

Though Climacus is interested in Christianity, he professes not to be a Christian. His discussions of ethical issues do not presuppose any specifically Christian beliefs. I believe that it can be shown, however, that the way he poses the questions of secular ethics helps us see how the claims made in *Works of Love* answer those questions. Another way of making the same point is to say that Climacus addresses what might be called the formal structure of ethics. He does not do so as a Christian. However, the way he does this allows Christian ethics into the conversation, so to speak, by showing how its content can be seen to fit that structure.

This is not to say that Climacus discusses ethics from some kind of neutral perspective. The claims he makes about the structure of the ethical life turn out to be substantive and even contentious. But they are claims that can be made and defended without any specific religious standpoint being assumed. If I am right in my conviction that his standpoint provides a way of seeing how Christian faith can be seen as giving answers to the central questions of ethics, then this shows how Christian ethics can become part of the contemporary ethical debate without first demanding that its debating partners accept some religious authority as the basis for discussion.

The genuinely pseudonymous character of *Concluding Unscientific Postscript* seems to me beyond doubt. Johannes Climacus is not a Christian believer, but a self-described 'humorist', a kind of philosophical thinker with his own religious stance.[1] Nevertheless, he is an individual interested in Christianity, and not merely in a disinterested academic sense. He wants to know how to become a Christian. This strong orientation towards Christianity does give Climacus a close link to Kierkegaard the Christian writer, a link that Kierkegaard signals by placing his own name on the title page as editor. One might say that Climacus gives an accurate account of how Christianity appears from the perspective of a sympathetic outsider, someone who could even be described as a 'seeker'. Such a view is far from an insider's perspective on faith. However, it often captures im-

---

[1] See Lippitt, *Humor and Irony*, and also ch. 10 of my *Kierkegaard's* Fragments *and* Postscript.

portant insights about faith that can be seen from both sides so to speak.

This close relation does not mean that Johannes Climacus is a closet Christian.[2] However, it does mean that he says many things that Kierkegaard could and did say in his own voice. One way to demonstrate this is by a comparison of *Concluding Unscientific Postscript* with some of the non-pseudonymous 'upbuilding' writings that Kierkegaard published under his own name. To this end I shall in this chapter look not only at *Concluding Unscientific Postscript* but at the first section of *Upbuilding Discourses in Various Spirits*, which I will henceforth refer to for the sake of conciseness and clarity as *Purity of Heart*. In this work, written shortly after *Concluding Unscientific Postscript*, Kierkegaard gives in his own voice the same kind of formal analysis of the structure of ethical life that we see in Climacus. This is not to say that *Purity of Heart* is intended as a work of ethical theory. It is rather an 'upbuilding' or edifying work that is written as preparation for confession. In serving this end, however, the book presents a clear picture of the ethical life, and we shall see significant parallels between that picture and the views of *Concluding Unscientific Postscript*.

THE 'ABSOLUTE' ETHICAL TASK: BECOMING A SELF

Formally, the account of the ethical offered by Johannes Climacus seems Aristotelian, in that he sees the ethical task in terms of the actualization of a distinctively human potentiality: 'Ethics concentrates upon the individual, and ethically understood it is every individual's task to become a whole human being,...' (p. 346). However, the concept of what a human being is differs in several respects from Aristotle's. We shall see that the self is understood in continuity with Socrates and Kant in a decidedly moral manner.[3]

---

[2] Though it could be argued that this is possible, since 'humour' is one of the 'incognitos' of the true Christian. See Kierkegaard, *Concluding Unscientific Postscript*, 504–9, 521. Subsequent references to this work in this chapter denoted by page nos. in parentheses.

[3] This section and the ones following draw on material from ch. 5, 'Existence and the Ethical', in my *Kierkegaard's* Fragments *and* Postscript.

It will not be hard to show that the conception of the ethical made possible by this view of the self is quite different from the picture presented in *Fear and Trembling*. The conception of the self offered by Climacus differs from Hegel even more strongly than from Aristotle. The conception of the ethical that Johannes Climacus holds is quite different from the Hegelian notion of *Sittlichkeit* that is contrasted with religious faith in *Fear and Trembling*. Far from regarding the ethical life as exhausted by the obligations created by social institutions, Climacus thinks that genuine ethical life only begins when an individual sees himself or herself as not being entirely defined by such social obligations. The ethical task is grounded in some kind of absolute requirement that lifts the individual out of the conformism involved in socially mediated duties. Climacus believes that every individual has a kind of awareness of this absolute ideal.

The encounter with this absolute ethical ideal is in fact an encounter with God; Climacus actually seems to identify God with the ethical at various points (p. 244). However, though an encounter with the ethical is an encounter with God, it is by no means always the case that the ethical individual recognizes this fact. On the contrary, a person may gain an impression of 'the infinitude of the ethical' without realizing that this involves an impression of God. However, the person who lacks an awareness of the ethical lacks an awareness of God, even though such a person may 'know how to bow his head every time God's name was mentioned' (p. 244). Climacus satirizes the person who lives without such an awareness of the infinite; such a person 'might very well live on, marry, be respected and esteemed as husband, father, and captain of the popinjay shooting club, . . . ' (p. 244).[4] This is of course more a caricature than a fair description of *Sittlichkeit*, but from the viewpoint of Climacus the satire captures what is objectionable about an ethic of 'my station and its duties'. *Sittlichkeit* does not really allow people to become individuals; they are defined by their social roles and unable to express that individual quality that Climacus calls 'primitivity' [*Primitivitet*], the unique self that God intended each person to become.[5] Instead, the ethical conformist manages life with

----

[4] For others as mystified by this reference as I was, popinjay shooting is apparently shooting at an artificial bird on a pole.

[5] See Kierkegaard, *Sickness Unto Death*, 33.

'custom and tradition', living the way a child must eat who does not yet know table manners, watching to see how 'the others' do it (p. 244).

Genuine ethical life then arises when an individual becomes aware of an absolute requirement that is rooted in something transcendent. There is obviously a close connection on this view between ethics and religion; religious life, at least in the 'natural' form Climacus calls 'Religiousness A', grows out of the ethical life.[6] The difference between the two is not that one involves belief in God or a relation to God and the other does not. It is rather a matter of how the individual relates to God. Both involve a relation to an 'absolute *telos*' or end, which is either God or something that stems from God (Climacus is not always clear about this), though as noted above, the individual may not realize that this is a God-relation. As Climacus describes the ethical life, the individual sees herself or himself as having an ability to realize the ethical task. The religious life begins when the individual recognizes the impossibility of doing so. The ethical life is characterized by 'struggle and victory', the religious life by guilt and suffering (pp. 288, 532–4).

What sense can we make of these remarks by Climacus? How can an awareness of the absolute ideal of ethics be or include an awareness of God? Of course we could think that 'God' here is just a symbol for unrealized human potential, a dramatic way of speaking about a requirement that human beings lay on themselves.[7] However, that is not how Climacus seems to think of God, and he clearly thinks that the individual requires some kind of transcendent basis for the ideal that distinguishes my potential ideal self from a set of social roles. Such a self cannot simply be invented by the self.

There is some looseness in the language of Climacus here, but I believe it is possible to see what he is getting at. If we take

[6] In saying that Religiousness A grows out of the ethical life, I do not mean thereby to distinguish it from Religiousness B, since there is also a sense in which this is true of B, at least in part. However, Religiousness B has as its ground an historical revelation and thus does not emerge solely out of human ethical-religious experience as does A.

[7] See Don Cupitt, *Taking Leave of God* (New York: Crossroad, 1981) for a clear example of such a view.

seriously the idea that God has created and is creating each self, then we can see the task of becoming one's self to be simultaneously the task of achieving a proper relation to God. In creating me God endows me with the potential to become a particular self, and he gives me the freedom to do so or fail to do so. I relate properly to God only by recognizing and assuming the task he has given to me, a task which is absolute in the sense that it overrides all other responsibilities I may have.

It is this conception of the human self as containing a potentiality that is given by God as a task that makes it possible for Climacus to combine a view of the ethical task that sounds formally like Aristotle's with a description of the ethical life that sounds very much like Kant's. He speaks of the ethical task in terms of self-actualization, but he also speaks of ethical obligations as absolute in character. In a Kantian spirit the ethical person seeks to do his or her duty, and does so without concern for results.[8] How can the ethical life be described in such diverse ways as 'Actualize yourself' and 'Do your duty for the sake of duty'? Both can be true if the self that is to be actualized is conceived in thoroughly moral terms. The true self is the morally virtuous self, and one becomes one's self by learning to care about moral virtue for its own sake.

One might worry that the religious character of the ethical task as Climacus conceives it undermines any claim that he is offering an ethical theory that can be taken seriously by philosophers. Obviously, the kind of ethic that Climacus proposes is likely to be rejected or regarded as implausible by the great majority of secular philosophers. However, that does not mean it is not a serious proposal that can be defended without appeal to religious authority.

As evidence for this I would cite the contemporary work of Robert Adams, particularly *Finite and Infinite Goods*. In this book Adams argues that ethics has a theistic basis. God as a loving personal being is identified with the Good, an infinite, transcendent reality. Finite goods are good because and to the degree that they resemble God. Moral obligations are identified

---

[8] For the unimportance of results, see Kierkegaard, *Concluding Unscientific Postscript*, 134–41. For a philosophical discussion of this point, see my *Kierkegaard's* Fragments *and* Postscript, 75–81.

with the commands of this loving God. Adams argues that such a view is perfectly consistent with the supposition that many people who are aware of the Good and of moral obligations do not recognize that these properties are related to God in the way they are. Nevertheless, he presents serious arguments that this view is superior to such secular rival theories as expressivism, utilitarianism, and other forms of ethical naturalism. Adams' view, like that of Climacus, is unlikely to be accepted by many secular philosophers. However, it is a view that is presented and argued by Adams without appeal to any religious tradition or authority. There seems to be no reason in principle why a religiously grounded ethic cannot be put forward into contemporary ethical debates.

THE CONTENT OF THE ETHICAL TASK: SELFHOOD, SOUL-MAKING, AND EQUALITY

A major constraint on the self-actualization ethic Climacus presents is a commitment to a principle of equality. In some sense every human being must have the opportunity to achieve the ethical task of becoming a self. This egalitarianism actually is a deep strand in Kierkegaard's thinking as well, and constitutes one of the points of agreement between Kierkegaard and Climacus. The commitment to equality shows itself at many points. For example, Climacus argues that since every person has the ethical task of becoming a whole person, 'it is the presupposition of ethics that every person is born in such a condition that he can become one' (p. 346). Paradoxically, the task of becoming 'the individual' is a universal task:

To want to be an individual human being (which is what one undeniably is) by help of and in power of one's differential distinctions is cowardice; but to want to be an individual human being (which is what one undeniably is) in the same sense that every other person can is the ethical victory over life and over all illusions (p. 309).[9]

This egalitarianism is a major factor that pushes this ethic of self-actualization in a Kantian direction. If we measure selfhood by such qualities as potentiality for artistic creation or scientific

---

[9] I have here modified the Hong translation.

achievement it is obvious that many people lack the ability to make much progress towards becoming a self, either because of their genetic endowments or environmental handicaps. Climacus affirms, rather, that the task of the individual 'is to transform himself into an instrument which clearly and definitely expresses the human in existence. To comfort oneself with respect to differences is a misunderstanding, for the business of having a little better mind and other such things is purely insignificant' (p. 309).[10]

There are two reasons why Climacus believes people are on an equal footing in the task of becoming selves. First, the ideal is, so to speak, relativized by being individualized. For each individual the task is to become the particular self God has created that person to be. If I have been given musical gifts, then I must reflect on whether I should develop those gifts and how I should use them. However, if I have little or nothing in the way of musical talent I have no such obligation. Secondly, the essential self that I must become is seen in moral terms and in this respect the task is the same for everyone. Every person has the responsibility to strive to become the self he or she should be; every person thus has essentially the same moral duty. Though the content of the task obviously is different for everyone, the character of moral striving can be the same. Every person can strive to do what is right (being obedient to the call to become the self he or she should be) because it is right. Every human person has the power to make responsible choices, to seek to do what he or she ought to do. Each of us has the power to develop moral character, and in fact, Climacus believes that simple, uneducated people are by no means disadvantaged in this task.[11]

It is in fact a general Kierkegaardian maxim that with respect to what he calls the 'passions' there is a kind of human equality. People are not equal in intellectual or artistic abilities. However, he believes that everyone has the capacity to care about what is morally right and strive to become morally good. If he is

---

[10] Again, this is my translation.

[11] See his discussion of 'the simple people', who 'feel the pressure of life', Kierkegaard, *Concluding Unscientific Postscript*, 170 n (my translation). The Hongs translate '*de Eenfoldige*' (literally 'the simple') as 'the simple folk'.

mistaken about this, and in fact people differ in their moral capacities, this inequality is mitigated by the way the moral task is individualized by God. Human persons must in some sense have an equal ability to achieve the task because the task is apportioned to their abilities. It might even be the case, for example, that for a person with deeply anti-social tendencies the self the person is assigned as a task would hardly be recognizable as having moral character by society generally.

One useful way to think about the kind of ethic presented by Climacus is in terms of a contrast between what we might call a 'soul-making' ethic as opposed to a 'society-transforming' ethic. There is a long tradition in philosophy of thinking of the ethical life as the development of moral character. The Socrates presented in Plato's dialogues seems to think this way, often characterizing life as something like 'sentry duty,' an assignment to a post by the gods in which we will be examined with respect to how well we have carried out the assignment.[12] If the achievement of moral character is *the* human task, then Socrates' claim in the *Apology* becomes intelligible: 'Nothing can harm a good man, either in life or after death, and his fortunes are not a matter of indifference to the gods.'[13] If the true self is the soul and the soul's destiny is linked to its character, then the only thing that can truly damage a person is wrongdoing. The most terrible calamity that can befall a person is not to suffer wrong or injury but to do wrong, for only wrongdoing can injure the soul.[14] People may be fortunate or unfortunate in the reception of such goods as health, wealth, and intelligence, but in the ethical realm goodness is more fairly distributed.[15]

Such a soul-making ethic is markedly different from the classical utilitarian perspective, that sees moral goodness

---

[12] See Plato's *Apology*, 28e–29b, in *The Collected Dialogues of Plato*, eds. Edith Hamilton and Huntington Cairns, trans. Hugh Tredennick (Princeton: Princeton University Press, 1963).

[13] Ibid. 41 c–d.

[14] Ibid. 30 d–e.

[15] Thus Socrates, like Kierkegaard and Climacus, would have to reject the idea that there is 'moral luck', an idea popularized by Bernard Williams. See Williams, *Moral Luck: Philosophical Papers* (New York: Cambridge University Press, 1981).

primarily as something that is instrumentally good, something that should be valued because it leads to happiness or other natural, non-moral goods. It is true that thinkers such as John Stuart Mill make a distinction between evaluation of the act and evaluation of the agent, but it is evident that most of Mill's attention goes to the former. John Dewey represents almost a pure example of the outlook that emphasizes the value of the results of moral action, rather than seeing moral character as an end in itself:

This constant throwing of emphasis back upon a change made in ourselves instead of one made in the world in which we live seems to me the essence of what is objectionable in 'subjectivism'. . . All the theories which put conversion 'of the eye of the soul' in the place of a conversion of natural and social objects that modifies goods actually experienced, is a retreat and escape from existence . . . The typical example is perhaps the other-worldliness found in religions whose chief concern is with the salvation of the personal soul.[16]

Such an attitude is about as different from the Socratic view of life as a 'sentry post' as can be imagined.

There is little doubt that all of Climacus's sympathies are with the Socratic type of view in this dispute, and he pointedly rejects what he calls 'eudaimonism'.[17] However, he takes as his direct target not merely utilitarianism, but any kind of theory that attempts to locate the ethical task by looking at what can be accomplished from a 'world-historical' point of view. Climacus certainly has Hegelians in mind as a primary target here. Perhaps we could characterize the kind of view he wishes to attack as one that sees the ethical task in the following way: we must seek to understand the progressive direction of history, ascertain where we are in the course of history, and do what we can to move the wheel of history one step further towards its goal.

---

[16] John Dewey, *The Quest for Certainty* (New York: G. P. Putnam's Sons, 1929), 275.

[17] It should be noted that Kierkegaard's understanding of 'eudaimonism' is somewhat idiosyncratic, and this is reflected in Climacus's usage as well. Kierkegaard uses the term for views that regard moral actions as justified by the achievement of non-moral results desired by the agent. An ethical view that links the moral life to happiness is not necessarily 'eudaimonistic' in this sense, since the happiness in view is not necessarily to be viewed as an external consequence to moral action but as a constituent of the moral life itself.

Some of Hegel's Marxist descendants might well fit this description pretty well, but it is not, I think, a mentality that is unknown among non-Marxists with serious social concerns. The particular version of Hegelianism that engenders ridicule from Climacus is one that sees the goal of history as already having been achieved. The only ethical task left for us would seem to be the intellectual task of contemplating and understanding this momentous achievement.

Climacus does not see world-history as in any way a source of moral guidance. He finds several things objectionable about such a view. First, as even Hegel admits, the world-historical process is only understandable in retrospect. It is only after the fact that one can see a revolution or election as one that advances the cause of freedom or prosperity or whatever one sees as the goal of history. Since the ethical must give us guidance for the future, such a retrospective understanding is of no help in deciding what we must do, even if it is possible to discern moral progress when we look back at history (pp. 146–7). In any case, the ethical task cannot consist simply in intellectual understanding, since the essence of the ethical life is the choosing of alternative actions.

Secondly, a concern for world-historical significance can compromise the purity of ethical intentions. The person who wills to achieve some great historical result does not will simply to be morally good. Rather, at best the person wishes to achieve some significant result through his goodness. But what about the case when that result requires some moral compromise? The person who aims at some world-historical result will at this point have a 'divided self,' and the purity of his moral resolve will be tarnished. This is, by the way, a major theme of *Purity of Heart* and constitutes one of the points of agreement between Climacus and Kierkegaard I will discuss later in the chapter.

One might object at this point that a truly moral person can have concerns with world-historical significance. Think, for example, of William Wilberforce and his struggle against slavery. The answer to this objection, I think, is to note that there is no reason why the moral tasks assigned to some individuals might not have world-historical significance. The individual's primary task must be to become the self he or she is supposed to become. For some, such as a William Wilberforce, famous for his campaign against slavery, a crucial component of that self's identity may be opposition to some great social evil. However, Wilberforce's moral greatness must not be measured simply by his world-historical success. A Wilberforce who attempted to do the same things but whose efforts were unsuccessful due to external circumstances would not be morally inferior to the actual Wilberforce. What is crucial is that in measuring Wilberforce's moral greatness we focus on the common human task: his fulfilling the task assigned to him and his becoming the person he should be.

If the ethical task is defined primarily in terms of world-historical achievement, then the principle of equality that Climacus accepts cannot be maintained. Some people (such as Wilberforce) are inevitably in a more advantageous position to achieve important world-historical results than others. Indeed, such a view of the ethical task seems to imply that the lives of most humans, who have lived in obscurity, are devoid of significance, except perhaps as 'fodder' for the world-historical process.

From a soul-making point of view, things look very different: '[T]here is no squandering [of human lives], for even if individuals are as innumerable as the sands of the sea, the task of becoming subjective is indeed assigned to each person' (p. 159)[18]. From an ethical point of view, people who are historically insignificant may accomplish more than a Napoleon:

> In relation to the cleverest, most daring plan to transform the whole world, the principle is valid that it becomes great by virtue of the result; in relation to the simple and loyal resolution of an obscure human being the principle holds that the plan is higher than any result, that its greatness is not dependent upon the result. (p. 398)[19]

Such a view can even give meaning to suffering, and it implies that the significance of a life cannot be measured by its length. From an ethical perspective 'the time itself is the task' with the time here meaning whatever lifespan one receives (p. 164). To somehow 'go beyond' the ethical task is to misunderstand the

---

[18] Translation modified.   [19] My translation.

task, since 'to become finished with life, before life is finished with one, is precisely not finishing the task' (p. 164).

It might appear that an ethic of self-actualization that characterizes the self that is to be actualized in moral terms is circular in a way that makes the account vacuous. It makes sense, one might think, that I might have certain potential qualities that I have an obligation to actualize. If I do actualize them, I am fulfilling my moral duty. However, if the self that is to be actualized is itself characterized as one that fulfils its moral duty, then it appears that 'moral duty' will not have any concrete content. What is a moral self? One that has fulfilled its obligation to become itself. What self am I to become? A moral self. This appears to be an unilluminating circle.

To escape this problem I believe that Climacus must posit some non-moral content to the self that a person must become. How can he do that and still claim that the true self is essentially the moral self? The key is to make a distinction between the essential form of the self and the material content of the self. Every actual self has some concrete qualities that ought to be actualized; we might call that the material content of the self. The moral obligation to become that self can be seen as the formal quality that all human persons share. A commitment to become the self I ought to become is thereby also a commitment to actualize those concrete material qualities. One cannot actualize one's moral potential without simultaneously actualizing the concrete qualities, including the non-moral ones, that are included in one's ideal self. The person who is truly committed to becoming the self he or she ought to be has in one sense become the self he or she ought to be, morally. But in becoming this self, he or she necessarily becomes something particular as well.

An example may help here. Suppose that I have prodigious musical talent. I reflect on this talent and arrive at some decision as to how I ought to develop it and use it. If I do so I am becoming my true self, the moral self, in exactly the same way that people can who have no musical talent whatsoever.

From a formal point of view the self I must become is simply the self who is willing to make the 'absolute venture' and commit to the good. However, every person who does make such a venture will find that it must express itself in concrete ways.

A careful look at the text will reveal that Climacus does indeed speak about the non-moral qualities of the self that must be actualized: 'Ethics focuses upon the individual, and ethically understood it is every individual's task to become a whole human being' (p. 346). What does it mean to become a whole human being? Climacus says that there are universal dimensions to the human self, qualities that every person must strive to develop. Every individual has the potential for thought, for imagination, and emotion, and one cannot become a whole person without the development of all these qualities: 'In existence, the important thing is that all elements are present simultaneously. With respect to existence, thinking is not at all superior to imagination and feeling but is coordinate' (pp. 346–7). Every person must attempt to unite 'the true, the good, and the beautiful' in their lives (p. 348). It is true that all of us are individuals and that in actual individuals there will always be a certain one-sidedness, but Climacus affirms that even in our one-sidedness we can affirm an ideal of wholeness: '[o]ne-sidedness should on the one hand not be regarded without sadness, and on the other hand should result from a strong resolution that would prefer to be something thoroughly than to dabble in everything' (p. 349).

These universal qualities that Climacus says we humans must strive to develop do not rule out the individual nature of the self each must become. Such qualities as thought and beauty are highly abstract and when present in actual humans must take on a particular quality. Perhaps one individual has the capacity to create great poetry, while another might be able only to appreciate the beauty of the poetry. A person's calling can include universal tasks but still be highly individual in the way those must be realized. Furthermore, though Climacus says that the individual self I must become includes these universal dimensions of humanness, he does not say that it is exhausted by them. The concrete self I must become includes individual qualities as well.

The 'soul-making' task is not vacuous. We can see how the human person who aims to become moral or virtuous necessarily aims at other ends as well.

THE ETHICAL AND 'RESULTS': CLIMACUS THE DEONTOLOGIST

Soul-making ethical views tend towards the deontological end of the ethical spectrum, and the soul-making ethic that Climacus sketches has a notably deontological character that has already shown itself in our discussion of its egalitarianism.[20] The ethical focus is primarily on the development of moral character, and Climacus by no means thinks that there is a necessary correlation between such character development and what we might call 'external' results. In fact, Climacus seems to go to an extreme by disparaging results altogether: 'True ethical enthusiasm consists in willing to the utmost of one's capability, but also, uplifted in divine jest, in never thinking whether or not one thereby achieves something' (p. 135). Climacus goes so far as to say that a truly great ethical individual would choose to remain in ignorance of external results: 'even in death he would *will* not to know that his life had any significance other than that of having ethically prepared the development of his soul' (p. 136).

One might wonder whether or not this ideal is even coherent, much less desirable. All action necessarily aims at some end, and insofar as one enthusiastically wills an end, it is difficult to see how the agent could be indifferent as to whether the end was achieved. I believe that a careful reading of this passage will show that this extreme lack of concern for results is not what Climacus has in mind.

The context makes it clear that the results Climacus has in mind are what we might call consequences with world-historical significance. The difficulty with respect to this kind of result is that such consequences are never fully within our

[20] I hope it is clear that in speaking of a deontological approach to ethics, I wish to emphasize an ethics that focuses on duty rather than simply the achieving of good consequences. I do not mean by 'deontological' to focus on actions rather than the achievement of character, since our duties include the duty to become a certain type of person, one who is loving.

power: 'Neither by willing the good to the utmost of his ability nor by willing evil with diabolical callousness is a person assured of becoming world-historical' (p. 134). This means that from an ethical perspective, a person who achieves such a world-historical result does so 'by accident' (p. 134). As soon as one aims directly at world-historical significance, rather than simply aiming at the ends that the ethical demands, the purity of one's ethical resolve is compromised.

On this reading, Climacus is not advancing the absurd thesis that a person could willingly choose to be ignorant of the direct results of his or her action. If I reach down from a bridge to lend a hand to help a drowning person escape from the water, I cannot possibly be indifferent to whether or not my action succeeds. What I cannot know is what long-range consequences my action will have, and the significance of those consequences. Perhaps I will be hailed as a hero and go on to be elected governor of my state, and use my political influence to help millions of people. Perhaps the person I save will go on to become a serial murderer. I cannot know, but it does not matter, for my ethical task in this situation is clear. I must do what I can to help the person who is drowning, and let the world-historical chips fall where they may.

Climacus makes it clear that the ethical individual must will his ends 'to the utmost of one's capability', and hence in one sense cannot be unconcerned about results. No one who wills an end sincerely can be indifferent about whether that end is realized. The comments about willed ignorance have, I believe, a contrary-to-fact ring, and are placed in the subjunctive mood. One might read the claim that the ethical individual would choose to remain ignorant of results as accompanied by a clause 'if this were possible', with the understanding that it is not in fact possible. The point is not that ethical people would literally prefer to be ignorant of the direct results of their actions, but that such people recognize that the ultimate world-historical significance of their actions is not within their control, and that it is dangerous to allow consideration of results to affect one's estimate of one's moral worth. If we begin to measure our lives ethically by such a world-historical measuring stick we are beginning to become unethical.

In a strict sense of the word, even fairly direct results are not entirely within our control. I cannot guarantee that if I stoop on the bridge to help the person who is drowning that the board on which I rest will not give way, causing both of us to drown. Even when I perform a simple action such as raising my hand I presuppose that I will not at that moment suffer a stroke that paralyses me, and yet I cannot by willing prevent such a stroke from occurring. There is a sense in which all people have the same moral power: to will to do what is ethically required. Morally speaking, what counts is what one wills, and the penniless person in a wheelchair may do exactly what the rich politician can do: will to do whatever she can, thus preserving the equality of the ethical. The results are never completely within our power, though we can and should strive for those results with all the power we have.

How should we think about the deontologism of Climacus? Textbook characterizations of a deontological perspective sometimes contrast this view with a teleological theory which links what is morally right to the good. The deontological view is described as a view that holds that certain actions are intrinsically right or wrong, independent of the goodness of the results.

This seems accurate as a description of Climacus' view as far as it goes, except for limiting our duties to actions and not including character traits as well. However, it seems misleading to me in that it fails to recognize that Climacus also has a vision of the good that is linked to his account of the ethical. It would not be accurate to say that a teleological theory has a concern for the good, while the kind of deontological view found in Climacus focuses only on the right. Climacus also is concerned about the good. There are recognizable parallels between Climacus and contemporary virtue ethicists, who regard the goodness of moral character to be the pre-eminent type of goodness.[21] Nor does he, I would claim, see moral goodness as the only type of goodness. There must be non-moral goods that shape the ends

---

[21] See Robert Roberts, 'Existence, Emotion, and Virtue: Classical Themes in Kierkegaard', in *The Cambridge Companion to Kierkegaard*, and John J. Davenport, 'Towards an Existential Virtue Ethics: Kierkegaard and MacIntyre', in *Kierkegaard After MacIntyre*.

that the ethical person wills. However, such non-moral goods have only a relative importance in relation to the goodness of moral character.

The real difference can be seen when Climacus' view is contrasted with utilitarian views that understand right actions as being those that maximize non-moral goodness. Even if one adds the goodness of moral character as one more factor to be weighed in the utilitarian decision, there is a clear difference between such a utilitarian view and the deontological view of Climacus. From his perspective, such a utilitarian view errs in seeing moral goodness as commensurable with the non-moral goods that are the typical utilitarian goals. Moral goodness, on such a view, would simply be one more factor to be added to the utilitarian calculus. Climacus, like Socrates, sees moral good-ness as 'the pearl of great price', a good for which all other goods, including even such significant goods as health and length of life, must be sacrificed if necessary.

This does not imply, as one might think, that the agent is concerned only with consequences for himself or herself. The ethical agent can and should certainly have a concern for the well-being of others. However, in estimating how others might be helped, the development of moral character is again the pre-eminent factor. There are strict limits on our ability to help another person develop such character, since ultimately a per-son's character is formed by his or her own choices. It is for this reason that Climacus says that the ethical communicator must use indirect means in helping another towards the truth. How-ever, within those limits it is still true that the highest thing one person can do for another is encourage the development of character.

To summarize, the ethical perspective of Climacus seems to be something like this. Every person has what might be called a vocation or calling, a self he or she ought to become. This ideal self is given by God to each individual as a potential to be actualized. To act ethically is to act in accordance with an obligation to move towards this ideal. Moral character is achieved by my willing to become the self God demands. Actions that this requires are right, and should be performed regardless of the world-historical significance they may possess or fail to possess.

There is a great deal that this picture leaves open. Climacus says little about the content of the ethical task. The task of becoming a self is universal, as is the moral character of the task. There is an abstract or formal quality to the virtue ethics of Climacus. Some of the incompleteness rests on what I would regard as an overly optimistic moral epistemology. For Climacus, 'the ethical is ... always very easy to understand, probably in order that no time will be wasted on understanding, but one will be able to begin right away' (p. 391). What is important to Climacus is not the differences in people's understanding of what the ethical requires. In any case, since ethical obligation is linked to my individual vocation or calling, it is not devastating if it should turn out to be the case that there are significant differences in obligations. What is crucial for him is simply that a person acquire a sense of the 'absoluteness' and 'infinity' of the moral requirement and begin to shape his or her life accordingly.

To anticipate the next chapter, we can I think see that Climacus leaves plenty of space for further discoveries about the nature of the self I am to become as well as the nature of the process by which I must become that self. We may also discover that the optimistic moral epistemology reflects the position of the pseudonym, a non-Christian who assumes that all humans have the potential to become aware of the self they ought to become, even if they are not able fully to realize the ideal. This assumption is one that Kierkegaard the Christian writer will challenge in certain respects.

PURITY OF HEART AND THE ETHICAL TASK

The pseudonymous character of *Concluding Unscientific Postscript* raises questions about the relation of Kierkegaard's views to those of Johannes Climacus. I shall argue that, despite the pseudonymous character of *Concluding Unscientific Postscript*, which requires us to take seriously the non-Christian character of Johannes Climacus, in many important respects the view of the ethical found in Climacus is shared by Kierkegaard. There are important differences, most related to the somewhat abstract and formal nature of the account of the ethical given by Climacus. However, the points of agreement are numerous and deep.

The best way to show this is, I believe, through a comparison on these points between *Concluding Unscientific Postscript* and *An Occasional Discourse*, part I of *Upbuilding Discourses in Various Spirits*, written shortly after *Concluding Unscientific Postscript* and published a little over a year later. This discourse was originally published in English separately under the title *Purity of Heart Is to Will One Thing*, in a translation by Douglas Steere.[22] This 'upbuilding' or edifying work, written 'On the Occasion of a Confession', is certainly not written as a piece of ethical theory. However, in this work Kierkegaard attempts to help 'that single individual' who is his reader prepare for confession by reflecting on the nature of the good and what it is to be totally committed to the good, thereby attaining 'purity of heart'. It does therefore contain a clear perspective on the ethical life written under Kierkegaard's own name from roughly the same time as *Concluding Unscientific Postscript*.

The fundamental structure of *Purity of Heart* can usefully be compared with Kant. Kant begins with a purely formal characterization of moral action as action in accordance with law and from this attempts to develop a touchstone of moral action, the Categorical Imperative, that can be used to decide which specific maxims are in accordance with morality. In *Purity of Heart* Kierkegaard also begins with what appears to be a formal and abstract characterization of a morally good person, namely that this person is not morally at war with herself. The person 'wills one thing', which means, I think, not that the person wills only one finite thing among others, but that there must be some overriding ultimate commitment that orders the person's life, something to which the person is unconditionally devoted. Kierkegaard argues that this 'one thing' can only be 'the

---

[22] Steere's translation of the first section of Kierkegaard's *Upbuilding Discourses in Various Spirits* was eventually published in a Harper Torchbook edition (New York: Harper and Brothers, 1956) and thus this Discourse of Kierkegaard has become well known under this title. It is for this reason that I have decided to refer to this work as *Purity of Heart,* although all references to the work will be taken from the Hong translation of Kierkegaard's *Upbuilding Discourses in Various Spirits* (Princeton: Princeton University Press, 1993). Subsequent references to this work in this chapter are denoted by page nos. in parentheses.

Good' (p. 24).[23] If a person attempts to make something such as wealth or money his or her ultimate value, that thing turns out not to be one thing at all, and therefore incapable of providing the moral ordering the good life requires (pp. 24–35).

It might appear that the ethical perspective found in *Purity of Heart* differs significantly from that in *Concluding Unscientific Postscript*. We have seen that *Concluding Unscientific Postscript* characterizes the ethical life primarily in terms of an ethic of self-actualization. *Purity of Heart*, on the other hand, characterizes the ethical life in terms of a commitment to the Good. This apparent difference is quite superficial, however. We have seen already that the self that Johannes Climacus thinks must be actualized is understood primarily in moral terms. I become myself by becoming morally good, though this means concretely that I must develop other specific qualities and perform specific actions. Kierkegaard's discussion of 'willing the Good' in *Purity of Heart* turns out to be essentially the same. For the Good that I must will turns out to be a commitment to become the self God requires me to be:

[A]t every person's birth there comes into existence an eternal purpose for that person, for that person in particular. Faithfulness to oneself with respect to this is the highest thing a person can do, and as that most profound poet has said, 'Worse than self-love is self-contempt'. (p. 93)[24]

To will the Good is therefore to will to fulfil this obligation to become one's true self, an obligation that is explicitly understood as involving a responsibility to God. 'But in eternity everyone as a single individual must make an accounting to

---

[23] Nineteenth-century Danish capitalized all nouns. It therefore calls for a decision on the part of a translator as to whether or not 'the Good' (*det Gode*) should be capitalized. The Hongs chose lower case initial, implying that 'the good' is simply a common noun. I am convinced that Douglas Steere was correct to translate '*det Gode*' as 'the Good', indicating the very specific character of what Kierkegaard is discussing. It seems clear enough in many cases that the Good is identical with 'the Eternal' or with God. One might compare Kierkegaard here with Robert Adams in *Finite and Infinite Goods*, who consciously evokes Plato by capitalizing 'the Good'.

[24] The 'profound poet' is Shakespeare; according to the Hongs the reference is to *King Henry the Fifth*.

God, that is, eternity requires of him that he must have lived as a single individual' (p. 128).

Kierkegaard explicitly recalls the Socratic view of the self's task as being 'sentry duty'. Even a person who because of physical or mental suffering can accomplish nothing in an outward and worldly sense can fulfil the task he has been given:

[H]e is participating in the great common enterprise of humankind; at his solitary post he is, so to speak, defending a difficult pass by rescuing his soul from the ensnaring difficulties of all suffering— even if no human being sees him, humankind feels with him, suffers with him, is victorious with him. (p. 117)

This soul-making ethic of Kierkegaard also shares the specific deontological character that we saw in *Concluding Unscientific Postscript*. Kierkegaard explicitly rejects the notion that means can be justified by the ends achieved. However, just as we noted when looking at Climacus on this point, he should not be understood as simply evidencing a concern for what is right in distinction from the good. Rather, it is the goodness of moral character itself that fundamentally grounds his claims. A person 'is not eternally responsible for achieving his end in temporality, but he is unconditionally eternally responsible for which means he uses. When he wills to use or uses only the means that truly is the good means, he is, eternally understood, at the end' (p. 141).

This deontology that is rooted in a teleological vision of the goodness of moral character also helps explain why Kierkegaard can insist, as did Kant, that a moral action must not be done for the sake of an external reward, and yet can be appropriately rewarded in eternity.[25] The person who wills the Good for the sake of an external reward cannot truly be said to will one thing, since the reward and the Good are heterogeneous. In this life, the Good and the reward 'are so different that, if the reward is coveted separately, the good is the ennobling and sanctifying element, and the reward is the tempting element' (p. 37). The reward that God has 'eternally joined with the Good' is quite different; it is neither dubious nor uncertain. (p. 37). The reason this is so is that the possession of the Good is itself the reward,

---

[25] The points that follow are discussed at greater length in Chapter 6 below.

and the link between the Good and God means that eternal life must not be understood superficially as merely consisting of sensuous delights. Rather, eternal life is simply the enjoyment—fragmentarily in this life and completely after death—of God, who is himself the Good, by those who have come to love the Good: 'That the Good is its own reward, yes, that is eternally certain. There is nothing more certain; it is not more certain that there is a God, because this is one and the same' (p. 39). What is morally right must be done for its own sake, not because right is independent of the good, but because the highest good, the good that is incommensurable with all other kinds, is moral goodness. Kierkegaard goes so far as to say that even what humans would commonly call 'useless suffering' can be good if it helps the person gain that moral character that is itself the highest good (p. 104).

Kierkegaard stresses, just as Johannes Climacus did, that this soul-making ethic is one that is profoundly egalitarian in spirit:

With respect to the highest, with respect to willing to do everything, it makes no difference at all, God be praised, how big or little the task. Oh, how merciful the eternal is to us human beings! The eternal does not recognize all the corruptive strife and comparison that condescends and insults, that sighs and envies. Its requirement is equal for everyone, the greatest who has lived and the lowliest. (p. 81)

The equality is possible because the task is individualized. Every person can make a decision for the Good, can will the Good (understood as the obligation to become the self God requires a person to be) not merely 'to a certain degree' but absolutely (p. 64). It is for this reason that Kierkegaard argues a chronic 'sufferer' who can accomplish nothing outwardly can still do as much ethically as anyone (p. 111). Such a person can will to be the self God wants him to be, and will be responsible when God questions him in eternity about his life (p. 128). No one can do more and no one should do less.

Kierkegaard's agreement with Climacus extends to the suspicion of 'world-historical significance' as well. Though Kierkegaard does not specifically use this language of Climacus, he advances a similar claim when he discusses the case of the double-minded person who wills the Good, but wills that the Good triumph through him. Such a person is double-minded because he 'self-willfully wills the good'. Though such a person can appear devoted to the Good, he is actually devoted to one other thing: his own importance. 'He does not will the good for the sake of reward; he wills that the good shall be victorious; but he wills that it shall be victorious *through him*, that he shall be the *instrument*, the *chosen one*' (p. 61).

Kierkegaard says that this self-willful person is presumptuous (p. 63). He is not willing to accept the fact that the Good 'has put on the slowness of time like a shabby suit of clothes' and that this means that all who serve the Good must see themselves as 'unprofitable servants' (pp. 63–4). We humans cannot by willing guarantee the victory of the Good in time. The victory of the Good in eternity is certain, but we must be faithful to our tasks and allow God to determine whether our efforts are to have world-historical significance, to use the language of Climacus.

Finally, Kierkegaard makes it plain that the formal commitment to the Good brings with it material changes in our form of life. To be committed to the Good is to recognize that one has a 'relationship in which you as a single individual relate yourself to yourself before God' (p. 129). This relationship, which Kierkegaard identifies as conscience, ought to permeate and shape every other relationship which a person has, whether that be a marriage relation, parenting relation, friendship relation, or whatever. It is conscience that makes it possible for an individual to go beyond conformity to accepted social practices: 'Eternity does not ask you whether you brought up your children the way you saw others doing it but asks you as an individual how *you* brought up your children' (pp. 130–1).

Interestingly, since Kierkegaard is sometimes accused of a lack of social concern, this concern for conscience is explicitly extended to broader civic responsibilities. The person who 'does not live in an out-of-the-way spot' but 'in a heavily populated city' must 'sympathetically give heed to people and events' (p. 131). Kierkegaard recognizes that many social issues are complex and says a person does not have to 'have an opinion about something that you do not understand'. However, individuals must take responsibility for the judgements of this type they make, and once more, conscience does not accept as an excuse that the position one took was popular at the time:

And in eternity you will not be pryingly and busily asked, as by a journalist, whether there were a great many who had the same—wrong opinion, but only whether you had it; whether you have pamperingly accustomed your soul to judge light-mindedly and unthinkingly along with the others because the crowd judged unthinkingly; ... (p. 132)

The ethical alternative to *Sittlichkeit* that Kierkegaard advances is therefore not a solitary individualism that ignores relations to other people. Being a 'single individual' is not to be understood as precluding but rather as demanding certain kinds of relations to other people. The relation a person has to himself and to God through conscience is rather a transforming component in every other relation, ensuring that those relations are truly humane. If a person is rightly 'allied with God' then that person will also be 'in concordance with all people' (pp. 144–5). In a passage that strongly anticipates a major theme of *Works of Love*, the relation an individual has with God is described as one that is enjoyed by all others, and hence all people, including 'strange people whose language and customs you do not know,' are 'blood relatives' (p. 144). This is not an ethic of 'my station and its duties', but it is an ethic that is supposed to transform my station and all its duties.

This includes one's duties in the area of work. Kierkegaard says that a person should view his or her work, assuming that it is 'something good and honorable', as a calling (p. 142). The same deontological standard is applied here as in other areas. Ultimately, one is not judged by how successful one may be in an external sense, but about the means one uses in pursuit of the particular ends that one's work involves (pp. 141–3). Kierkegaard's egalitarianism comes into play here as well. It does not matter whether one's calling is prestigious or insignificant. From the perspective of eternity the only question is whether one has through one's calling willed the Good.

CONCLUSIONS: GOD AND THE ETHICAL

Having seen the profound similarities, what differences appear between Climacus and the Kierkegaard of *Purity of Heart* with respect to the ethical? One would expect the non-Christian character of Climacus to make some differences, and I believe that it does. *Purity of Heart* is a book intended as a preparation for Christian confession. Accordingly, it is proper that ethical responsibility is here described much more definitely as a responsibility to God and before God. Much that in *Concluding Unscientific Postscript* is vague and implicit is now clear and explicit. One might say that Climacus realizes that people are aware of God when they become aware of the responsibility to become a self, but he also realizes that they may be only vaguely aware of God, not aware of God as God. The tone of *Purity of Heart* is quite different.

Nevertheless, though *Purity of Heart* is in one sense a Christian book, it does not really employ what Kierkegaard himself would call 'the distinctively Christian categories'. The prayer that begins the book is not Trinitarian, unlike the prayer that begins *Works of Love*. The book discusses repentance, and one could argue that it implicitly is linked to the atonement, since the individual reading the book is preparing for Christian confession. However, there is no discussion of the atonement and no real discussion of the saving work of Jesus or the sanctifying work of the Holy Spirit. Though the book begins, as do Kierkegaard's earlier *Upbuilding Discourses*, with a scriptural text (from James), it takes as its main theme the knowledge of God that is rooted in conscience. No claims are made that such knowledge requires or is rooted in a special revelation from God, and in this respect, *Purity of Heart* is close to the perspective of *Concluding Unscientific Postscript*. To use traditional theological language, one could say that both books examine what can be known about the ethical life on the basis of general revelation, though one looks at that revelation from an explicitly Christian perspective and the other does not.

Works of Love, as we shall see, is quite different. It offers a perspective on the ethical life that self-consciously begins with an historical revelation viewed as authoritative. On the surface, much of *Works of Love* seems to be a polemical blast against natural ethical knowledge. I will argue, however, that the book does not assume that there is no natural ethical knowledge. It rather assumes that our natural ethical knowledge is vague and subject to error, in need of an historical revelation for clarification and correction. The question of the relation of that historical revelation to general revelation is a crucial one. If the ethic of *Works of Love* has no positive relation to the kind of ethic developed in *Concluding Unscientific Postscript* and *Purity of Heart*, then it will be difficult to argue that it deserves a hearing in a pluralistic society such as our own.

I believe there is such a positive relation. It is possible to see *Works of Love* as giving specific content to the formal accounts of the ethical given in the earlier works. Both *Concluding Unscientific Postscript* and *Purity of Heart* see the ethical life as involving a relation with God, but the God to whom one is related is known only through conscience. One of the shortcomings of the account of the ethical found in both *Concluding Unscientific Postscript* and *Purity of Heart* is the vagueness of the content of the ethical life. One might say that we have in these works a divine command ethic, but the commander does not come into clear view. From a Christian point of view, the God whom we know in conscience is a God who has spoken more clearly and definitely in history. The questions the ethical person must ask are given definitive answers; the vague, implicit and subject-to-error knowledge that is possible through conscience is corrected and sharpened. Nevertheless, it is of fundamental importance that the answers given by an historical revelation (though perhaps not only by such a revelation) are answers to the questions humans must ask as humans. The clarifying and correcting insights are insights that clarify and correct the knowledge that is possible independently of that revelation.

5

Divine Commands as the Basis for Moral Obligation

In this chapter and the ones following I shall develop an account of the ethical life found in Kierkegaard's *Works of Love*. It is, I shall argue, a view that unites an ethic of self-actualization and a divine command theory of moral obligation by viewing the self a person must become as constituted by a relationship with God, a relationship that requires obedience to divine commands. Some of the basic structure of this view is already present in *Concluding Unscientific Postscript* and *Purity of Heart*, as we have seen. In *Works of Love* this kind of view is given concreteness: both the self I must become and the divine command I must obey are specified in terms of biblical teachings about love. I am commanded to love my neighbour as myself, and it is only when I learn to love in this way that I can become the self I was created to be and truly want to be (though in my sinfulness it is also the self I am fleeing from). I can only love my neighbour as myself when I have a relation to God, who becomes the 'middle term' in every true love-relationship. Neighbour-love is not exhausted by nor is it reducible to such natural human forms of love as erotic love and friendship. Rather, these merely human forms of love require neighbour-love if they are to become transformed and purified from selfishness. This ethic of neighbour-love has concrete implications for all human relations, including those defined by such things as race, class, and gender, though I shall argue that Kierkegaard does not always rightly trace these implications.

One might object that Kierkegaard gets Christian ethics wrong by focusing so strongly on love for neighbour, since Christianity teaches that the most fundamental obligation is the obligation to love God. Kierkegaard recognizes this duty to God as primary quite explicitly. In fact it is because we have a fundamental duty to love God that we are obligated to obey his command to love the neighbour. However, his major focus in *Works of Love* is on human obligations towards fellow humans, and thus love for neighbour gets most of Kierkegaard's attention. The duty to love God is not ignored, however. Not only does Kierkegaard explicitly mention this duty at times; it is always presupposed by virtue of his thesis that it is only possible to love the neighbour when God is loved as a 'middle-term'. Love for the neighbour is not merely what God requires; it is something that presupposes love for God.

All of these themes are connected in intimate ways, and there is a sense in which the whole account should be given all at once. Unfortunately, this is obviously not possible. I shall therefore attempt to discuss the most important issues in what seems to me to be a logical order, though one could easily treat them in a different order. The interconnections will, however, require some repetition, as concepts require discussion of other concepts to be made intelligible. In this chapter, after a look at the polemical targets of *Works of Love*, the primary focus will be on the way in which the obligation to love the neighbour is rooted in a command. I shall argue that such a foundation for moral obligation does not make morality pointless and arbitrary, as critics of divine command theories of obligation allege, but actually safeguards the humanistic character of morality.

This argument will be completed in Chapter 6 by looking at the relation between the self-denial demanded by the command to love the neighbour and human happiness. I shall try to show that though the person who follows the command is not seeking his or her own happiness, it still makes sense to see the command, which is directed by God towards the good, as issued by God with an understanding that human happiness is best found by living in accord with the command. God's commands are linked with human happiness, though that link may be one that can be discerned in this life only through faith and hope.

In Chapter 7 I extend and develop this divine command theory of obligation by reflecting on how the divine commands are promulgated and on the nature of the commands. God's commands turn out to be both universal and individual in character, and are promulgated through both special and general revelation, though Kierkegaard's emphasis is decidedly on the former. A strong view of human sinfulness explains why Kierkegaard thinks that the knowledge that is in principle available through general revelation must usually be derived from special revelation, although I argue that Kierkegaard's emphasis on sinfulness is exaggerated and inconsistent with other claims he makes.

In Chapter 8 I begin to look at the content of the command by focusing primarily on the concept of the neighbour and the character of the love a person must show to the neighbour. In Chapter 9 I look more closely at the relation between neighbour-love and natural human loves such as erotic love and friendship. Chapter 9 will conclude with an examination of the implications of the account for social theory, with a focus on the kind of equality love demands and what this means for concrete social relations. Chapters 10 to 12 will go on to compare the account with some selected contemporary secular alternatives, so as to defend its plausibility. The final chapter will look at the viability of a divine command theory in a pluralistic, secular society by looking critically at some common arguments that such a religiously grounded ethic cannot work in such a society.

THE POLEMICAL TARGETS OF *WORKS OF LOVE*

It is well known that Kierkegaard is a thoroughly polemical writer. It is no accident that he was nicknamed 'the Fork' as a child, and his combative tendencies did not lessen with the years. *Works of Love*, though its subject is love, is by no means an exception to this characteristic, and it is important to identify clearly the implied objects of criticism in the book if it is to be understood.

There are, I believe, three main targets, whom I shall call the unspoiled pagan, the spoiled pagan, and the deluded pagan, respectively. The concept of the 'unspoiled pagan' is directly introduced early in the book, in a passage in which Kierkegaard stresses the originality and uniqueness of the Christian command to love the neighbour: 'Take a pagan who is not spoiled by having learned thoughtlessly to patter Christianity by rote or has not been spoiled by the delusion of being a Christian—and this commandment, "You *shall* love", will not only surprise him but will disturb him, will be an offense to him.'[1] Kierkegaard almost always has in mind the culture of ancient Greece when he discusses this kind of paganism, and he generally argues (with, as we shall see later, some interesting exceptions) that this culture did not even contain a 'hint' of the Christian concept of neighbour-love as commanded (p. 44). As one might expect, Kierkegaard spends relatively little time attacking this form of paganism, since it is extinct. In fact, even while stressing the differences between Christianity and paganism properly so-called, he often compares contemporary forms of paganism within 'Christendom' to Greek thought in ways that are unflattering to the contemporary versions.

The other two forms of paganism are the more serious objects of his polemical attention, and both of these forms occur within Christendom. Actually, both could have been labelled as forms of 'spoiled' paganism, because in both cases Kierkegaard thinks the paganism present is confusedly mixed with Christianity to the detriment of both Christian and pagan views. Nevertheless, there are two different figures that meet this description and I think it is important to distinguish them. I have therefore chosen to describe one as the 'spoiled pagan' and the other, who seems more deeply deceived, as the 'deluded pagan'.

The person I designate as the spoiled pagan could be best described as a kind of secular, 'emancipated' thinker who attempts to take over the substance of Judaeo-Christian ethics without its foundation. This thinker is different from the unspoiled pagan who finds the idea that love is commanded shocking. The spoiled pagan has learned from Christianity that love is a duty. The difference between this view and genuine Christianity is that the moral law is seen by the spoiled pagan as something we do not need God for: 'God and the world agree in this, that love is the fulfilling of the Law; the difference is that the world understands the Law as something it thinks up by itself, ...' (p. 128).

Kierkegaard describes the spoiled pagan in the language of emancipation and progress beloved by the Enlightenment. The human race has made great moral progress, according to this

---

[1] Kierkegaard, *Works of Love*, 25. Subsequent references to this work in this chapter are denoted by page nos. in parentheses.

view. Feudalism and slavery have been abolished. Human beings are no longer bond servants to other human beings. The next step in human emancipation is to be free from divine authority, which is found to be a 'burdensome encumbrance'. Modern culture is defined by a kind of mutiny against God, a desire to assume the place of God: '[T]here is a more or less open intent to depose God in order to install human beings—in the rights of humanity? No, that is not needed; God has already done that—in the rights of God. If God is dismissed, the place will indeed be vacant' (p. 115).

I think it is important to distinguish this secular spoiled pagan, who does have some understanding that his view is a challenge to traditional Christianity, from the figure I call the deluded pagan. The deluded pagan is the person in Christendom who essentially thinks and lives as a pagan, but confusedly and perhaps self-deceptively thinks of himself as a Christian. The deluded pagan is the individual who believes that neighbour-love can be identified with such natural, merely human loves celebrated by the poet as friendship or romantic love, or at best sees neighbour-love as something that one has alongside or in addition to these natural forms of love. (Of course the figure I call the 'spoiled pagan' can make this same identification, and thus there is some common ground between these categories.) Christian love is thereby, according to Kierkegaard, domesticated.

Kierkegaard thinks that such a view really does justice neither to these natural forms of love nor to Christian love. The power of romantic love and friendship lies in their exclusivity. If a person thinks that it is a good thing to lower the intensity of this preferential love so that one can extend it to more people, the result is neither poetic nor Christian. Christianity does not demand having lots of friends and several romantic lovers; it demands that one love every human person. The deluded pagan confuses this stringent requirement with an obligation to love a number of people:

Christian love yields, slackens the tension of eternity, scales down, and is of the opinion that when a great many are loved, then it is Christian love. Thus *both* poetic *and* Christian love have become confused, and what has stepped in as a replacement is *neither* poetic *nor* Christian love. (p. 50)

Kierkegaard distinguishes between natural human loves and neighbour-love so stridently that it would be easy to conclude that they are mutually exclusive. In Chapter 8 I shall try to show that this is a misreading. However, it is not an accident that Kierkegaard is strident on this point, for of the three polemical targets, there is little doubt that it is the deluded pagan in Christendom, who thinks of himself as a Christian but who emasculates Christianity by reducing it to the 'merely human', who draws the greatest share of criticism.

It is not surprising that Kierkegaard's polemical fire should be directed primarily at this target, since he lived in an officially Christian culture. However, I think it is important to recognize that contemporary western societies are quite different from the one in which Kierkegaard lived. In many ways the kind of secular view embodied in the spoiled pagan has become the 'establishment', at least within academic circles and the world of 'high culture'. In Kierkegaard's own day the figure I am calling the deluded pagan occupied this cultural place. Hence Kierkegaard's critique of the spoiled pagan may have much more relevance today than it did in his own time. We will see in what follows that all of these three 'pagan' figures appear repeatedly in Kierkegaard's account of the obligation to love the neighbour.

THE NATURE OF A DIVINE COMMAND THEORY OF MORAL OBLIGATION

To explicate the role of divine commands in *Works of Love* it is first important to become clear about how pervasive a role is played in the book by the notion of a command that is rooted in divine authority.[2] Authority is so ubiquitous in *Works of Love* that it is sometimes hard to see. Much as God's omnipresence in the world makes him invisible, authority permeates the book in such a way that it is easy to miss its fundamental significance. In fact, in a generally excellent recent book, Jamie Ferreira, while hardly failing to notice the role of divine commands in *Works of*

[2] Much of this section draws on my article, 'Authority and Transcendence in *Works of Love*,' in Niels Jørgen Cappelørn (ed.), *The Kierkegaard Studies Yearbook 1998* (Berlin and New York: Walter de Gruyter, 1998).

Love, actually goes so far as to deny that the book contains a divine command account of moral obligation at all.[3] That such a denial can be made by a commentator as astute and well-versed as Ferreira is evidence of the low esteem a divine command theory of moral obligation generally enjoys. Such views are often regarded as theories that make morality arbitrary and even inhuman. It seems to me that Ferreira simply reasons that since moral obligations do not appear to be arbitrary for Kierkegaard, then he could not hold a divine command theory of obligation. I shall try to show that it makes more sense to recognize that Kierkegaard's account is a divine command theory of obligation and question whether such a theory must have the negative consequences it is often alleged to have.

How shall we understand a divine command theory of moral obligation? We must begin by recognizing the limited scope of such a theory. First of all, the account is not intended as an account of the whole of ethics, but only of *obligation*. Specifically, the account I will present on behalf of Kierkegaard presupposes an account of the good, and therefore does not attempt to explain the good in terms of divine commands.

Secondly, even within the sphere of obligation, the account is limited to *moral* obligations. In the first chapter, I committed myself to the account of obligations as generated by social relations developed by Robert Adams.[4] On this account social relations, such as those of parent and child, husband and wife, generate obligations of various types. This makes it possible for the relation to God, a relation of creature to Creator, to generate obligations as well. As my Creator, God creates obligations for me by giving authoritative commands. Obviously, the account then assumes that certain obligations hold independently of whether God commands the relevant actions, since these facts about the genesis of obligations form the basis of the theory. However, the legal, social, and familial obligations generated by relationships humans have to each other are not necessarily moral obligations. Adams calls them 'pre-moral'.[5] While they may, in most societies, substantially overlap with our moral

---

[3] See Ferreira, *Love's Grateful Striving*, 40–2, 243.

[4] See pp. 12–16, above, and Adams, *Finite and Infinite Goods*, ch. 10.

[5] Ibid. 243.

obligations, some of them may actually be contradictory to morality.

Consider, for example, the obligation of a widow in a traditional Hindu society to allow herself to be burned to death along with her husband's corpse, or the obligation parents have in some traditional African societies to have female children genitally mutilated (so-called 'female circumcision'). It is at least arguable that such obligations, while deeply rooted in certain social relations and practices, are not morally obligatory but are actually morally wrong. Those obligations that we term 'moral' must be obligations that are objective in character, meaning that they do not hold merely because of the customs, practices, and beliefs of particular cultural groups or societies (or individuals for that matter). Besides objectivity, moral obligations also have the character of being ultimate in the sense that they override other kinds of obligations. Another characteristic that I affirmed in Chapter 1 to be linked to moral obligations is universality. It is not that all moral obligations are universal, since God's commands, which provide the basis for moral obligations, can be addressed to specific individiuals or groups. However, there is an important subgroup of moral obligations that are universal. I shall try to show that thinking of moral obligations as divine commands also explains why there can be these universal duties. The version of divine command morality I shall develop is therefore one that claims that the particular obligations generated by divine commands have precisely the characteristics we think moral obligations must have.

What characteristics must a theory possess to be designated as a divine command theory of obligation? There are many different types of such theories, and we could obviously define the concept in different ways. The root idea is that moral obligations are in some way dependent on God's commanding certain actions to be done or not to be done, or, on some accounts, God's willing that certain actions be performed and others not performed, or that certain character traits be acquired and maintained and others avoided. (In what follows I shall usually speak only of actions so as not to be unduly cumbersome, but it is important not to forget that duties include more than actions.) There are a variety of ways of construing the metaphysical relation between divine commands and moral obligations on such a view. As Philip Quinn has suggested, these range from identity (moral obligations simply are divine commands) to causal dependence (God's commands cause certain acts to be morally obligatory), to the notion of 'supervenience'.[6]

So far as I can see, the account that Kierkegaard assumes does not commit him to any one of these options in particular. It seems to me that he is committed, however, to the claim that God's commands are both necessary and sufficient to constitute acts as moral obligations. To say that God's commanding an action is necessary for it to be a moral obligation is to say that all actions that are morally obligatory are actions that God commands; there are no genuine moral obligations that are not commanded by God. To say that God's commanding an action is sufficient for moral obligation is to say that any act that God commands is thereby morally obligatory. If moral obligations are simply identical to divine commands, then it is clear that divine commands will indeed be necessary and sufficient for moral obligations. If God's commands in some way cause or create moral obligations, then divine commands are clearly sufficient for moral obligations, and, if it turns out that there is no other adequate cause or ground of moral obligations, necessary as well. Similar things can be said if moral obligations can be said to 'supervene' on divine commands in one of the senses commonly given to this vexed and controversial philosophical concept.

A divine command theory of moral obligation, as I shall understand the term, is therefore committed to the following two propositions: (1) Any action God (understood as a perfectly good, all-powerful, and all-knowing Creator) commands his human creatures to do is morally obligatory for them. (2) Any action that is morally obligatory for humans has the status of

---

[6] Philip Quinn, 'The Recent Revival of Divine Command Ethics', 347–9. Quinn himself defends a causal theory in 'Divine Command Ethics: A Causal Theory', in Janine M. Idziak (ed.), *Divine Command Morality: Historical and Contemporary Readings* (New York: Edwin Mellem Press, 1979). One of the best treatments of divine command theories can be found in Edward Wierenga, 'A Defensible Divine Command Theory,' *Nous*, 17 (Jan. 1983), 383–407. Also see Wierenga's treatment of the subject in his *The Nature of God* (Ithaca, NY: Cornell University Press, 1989).

moral obligation because God commands it. Note that the account is compatible with the claim that some of the acts that are in fact morally obligatory would be obligatory in some non-moral sense even apart from God's command. And it is also consistent with the claim that even apart from God's commands, at least some (perhaps most) of the acts God commands would be 'good to do'. The latter claim is particularly important, since it makes it possible for God's commands to be free from arbitrariness. However, it is also possible that some actions that are morally obligatory for humans would not be obligatory at all (even in a non-moral sense) if God did not command them, and that some of these may be acts that would not even have the character of being 'good to do' apart from God's commands. It might be the case, for example, that some acts that would otherwise be morally indifferent become morally obligatory because God commands them.

Proposition (1) should be read as a claim that any action God commanded, including an action such as killing one's child, would become morally obligatory if God commanded the action. Thus, if we assume that the biblical story that God commanded Abraham to sacrifice Isaac is historically true, Abraham's action in being willing to obey God would be morally right. This is of course contrary to the view of Johannes de Silentio in *Fear and Trembling*, who holds that there is no ethical or moral justification for Abraham's act. However, as we have seen, in making this claim de Silentio seems to assume that 'the ethical' is to be understood in an Hegelian fashion. Someone who holds a divine command theory of ethical obligation obviously is not required to think of 'the ethical' in this limited way.

It is worth noting that the claim that whatever God commands is morally right is logically consistent with the claim that there are some actions that God would not or perhaps could not command because his nature is essentially good. Some philosophers would undoubtedly hold that the act of killing a child would be one of those. If this is so, then the proposition 'If God commanded killing a child, it would be morally right to do so' would still be true, but it would be a conditional proposition with an impossible antecedent. In Chapter 13 I address the question as to what a proponent of a divine command theory should say about such a case if the biblical story is regarded as true or possibly true.

Proposition (2) should be read as the claim that: (a) all morally obligatory actions are commanded by God; and (b) his commanding them is the reason they are *morally* obligatory. This leaves open the possibility that such actions might be obligatory in other senses for other reasons, and of course it is consistent with the claim that there are reasons for God's commanding the actions.

I believe that a theory that claims that divine commands are necessary and sufficient for moral obligation is certainly strong enough to be an interesting version of a divine command theory. There could of course be both stronger and weaker versions of a divine command theory of obligation than one that satisfies this test. For example, a stronger theory might hold that all obligations, rather than simply those that are moral in character, are duties solely because they are commanded by God. Or a theory might even hold that God's command somehow bestows upon an act the character of being 'good to do'. A theory might hold then that other aspects of morality, such as the good, and not just obligations, depend on divine commands. However, although stronger views are conceivable, it seems to me that any account that implies that divine commands are both necessary and sufficient to make acts morally obligatory is one that should count as a divine command theory of obligation. For such a theory is committed to holding that any action God commands is morally obligatory, and that any action that is morally obligatory has that status because God commands the action. In addition to this, such a view may also have the consequence that there are some actions that would not be obligatory in any sense or even good if God did not command them. These claims seem sufficiently strong to warrant the label 'divine command theory of moral obligation'. I shall leave open the question as to whether weaker theories that do not satisfy this test—for example, ones that hold only that God's commands are necessary for moral obligation without being sufficient, or ones that hold that God's commands are sufficient without being necessary—might legitimately be considered divine command theories of obligation.

When measured by my test, it seems undeniable to me that Kierkegaard does hold a divine command theory of obligation.

For Kierkegaard, love for the neighbour is *commanded*, and its status as a serious moral duty depends on its being commanded. Furthermore, Kierkegaard believes that the concept of a command logically presupposes a commander with the authority to issue the command. God is the one who has this authority, and Kierkegaard does not flinch from the consequence of a divine command account of moral obligation that many people consider most offensive, which is that it implies that whatever God commands is obligatory:

> But you shall love God in unconditional obedience, even if what he requires of you might seem to you to be to your own harm, indeed, harmful to his cause; for God's wisdom is beyond all comparison with yours, and God's governance has no obligation of responsibility in relation to your sagacity. All you have to do is obey in love. (p. 20)

I will address in my final chapter the question whether it is defensible to hold that an action that we now think immoral would be obligatory if God commands it. My point here is simply that Kierkegaard does not shy away from such a claim, and he is therefore committed to the view that a divine command is sufficient to make an action morally obligatory.

It is not hard, I think, to show that Kierkegaard also accepts the claim that all our moral obligations are divine commands as well, and that there are no other adequate grounds for moral obligation. Kierkegaard holds that our moral duties to our fellow humans are both grounded in the command God gives us to love our neighbours as ourselves and are fulfilled by obeying this command. All our moral duties are therefore commanded by God or derived from such a command. Later in this chapter I will examine his sustained polemic against the claim that any finite reality, such as human emotions or social agreements, could be the basis of moral obligations.

It can also be shown that the notion of a divine command is not merely window dressing for Kierkegaard. Divine commands give actions that would only have the status of being 'good to do' the status of moral obligations. This is perhaps easiest to see if we consider Kierkegaard's notion of an individual call. God's requirements for individuals reflect the individual vocations he has given them, a theme that I shall discuss in Chapter 7. Acts may be obligatory for one individual that are not obligatory for

another because of the individual nature of some of God's commands.[7] I think it is clear therefore that Kierkegaard is indeed
committed to a divine command theory of obligation.

DIVINE AND APOSTOLIC AUTHORITY

Though Kierkegaard is careful to say that his own words are
'without authority' (p. 47) he constantly appeals to Scripture,
Christ, or various apostles' words as authoritative. 'The *fulfilling* of the law—but what law is referred to here? Our text is the
apostolic word, we are speaking about Christian love; therefore
here the law can be only *God's law*' (p. 106). What Christ says is
'infinitely important' simply because it is Christ, the one with
authority, who has said it (p. 97). An apostle's authority makes
him a reliable guide for life: 'But if no one else can or will, an
apostle will always know how to lead us along the right road in
this regard, the right road that guides us both to do what is right
to others and to make ourselves happy' (p. 159).[8]

The apostle's authority here is of course derived from God.
Works of Love is closely linked to another work Kierkegaard
wrote at roughly the same time but never published, *The Book
on Adler*. This work was occasioned by the strange case of a
Danish pastor who claimed to have had a direct revelation from
Christ and was eventually removed from his pastorate, and the
case stimulated Kierkegaard to think hard about the importance
of authority and how one might recognize a genuine religious
authority. One similarity between *The Book on Adler* and *Works
of Love* is the prominence in both of the concept of an apostle,
understood as a person who has received divine authority, a
characteristic that must be sharply distinguished from human

[7] I do not mean to imply here that an individual may have a life-course that
is 'good to do' that later becomes obligatory because of God's call, because I
do not believe that individuals exist independently of God's call. The point is
logical, and not temporal. A life-course that would be merely 'good to do' can
be obligatory by virtue of God's call. For a similar individual with a different
call, the same life-course might be merely 'good to do'.

[8] Kierkegaard is clearly thinking of the biblical apostles in this quotation.
Yet it is important to note that the category of 'apostle' is just that: a category.
Even if God in actuality only calls and authorizes the twelve disciples of Jesus
to be apostles, as many traditional Christians believe, it is possible for God to
give other humans this status.

philosophical or artistic genius.[9] It is 'God in heaven' who speaks through the apostle (p. 336). The more insignificant an apostle is from a merely human point of view, 'the stronger the impression ... of divine authority granted him' (p. 122). Since the authority of God lies behind the apostle, it is God's law that the apostle proclaims.

In *Works of Love*, Kierkegaard argues that the mere fact that love is commanded suffices to distinguish Christian love from merely human conceptions of love. The natural human conception of love is one that glorifies spontaneity and sees duty and love as incompatible.[10] Hence the Christian command to love the neighbour as oneself could only have arisen through revelation. It 'did not arise in any human being's heart' (p. 27). and it contains the mark of a genuine divine revelation, the possibility of offence, notable in the passage about the 'spoiled pagan' we have already examined:

What courage it takes to say for the first time, 'You *shall* love', or, more correctly, what divine authority it takes to turn the natural man's conceptions and ideas upside down with this phrase! There at the boundary where human language halts and courage fails, there revelation breaks forth with divine origination and proclaims what is not difficult to understand in the sense of profundity ... Take a pagan who is not spoiled by having learned thoughtlessly to patter Christianity by rote or has not been spoiled by the delusion of being a Christian—and this commandment, 'You *shall* love', will not only surprise him but will disturb him, will be an offense to him. (pp. 24–5)

One might object to Kierkegaard here that a purely human ethic of love does not necessarily reject the notion that love is a duty. It does not throw out the concept of law altogether, but rather denies that such a duty to love requires a divine law as its foundation.

Kierkegaard gives explicit consideration to this type of objection. In effect the objection does not stem from the unspoiled pagan, for whom Christianity is genuinely new and genuinely disturbing, but rather from the spoiled pagan, who

---

[9] Søren Kierkegaard, *The Book on Adler*, ed. and trans. Howard V. Hong and Edna H. Hong (Princeton: Princeton University Press, 1998), 80–90, 173–8.

[10] I shall discuss in Chapters 6 and 8 whether it is possible for love to be commanded in this way.

has appropriated Christian ideas but in a confused manner, failing to notice the inconsistency between them and pagan ideas. Kierkegaard considers both types of 'pagans' but of course cannot reply to them simultaneously. That is, he looks both at the claim that love should be spontaneous rather than a duty to obey a law (the view of the unspoiled pagan), *and* the claim that love can be a duty to obey a law without invoking divine authority (the view of the spoiled pagan). After telling us that the world (in the figure of the unspoiled pagan) finds the concept of a law that demands love shocking, he later admits that the world (in the figure of the spoiled pagan) itself admits the need for love to be a law (p. 128).

I don't think Kierkegaard's characterizations of the 'world' here are inconsistent. He is simply thinking of two different 'worlds'. The world that finds the concept of law offensive is the world of the person who has not been exposed to Christian ideas at all. Such a view of the pagan world is quite consistent with the claim that within Christendom, a word that properly should be used to denote a specifically Christian concept can be hijacked, as it were, and used to denote a view that is inconsistent with Christianity. Kierkegaard's view here is rather similar to that developed in a well-known article by Elizabeth Anscombe, in which she argues that, although the law conception of ethics requires a divine lawgiver, in a culture that has been shaped by Jewish and Christian beliefs, it is natural for this concept to survive, albeit in a confused form:

Naturally, it is not possible to have such a conception [a law conception of ethics] unless you believe in God as a law-giver; like Jews, Stoics, and Christians. But if such a conception is dominant for many centuries, and then is given up, it is a natural result that the concepts of 'obligation,' of being bound or required as by a law, should remain though they had lost their root.[11]

So Kierkegaard can consistently attribute to the world both the view that an ethic of love should not be law-based and also the view that such an ethic can be law-based but that the law in question is human in origin. The trick is to see these claims as

---

[11] G. E. M. Anscombe, 'Modern Philosophy', in Steven Cahn and Joram G. Haber (eds.), *Twentieth Century Ethical Theory* (Englewood Cliffs, NJ: Prentice-Hall, 1995), 355. Reprinted from *Philosophy*, 33/124 (Jan. 1958).

made by different versions of the 'world'. Naturally, Kierkegaard finds both claims wanting. I shall consider in some detail later in this chapter why he thinks it is crucial that love be a duty grounded in law. First, I want to look at his thoughts on the question as to whether or not a duty to love can be seen as grounded in a humanly created law.

CAN HUMAN BEINGS BE THE FOUNDATION OF THE MORAL LAW?

An attempt to create an ethic without a foundation of divine law is seen by Kierkegaard, as we noted earlier, as a kind of 'mutiny' (p. 115). Kierkegaard rightly sees that the heart of modernity, insofar as it is the product of the Enlightenment call to autonomy, is a claim that human beings should recognize no higher authority than human reason itself. It is a good thing that serfdom has been abolished; now humankind is ready to go further in the cause of liberation by making people independent of divine authority (p. 115). Kierkegaard, however, thinks that this revolt against divine authority is the source of many of the ills of modernity: 'As a reward for such presumption, all existence will in that way probably come closer and closer to being transformed into doubt or into a vortex' (p. 115).

What is wrong with a humanly constructed moral law? There are several ways humans might try to create a moral law, and the critique of these strategies must be tailored to specifics. One move is the Kantian one of regarding morality as self-legislation. This particular strategy is cryptically described as 'pure arbitrariness' in *Works of Love* (p. 116). The criticism is explained more clearly in some other places in the Kierkegaardian writings. Perhaps the most notable is a journal entry from about 1850:

Kant was of the opinion that man is his own law (autonomy)—that is, he binds himself under the law which he himself gives himself. Actually, in a profounder sense, this is how lawlessness or experimentation are established. This is not being rigorously earnest any more than Sancho Panza's self-administered blows to his own bottom were vigorous.[12]

---

[12] *Søren Kierkegaard's Journals and Papers*, ed. and trans. Howard V. Hong and Edna H. Hong (Bloomington: Indiana University Press, 1967), i. entry 188, p. 76.

A law must be able to bind to be a law, but a law that I give myself cannot have this binding power, since the self that has the authority to issue the law would retain the authority to repeal it, and would of course be tempted to do just that precisely when the law constrains desires.[13] Kierkegaard's thought here is paralleled by Anscombe when she argues that 'the concept of legislation requires superior power in the legislator' and so Kant's idea of 'legislating for oneself' is as absurd as it would be to call every reflective decision of a person a 'vote' that always turns out to be a solid majority of $1:0$.[14]

This same thought is expressed in *Sickness Unto Death* by Anti-Climacus, who characterizes the commitments of the active, despairing self as 'experiments', regardless of what such a self undertakes.[15] Such a self lacks 'earnestness', since it 'recognizes no power over itself', but tries to substitute for the earnestness of God's attention to the self, the attention of the self to itself.[16]

Works of Love clearly holds this same view of moral obligation as linked to recognition of some binding authority. Contrary to the call for liberation from divine authority issued by the secular humanist, Kierkegaard argues that conscience requires that a person be bound by a higher power: 'a pure heart is first and last a *bound heart*', and it is only when there is 'infinite boundedness' that there can be genuine freedom (p. 148). The idea that genuine morality requires a sense that there is one to whom one is accountable and responsible permeates the book.

---

[13] I think it is important to note that Kant himself did not think of the self-legislated moral law as something that the self could repeal or revoke, and so Kierkegaard's reading of Kant here is not historically accurate. Rather, the Kant he describes seems closer to an 'existentialist' view of the self as creating morality. I agree with John Hare that this is not Kant's own picture at all. However, it is very natural to interpret the image of 'self-legislation' in the way that Kierkegaard does, and I think a strict reading of Kant raises questions about the appropriateness of the image of self-legislation in his thought, for the image suggests that the self is the author of the moral law in a sense that is not true for Kant.

[14] Anscombe, 'Modern Moral Philosophy', 352.

[15] Kierkegaard, *Sickness Unto Death*, 68. I prefer to translate the Danish *Experimenter* as 'experiments' rather than the Hong's 'imaginary constructions'.

[16] Ibid. 68–9.

In a powerful illustration, Christian love is compared to an 'earnestly brought-up child'. When such a child is away from home, it does not adjust its behaviour to conform to those of other children who may lack the same standards of behaviour, since such a child 'never forgets that the judgment is at home, where the parents do the judging' (p. 189). Similarly, Christian love 'never for a moment forgets where it is to be judged' (p. 190).

In comparing neighbour-love to a child, Kierkegaard may appear to be playing into the hands of the critics of divine command theory, who often object that such a view infantilizes human beings.[17] A full reply to this objection requires an account of whether or not it is possible for humans to become fully or completely autonomous. As we saw in our examination of MacIntyre's notion of 'criterionless choice' in Chapter 2, Kierkegaard believes that such an ideal of total autonomy is a chimera. Such an autonomous self turns out to be a king with no substantive country to reign over, a government that is subject to the revolution of an arbitrary will at any time. Liberation from unjust and oppressive human authority is indeed a good, but liberation from the transcendent power whose commands are directed towards the Good itself is quite another matter. It is also worth pointing out that a God who commands humans to love can be a God who values human freedom. Not only could God allow humans the freedom to obey or not to obey his command. He could also issue commands that they must freely interpret, and creatively and imaginatively apply, tasks that require maturity and even a kind of autonomy. And this is precisely how Kierkegaard pictures God, not as a tyrant who eliminates human freedom, but as a ruler who extends to his subjects the dignity of becoming what we might call his partners. So the rejection of self-legislation is not a rejection of the ideal of human freedom.

However, if individual self-legislation fails to provide the higher authority needed for the ethical life, cannot this be provided by society? Perhaps the most popular form of this

---

[17] See James Rachels, *The Elements of Moral Philosophy*, 2nd edn. (New York: McGraw-Hill, 1993) and Patrick Nowell-Smith, *Ethics* (Baltimore: Penguin, 1961), for examples.

idea is that provided by contract theories of ethics, in which morality is essentially a matter of social agreement.[18] Kierkegaard believes that it is precisely such an idea that produces the 'doubt and vortex' he sees as characteristic of modernity. Doubt results partly because it is unclear which social group of the many to which I belong has the relevant authority: 'What, after all, is the Law, what is the Law's requirement of a person? Well, that is for people to decide. Which people? Here the doubt begins' (p. 115).

Perhaps this problem can be resolved through the strategy of Jurgen Habermas, in which the agreement that counts is the result of a free and fair conversation in which everyone may participate.[19] However, aside from the problem as to what constitutes a free and fair conversation, and the problem of whether everyone is really welcome to participate, since Habermas requires that people who participate accept ground rules that rule out substantive conceptions of the good as a basis for discussion, Kierkegaard does not think a merely *hypothetical* agreement can be binding on actual, existing beings:

> Or should the determination of what is the Law's requirement perhaps be an agreement among, a common decision by, all people, to which the individual has to submit? Splendid—that is, if it is possible to find the place and fix a date for this assembling of all people (all the living, all of them?—but what about the dead?), and if it is possible, something that is equally impossible, for all of them to agree on one thing! (p. 115)

The claim that such a convocation could never reach an agreement if all people were included seems very plausible to me, which is why the proposals of 'procedural liberals', such as John Rawls, for a social contract, invariably specify the situation of the participants in the conversation (in Rawls' case the 'original position') in such a way that actual concrete individuals are excluded.[20] What agreement could we actually expect if to

---

[18] I explain and critique a fuller version of this type of meta-ethical theory in Chapter 11.

[19] See, for example, Jurgen Habermas, *Moral Consciousness and Communicative Action*, trans. Christian Lenhardt and Shierry Weber Nicholsen (Cambridge, Mass.: MIT Press, 1992).

[20] For the classical statement of John Rawls's view, see his A *Theory of Justice* (Cambridge, Mass.: Harvard University Press, 1971). In this work

discuss moral obligations we brought together Muslim funda-
mentalists, theosophists, radical Marxists, Catholic Christians,
radical feminists, faith-healing Pentecostals, and consumer-
oriented, live-for-today materialists? One can of course add to
this group indefinitely. In Rawls's 'original position' the hypothetical discussion requires a 'veil of ignorance' in which the
participants are ignorant both of their position in society and
their own substantive views of the good. But such a requirement
adds to the hypothetical character of the conversation and any
agreement it could produce.

However, even if we imagine such a hypothetical meeting
would lead to an agreement, it simply is not clear how a hypothetical agreement could produce *actual* obligations. Suppose it
to be true that if I were to attend a meeting in the Vatican, I
would be moved to promise to give money to support the
restoration of the Sistine Chapel, and that if this occurred I
would have an obligation to give the money. Does this hypothetical fact mean that I now actually have this obligation, when
no such promise has been made? Surely not. One might object
that if I were fully informed about the needs of the Vatican, I
would indeed wish to help, given my current beliefs and values.
The hypothetical agreement in such a case would get its force
from my current beliefs and values. However, I still do not see
how such hypothetical facts could make it a *duty* for me to make
a contribution; at most such hypothetical facts suggest that I
might in fact have some good reasons to contribute.

In addition to this problem, there are at least two other
difficulties with a contract view of morality. One is that a social
agreement, like an individual decision, would be subject to
change and would therefore lack the relevant firmness: 'The
love commandment is not like a human commandment, which
becomes old and dulled over the years or is changed by the
mutual agreement of those who should obey it' (p. 375). Yet
another, even more fundamental issue is this: the obligation to

---

Rawls does not attempt to develop a theory of moral obligations in general,
but only a theory of justice. However, it is easy enough to imagine someone
employing a Rawlsian strategy for this more ambitious theory, though I
do not think Rawls himself tries to do this or would endorse such an attempt.

keep one's promises is itself a form of moral obligation, arguably one of the most fundamental forms. Even if other moral
obligations could be grounded in something like a mutual
promise, it is hard to see how the obligation to keep the promise
itself could be derived from such a promise.

We thus see that for Kierkegaard a genuine obligation requires a divine authority, or something analogous to divine
authority in being 'transcendent' or 'infinite' in character. It is
interesting to note that at one point he acknowledges that what
he calls divine authority has been called 'by thinkers' something
else: 'the idea' or 'the true' or 'the good' (p. 339). In fact, as we
have seen, Kierkegaard himself uses the language of 'the Good'
in *Purity of Heart.* I believe this point about alternative languages is important, since it implies that the divine command
that is the basis of morality has been promulgated by natural or
general revelation, and not simply in some particular historical
revelation.[21] It seems possible then for people to be aware of a
divine command without being clearly aware that it is a divine
command. Nevertheless, Kierkegaard claims that this transcendent reality that humans can be aware of is described
'more accurately' as 'the God-relationship' (p. 339). It is clear
that for Kierkegaard the relationship of personal accountability
grounded in the notion of God is by far the most fitting way of
thinking about the moral life.

THE PROBLEMATIC CHARACTER OF AUTHORITY

If I am right in my contention that the concept of divine
authority is central to *Works of Love*, this will hardly be perceived as a virtue by many. For claims to religious authority are
regarded with suspicion in the contemporary world. Such tragedies as Heaven's Gate, in which forty-one people committed
to the authority of Marshall Applewhite committed suicide, or
the Branch Davidian inferno in Waco, clearly show the dangers
of uncritically accepting a religious authority. Such tragedies
raise pressing questions about whether it is possible to distinguish legitimate and illegitimate forms of religious authority,
and if it is possible, how to make the distinction. Kierkegaard's

---

[21] I shall expand on this point in Chapter 7.

view of authority, as developed in *The Book on Adler*, in some ways makes this problem more difficult.[22]

However, the contemporary suspicion of authority goes beyond merely demanding rational criteria for determining when authority is legitimate. Rather, it extends to the question as to whether there can be anything like a legitimate authority, of whether claims to authority are intrinsically dubious. For those who have a general suspicion of authority, a legitimate authority may seem a bit like an honest thief.

One might think that so-called 'postmodern' or post-Enlightenment thinking could be more open to authority. After all, the Enlightenment was partly born out of the recognition that claims to authority, especially religious authority, breed intolerance, persecution, and bloody wars. In reaction to this, the Enlightenment tried to substitute the authority of reason, understood as universal and impersonal, for particular authorities. Postmodernism has in turn criticized Enlightenment appeals to reason as disguised attempts on the part of one social group to exercise power over another. Faith in reason is replaced by the claim that we must learn to live with the 'flux', employing a different metaphor than the image of the 'vortex' Kierkegaard employs to describe the contemporary period.[23] Both metaphors, however, may be understood as characterizing a culture where doubt is rampant and nothing seems to stand firm.

However, the postmodernist critique of impersonal reason can be seen as inspired by the same desire to produce a tolerant community that drove the Enlightenment critique of authority. The danger with a reason that discovers the final truth is that such a truth can, like claims of authority, once more be the ground of oppression and violence. However, if postmodernists have come to believe that intolerance and oppression can masquerade under the label of reason, it does not mean that they are inherently friendly to the claims of authority that reason was supposed to subvert. John Caputo is on this point a

[22] See my article 'Kierkegaard on Religious Authority: The Problem of the Criterion', in *Faith and Philosophy*, 17/1 (Jan. 2000), 48–66.
[23] This term is used frequently by John Caputo in *Radical Hermeneutics* (Bloomington, Ind.: Indiana University Press, 1987).

representative postmodern thinker when he rejects the notion of a privileged standpoint: 'No form of *Wahrheit* has any rights or privileges over any other. We lack the standpoint and the right to make such a judgment.'[24] However, one might think that the essence of authority lies in the privileging of some voice, since that voice is recognized as 'higher' and therefore rightfully calling for submission.

The problem is not merely that claims to final truth lead to violence, since 'blood is usually shed in the name of Being, God, or truth ...'[25] Rather, for some the whole idea of submission to a higher power is felt to be inherently dehumanizing. Kierkegaard himself understands the thought behind this when he notes that the idea of liberation from divine authority is seen as 'going further', the next step after liberation from slavery or serfdom (p. 115). The power of this idea can be seen in the work of theologian Don Cupitt, who says that a God who is conceived of as a transcendent reality to whom I must answer would violate the autonomy that lies at the essence of the moral life.[26] So although Cupitt speaks of the unconditional authority of the religious requirement, the authority here rests on a person's own ideals, and talk of God is simply a pictorial and expressive way of talking about the force of those ideals.[27] We thus have in Cupitt another example of the view discussed above, in which the individual himself is ultimately the source of the 'Law'. From this perspective, an authority that comes from outside the self seems deeply anti-humanistic.

I wish to put to one side for now the epistemological question as to how one might recognize a legitimate religious authority

---

[24] Ibid. 182.

[25] Ibid. 195.

[26] The following passage is a good illustration of this attitude: 'The religious requirement is not heteronomy, in the sense of being an odious subjection to the will of another such as is incompatible with the dignity of a conscious rational self. It is true that I cast myself on God's mercy, knowing that the false self I have made of myself must die before I can attain my spiritual destiny. But I do not suppose God to be an objective individual over and above the religious requirement. The religious requirement has been radically internalized and made my own, so that *I* will its judgment upon myself.' Don Cupitt, *Taking Leave of God*, 87.

[27] 'God *is* the religious requirement personified, and his attributes are a kind of projection of its main features as we experience them.' Ibid. 85.

and know that a command is really divine in origin. The more fundamental question for ethics is whether such a command, even if known to be divine in origin, could be the ground of genuine moral obligations. To put the matter bluntly, why should I obey God, even if he does issue commands to me?

WHY SHOULD GOD BE OBEYED?

I have already suggested that the answer to the question as to why a person should obey God is given by the identity of the self. A divine command theory of moral obligation can and should be linked to an ethic of self-actualization. I should obey God because I should love God and be grateful to him for the good he has manifested to me in creating me and sustaining me. The gratitude in this case is both sustained by love for God and is a manifestation of that love. When I manifest this grateful obedience I become my true self and find the satisfaction and happiness God intends me to have. This means that the ethical view presented in *Works of Love* is, in the final analysis, a humanistic ethic, not in the sense that it is an ethic that rests on humanity conceived independently of God, but that it is an ethic directed to human flourishing.

That the command to love the neighbour is aimed at helping people find fulfilment by becoming the selves they were intended to become may appear implausible. It looks as if I am claiming that the obligation to love the neighbour as oneself is rooted in a form of eudaimonism. However, this is not the case at all. Kierkegaard stresses continually in *Works of Love* that genuine love for the neighbour requires self-denial, and this looks quite foreign to the outlook of eudaimonism (p. 56). Ultimately, when we look closely at the nature of self-fulfilment and happiness as well as self-denial, we will see that the opposition between self-denial and self-fulfilment breaks down when both are understood properly. This is a task I will undertake in the next chapter.

However, though we will see that Kierkegaard does give an important place to human happiness and fulfilment in his account and shows that they are linked to love for the neighbour, that happiness does not serve as the direct motivation for obeying God, and thus the account he develops does not root human obligations in something like prudence. The fact that obedience to God leads to happiness does not imply that my obedience to God must be motivated by a search for my own happiness. The immediate ground of the obligation to obey God for us humans is not that we thereby seek to secure our own happiness. An analogy with a humanly grounded obligation will be helpful here. For the moment let us consider the obligations children have towards parents who have lovingly cared for them. Any such obligations children have towards their parents are rooted in the history of their relationship. Because of the love and sacrifices of the parents, the children owe them a debt of gratitude, and when the children seek to honour and show appreciation for the parents they are moved primarily by love and gratitude, rather than a concern for their own happiness. Nevertheless, it is true that children who generously manifest such love and gratitude find this fulfilling. The relationship with their parents is one that is conducive to their own happiness.

We can say then that the question of why children should honour and respect their parents can be answered in two ways. The question is ambiguous and the answer depends upon how we understand the question. If we mean to ask 'What should motivate children to honour and respect their parents?' the answer is 'love and gratitude in response to the goodness of the parents toward the children.' The children value the parents and they value the relationship, and both are valued in themselves and not merely as a means to the children's own happiness. However, if we mean to ask, 'Why is it a good thing for children to honour and respect their parents?', a legitimate part of the answer is that such a practice advances the happiness and well-being of the children. This fact helps explain why *parents* might legitimately expect and even require this of their children. The parents do not necessarily do this for selfish reasons but because they realize it is what is best for their children. We can thus see the children's obedience as linked to their happiness, not prudentially as a motive for the children to be obedient, but as a reason why the parents should have such expectations.

In a similar way, Kierkegaard argues that our obligation to obey God is grounded in the specific relationship we have with God, a relationship that is historical, beginning with our birth

and continuing beyond our death. Just as the obligations romantic lovers have to each other are rooted in their history with
each other, grounded in the promises they have made and the
loving actions they have performed, so our duties to God are
rooted in our history with God, a history that precedes any
obligations created by human actions: 'But that eternal love-
history has begun much earlier; it began with your beginning,
when you came into existence out of nothing, and just as surely
as you do not become nothing, it does not end at a grave' (pp.
149–50). My obligations to God stem from the fact that God
has created me and intends me to have a life of eternal happiness. I should love such a being and one way my love will
express itself is in gratitude.

It is noteworthy that Kierkegaard refrains from any claim
that God should be obeyed because he is all-powerful. In *Purity
of Heart* he explicitly rejects the claim that anyone can will the
good out of fear of divine punishment, on the grounds that
God's punishments are not really punishments. Rather, when
God chastens an individual it is for the individual's own good.
In sending such discipline, God is motivated by love, and thus,
far from fearing divine punishment, the person who truly wills
the good should welcome this correction.[28] This avoidance of
any appeal to power is significant. It means that the ground of
the obligation to obey God is not rooted solely in the fact that
God, as the all-powerful Creator, has made me from nothing.
A God who created me for his own amusement would have no
claim on my love and gratitude. My obligations to God are
rooted in the fact that the God who created me loves me and
wants only my good. It is to this loving Creator, who has given
me everything that I have, that I owe ultimate loyalty. This
claim that I should obey God out of love and gratitude for the
good he has bestowed upon me is consistent, however, with the
claim that my own deepest happiness lies in doing so. And if this
is so, then God's commands do not have to be seen as arbitrary,
but as rooted in God's desire for human flourishing, and I shall
argue below that this is what Kierkegaard maintains.

I think then that Kierkegaard's answer to the question as to
why a person should obey God is similar to that given by Robert

[28] See Kierkegaard, *Upbuilding Discourses in Various Spirits*, 44–60.

Adams in his well-known paper, 'A Modified Divine Command Theory of Ethical Wrongness'.[29] In this paper, Adams concedes that not all aspects of ethics can be accounted for in terms of commands, and that not just any god's commands would be worthy of obedience. Instead, he argues that ethical wrongness can be identified with the property of being contrary to the commands of a *loving* God. Obligations as such are rooted in social relationships, and the particular relation humans have with God is the ground of those overriding obligations that we call moral. Of course, if God's nature is such that he is necessarily loving, as Adams suggests in his more recent book, *Finite and Infinite Goods*, the adjective can be omitted and we can say simply that moral wrongness is the property of being contrary to the commands of God.[30]

Kierkegaard's view is very similar. It is the fact that God is love and that love is ultimately the foundation of all that is really valuable in human existence that makes God's commands such that they should be obeyed. It is true that the God to whom I am responsible, whose rigorous gaze falls upon me, is all-powerful, but there is no appeal in Kierkegaard to sheer, naked power, since such an appeal would truly subvert love by transforming it to self-interest. Rather, the gaze of the one to whom I am responsible is the gaze of love. 'Would that I could describe how the one who loves looks at the one overcome, how joy beams from his eyes, how this loving look rests so gently on him, how it seeks, alluring and inviting to win him' (p. 342).[31] This description of the loving gaze is of a human lover, but it surely applies even more aptly to God. The gaze of God upon his creatures has precisely this gentle, alluring quality, and it is this, I think, that makes all the difference. The command of

[29] Robert Adams, 'A Modified Divine Command Theory of Ethical Wrongness', in *The Virtue of Faith and Other Essays* (Oxford: Oxford University Press, 1987), 97–122.

[30] See Adams, *Finite and Infinite Goods*, 281.

[31] It is very striking to compare this description of the 'look' or 'gaze' of the lover with the description Sartre gives of the look or gaze of the other in *Being and Nothingness*, trans. Hazel E. Barnes (New York: Washington Square Press, 1966), 310–70. I think that the whole difference between the philosophies of Kierkegaard and Sartre could be seen as stemming from their contrasting perception of what it would mean to have God's gaze rest upon a person.

God does not crush human autonomy, because the one who issues the command is the one whose gaze invites and allures, the one who does not compel faith in himself and love for himself, but invites it by the gift of creation, and, according to Christian belief, himself suffering and dying with us.

6

The Humanistic Character of Commanded Love

In Chapter 5 I argued that Kierkegaard does hold a divine command theory of moral obligation. He believes both that all genuine moral duties are divine commands, and that whatever God commands for humans is morally obligatory for them. God's commands give human actions and virtues the character of being duties. However, on Kierkegaard's view the moral obligations that are grounded in God's commands are not arbitrary, because the commands are directed to our good. The commands come from a loving God and have love as their goal, and this God has created us so that our own deepest happiness depends on our coming to love in this way. In this chapter I will extend this argument by discussing in more depth the relation between neighbour-love and human happiness. I will then develop Kierkegaard's argument for the humanistic character of this love by detailing the human goods that it secures and safeguards.

SELF-DENIAL AND HUMAN HAPPINESS

This reading of Kierkegaard does not, however, convert his view into a form of ethical eudaimonism, at least not of any ordinary sort. Kierkegaard seems resolutely anti-eudaimonistic. Rather, he stresses the need for self-denial as the dominant characteristic of the person who is following God's command to love the neighbour. God's command to love the neighbour is not a command that a person could conceivably be motivated to obey by what we might call natural self-regarding considerations. This is because the command is a command to love the neighbour, and the neighbour is not the 'other-I' but the 'first-you'.[1] My love for

---

[1] Kierkegaard, *Works of Love*, 57. Subsequent references to this work in this chapter are denoted by page nos. in parentheses.

the neighbour cannot plausibly be understood as directed at my own happiness, even when I understand my happiness as linked to the happiness of others, such as friends and kinspeople, with whom I share natural bonds. For the neighbour is any person and every person, even those who consider themselves my enemies. The command to love the neighbour creates an obligation to love those I am not naturally disposed to love, and the satisfaction of such a command does not appear to be something a person seeking to satisfy natural desires would aim at. I am obligated to love others in a selfless manner and this certainly requires self-denial. Is such an ethic of self-denial consistent with the claim that God's commands are oriented towards our happiness?

It is important to see that despite Kierkegaard's talk of the necessity of self denial, in the end he does wish to affirm a link between love of neighbour and human happiness and fulfilment. Early on in the book he affirms very clearly that love is what makes life worth living, and that this is true in the deepest sense of Christian neighbour-love, rather than romantic love and friendship (p. 38). The book concludes by arguing that the satisfying character of love is such that we *ought* not to require a command at all. Love must be a duty only because of our own fallenness. In the conclusion, Kierkegaard puts into the mouth of the 'apostle of love' the following words, which serve as an apt summary for the deeply humanistic character of Christian love:

Dear me, what is all this that would hinder you in loving, what is all this that you can win by self-love! The commandment is that you *shall* love, but ah, if you will understand yourself and life, then it seems that it should not need to be commanded, because to love people is the only thing worth living for, and without this love you are not really living. (p. 375)

We cannot thereby eliminate the tension between self-actualization and self-denial by pretending that the former is not important for Kierkegaard.

The question as to how to reconcile the ethical demand for self-denial with the idea that the ethical life properly is rewarded with happiness is of course not unique to Kierkegaard. The same issue arises in Kant, who claims both that duty must be done for the sake of duty but also that the ethical person's highest end is a world where people are virtuous and where their virtue is rewarded with happiness.[2] Kierkegaard himself raises the issue explicitly in *Purity of Heart* and I believe he develops a successful solution there.

Purity of Heart appears to develop an ethic that allows no room for rewards at all, for Kierkegaard claims that 'the person who wills the Good for the sake of reward does not will one thing but is double-minded.'[3] If this line of thought is pushed, it could easily develop into a rigorous asceticism that leaves no room for an individual's own happiness as a legitimate end. However, it is easy to see that this is not Kierkegaard's view, for he qualifies the claim about rewards very carefully by making it clear that God has linked a legitimate reward to the ethical quest: 'The reward we are speaking of here [that cannot provide legitimate motivation for willing the Good] is the world's reward, because the reward that God has eternally joined together with the Good has nothing dubious about it and is also adequately sure.'[4]

What is the difference between the world's reward and God's reward? The worldly reward is externally related to the Good: 'The Good is one thing; the reward is something else.' The person pictured here is the individual who wants to be rewarded for goodness by such things as wealth and a good reputation. The individual who is seeking the divine reward however finds happiness in the Good itself; the reward is internally linked to the God and is not an external consequence that may or may not accompany it: 'That the Good is its own reward, yes that is eternally certain. There is nothing more certain; it is not more certain that there is a God, because this is one and the same.'[5]

One might read this last quotation reductionistically as a claim that God is for Kierkegaard merely a symbol of the Good itself, with eternal happiness merely the happiness to be found in this life when one learns to value the Good. However,

---

[2] See Immanuel Kant, *Critique of Practical Reason and Other Writings in Moral Philosophy*, trans. Lewis White Beck (Chicago: University of Chicago Press, 1949), 214–20.

[3] Kierkegaard, *Upbuilding Discourses in Various Spirits*, 37.

[4] Ibid.

[5] Ibid. 39.

it is surely more plausible, in light of Kierkegaard's robust faith in God as the Creator and as the one who offers hope beyond the grave, to see this quote as an expression of Kierkegaard's view of the nature of eternal happiness and its link to God. God is the Good, but this identification requires us to rethink the Good as embodied in a person rather than reductionistically to understand God as an abstraction. Because of this identity, the one who wills the Good sincerely wills an alliance with God. God's own reality as Creator and providential sustainer of the universe guarantees that the one who wills the Good in this way will be happy eternally. Even in time such a person can have a kind of happiness, in spite of the 'temporary' ingratitude, lack of appreciation, poverty, contempt, suffering, and even premature death that this life typically offers the person truly committed to the Good. This is so because this person already possesses a relation to God, though this kind of happiness is not what is ordinarily thought of as happiness. Such a person can in eternity receive genuine happiness in full. This happiness, both in this life and in the life to come, is not an external reward that taints or compromises the commitment to the Good, because the happiness will consist in the opportunity to share fully in the Good, to experience union with God, who is the Good.

Kierkegaard illustrates this with a simple example of earthly love. He considers the case of a young man who falls in love with a young woman who is wealthy.[6] If the young man 'loves' the woman for her money, then his love is not genuine love at all. A couple in love who understood the temptations and difficulties occasioned by such wealth might decide to give the money away. Clearly, money is an external reward that can corrupt the purity of love. However, if the young man simply loves the woman and finds happiness in their life together, his reward is not external to his love and does not taint or corrupt it. Rather, the love is a condition for the happiness.

In a similar way, a desire for heaven does not have to be seen as an external reward that taints or corrupts the love of the Good. If heaven is simply a designation for life together with God, and God is the Good, then it is only those who truly love

---

[6] Ibid. 38–9.

the Good who will find heaven desirable. In Matthew's Gospel Jesus teaches that the 'pure in heart' are blessed because they will see God. Perhaps they are blessed because they are the only ones who will want to see God or can even endure the sight of God. A connection between human happiness and moral virtue can be seen as intrinsic if we have the right conception of human nature and how it may be fulfilled.

THE MOTIVATION FOR LOVE OF THE NEIGHBOUR

We saw in the last chapter that on Kierkegaard's view the motivation for love of the neighbour is not that one thereby seeks one's own happiness. Rather, the motivation is love for God and gratitude stemming out of that love for the goodness God has bestowed. This view is quite consistent with the claim that God has created the human self in such a way that when humans do love God and their neighbours in this way, they find themselves happy and fulfilled. As Kierkegaard puts it, 'the one who loves saves another from death, and in quite the same or yet in another sense he saves himself from death' (p. 281). However, though he does save himself, 'love never thinks of the latter, of saving itself.' Thus, human happiness may be one of God's aims in commanding love of the neighbour, but the one who loves in this way is not primarily seeking his or her own happiness.

However, if a human being comes to recognize this link between his or her own happiness and obedience, will this not compromise this selflessness? Can self-denial survive the discovery that God ultimately wills the happiness and fulfilment of the lover? At this point, the claim that the person who loves the neighbour does not aim at his or her own fulfilment must be qualified. All depends on how the self and its fulfilment are understood.

If we assume what we might call a 'natural' understanding of the self and its happiness, then a tension between seeking one's own happiness and seeking to love the neighbour seems ineradicable. From this perspective, love for the neighbour must be motivated by God's love and goodness and the love for God that God inspires and creates in the self. It is only when God is loved in this way that one can love the neighbour, for God is the 'middle term' in all such love.[7] To love the neighbour is to love him or her because he or she is created by God in God's own image. Kierkegaard himself, surprisingly, does not really use the language of the *imago dei* in *Works of Love*.[8] The closest he comes is the assertion that humanity has an 'inherent kinship with God' and so Christianity posits as a task 'humanity's likeness to God' (p. 62). However, the concept of the image of God often seems to be presupposed. God is love and when I love my neighbour, I image God by loving my neighbour. That neighbour is also like God because God has placed love within all of my neighbours, 'in the foundation'. Such love clearly is a reflection of God's nature. I cannot love God without loving those whom God has made who reflect God's nature. Love for God and not a desire for my own natural happiness must motivate such neighbour-love.

However, when we come to understand that this self, with its 'unnatural' love of the neighbour, including the enemy, is what God intended the self to become, the situation is transformed. The opposition between the self's quest for happiness and the obligation to love in a selfless way is undermined. For the happiness of the self is no longer understood as a good external to the love of God and the love of neighbour but rather as consisting of such love and the opportunity to develop and exercise it in a loving community. When a human person gains the right understanding of his or her own true nature and happiness, then it becomes true that 'it is as though it should not need to be commanded' that the person love in this manner, because loving selflessly is precisely the route to happiness and fulfilment (p. 375).[9] It is of course only 'almost' because we do not in this life attain to such perfect selflessness.

Thus in this life duty remains duty. The self's 'natural' desires are currently not oriented towards the love of God that would lead to genuine happiness but towards selfish ends.[10] As long as humans are in this state it cannot be true that doing my

---

[7] See Chapter 8 for a fuller discussion of this point.

[8] At least the Hong index shows no entry for 'image of God' or '*imago Dei*'.

[9] This is my translation.

[10] It ought to be clear then that the tension between the quest for happiness and the demands of love reflects the sinful human condition. See the discussion of sinfulness in Chapter 7, pp. 164–9.

moral duty can simply be identified with the search for my own happiness. Perhaps in eternity, my desires will be transformed entirely. Duty will cease to exist as duty and I will love my neighbour and at the same time thereby fulfil my own deepest desires. Those desires will perfectly correspond with what is now experienced as duty.

This is not eudaimonism, at least of the ordinary sort, because the recognition of my own deepest happiness requires a transformation of the self; it is only when I have learned to practise self-denial with respect to those goods that I currently naturally seek that I can be truly happy. It is only when my understanding of my self has been transformed that I can understand where my deepest happiness lies. It is not inconsistent, then, for Kierkegaard to argue that the self-denial demanded by love of the neighbour ultimately leads in the direction of human fulfilment. The central thrust of his argument in each case is a contention that it is the commanded character of neighbour-love that enables it to secure an important good, a good that even unloving people can recognize as good. The humanistic character of neighbour-love is thus not achieved in spite of its commanded status but because of that status. In the next section of this chapter I shall review some of the arguments Kierkegaard gives that neighbour-love is fulfilling in just this way.

THE SUPERIORITY OF COMMANDED LOVE: THREE
FUNDAMENTAL HUMAN GOODS

A good deal of *Works of Love* can be read as a series of arguments that, despite the contempt that the world has for Christian love, and despite the fact that this love requires self-denial, neighbour-love, grounded as it is in authority, provides a basis for genuine human flourishing. This fact does not directly ground the obligation to obey God. Those obligations are, as we have seen, rooted in God's loving creation of the individual. My obedience to God stems from the love and gratitude I owe to him in response to the love he has shown to me in creating me and destining me for eternal life. Understanding the humanistic character of God's commands does, however, help us understand better God's loving purposes in issuing his commands and also helps us see that those commands are not arbitrary. And, to the degree that I have become transformed both in my understanding of myself and my happiness, the opposition between the demands of duty for self-denial and my own happiness begins to disappear. I will in the remainder of this chapter review several of the lines of argument that Kierkegaard presents for this thesis.

Kierkegaard identifies three goods that he maintains are fostered by neighbour-love, along with three counterpart evils against which this love serves as a kind of protection. The first good is what we might call steadfastness or continuity in loving; its counterpart evil is the dimming or extinction of love over time. The second good is a kind of autonomy or independence that is linked to freedom; the counterpart evil is an unhealthy kind of dependence that can lead to oppression and victimization. The third good might be described simply as significance, a kind of happiness over the fact that a person sees his or her life as worthwhile; the counterpart evil is despair. All three goods are listed in a summary in Chapter IIA in Part I, which Kierkegaard highlights in bold: '**Only when it is a duty to love, only then is love eternally secured against every change, eternally made free in blessed independence, eternally and happily secured against despair**' (p. 29). I shall discuss each of these three points in some detail.

1. *Steadfastness.* One persistent line of argument is that basing love on an authoritative commandment gives love protection against the changes and insecurities inherent in temporal relationships. This theme is sounded both early and late. We have already seen it in the summary statement above. Exactly the same note is sounded in the last chapter of the book:

The love commandment is not like a human commandment, which becomes old and dulled over the years or is changed by the mutual agreement of those who should obey it. No, the love commandment remains new until the last day, just as new even on the last day when it has become oldest. Thus the commandment is not changed in the slightest way, least of all by an apostle. (pp. 375–6)

Merely human loves that rest on natural spontaneity are prisoners of 'drives and inclinations' or 'feelings' or simply 'intellectual calculation'. Nothing that rests on such changeable

entities can be secure. Contrariwise, eternal faithfulness requires as its basis something eternal, and a command of God,
who is eternal, has this quality (p. 313).

One might think that the mere fact that love is eternally
commanded would hardly establish it as secure against time.
For it is one thing for love to be commanded; another for it to be
realized. Surely, even if love is eternally commanded, it is not
eternally actualized by humans. It seems plausible that the love
for the neighbour that actual, temporal human beings have for
each other is not unchangeable, any more than romantic love is
unchangeable.

I think Kierkegaard's response to this objection is twofold. I
do not see how he could be under any illusion about the frailty
of temporal human beings, since *Works of Love* is full of laments
for how unloving we humans are. In arguing that neighbour-
love is not subject to change, he cannot therefore mean that we
human beings cannot cease to love as we ought.

Actually, Kierkegaard does say that to the degree we allow
our love to change this shows that it was never genuine neighbour-love at all, because 'love abides' (p. 303). However, this
claim does not seem to me to be consistent with taking seriously
the temporal character of human life. No matter how deep and
genuine a person's virtuous character at a particular time may
be, it seems to me that if this virtue is to endure it must be
reaffirmed. On Kierkegaard's own account of human existence,
spiritual qualities are not the kind of thing that can be taken for
granted; they must be continually renewed. However, if the
possession of a virtue at some particular time, no matter how
deep and genuine, is not sufficient to guarantee that this virtue
will last, then it follows that a failure of a virtue to endure does
not entail that it was never genuine at some past time. Perhaps it
implies that there was some defect within the character of the
person whose love has waned, but it does not seem to me that a
failure to continue to love one's neigbour shows that one never
had such love at all.

However, though I do not think Kierkegaard can reasonably
argue that neighbour-love in finite, temporal human beings is
impervious to change, he can argue that there is something
about neighbour-love that resists such change. There is still a
significant difference between neighbour-love and such natural

human loves as romantic love and friendship. These latter have as their ground or basis human desires and inclinations which arc essentially subject to flux. Neighbour-love at least has as its basis or foundation the eternal command of God. Though our love for the neighbour may wane, at least the possibility of a constant love is provided by the fact that the love itself is rooted in something that is eternal. If our love for the neighbour does vanish, this is for Kierkegaard a sign that the love was not fully present as neighbour-love, for such love is grounded in that which does not change (p. 305).[11] Even one who does not accept the claim that it would be impossible for a genuine lover to change and cease to love can accept something in the neighbourhood, which is that such a change would reveal that the person either was not or did not remain fully committed to the eternal. The ground of the love did not change; any change must therefore be in the person's relation to that ground, and reveals a defect in that relation.

I think the second part of Kierkegaard's answer to this objection involves an implicit appeal to Kant's principle that 'ought implies can'. If the eternal God, who is the creator, has commanded love, then God must also provide the condition for making that love a reality and God is fully capable of doing so. This is, I think, one of the reasons Kierkegaard says that love must presuppose the presence of love in everyone (p. 216). God himself is love, and as the Creator he is the ground of all existence. The true lover then always presupposes that love is present in others (and himself) *i Grunden*, 'in the foundation', or literally 'in the ground' (pp. 216–17). Since love is eternally commanded by an eternal being who must make it possible to obey the command, love is an eternal reality, at least as a *real possibility* that is present in the foundation of every individual, and this gives love a certain invulnerability to the whims and vagaries of inclinations and feelings. The possibility is real in the Kantian sense that it is grounded in something actual in the person; it is not merely a logical or abstract possibility.

It is crucial to see that this argument does not beg the question by simply presupposing the superiority of neighbour-love. Rather, it is a claim that neighbour-love is better able to secure a

---

[11] Note the claim that 'the one who loves is in covenant with the eternal'.

human good (protection against change) which natural human lovers themselves value and seek. If we look at romantic love, Kierkegaard notes, it is clear that this love is aware of the possibility of alteration, and that the lovers seek to prevent such change by such actions as swearing to be faithful to each other (p. 29). However, Kierkegaard argues that such an oath contains a 'poetic misunderstanding', because an oath requires something 'higher' for its foundation, and in this case, when the lovers swear by the moon or the stars, their love is actually what gives the oath its meaning, since they have nothing higher than that love that can serve as a basis for the oath. Only neighbour-love, which is grounded in God and God's command, has this root in something higher and is thus impervious to change. Shakespeare famously says that 'love is not love which alters when it alteration finds.'[12] It is only neighbour-love that is capable of being a love which steadfastly abides when it discovers change in the beloved. Thus Kierkegaard argues, in a way that actually parallels Judge William's argument in favour of marriage in *Either/Or II*, that commanded love provides the possibility of realizing an ideal that romantic love itself acknowledges as valid.

Does Kierkegaard think that other kinds of loves, such as marriage and friendship, cannot abide? I will discuss the relation between neighbour-love and other kinds of love in Chapter 9. I will merely add here, by way of anticipation, that it would be a mistake to think of neighbour-love and other kinds of love as mutually exclusive rivals. Rather, neighbour-love can be present as a foundational and transformative component in these other kinds. Insofar as neighbour-love is genuinely present in these loves, they can share in the steadfast character of neighbour-love. Perhaps the degree to which they are steadfast is itself a sign of the degree to which they embody neighbour-love.

It does not seem to me that love that is steadfast is incapable of any kind of change at all. Kierkegaard repeatedly recognizes the many varied forms that neighbour-love itself can take. It would be wrong to think that a steadfast love could not take on new forms in different circumstances. Suppose I love a friend,

---

[12] Shakespeare, Sonnet 116.

but my friend decides to spurn me out of a desire to have friends who are richer and more influential than I am. In that case I must go on loving my friend, but my love will not take the form of day-to-day encouragement and fellowship, but of a constant willingness to renew the friendship. A love that is steadfast may change its form of expression; what it cannot do is change from love to unlove.

2. *Autonomy*. A second line of argument for the deeply humanistic character of the love that is grounded in divine authority stresses that this love (and its underlying authority) is one that liberates and frees from human oppression. The pattern of argument that underlies this line of thought is similar to the one given above. Kierkegaard identifies a recognizable human good, in this case autonomy or independence, and argues that it is commanded love that offers the best possibility for achieving it. Somewhat surprisingly, the response to the Enlightenment worry that submission to divine authority is a violation of autonomy is not a complete rejection of autonomy, but an argument that genuine autonomy requires divine authority. There is then for Kierkegaard a valid ideal of autonomy: 'But also in the world of spirit, precisely this, to become one's own master, is the highest—and in love to help someone toward that, to become himself, free, independent, his own master, to help him stand alone—that is the greatest beneficence' (p. 274).

How is this possible? The 'spoiled pagan' who has emerged from the Enlightenment sees autonomy over against God as the logical next step after liberation from human masters. However, as Kierkegaard sees things, the relation to God equalizes and humanizes all relationships among humans, and without that God-relation there is no protection against human domination of other humans. Even well-intentioned human beneficence can introduce a subtle hierarchy by introducing a relationship of dependence. I cannot truly help another to stand alone if I see my actions as completely autonomous, because if I become the other's benefactor I introduce a relation of dependence. I am superior to the other because the other's situation has been advanced by my actions. However, if I help the other to stand alone with God's help, the same help that allows me to stand, then the relationship of superiority I have to the other is undermined (pp. 274–9).

Part of the independence given by neighbour-love consists in the freedom from the need for reciprocation. Love of course welcomes reciprocal love, for love for another expresses itself in helping the other to become more loving. However, when love is rooted in God's command, then it does not demand or presuppose reciprocation. In this way, Kierkegaard argues 'only law can give freedom' (p. 38). Romantic love and friendship are limited by the demand for reciprocity: 'If when another person says, "I cannot love you any longer", one proudly answers, "Then I can also stop loving you"—is this independence?' Neighbour-love, however, which is rooted in God's command to love, has the independence that natural human love itself desires. When told by another that love will no longer be forthcoming, the true lover can say, 'In that case I *shall* still continue to love you' (p. 39). Neighbour-love thus protects against the unhealthy kind of dependence on another.

This humanizing character of the relationship to God is seen particularly in the case of a conflict between good and evil. It is just such conflicts that often create the kind of violence that John Caputo rightly fears and wrongly believes to be necessarily linked to claims to authority. The person (or group) who *is* in fact in the right easily demonizes the opposition, who is not merely seen as wrong but becomes thought of as the embodiment of evil.[13] Even short of such demonization, those who fight for the good naturally see themselves as superior to the opponent. However, if the one who battles for the good sees himself as under divine authority, the relationship to the opponent is transformed:

The one who loves does not give the impression at all, nor does it occur to him that it is he who has conquered, that he is the victor—no, it is the Good that has conquered. In order to take away the humiliating and the insulting, the one who loves introduces something higher between himself and the unloving one and in that way removes himself. (p. 339)

The God-relationship makes possible a kind of 'holy modesty' in an individual that prevents the embarrassment of superiority.

---

[13] See John Caputo, *Radical Hermeneutics*, 195, and the discussion of this point on pp. 133–5 in the previous chapter.

This modesty can be seen, for example, in the way that a person receives the expressions of repentance on the part of another:

> Expressions of grief over the past, sorrow over his wrong, pleas for forgiveness—in a certain sense the loving one accepts all this, but in a holy abhorrence he promptly lays it aside, just as one lays aside something that is not one's due—that is, he intimates that this is not his due; he assigns it all to a higher category and gives it to God as the one to whom it is due. (p. 341)

When love is grounded solely in human decisions, as in a contractual model of love, then some humans are inevitably victims of the decisions of others. Two people can be in love, but one party breaks the relationship, and therefore appears to 'have the upper hand' (p. 304). Kierkegaard argues that from the perspective of eternity, the true lover does not suffer this fate. Undoubtedly, human beings still remain subject to victimization; 'it certainly is that way in the world, but in the eternal sense it can never be that way' (p. 304). If love is grounded in God's eternal command, if God as love is present as 'the third term' in a love relationship, then the person who has been deceived can continue to love. From an earthly point of view, the person is a victim, but eternally it is the one who broke the relationship who has been harmed. From the point of view of the genuine lover, the relationship is not even broken; it remains as a possibility. The true lover is oriented towards the future, and does not see only the past, and from this future perspective, the relationship is not necessarily broken. It is simply 'a relationship that has not yet been finished' (p. 306). The true lover continues to hope for reconciliation and believe in that possibility.

3. *Significance*. Finally, Kierkegaard argues that the love commanded by God is linked in the most direct way to human fulfilment by securing human life against the opposite of happiness: despair. This third line of thought takes the same form as the first two. Again Kierkegaard identifies a human good, in this case a sense of significance, a kind of happiness understood as freedom from despair, and argues that it is divinely commanded love that makes it possible to realize this good. In an argument that closely parallels one given by Anti-Climacus in *The Sickness Unto Death*, Kierkegaard claims that despair

cannot be an accident that befalls a person.[14] If a person loses a
job, loses a friend, or suffers a painful divorce, and then des-
pairs, it appears that the person's despair is precipitated by the
particular event.

However, Kierkegaard claims that despair is 'a misrelation in
a person's inner being', and that what has really happened in
such a case is that the event in question has revealed a state
of despair that was present all along (p. 40). The despair
is grounded in the fact that the person's identity as a self is
grounded solely in the temporal: 'In other words, what makes a
person despair is not misfortune but the lack of the eternal.
Despair is to lack the eternal; despair is not to have undergone
the change of eternity through duty's *shall*' (pp. 40–1). This
does not mean, of course, that an individual should not grieve
and sorrow over the loss of a friend or a lover. It means,
however, that for the one whose identity is given by God's
command to love the neighbour, such a loss does not make life
worthless or pointless. In the midst of disappointment and
sorrow, the individual who loves others continues to believe
that his or her own life is meaningful and worthwhile. When
God commands us to love, he in effect says to us, 'Your love has
an eternal worth', and this means that our lives have this worth
as well. (p. 41). God commands us to love because he has
created us in such a way that we can only fulfil ourselves by
loving. The person who is commanded to love is 'eternally and
happily' saved from despair (p. 42).

One might say that when we truly understand our nature and
destiny, the tension between the requirement of self-denial and
the humanistic need for happiness can be seen to rest on a
misunderstanding. We discover that our true human fulfilment
and happiness is found, not when we aim at our own happiness,
but when we discover God's love for us and respond with love
and gratitude. Our obedience to God is motivated by this
love and gratitude, not by any quest for happiness. However,
by seeing the link between our happiness and those commands
we are better able to understand God's character in commanding them, and our love for God is increased.

[14] Kierkegaard, See *Sickness Unto Death*, 20–8, 49–60.

When we love God in the right way, we will want to obey his command—the command to love our neighbours as ourselves that requires self-denial. Paradoxically, this self-denying love turns out to be what leads to true happiness. The person who would save his life is the person who is willing to lose it.

7

Divine Commands: How Given and To Whom?

If moral obligations are rooted in divine commands, these commands must be promulgated and received. For a law to be valid, it must not only stem from the relevant authority, but must publicly be made known by that authority. How does Kierkegaard see the divine command to love the neighbour as oneself as being issued? How is the command known? Is the command the same for every human being, or are God's requirements particularized for the individual? In this chapter I shall try to extend the account of moral obligation as rooted in divine commands developed in Chapters 5 and 6 by answering these questions.

SPECIAL AND GENERAL REVELATION: ARE CHRISTIAN CLAIMS UNIQUE?

Theologians commonly distinguish between special and general revelation, understood as two ways God might make himself known. Very roughly, general revelation is the knowledge of God that God makes possible through observation of the natural world or through reflection on human experiences that are universal or commonly accessible. Special revelation is knowledge of God made possible by specific communications from God or specific historical events.

On the surface it might appear that Kierkegaard wishes to claim that God's command to love the neighbour is promulgated solely through special revelation. *Works of Love* continually focuses on biblical texts and affirms, as we have seen, that such texts have divine authority because they stem from apostles, divinely authorized messengers.[1] There is a running

---

[1] I do not think Kierkegaard's claim here depends on accepting traditional authorship of the relevant New Testament texts, though I think it does

argument that the content of this biblical revelation is some-thing that humans, relying on their own natural powers, would not have discovered without a special revelation from God.

The primacy of special revelation is emphasized most strongly in Kierkegaard's claim that the Christian command to love the neighbour as yourself was unknown in paganism. When Kierke-gaard speaks of paganism, it is almost always the culture of ancient Greece he has in mind. He is clearly not thinking about other major world religions such as Hinduism and Buddhism, which do not appear to be very evident on his radar screen, when he claims that there was 'no hint of neighbor love in paganism'.[2] Though he admits that love was present in paganism, and so the Christian understanding of love is not new in the sense of a 'novelty', he still wants to maintain that within Christianity 'everything is made new' (pp. 24–5). Greek paganism knew about special relations such as erotic love and friendship, but did not understand the obligation to love the neighbour in the sense that every human being is one's neighbour.

The originality of Christian teachings is appealed to as one sign of its divine origin. The Christian command to love, like other aspects of Christianity, is something that 'did not arise in any human being's heart'.[3] His polemical target here is clearly, however, not paganism itself, but the person within Christen-dom who has allowed himself to become indifferent to the power of Christian ideas. Such a Christian simply takes for granted the teachings of Christianity (and Judaism, Kierke-gaard significantly adds), and ungratefully fails to consider 'what his condition might be if Christianity had not come into the world' (p. 24). Kierkegaard urges such a person to reflect on the difference Christianity makes in his life, if the person is genuinely a Christian. Nor should this be difficult, 'for it is indeed not so very long since both you and I, my listener, were pagans—that is, if we have become Christians' (p. 26). Chris-

require that those texts stem from the teachings of the apostles and thus are linked to them.

[2] Kierkegaard, *Works of Love*, 44. Subsequent references to this work in this chapter are denoted by page nos. in parentheses.

[3] An allusion to I Corinthians 2: 9, a verse that Kierkegaard loves to cite. See, for example, the references to it by Johannes Climacus in *Philosophical Fragments*, 36, 109.

tian teachings are not only unique and unknown in paganism, but contain within themselves the 'possibility of offence', a natural tendency to shock and disturb the person who has not been fully transformed by Christianity, a description which for Kierkegaard fits just about everyone (pp. 56–9).

These claims for the uniqueness of Christianity will strike many contemporary readers as problematic. There is first the question of their correctness. Is it true that in paganism there was not even a 'hint' of the Christian teaching that one is obligated to love all human beings, and not merely one's family, friends and romantic partners? If we conceive of 'paganism' as including the great non-Christian religions, such a claim appears dubious, since in Buddhism at least there clearly seem to be obligations that extend to all other human beings.

Even if we restrict ourselves to the ancient Greek culture that Kierkegaard has in mind, the uniqueness claim may appear exaggerated. It is true that in general Plato and Aristotle do not seem to think of a class of moral obligations that apply to human beings as such.[4] However, there is a passage in Aristotle, in which he says that 'there seems to be some justice between any man and any other who can share in a system of law or be a party to an agreement; therefore there can also be friendship with him in so far as he is a man.'[5] This passage is hardly a model of clarity; it may well imply that some human beings, who are 'natural slaves', fall outside the obligation under discussion, and so may not be a real exception to Kierkegaard's claim. But it could be read as implying there is a class of moral obligations that hold between humans as humans.

A more plausible counter-example is provided by the Stoics, who clearly have a conception that the concern Aristotle says should be shown for one's friends can be gradually widened and eventually extended to all of humankind.[6] This certainly appears to me to contain at least a 'hint' of the Christian conception of

[4] The following discussion draws heavily on the advice of John Hare, who knows the classical world far better than I do, and I am grateful for his help.

[5] Aristotle, *Nicomachean Ethics*, 1161^{a}33–^{b}10, *The Basic Works of Aristotle*, trans. W. D. Ross (New York: Random House, 1941), 1071.

[6] For a discussion of the Stoic notion of impartiality and how it developed, see Julia Annas, *The Morality of Happiness* (Oxford: Oxford University Press, 1993), 262–76.

neighbour-love, and thus it does not appear to me that Kierkegaard's stronger claims for the uniqueness of Christianity can be defended, even for classical Greece, though of course in the later Stoics one cannot rule out the possibility of some influence from Jewish and Christian ideas that were by then prevalent in the Roman empire. Nevertheless the Stoics do appear to be a counter-example to Kierkegaard's claim. In fact, it is not clear that Kierkegaard himself believes his claim, for in *Works of Love* he continually uses the figure of Socrates as embodying a kind of prefigurement of Christian love (pp. 128–9, 373).

There are of course differences between the concern Socrates had for others and Christian love, and Kierkegaard duly notes these, using both the similarities and differences between Socrates and Christianity to illuminate the latter. And there are differences between the Stoic ideal of concern for all humankind and Christian love as well. Chief among these is that the Stoic obligation is derived from an extension of the notion of friendship, and it explicitly builds on the Aristotelian conception of the friend as an extension of the self, the 'other-I'. The obligation to care for the other is thus grounded in self-love; my own happiness requires me to care for all other human beings. Christian love, by contrast, as I shall emphasize in Chapter 9, stresses the *otherness* of the neighbour, and my duty to love the neighbour is not directly aimed at my own happiness but requires self-denial on my part, a theme already discussed in Chapter 6.

Nevertheless, such differences do not show that there are not significant parallels as well. In the end, I do not think the uniqueness claim, at least in its stronger forms, is important for Kierkegaard. In fact, he explicitly admits that since Christianity is nothing new in the sense of a 'novelty', that there are parallels of a sort between Christian teachings and paganism (p. 25). Hence I see no reason why Kierkegaard should deny that there is some knowledge of God's command to love the neighbour present in Greek culture, as well as in other cultures. There is no principled reason why Kierkegaard should not admit that God's command to love the neighbour is promulgated through general revelation. In fact, if Kierkegaard did wish to maintain that the moral law could be known only through a special historical revelation, this would create grave problems for him, and it is hard to see how such a view could be reconciled with his claim that God has placed love 'within the ground' of every human person (p. 216).

Kierkegaard agrees with the common traditional view that at least some moral obligations apply universally; they are part of what he calls the 'universally-human' (p. 364). However, it is difficult to see how a command that is issued only through a special revelation could be binding on those who have no access to the command and therefore no possibility of knowledge of it. Perhaps ignorance of my duty is not always an excuse; there may be such a thing as morally culpable ignorance of obligations. However, surely it must at least be possible for a human being to come to know about an obligation if that obligation is truly binding. Without such a possibility, there could not even be such a thing as culpable ignorance of the moral requirement.

There is yet another problem that arises, at least for us, in limiting the promulgation of a divine command that is supposed to give rise to moral obligations to special revelation. In a pluralistic society such as that in the United States, with a clear tradition of the separation of church and state, a claim that morality can only be known through a special revelation appears sectarian. It is difficult to argue that obligations that are revealed in this way apply to all people and not just to those who accept the authority of the revelation in question, if those who do not accept the revelation have no way of coming to know about the obligations.

Fortunately, I do not believe that Kierkegaard wishes to claim that the moral law can only be known through special revelation. It is clear that he thinks it has been made known through such a revelation, and that within Christendom those who claim to be Christians should recognize the authority of this revelation. It must be remembered that it is this kind of professedly Christian audience that he is addressing. However, when we look carefully at his text, we find that he affirms the possibility of a knowledge of the divine command to love the neighbour that is rooted in creation and not just in a special revelation. It is true that he thinks that this possible knowledge through creation is defective in various ways in comparison with that gained through special revelation. Chiefly, the problem is that this knowledge is for most people only possible and not actual. Though humans have the ability to know God's law, it is an ability that they generally do not exercise. And even when some natural knowledge of the divine is gained, it is not equal to that gained through special revelation. It is both more vague and more subject to error. However, the possibility of such knowledge is real and it is unambiguously affirmed by Kierkegaard.

The knowledge of the love that God commands us to have is, says Kierkegaard, a knowledge that everyone can have and should have: 'Thus every human being can come to know everything about love, just as every human being can come to know he, like every other human being, is loved by God' (p. 364). This is a knowledge that is rooted, not in special revelation, but in creation, for Kierkegaard affirms that within every human being God has placed love 'in the ground' of the self: 'It is God, the Creator, who must implant love in each human being, he who himself is Love' (p. 216). And God has done this, which allows the one who loves to presuppose 'that love is in the other person's heart', a presupposition that allows the true lover to build on this foundation and build up love in the other (pp. 216–17).[7] Since Kierkegaard consistently holds that 'like is known by like' it is this presence of love in every person, at least as a real possibility, that accounts for the possibility of a natural knowledge of our duty to love our neighbours as ourselves.[8] Of course to say that this potential knowledge is 'natural' is not to say that it is something humans can achieve apart from God's help. General revelation is still a form of revelation.

Since God is love, an awareness of genuine love is at least implicitly an awareness of God. Essentially, the knowledge of God and the knowledge of God's command to love are linked. Surprisingly to those who only know Kierkegaard as a textbook-caricature figure, who abandons any hope of knowledge of God and takes refuge in a desperate, irrational leap of faith to

---

[7] In Kierkegaard's text these words are in italics.

[8] For a typical argument that knowledge requires some similarity to what is known, see *Works of Love*, 285–6, where Kierkegaard argues that a truly innocent person cannot understand evil. By 'real possibility' I mean a possibility that is grounded in something that is actual. Kierkegaard's thinking here seems similar to the idea, found in Calvin and Kant, among others, that there is a 'seed of goodness' in all human beings, and he sees this seed as providing us the precondition for understanding our duty to love.

believe in God, Kierkegaard affirms the possibility of what we should call a natural knowledge of God. Such a knowledge is not grounded in reasons or arguments; it is not gained through philosophical proofs. Rather, it is a knowledge made possible by human spiritual striving: 'But if someone does not, precisely by choosing the inward direction, strain his spiritual powers as such, he does not discover at all, or he does not discover in the deeper sense, that God is' (p. 361). This clearly implies that the person who *does* exercise his or her spiritual powers in the right way can come to know God's reality.

Kierkegaard identifies *conscience* as the place where this natural knowledge occurs: 'The relationship between the individual and God, the God-relationship, is the conscience' (p. 143). Every human being can come to know God, and every human being can come to know the obligation to love, because every human being has a conscience: 'What is conscience? In the conscience it is God who looks at a person; so now in everything the person must look at him' (p. 377). He is not affirming here that conscience is infallible, or denying that it is culturally conditioned. He is simply affirming that in and through a person's cultural situation, the person can become aware of God's reality, can become aware *that* there are objective duties, even if the person's understanding of what those duties are is defective. One way Kierkegaard can deal with cultural relativity is through the notion of an individual calling, an idea discussed later in this chapter. If God's requirements are individualized, then a person's duties in one culture may genuinely be different from those of a different individual in another culture.

The point is that a person who is aware of the absoluteness of duty is aware of God. Such a person has an awareness of what John Hare has called 'God's call', though of course the individual may not realize that this awareness is an awareness of God.[9] It is one thing to be aware of God and another to be aware of God as God. In affirming the possibility of a knowledge of God Kierkegaard also wants to affirm at least the possibility that humans can come to see the value and goodness of human beings as such. A person who knows God naturally has his view of human beings transformed, since God is the one who

---

[9] See John Hare, *God's Call*.

has created humans and has placed love within them 'in the ground'. Such an awareness is at least an implicit awareness of the obligation to love my neighbour as myself.

The possibility of such a natural knowledge of God is affirmed by Kierkegaard when he says that what he describes (more accurately) as 'the God-relationship' has been called 'by thinkers' other names: 'the idea, the true, the good' (p. 339). In effect, Kierkegaard here attempts to turn the tables on Hegelian treatments of religion. As Kierkegaard sees things, the Hegelian view of religious faith is condescending. The Hegelian thinks that the pictorial language of religion, which speaks of a personal deity, is a less-clear attempt to articulate what philosophy conceives in a more rigorous and profound way. Kierkegaard's rival thesis is that the philosophical language used to describe what is ultimate and absolute (the idea, the true, the good) is simply a less clear and less-illuminating description of the reality that is better captured by explicitly religious language. However, despite the polemic against philosophy in the quotation just cited, it is important to see that Kierkegaard is affirming the possibility of a kind of awareness of God that is less than fully explicit and that can be expressed through philosophy.

The possibility of such knowledge is exemplified by the life of Socrates, that 'simple wise man of old', who had 'loved people in something higher', and, though a pagan, loved young people because he sensed that they still had 'a receptivity to the divine' that had not yet been dulled by society (pp. 128–9). Socrates is not credited with a full and explicit understanding of the biblical demand to love the neighbour, but he does have some knowledge of what God expects, and Kierkegaard evidently thinks this knowledge is derived from God.

I realize that some readers may not be entirely convinced by my argument that Kierkegaard proposes that the moral law can be known by general revelation as well as special revelation, in view of the pessimism Kierkegaard exudes about our natural capacities. I believe that my case is strong. The pessimism is, I believe, grounded in Kierkegaard's Lutheran conception of the pervasiveness and depth of human sin. Sinfulness does not mean, however, that it is impossible for humans to know the moral law, but rather that many of us will not in fact do so. In any case, if someone is not convinced that Kierkegaard allows for such natural knowledge, I would urge that it is the view he should have held, whether he actually did or not. For one cannot argue that people have a duty to obey a law that has not been promulgated. Kierkegaard, however, believes that every person should have love for the neighbour.

SINFULNESS AND OPPOSITION TO THE WORLD

If the knowledge of God and the command to love can be gained by anyone, why is special revelation so important? The answer is implicit in the last paragraph, which highlighted Kierkegaard's characteristic emphasis on human sinfulness. Though the possibility of the knowledge of God and the obligation to love is real, it is a possibility that is not exercised by most people. In fact, this knowledge is one that is actively suppressed. *Works of Love* contains a sustained critique of what Kierkegaard calls 'the world', which should not be equated with created reality but with the dominant patterns of thinking and acting that shape human societies. There is a polemical relation, one that Reformed theologians would call a relation of 'antithesis', between worldly patterns of thought and action and genuine Christianity.[10]

This antithesis shows itself in various ways. The sharp opposition between worldly ways of thinking and Christianity implies that Christianity will not be immediately attractive to the worldly mind, and thus Kierkegaard worries that the apologist who wants to make Christianity acceptable to its 'cultured despisers' will alter the message to avoid a confrontation.[11] Instead, Kierkegaard insists that 'the possibility of offence' is a defining characteristic of what is genuinely Christian, and that the proclaimer of Christianity must take care not to eliminate this possibility (pp. 58–9). (Though of course he does not think offence itself is good or praiseworthy.)

---

[10] For a good expression of the importance of 'the antithesis' for Christian thinking, see Abraham Kuyper, *Lectures on Calvinism* (Grand Rapids, Mich.: Eerdmans, 1931), 11–12, 34, 89–91, 198–9.

[11] The allusion is, of course, to Friedrich Schleiermacher's famous *On Religion: Speeches to its Cultured Despisers*, ed. Richard Crouter (Cambridge: Cambridge University Press, 1988). Schliermacher's work first appeared in 1799.

Kierkegaard also thinks that this antithesis will manifest itself in scorn and persecution from the world for the person who is truly loving. Such an individual can expect no temporal reward for his or her self-sacrificing love of others. To the contrary, the true lover should expect opposition, contempt, persecution, even death as a reward for his or her labours. Kierkegaard exhorts his reader to love and warns at the same time: 'Oh, do this! And then just one more thing! "Remember in good time that if you do this or at least strive to act accordingly, you will fare badly in the world"' (p. 191).

Christian love requires a twofold struggle and carries with it what Kierkegaard calls 'the double danger' (p. 194). The lover must struggle to overcome his or her own selfishness and natural resistance to this strenuous form of love, but if the lover makes progress in this regard, he or she will also have to contend with, 'at the very least' the 'ingratitude' of the world' (p. 193). The sinfulness of the world means that 'the world's opposition stands in an *essential* relationship to the inwardness of Christianity' (p. 194). It is impossible for either 'the world or Christendom' to become essentially good, and as long as this is true, the relationship of antithesis is necessary.

It is hard not to think that at times Kierkegaard's sense of the depths of human depravity threatens to overwhelm his sense of the created goodness of God's world. The world is seen as almost unambiguously evil. However, is such a stance consistent with the love Kierkegaard says God expects from us? Kierkegaard himself argues that the genuine lover always seeks to view others in the best possible light. The lover 'believes all things' in the sense of always, when it is possible to do so, interpreting the actions of others in a charitable way (pp. 221, 225–45). Even when the other has done wrong, the lover stands ready to 'cover the sin' with 'a mitigating explanation' (pp. 291–4). Kierkegaard himself seems aware that there is a tension between this loving duty to see good in others and his own harsh disparagement of 'the world'. He attempts to resolve the tension by saying that 'it would be a different matter if a person were to talk about his own relationship to the world; then it is a duty to speak as gently and as extenuatingly as possible, ...' (p. 197).

His view then seems to be that in the abstract a person must recognize and affirm that the world is evil and stands in an essential relationship of opposition to the good. However, the loving person has a duty to view the actual world he or she encounters differently. It seems hard, however, to maintain such a view: to consistently view the actual world I encounter in a charitable manner while remembering that in general 'the world' stands in opposition to the good. How can I consistently view the world I encounter as good when I have been warned that I must continually expect persecution if I am loving because the world is evil?

Another way of putting this tension would be to focus on the different attitudes Kierkegaard seems to take to individuals as opposed to the 'world'. With respect to individuals, Kierkegaard stresses that the loving person must 'believe all things' by seeking to give a charitable interpretation of other's actions (pp. 221, 225–45). The loving person must 'hide' sin by not seeking to discover it and by always looking for a 'mitigating explanation' (pp. 291–4). Kierkegaard does not seem to adopt this same charitable stance with respect to the 'world', at least the world understood in abstraction. However, the world we actually encounter is a product in part of the individuals we encounter, and it is hard to see how a person can maintain the charitable stance towards these individuals that Kierkegaard recommends while taking the extremely pessimistic stance he takes toward that world.

I think Kierkegaard senses the problem here. He affirms that 'we are truly reluctant to make a young person arrogant and prematurely teach him to get busy judging the world' (p. 193). However, it is hard to see how his pervasive claims about the world will not have this very effect. It seems to me that Kierkegaard at times almost seems to relish opposition and persecution from the world, and this has given his critics an opening to claim that Kierkegaard sees genuine Christianity as indistinguishable from misery.[12] Again, Kierkegaard senses the

---

[12] A prominent example is Knud E. Løgstrup. See his 'Settling Accounts with Kierkegaard's *Works of Love*', which appears as a 'Polemical Epilogue' in Hans Fink and Alasdair MacIntyre (eds.), *The Ethical Demand* (Notre Dame, Ind.: University of Notre Dame Press, 1997), 218–64. This essay originally appeared as 'Opgør med Kierkegaards *Kaerlighedens Gerninger*', in *Den Ethiske Fordring* (Copenhagen: Gyldendal, 1956). Jamie Ferreira presents a very fine exposition of Løgstrup's critique and gives a splendid response on behalf of Kierkegaard in her *Love's Grateful Striving*, 76–83.

potential problem and tries to head it off. He warns against a 'morbid hatred of the world' and insists that one should not desire persecution, because of the 'enormous responsibility' of the guilt incurred by the persecutor (p. 193). However, at the same time he seems to imply that someone who is not suffering in this way should worry that he or she is not truly loving, and at times goes so far as to suggest that this in fact is true.

I think that Kierkegaard could temper his attitude towards the 'world' without really undermining the antithesis between human sinfulness and Christian love that he wants to maintain and that his Lutheran conception of sin implies. This does not mean that he must repudiate the doctrine of original sin, to which he is firmly committed. After all, as G. K. Chesterton noted long ago, original sin is probably the only Christian doctrine that enjoys massive empirical support. That there is something radically wrong with human nature can be seen both written large in the horrors we see on the news, and also delicately printed in our own hearts, when we reflect on the pettiness and self-centredness that characterizes even our most altruistic acts. It is for good reasons that Kant warns about the human tendency to overvalue 'the dear self' and Iris Murdoch icily portrays the 'fat, relentless ego' in her fiction.[13]

To resolve the tension in his thought Kierkegaard does not need to deny or minimize human sinfulness. What is needed is rather a counterbalancing emphasis on the goodness of the created order and the loving activity of God within that order. Though the world may be fallen and sinful, it remains God's world. Kierkegaard himself insists that this is the case and that this implies that God's love is present 'in the ground' of every human self. This does not lessen the tragic character of human fallenness. However, it does mean that the fallen world is one that is open to possibilities of redemption.

What I am suggesting is not then that Kierkegaard should give up what I have called his principle of antithesis. As long as the world is characterized by sinfulness that manifests itself as selfishness, love must define itself in opposition to the dominant patterns of human thought and behaviour.

---

[13] See Iris Murdoch, *The Sovereignty of Good* (New York: Shocken Books, 1971), 52.

However, we do not have to think of this opposition as one that is universal and necessary. Hence love does not have to despair of any positive achievements in the world and darkly resign itself to ineffective action that is rewarded by suffering. Kierkegaard himself seems to think of the opposition of the world to true love as one that will be pervasive until eternity transforms human nature and human relationships. However, if God is active within the temporal order, both as Creator and Redeemer, then this transformation must be understood as one that can begin to occur in time. It is true that in time the transformations are never complete and final. The true lover must always be *willing* to suffer opposition and *willing* to endure opposition. However, the true lover must not pessim- istically assume that love cannot make any headway in this world, for this would be unloving, and a denial of the power of God, for whom all things are possible. Without any triumphal expectation that the Kingdom of God can be realized in time, the one who believes in love must believe in the possibility that love can transform the sinful structures of the human heart and human society, at least in partial and fragmentary ways, just as the lover believes in the power of love to trans- form the individuals whom one loves.

If this possibility is real, then someone who is committed to the truth of a special revelation, such as the one Kierkegaard finds in the New Testament, can dare to speak of the content of that revelation in a pluralistic public arena. Such an individual can hope that the truth of what he or she believes can be seen by those who are not committed to that revelation and defended without an appeal to authority. This hope must be tempered by a realism that is grounded in a recognition of the power of sin, and the difficulty of making common cause, even with those who in principle seem to be heading in the same direction. The individual must hear Kierkegaard's warnings about the possi- bility that the world will respond with ingratitude to a message of love, even with contempt and persecution. The individual must be committed to doing what is loving and good without any guarantee of temporal reward. However, the loving indi- vidual does not hope for persecution, as Kierkegaard himself affirms, and must believe in the possibility that love can make headway here and now.

I think that Kierkegaard's actual practice is consistent with this recommended policy. We have seen in Chapter 5 that he appeals to authority, and such an appeal is legitimate given that his intended audience consists mainly of those within Christendom who claim they are committed to that authority. However, we also saw in Chapters 5 and 6 that he argues for the humanistic character of neighbour-love by trying to show that this commanded love provides a basis for human flourishing. Neighbour-love actually does a better job of realizing the human goods that natural human loves, such as romantic love and friendship seek—goods such as steadfastness, autonomy, and the significance that consists in freedom from despair—than do those natural loves themselves. Kierkegaard certainly does not assume that the superiority of neighbour-love will be immediately apparent. However, he does seem to assume that a principled argument for the superiority of neighbour-love can be given, and that such an argument might be effective for a person who is honest, reflective, and open, even if that person is not committed to the authority of the Christian revelation.

At one point his procedure becomes completely explicit. He considers the situation of a person, such as a jilted lover or a deserted spouse, who has been hurt as a result of a love relation. Such a person is naturally full of grief. Kierkegaard says that the divine command to love, when offered to a person in such a situation, appears to be the wrong thing to do. One might think that the last thing a person who has been hurt in this way needs to hear is that he or she must continue to love the person who has hurt him or her, that he or she is commanded to do so. Nevertheless, Kierkegaard affirms that the Christian perspective can be put to an *empirical* test (pp. 32, 34). He claims that the one who has been in such a situation, if challenged by the Christian requirement, can come to see that the Christian view is genuinely comforting and upbuilding. Kierkegaard does not, then, deny the possibility that the goodness of neighbour-love is something that humans can recognize even apart from a commitment to special revelation, even if he is more pessimistic about this occurring than he should be.

LOVE AS UNIVERSAL DUTY AND
PARTICULAR CALLING

In the Discourse entitled 'The Work of Love in Praising Love' Kierkegaard makes a comment in a discussion of self-denial about the universal and the particular. Although the comment appears to be made in passing, I believe the concepts employed are of fundamental importance for his understanding of moral obligation:

> What a human being knows by himself about love is very superficial; he must come to know the deeper love from God—that is, in self-denial he must become what every human being can become (since self-denial is related to the universally human and thus is distinguished from the particular call and election), an instrument for God. Thus every human being can come to know everything about love, just as every human being can come to know that he, like every other human being, is loved by God. (p. 364)

Nowhere in *Works of Love* is there a sustained discussion of this contrast between the 'universally human' and an individual's 'particular call and election'. Nevertheless, I believe that this contrast is one of fundamental importance to this work and to Kierkegaard's ethical outlook in general.

This notion of an 'individual call' is linked to the issue of whether the obligation to love can be known only through special revelation. Scriptural teachings of an ethical type often take the form of general principles. Of course Scripture also contains commands directed to specific individuals and groups, and also teaches through stories and other means. All such teachings can certainly be applicable to individuals in very specific situations. However, if God also speaks directly to individuals, then commands can be given that are directed specifically to the unique circumstances of an individual at a particular time. A particular individual can be asked by God to do a particular action at a particular time, thus making it possible for God's requirements to be highly individualized.

Something like the contrast between general obligations and individual call is already present in some of the pseudonymous works, particularly *Concluding Unscientific Postscript*. In fact, it is striking that Kierkegaard, widely known as the philosopher whose category is 'the individual', is deeply committed to human equality as a universal ideal. In Chapter 1 I briefly looked at the theme of 'becoming a self' as articulated in *Concluding Unscientific Postscript*, and then expanded on this theme at some length in Chapter 4.[14] Johannes Climacus thinks that there are universal dimensions to the task of becoming a self; it is in one sense a universal task. Every person, Climacus says, must be assumed to be in possession of what essentially belongs to being human.[15] The ethical task of becoming a self is precisely what is essentially human, and thus '[t]here is no wastefulness [of human lives], for even if individuals were as numberless as the sand of the sea, the task of becoming subjective is given to each.'[16] All of us have the task of actualizing our potential to think, to imagine, to have emotions.[17] All of us have the task of developing ethical and religious passion, and ultimately the passion of faith. Nevertheless, the self that each of us must become is an individual self, with its own unique situation and set of potentialities and tasks arising from that uniqueness.

In *The Sickness Unto Death* Anti-Climacus, the Christian pseudonym that Kierkegaard invented due to his anxiety that he was personally unworthy to represent the highest Christian ideals, speaks of the 'essential contingency' of each person.[18] Though there are universal tasks, one of the universal tasks is precisely that each of us has a responsibility to recognize and discern what our individual situation requires of us. What is contingent is thus an essential part of our humanness; the 'universally human' is not therefore seen simply as contrasting with what is particular and individual but as encompassing it.

Kierkegaard's category of the 'individual' is therefore by no means an 'existentialist' repudiation of a universal human nature, but rather an insistence that part—and only part—of what we share as human beings is our uniqueness. However, underlying this uniqueness is our shared humanity. We are commanded to love our neighbours as ourselves, and both the one to whom the command is addressed and the one we are commanded to love must be understood in universal terms:

---

[14] See pp. 91–103.
[15] Kierkegaard, *Concluding Unscientific Postscript*, 356.
[16] Ibid., 159.
[17] Ibid., 346–9.
[18] Kierkegaard, *Sickness Unto Death*, 33.

The category 'neighbour' is like the category 'human being'. Each one of us is a human being and then in turn the distinctive individual that he is in particular, but to be a human being is the fundamental category. No one should become so enamored of his dissimilarity that he cravenly or presumptuously forgets that he is a human being. No person is an exception to being a human being because of his particular dissimilarity but is a human being and then what he is in particular. (p. 141)

God has created human beings and placed love within them as their 'ground'. Since this is how God has created them, when God commands humans to love, God is really commanding them to become themselves, to actualize their own potential to become the persons God created them to be. In one sense the command is the same for everyone: to love the neighbour as oneself. Whether promulgated by special revelation or by an understanding of our common status as creatures of God, the command is the same. However, the particular character of the self each of us is commanded to become individualizes the command. This gives rise to the 'individual call' of the person, which is part of the 'universally human' in the sense that every person has such a call but cannot be captured in its material content by universal rules.

How do people become aware of such individual calls? Kierkegaard says little about the question, but it seems likely that he does not have in mind mystical visions or voices as the normal means whereby God communicates his call to individuals. Though supernatural experiences are not ruled out, the normal situation seems to be one in which an individual becomes aware of God's will for her life as a result of reflection on her particular situation and circumstances. Naturally, these circumstances can include reflection on some biblical passage that has come to seem specially relevant, at least for those who take the Bible to contain a revelation from God.

In thinking about her situation, the person naturally asks such questions as these: What are the human needs God has brought to my awareness? What are my particular gifts and how can they be used for the good? How can I creatively bring my gifts to bear to accomplish what could not be done, or done so well, by others? In this way a person's awareness of God's call can be understood as the result of God's providential care, but it does not necessarily involve any unusual experiences.

Kierkegaard takes these individual differences seriously. He denounces the 'small-minded person', who, because of fear of what other people might say, does not dare to express his own distinctiveness (p. 271). Every individual should have the courage to be himself or herself before God. God has created human beings as individuals and the person who truly lives 'before God' is free to accept and even relish his or her distinctiveness. In effect, Kierkegaard seems committed to the Scotist doctrine of 'individual essences'.[19] God does not simply create individuals with a common nature, but individuals who share a common nature and who are also essentially different in their individuality.

And now the differences between human beings! How infinite! If it were not so, then humanity would be degraded, because humanity's superiority over animals is not the one most often mentioned, the universally human, but is also what is most often forgotten, that within the species each individual is the essentially different or distinctive. (p. 230)

These individual differences mean that when God asks each individual to become himself or herself, the material content of the task will reflect those differences, even though the task will be formally the same.

Kierkegaard actually draws the radical conclusion that God's commands to different individuals will not only be different but can actually be contradictory: '[O]ne human being, honest, upright, respectable, God-fearing, can under the very same circumstances do the very opposite of what another human being does who is also honest, upright, respectable, God-fearing' (p. 230). Were this not the case, Kierkegaard says that 'the God-relationship would be essentially abolished' and 'everything would be oriented exteriorly and find its completion paganly in political and social life' (p. 230).

---

[19] See John Duns Scotus, 'Individuation, Universals, and Common Nature', Ordinatio, II, d. 3, no. 172 (vol. 7, 476). This reference came from William A. Frank and Allan Wolter (eds.), *Duns Scotus, Metaphysician* (West Lafayette, IN: Purdue University Press, 1995), 184–6. The reference to Scotus is only meant to be suggestive, and I do not claim that Scotus's concept captures all that Kierkegaard means when he thinks of God as the creator of individuals in their uniqueness.

Is this claim plausible? The answer depends, I think, on how broadly we interpret 'under the same circumstances'. If we include in 'same circumstances' having the same history and individual calling, then it is probably incoherent to imagine two individuals who could have opposite duties. However, perhaps in such a case we would not really have two individuals at all. Probably what Kierkegaard means is that two individuals, in outwardly similar circumstances, might be obligated to do opposite things. Jim, who is called by God to work in a dangerous area of the world, might be called by God to renounce the joys of family life. Joe, who is a loner who struggles to connect with people, might be called to give up what seems to him to be an exciting dream of working for justice in a dangerous part of the world by being called to learn to love in a concrete way by getting married, with the resulting obligations to care for a family. Both Joe and Jim have the task of loving their neighbours as themselves, but what this means for them as individuals cannot be determined by any universal rules that could function algorithmically for them.

It is worth noting that the task of becoming one's self is a task that Kierkegaard says is equally assigned for both women and men. Given that Kierkegaard is quite unenthusiastic about women's emancipation and other nineteenth-century social reforms for women, it is remarkable that he is clear about this. The category of 'neighbour' is the universal category that coincides with 'human being' for him. All human beings must be the object of neighbour-love and all human beings must become the neighbour who loves in this way. This is not to deny the dissimilarities that exist among human beings: 'In being king, beggar, rich man, poor man, male, female, etc. we are not like each other' (p. 89). However, none of these differences are essential differences. People in all of these categories have the same obligation to love, and they are to love people in all of these categories.

MERCIFULNESS AS ILLUSTRATION OF UNIVERSAL DUTY AND PARTICULAR VOCATION

I believe that Kierkegaard's understanding of the relation between the 'universal human' and the 'particular call' is very well exemplified in Discourse VII in Part II of *Works of Love*, entitled 'Mercifulness, a Work of Love Even If It Can Give Nothing and Is Able to Do Nothing'. This discourse has been the focus of some of the harshest criticisms of Kierkegaard. To some critics it appears to manifest an indifference to concrete human need by downplaying the value of generosity and benevolence towards the poor.[20] The Discourse is grounded in a distinction between generosity (*Gavmildhed*) and mercifulness (*Barmhjertighed*) and most of the attention is focused on the latter. Much of the scandal stems from the fact that the Discourse begs the poor to be merciful towards those rich people who have been indifferent to their needs (p. 223).

I believe the criticisms of this Discourse have failed to take into account its intended audience. It is clear enough that Kierkegaard, in arguing for the possibility of merciful action on the part of the poor, does not intend to relieve the rich of their obligation to show concern for those less fortunate. Kierkegaard says explicitly that when mercifulness is present 'then generosity will follow of itself and come by itself accordingly as the individual is capable of it' (p. 315). The person who is merciful will express that quality in concrete ways if the person has the means to do so: 'It follows naturally of itself that if the merciful person is able to do something, he is only too glad to do it' (p. 324).

However, Kierkegaard chooses not to emphasize generosity in this Discourse. He says that it is not generosity he wants 'to focus attention upon, but rather upon this, that one can be merciful without being able to do the least thing' (p. 324). His reason for doing so seems to be a conviction that generosity, by which he seems to mean the actual practice of philanthropy rather than simply a willing spirit to give as one is able, is a quality that cannot be part of our universal task since it presupposes financial resources that many do not have.[21] A constant

---

[20] For an example of this type of criticism, see Theodore Adorno, 'On Kierkegaard's Doctrine of Love', *Studies in Philosophy and Social Science*, 8 (1939–40), 413–29. Jamie Ferreira gives a clear exposition of Adorno's critique and a strong response in her *Love's Grateful Striving*, 188–99. Ferreira's admirable analysis of this Discourse in *Works of Love* highlights the intended audience, and my own discussion is indebted to her.

[21] It seems to me that the English term 'generosity' does not capture all the nuances of the Danish *Gavmildhed*. In English it seems more natural to think

176 Divine Commands: How Given and to Whom?

emphasis on such generosity is seen by him as inhuman since it excludes the poor from the universal task of showing love to the neighbour. A pastor who preaches only about our duty to be financial benefactors is being merciless towards the poor person in the pew who hears the sermon but has no opportunity to practise philanthropy. Such moral exhortation is inhumane because it implicitly denies that those who are extremely poor are moral agents. The poor are thus doubly victimized, by their poverty and by being excluded from the possibility of meaningful moral activity:

In this way the poor person is needy in his poverty, then in turn is abandoned by the world's conception of his ability to practice mercifulness and therefore is singled out, given up, as the pitiable object of mercifulness, who at most is able to bow and thank—if the rich person is so kind as to practice mercifulness. Merciful God, what mercilessness! (p. 322)

Kierkegaard therefore chooses to focus on mercifulness, a moral quality that excludes no one and therefore can be part of our universal human task. How mercifulness expresses itself concretely is partly a matter of the individual's particular situation and calling. By focusing on the case of someone who is extremely poor, he demonstrates that no one is excluded from the task of mercifulness. Even the poor person who is paralysed can silently utter a prayer for others, showing compassion for the hard-hearted individual who has failed to be merciful.

The Discourse is therefore directed to a specific audience, the 'poor and wretched' (p. 322). Though Kierkegaard affirms that mercifulness must manifest itself in generosity for those who have material means, he is not in this Discourse addressing those for whom this is a real possibility, but rather those who are desperately poor, those for whom daily life is a struggle to survive. He is speaking to those who 'from childhood or from some time later in life have been so tragically devastated, so badly ravaged, that they are unable to do anything at all, perhaps are even scarcely able to express sympathy in clear words'

of generosity as a disposition to give to others that could be possessed whether exercised or not, and thus as a quality that the poor can have. This is especially true inasmuch as people can also be generous with their time and energy, and not simply their finances.

(p. 325). The 'comfort' he offers is specifically addressed to such people, and he goes so far as to say that what he has to say is offered to this audience 'in confidence', even if the rich are allowed to listen to the conversation (p. 322).

It is therefore a mistake to criticize Kierkegaard for not stressing more than he does the duty to express our mercifulness in financial generosity. He has decided to address an audience for whom this is not a live possibility. (Though of course one might criticize his decision to address such an audience.) In so doing he illustrates both the universal character of the duty to love, as well as the particular ways in which the individual is called to express that love. No one is excused from the duty to be merciful. However, the rich are called to express that mercifulness in part by being financially generous, though of course such generosity does not exhaust what it means for them to be merciful. Those who are extremely poor are equally called to be merciful, though their mercifulness must express itself differently.

Kierkegaard illustrates this with a series of variations on the story of the Good Samaritan, which he retitles 'the merciful Samaritan'. Suppose the Samaritan had no money to pay the innkeeper to whom he carried the unfortunate victim, and could only beg the innkeeper to help the poor man? Suppose the Samaritan had not been able to save the victim of the attack, but had only 'gone away carrying the unfortunate man, had sought a softer resting place for the wounded one, had sat by his side, had done everything to stanch the flow of blood—but the unfortunate one died in his hands?' (p. 317). Such a Samaritan would have been equally merciful, even though he was unable to accomplish very much outwardly. The form that mercifulness takes in a person's life reflects that person's calling, which in turn is related to the person's life situation. Mercifulness in those whose life situation includes severe poverty may therefore express itself quite differently than in those with more means, even though mercifulness is something all are called to manifest.

CONCLUSION: LOVE FOR THE DISTINCTIVE THAT MAKES NO DISTINCTIONS

I believe there are two dimensions to Kierkegaard's notion of the 'individual calling'. There is first, the way in which the

universal human tasks are individualized for each person. It is
this aspect that Kierkegaard's discussion of mercifulness illustrates. However, the notion of an individual calling is not exhausted by this dimension. Kierkegaard also stresses the idea
that God has created each person with an individual 'distinctiveness' and that this means that there will be genuinely individual aspects to a person's vocation (p. 271).

It is not only our own distinctiveness that shapes our duties.
Our duty to love others must express itself in helping them to
become themselves. We must therefore pay close attention to
the distinctiveness of each individual and try to block our natural human tendency to want others to be like ourselves (p.
270). Love must seek the good of the other, and that means
that we must pay attention to how the other is genuinely different. We should take delight in the variety of God's creation and
seek to allow that variety to flourish.

Some commentators have criticized Kierkegaard for his
claim that the genuine lover must 'close his eyes' to differences
and look at the essential humanity of each person (pp. 68–9).[22]
These critics allege that Kierkegaard's love is too abstract and
does not connect with concrete individualities. However, this
criticism simply fails to grasp the point Kierkegaard is making.
What he means is simply that no one must be excluded from
love because of differences. The genuine lover must not distinguish between whom he loves and whom he does not on the
basis of such factors as nationality, social class, race, and
gender. But there is no contradiction between this claim and
the view that when one loves people in all of these categories one
must pay special attention to their concrete distinctiveness.
A love that makes no distinctions can be devoted to the distinctiveness of each individual. It is not that love looks for that
distinctiveness to find a basis for loving the other. We should
not love others solely *because* of the special characteristics that
distinguish them from others. Nevertheless, when we love
others, we must love them *with* all of their special characteris-

---

[22] Theodore Adorno once again would be a good example of a critic of this
Kierkegaardian advice to 'love with closed eyes'. See his 'On Kierkegaard's
Doctrine of Love', 418–19. Jamie Ferreira once again gives a clear explanation
of the critical problem and a convincing response in *Love's Grateful Striving*,
55–64, 109–10.

tics. The task is not to find the person who is lovable because of some differentiating characteristic, but to find the persons around us who are 'given' to us or chosen by us to be lovable in all their particularity (p. 166).

8

Who Is My Neighbour? Can Love
Be a Duty?

In Chapter 5 I began to explicate the ethic Kierkegaard develops in *Works of Love* by focusing on the divine commands that are the basis of our moral obligations. The primary theme was that such an ethic is not one that views moral obligations as rooted in the arbitrary commands of an all-powerful deity, but one that sees moral obligations as grounded in the love and gratitude owed to a loving Creator, whose commands are aimed at our own well-being and flourishing. In Chapter 6 I tried to show how a command to self-denial could be understood as directed to our happiness and flourishing. In Chapter 7 I argued that these commands are promulgated through general as well as special revelation, and that God's commands to us are partly universal in nature, but also directed to individuals as individuals. I have not as yet, however, given much attention to the content of God's commands. In this chapter I intend to focus on the nature of the love that we humans are commanded to show, as well as the person whom we are commanded to love: the neighbour. Who is the neighbour? How can he or she be loved? Can love be a duty and still retain the freedom we think love must have to be genuine?

SELF-LOVE AND NEIGHBOUR-LOVE

The command is to love one's neighbour as oneself. Kierkegaard begins by noting that this command presupposes or assumes that humans love themselves, with a satirical aside that Christianity thereby differentiates itself from philosophical systems that pretend to be presuppositionless.[1] One might

---

[1] Kierkegaard, *Works of Love*, 7. Subsequent references to this work in this chapter are denoted by page nos. in parentheses.

think that this means that an understanding of what it means to love the neighbour would be easy for us. Presumably we humans already know what it means to love ourselves; hence we know what love is. We only have to extend this love we naturally have for ourselves to others.

Kierkegaard disagrees with the above line of thought most emphatically. The extension of our existing self-love to others is what constitutes 'preferential love', the kind of love that Kierkegaard contrasts with neighbour-love. The problem with actual human self-love is not simply that it is too narrowly focused and needs to be extended to others. The problem with actual human self-love is that it is a selfish kind of love. It needs to be transformed. Even when that self-love is extended to others, as is the case in friendship and romantic love, the selfishness is not eliminated.

It might seem that Kierkegaard's presupposition that humans love themselves along with his critique of selfishness is a 'one size fits all' ethical prescription that does not take into account the variety of defects in human character. Certainly many people, perhaps even most, appear to be overly selfish, too concerned with their own happiness and too little concerned about the happiness of others. However, are there not also people who are overly concerned with the well-being of others and too quick to sacrifice their own happiness? Are there not people who fail to see the worth and value of their own existence, the sort of people who are sometimes said to suffer from 'low self-esteem'? Can such people simply be told that their task is to love others as they love themselves? Don't they need to learn to love themselves?

Kierkegaard recognizes this problem. He says plainly that the command to love one's neighbour as oneself should not be interpreted simply as an obligation to treat the neighbour as one treats oneself. For many people treat themselves very badly. 'Whoever has any knowledge of people will certainly admit that just as he has often wished to be able to move them to relinquish self-love, he has also had to wish that it were possible to teach them to love themselves' (p. 23). He gives a variety of examples of people who fail to love themselves properly. There is 'the light-minded person' who 'throws himself almost like a nonentity into the folly of the moment'. There is 'the depressed person' who 'desires to be rid of life, indeed, of himself'. There is the individual who 'self-tormentingly thinks to do God a service by torturing himself' (p. 23).

Kierkegaard thinks, therefore, that though Christianity presupposes that every person has a kind of self-love, it is by no means true that people always love themselves as they ought. The command to love the neighbour as oneself is not merely a formal prescription that is satisfied when self and others are treated in the same way. The task is to learn to love the neighbour *and* to love one's own self *properly*. In fact, they are not really two different tasks at all: 'To love yourself in the right way and to love the neighbor correspond perfectly to one another; fundamentally they are one and the same thing' (p. 22). The commandment is not merely to learn to love the neighbour, but 'properly understood' it may be read as follows: '*You shall love yourself in the right way*' (p. 22).[2]

Christianity therefore presupposes a certain form of self-love as present in everyone, but by no means assumes that this self-love is always a good quality that merely needs to be extended to others. What is the nature of the right kind of love, whether for oneself or for others? Kierkegaard characterizes it in a variety of ways. Initially, he characterizes love for someone as a concern for the good of that person. To love someone is to care for that person so that one seeks the person's well-being. It is, for example, not genuine love for a person if you satisfy a person's desire or wish when you know that doing so will be harmful to that person (p. 20). Kierkegaard warns against satisfying a person's desire when that leads to the person's harm: 'you expressly have no right to do this; you have the responsibility if you do it, just as the other has the responsibility if he wants to misuse his relation to you in such a way' (p. 20). To act towards another in this way would be to treat the other as God, who alone should be loved in obedience and adoration.

Later in *Works of Love*, Kierkegaard gives a more theological account of what it means properly to love: '*To love God is to love oneself truly; to help another person to love God is to love another person; to be helped by another person to love God is to be loved*'

---

[2] Kierkegaard's italics.

(p. 107).[3] One might think that this is a different account of what it is to love. However, for Kierkegaard, a loving relationship to God is the self's intended destiny and is the self's true happiness. Hence, to help another person or oneself to love God is to be concerned for the good of the other or oneself. However, even if this is true, can it make sense to identify a concern with a person's well-being with a concern for a person's God-relation? For Kierkegaard, the two are identical, but he realizes that the identity is not easy to discern. To recognize the link one must have the right understanding of the nature of God as well as a right understanding of the nature of the self.

In fact, I believe that implicit in *Works of Love* is an identification of God with the Good, an identification that we have seen is made explicitly in *Purity of Heart*.[4] God is love and he loves impartially and without distinctions (p. 63). God has no selfish ends of his own. His only desire is for those qualities we humans describe as good. One might object here that one cannot identify the good with a particular being, God, if the good is in fact a universal quality. An identification of God and the Good might threaten the personhood of God by reducing God to an abstract quality. However, another possibility is that what we might initially understand as an abstraction is better understood as a personal reality. Such an identification may be surprising to us, but there are lots of surprising truths in our universe.

Robert Adams has developed such a line of argument by claiming that one may think of God as the supreme and infinite Good, while viewing finite goods as good to the degree that they resemble God. Finite goods all have God as their source and thus reflect the goodness of that source. God can in the deepest sense be identical with the Good, without denying that we correctly apply the term to the qualities possessed by many finite objects as well as the qualities of God himself. For Kierkegaard, God 'seeks his own, which is love; he seeks it by giving

<hr />

[3] Kierkegaard's italics.

[4] See my discussion of *Purity of Heart* in Chapter 4, Robert Adams' discussion of 'the Good' in *Finite and Infinite Goods*, and also William Alston, 'Some Suggestions for Divine Command Theorists', in *Divine Nature and Human Language: Essays in Philosophical Theology* (Ithaca, NY: Cornell University Press, 1989), 253–73.

all things. God is good, and there is only one who is good—God, who gives all things' (p. 264).

We thus can see how for Kierkegaard a love for God is essentially a love for the Good, and a love for the Good is implicitly a love for God. To help another person to love God is to help that other person acquire a concern for the Good, a concern that must be impartially extended both to himself or herself and others, for that is the nature of God's goodness. Love for God cannot therefore become a rival for the love of other things or persons when those others are loved properly, for God is not a finite good that can compete with other finite goods:

God does not have a share in existence in such a way that he asks for his share for himself; he asks for everything, but as you bring it to him you immediately receive, if I may put it this way, a notice designating where it should be forwarded, because God does not ask for anything for himself, although he asks for everything from you. (p. 161, my translation)

This is not to say that Kierkegaard's view about the good of the other is uncontroversial. He is committed, I think, to the kind of view expressed by Socrates in the *Apology*, which stresses that a person's ultimate well-being consists in the possession of a good character, the kind of view I described in Chapter 4 as a 'soul-making' ethic. In the *Apology* Socrates argues that the worst fate that can befall a person is to do evil.[5] To suffer punishment or even death at the hands of others is not as bad, for it is only doing evil that damages the soul, and only such damage is eternal in its consequences. Socrates therefore robustly affirms that 'nothing can harm a good man in life or death, and his fortunes are not a matter of indifference to the gods.'[6]

Kierkegaard is committed to the same kind of soul-making ethic, which holds that the ultimate good is the acquisition of the right kind of character. He does not, of course, think that

---

[5] It is worth noting that there are differences between Kierkegaard and Socrates too. Socrates' view seems more extreme in holding that 'nothing' can harm a good person. Kierkegaard certainly holds that the good person can be harmed by the world, but that eternally such harms are not significant.

[6] Plato, *Apology*, 41 c–d.

character is the sole good; just that it is the supreme good, one that is incommensurate with other goods.[7]

At one point he expresses this idea in a somewhat misleading way, in a passage that has been seized on by critics as evidence that Kierkegaard's ethic is one of indifference to human temporal well-being: 'From the point of view of eternity, that someone dies is no misfortune, but that mercifulness is not practiced certainly is' (p. 326). Taken out of context and read carelessly, this sentence is indeed shocking. But I believe that the intended meaning is defensible. Kierkegaard does not mean that a person's death cannot be a tragic and grievous event, one that merits our deepest sorrow. The key qualification in the sentence is 'from the point of view of eternity'. It is of course the sober truth that every human being dies. It will be no special tragedy in eternity that someone has suffered death, since all will have suffered this fate, though of course the circumstances and timing of a person's death may be tragic.

Nevertheless, if we take the idea of an eternal life after death seriously, as does Kierkegaard, the tragedy of an early death cannot be compared with the horror of a soul that is eternally lost. In eternity all will have died, and thus having suffered death cannot be a special tragedy. What will be tragic will be a person's loss of goodness, a loss that is irredeemable. Both Socrates and Kierkegaard hold a religious view of the self that links the self's ultimate happiness with moral goodness. If this conception of the self is the true one, then it makes sense to identify love as a concern for the person's well-being with a concern for a person's God-relation, with God understood as the Good. Such a concern does not have to be understood as a purely spiritual one that excludes caring about a person's temporal and material well-being. Genuine love understands that persons are concrete beings with material needs. If love for God is love for the Good, then that love must express itself in a concern for the good of the whole person.

---

[7] In saying that Kierkegaard links the ultimate good with the acquisition of character, I am not of course saying that Kierkegaard is committed to 'salvation by works'. It is not that people secure the ultimate good by becoming morally good through their own efforts, but that God's ultimate purpose for each individual, and the good for that individual, involves becoming a certain kind of person.

LOVE AND GOD AS THE 'MIDDLE TERM'

Kierkegaard is committed to all of the following claims: (1) Every person loves himself or herself; self-love is universal; (2) Not all self-love is the proper kind of self-love; many people do not love themselves in the right way; (3) The right kind of love is love for the neighbour; one loves in the right way when one loves the neighbour as oneself.

No tension arises between these claims as long as it is understood that it is possible for a person to have a kind of self-love without loving himself or herself in the right way. One way of putting this point would be that it is possible for people to be selfish in some sense without loving themselves properly. The man who is in despair and does not value himself as he should may still be preoccupied with himself. The woman who masochistically torments herself may still focus on herself in an inappropriate and inordinate manner.

The third claim might be taken, as I have noted, as a purely formal prescription demanding equal treatment for the self and others, a prescription that might be satisfied by a person who treats both himself and others badly. We have seen, however, that Kierkegaard rejects this formal characterization of the prescription and says that there is material content to the command. Neighbour-love is a specific kind of love that one must show both towards oneself and others. Why is it that Kierkegaard thinks that the prescription has this substantive content?

I believe that the justification lies in the concept of the neighbour. When this concept is understood properly, Kierkegaard believes that what we might call the empty formal understanding of the prescription is precluded. The formal characterization of love for the neighbour in terms of equality is logically linked to the nature of the love that must be shown to the neighbour, as well as oneself. It turns out that it is impossible truly to love the neighbour as oneself without recognizing the value and worth of the neighbour and of oneself. A person who treats himself and others equally badly does not love either as he should. Love for the neighbour is not grounded in an abstract, formal ideal of equality. Rather, the ideal of equality is itself grounded in a substantive understanding of who the neighbour is. Once I understand my neighbour as my neighbour, I necessarily recognize the equality between all human beings, including myself.

Who then is the neighbour? The neighbour is any human being, understood not in terms of any distinctive relation that might serve as a ground for a preferential relationship, but in terms of the neighbour's relation to God. 'In order to determine what love is, it [Christianity] begins either with God or with the neighbor, a doctrine about love that is the essentially Christian doctrine, since one, in order in love to find the neighbor, must start from God and must find God in love to the neighbor' (p. 140). Kierkegaard explains neighbour-love initially by contrasting it with those forms of natural love with which humans are familiar, particularly romantic love and friendship. His discussion here has misled many commentators into assuming that neighbour-love and such natural loves are mutually exclusive rivals, though I shall show in the next chapter that this is a mistake. However, though neighbour-love is not a rival for such natural loves in the sense of being a replacement, it is a form of love that must be sharply distinguished from all natural forms.

Such natural forms of love are 'preferential'. They require a selection. Some people are my friends, and others are not. I am in love with one individual but not another. What is the basis of the selection? Kierkegaard agrees with Aristotle that the basis of such loves is some natural determinant, some respect in which two individuals are similar or alike. Aristotle holds that a friend must be someone one finds admirable, someone who shares one's own likes and dislikes. The friend is like 'another I'.[8] The admiration and devotion shown to the friend and the lover certainly appear to be different from selfishness. Kierkegaard, however, argues that from a Christian perspective such devotion is indeed devotion to the 'Other I' and it is not completely unselfish, since the person to whom the lover is devoted is chosen on the basis of a relation to the self: 'Well, now, to admire another person is certainly not self-love; but to be loved by the one and only admired one, would not this relation turn back in a selfish way into the *I* who loves—his other *I*' (p. 54).

---

[8] Compare Aristotle's discussion of friendship in the *Nicomachean Ethics*, 1166[a], where he says that a friend is 'another self'.

It is only when one loves the neighbour that true alterity is discovered. 'Whether we speak of the *first I* or the *other I*, we do not come a step closer to the neighbor, because the neighbor is the *first you*' (p. 57). How is this alterity discovered? It is only when the neighbour is loved, not by virtue of any characteristic that links him or her to you, but by virtue of being a creature of God:

In erotic love and friendship, preferential love is the middle term; in love for the neighbor, God is the middle term. Love God above all else; then you also love the neighbor and in the neighbor every human being. Only by loving God above all else can one love the neighbor in the other human being. The other human being, this is the neighbor who is the other human being in the sense that the other human being is every other human being. (pp. 57–8)

Kierkegaard takes seriously the idea that every human being has been created by God and endowed by God with the potential to love. Anyone who loves God truly must love those creatures whom God who is love has made in his own image by endowing them with the capacity for love.

Kierkegaard says that neighbour-love is purely 'spiritually determined' (p. 57). I think this means that the love is grounded solely in the relation human beings have to God and to each other by virtue of the relation to God. Such a spiritual love does not make myself and my beloved into a 'group I', because in neighbour-love we are not tied together by any natural determinant. Neighbour-love thus allows for the other to remain an other (p. 56). It does not demand that the other conform to my ideals, be part of my group, or share my ideology, but insists that the other should express his or her own distinctiveness (p. 269).

One might object that such a spiritual love does not reach true alterity, because what is discovered in the other is sameness, not difference. How can the relation to God which is the same for everyone be a way of discovering the otherness of the other? John Hare has suggested, in response to this problem, that the love of God in each person may be unique.[9] Every person is

---

[9] John Hare made this suggestion to me in commenting on this chapter. Similar thoughts may be found in Hare's *Why Bother Being Good* (Downers Grove, Ill.: InterVarsity Press, 2002), 66–70, 168–72.

alike in being a creature of God and in possessing the love that God has placed 'in the ground' of that person. But that love itself takes form in a person who is unique and must express itself in unique and distinctive ways. If I love people because of their relation to God I must love all people, because all are made with an ability to image God's love. However, to love those people is to love them as the concrete individuals they have been made to be; I cannot love them without loving their particularities.

But how is it possible to love our neighbours when every human person is in fact my neighbour? One response to this charge might simply be to concede the impossibility of the task. We cannot possibly do it, and the recognition of our failure will quickly drive us towards grace and forgiveness. Such a line is tempting, because as sinful human beings it is certain that we will indeed fail to love our neighbours as we ought. However, I think such a response is a mistake, and it is not the response Kierkegaard himself gives. The reason for this is that Kierkegaard accepts the ethical principle that 'ought implies can'. I cannot be obligated to do what it is not possible for me to do.

Kierkegaard actually says very little about how such love is possible. He does say that we must depend on God. 'Ought implies can' does not entail that we can do what we ought to do all by ourselves without any aid. We are entitled to trust that the God who commands us to love in this way will help us in the task: 'When eternity says 'You shall love', it is responsible for making sure this can be done' (p. 41). But in addition to faith *that* the task can be accomplished, we would look like to know *how* it is to be done. To make progress towards this end, I want to break the task into components. First, I shall ask how neighbour-love is possible at all, particularly when we see that such love is a duty, something that is commanded. At the conclusion of the chapter I shall discuss the question as to how it is possible to have such love for all people.

Kierkegaard's answer to this question as to how neighbour-love is possible is implicit in his remarks about God as the 'middle term' in all love for the neighbour. To understand his answer we must first think a bit about the nature of love. I assume that love is an emotion, as does Kierkegaard

(p. 112),[10] and so to understand what love is, we must first ask what an emotion is. An initial question concerns whether emotions must be episodic in character or can be long-term states that might be dispositional in character. Robert Roberts, on whose account of emotion I shall shortly draw, restricts the term 'emotion' to what I should term occurrent or episodic emotions, since he thinks that an emotion is something analogous to a perception.[11] Roberts would say, therefore, that love is either an emotion or a disposition to emotions, rather than an emotion per se. However, I would argue that emotions are analogous to beliefs, which can be both occurrent (as when a person has an experience of 'assenting') and also dispositional. I have many beliefs that I am not currently thinking about, but which manifest themselves in dispositions both to have the experiential kind of belief on relevant occasions, and also in complex tendencies to behave and think in various ways.

I believe that emotions can be similarly dispositional in character. It seems to me quite proper to say that I love my wife even when I am not thinking about her or having any special feelings about her. Such a love consists partly in a disposition to have the episodic experience of felt love, as well as a disposition to have other relevant emotions, such as joy in her presence, and a disposition to act and think in distinctive ways. If love such as this is a paradigmatic emotion, as it surely is, then I see no reason why emotions must be episodic. Allowing for emotions that are dispositional also makes it easier to understand how emotions can be unconscious, and it helps makes sense of Kierkegaard's claim that we can have love for people whom we do not even know.

I shall assume then that the love Kierkegaard thinks we are commanded to have for our neighbour is an emotion, and that this emotion can be, at least sometimes, dispositional in character. If we do not focus on love as an emotion, we make the task somewhat easier, I think, but we misunderstand Kierkegaard's account if we conflate it with Kant's understanding of

---

[10] 'Love is a passion of the emotions'.

[11] See Robert Roberts, 'Existence, Emotion, and Virtue: Classical Themes in Kierkegaard', in Hannay and Marino (eds.), *The Cambridge Companion to Kierkegaard*.

neighbour-love as a purely practical 'love' that consists solely of actions.[12] For Kant, to love our neighbours as ourselves is simply to act in a loving manner towards our neighbours, regardless of how we may feel about them. Kierkegaard's account of love does not allow such a focus on action alone. Though his concern in *Works of Love* is on action, understood as the outward expression of love, he insists that such actions stem from love as an inner reality, and it is this love we are commanded to have (pp. 8–10). It is true that for Kant action has an 'inner' dimension as well, since actions stem from the will. Still, what seems missing from Kant is the notion that the moral worth of an action might be related to an emotion that is the basis for the action. For Kierkegaard, we must strive to develop emotions of this kind. The task is the hard one of actually loving the neighbour, not merely acting towards the neighbour in a loving manner. But how is this possible?

EMOTIONS AS CONCERN-BASED CONSTRUALS

What can be said about the nature of an emotion? I think the best account of an emotion that we have has been provided by Robert Roberts, who says that an emotion is a 'concern-based construal'.[13] A construal is a kind of 'seeing-as'.[14] Many of us have seen pictures that can be 'seen' in two different ways, such as Jastrow's 'duck-rabbit' made famous by Wittgenstein.[15] Looked at one way the picture is a duck; when we look at it another way it is a rabbit. How we see other people and other situations is often analogously rooted in a certain perspective. My teen-age son's room is typically a mess. I can, if I wish, see him as lazy and sloppy. But perhaps I can also choose to

[12] Immanuel Kant, *Groundwork of the Metaphysic of Morals*, trans. H. J. Paton (New York: Harper and Row, 1964), 67.

[13] See Roberts, 'What is an Emotion?'. Also see 'Existence, Emotion and Virtue'. Since Roberts restricts emotions to emotions that are episodic and thus that are linked to experience, he also characterizes emotions as 'aspect-perceptions'.

[14] Though it should be remembered that I include in my account of an emotion dispositions to such construals, and do not limit emotions to occurrent construals.

[15] See Wittgenstein, *Philosophical Investigations*, 194e.

perceive him as an emerging adult who is attempting to demonstrate some independence by making his own decisions about 'his' space. Which way I see him and the room will determine the emotional response I have.

This view of Roberts explains two features of an emotion. First, an emotion, like a belief, typically has intentional content. An emotion is typically 'about' something, and this something can be expressed in propositional form, usually by a clause beginning with 'that'. I am afraid that I will owe a large amount of income tax this year. I am hopeful that I will get a large tax refund this year. Secondly, though emotions have propositional content in the way beliefs do, it is possible for an emotion to take as its intentional object something that is not the object of a belief. I can hope and fear possibilities that I do not believe will occur, although I clearly must believe they are possible.

It is important to realize that at least sometimes construals are subject to voluntary control. Even 'involuntary' construals that occur more or less spontaneously can over time be modified and shaped by our repeated actions. I can consciously work at construing my son's messy room in one way rather than another.

Not just any construal of a situation will count as an emotion. For a construal to constitute an emotion, it must impinge on my concerns; I must care about what I am construing. Typically, if I am afraid it is because I construe something as threatening something I care about. If I am hopeful it is because I construe the future as possibly leading to a good that I desire. If I am anxious it is because I construe a situation as uncertain, and I care very much about which possibility will be realized and how it will impact me or something I care about.

Given this all-too-brief account of an emotion, what will neighbour-love look like? What account does Kierkegaard give as to how it is possible to love the neighbour? His answer, we have seen, is somewhat cryptic. We must learn to love others by having God as the 'middle term' connecting us to the people we love, rather than some natural determinant. The 'determinant' in the case of preferential love will be some distinguishing feature that is the ground of an 'inclination' on the part of the lover. Given Roberts' understanding of emotion, one might say that in the case of preferential love one construes the other on the basis of some distinguishing feature that generates or is at least the ground of an emotion. I love the other person because I construe that person as beautiful, as distinguished, as fun to be with, as exciting and mysterious, and I am naturally attracted by this person when so construed. However, in the case of the neighbour there is no distinguishing feature of the person that is the ground of some preferential emotion. I do not love my neighbour because she is beautiful, rich, mysterious, or exciting, for if I love only people who fit such a description, I do not love my neighbour.

I think we should understand Kierkegaard's remarks about God as the basis for love of the neighbour in the following way. To love my neighbours as my neighbours is to love them because they are God's creatures, made in his image. This relation to God constitutes what Kierkegaard calls the 'inner glory' that all humans possess equally, and so to construe humans as creatures of God is to construe them in terms of this inner glory that is not visible to the senses (pp. 87–8). Such a construal is still a construal, but it is grounded not in a characteristic that distinguishes some humans from others, but in a characteristic equally possessed by all. This 'inner glory' that is the same in all people is a formal quality; it does not mean that the material characteristics that constitute this 'inner glory' are not unique or that this uniqueness is not important.[16]

When I love my cranky neighbour Ed as my neighbour, Christianly understood, I do not construe him merely as the grouch who yells at my kids when they are just being kids. Rather, I must construe him as a child of God, made in God's image. If I love God unconditionally I cannot be indifferent to that which God has made, particularly not to that which he has made that resembles himself. It is, I think, actually possible to construe others in this way: consciously to focus on our neighbours as persons made in God's image (and be disposed to do this as well). We can construe them not merely as the particular people they are with their faults and virtues, but also as the

---

[16] See the discussion above about the suggestion from John Hare that I wish to endorse, that God's love in every individual is unique since the individual is unique.

objects of God's love and concern, people for whom Christ
became incarnate and died to save. And if we truly love God
and care about what God cares about, such a construal will
indeed ground an emotion. When we construe others in this
way in light of the image of God they bear, then God is indeed
the 'middle term'. God provides the perspective from which we
can see the other as someone whose good I can care about and
will.

We can now understand in a deeper way why neighbour-love
is linked to proper self-love. When I love myself properly, I
construe myself in the same way I construe my neighbour, as
one of God's creatures. When I devalue myself, I fail to honour
God's creative goodness as this is expressed in me, just as when
I selfishly make myself the centre of the universe, I fail to
recognize God as God. The equality I must strive to realize in
my love for others is grounded in a recognition of a common
relation to God that is a barrier to self-hatred as well as to
selfishness.

CAN LOVE BE A DUTY?

In dealing with the problem of how it is possible to love the
neighbour, we have begun to answer an objection that the
'unspoiled pagan', as well as many people today, might make
against neighbour-love. This problem is that it does not seem
possible for genuine love to be commanded. Surely, genuine
love must be spontaneous and free. This problem is certainly
one of the reasons Kant believed that the task of loving the
neighbour as myself cannot actually be understood as an obligation to feel the emotion of love. For Kant viewed emotions as
'inclinations', feelings that we cannot control. The duty to love
he saw as a *practical* duty, and it is accomplished by *acting*
towards the other in a way that seeks the other's good by
following the principles of morality. This is all that morality
requires, and it is, he thought, quite enough.

If the account I have given of emotions is right, then I believe
an alternative to Kant's view is viable. If we see how it is
possible to construe all human beings as creatures made in
God's image so that my love for God engenders love for them
as well, then we can see how it is possible to have a duty to love.

It is certainly not easy to construe our neighbours—all of them that we come into contact with—in this way. However, it is not impossible, either. It is a goal that we can work towards, because we can exercise some control over our construals, at least over time. Some might prefer to say that our obligation, strictly speaking, is not to love—since having such an emotion may not be within our immediate power—but rather to work towards loving or to try to love the other. However, since achieving the goal of actually loving other people is a real possibility, I do not see why we should not say, as Kierkegaard does, that we have a genuine obligation to love the other. After all, there are many obligations whose fulfilment takes time and cannot be done all at once.

We live in a culture that in many ways is dominated by a cult of spontaneity. Divorce is justified on the grounds that 'I don't feel the same way anymore' and it would be somehow false or hypocritical to continue to be married when feelings have changed. We believe it is important to 'be in touch with our feelings' and yet we see our emotions, curiously enough, as things that just happen to us. It is often said that we cannot control our emotions and are not responsible for them.

If we accept Roberts' account of emotion, this is much too simple. There are emotions and there are emotions. It is true that some emotions are fairly 'immediate' and involuntary. When I hear a loud crash in a dark room, the fear I feel is not something I choose to have or not to have. There are, however, such things as enduring emotions, emotions that can be nurtured over time, and that presuppose a reflective framework. Such enduring emotions are close to what Kierkegaard termed the 'passions', the most important of which for him are faith, hope, and love. For Kierkegaard these passions have a kind of immediacy, but this is not the 'first immediacy,' but 'an immediacy after reflection'.[17] I think that the reason Kant denied that we can actually have love for our neighbours is that Kant did not grasp this distinction between immediate emotions and what we might call formed emotions. Kant thought of all emotions as immediate and thus concluded that emotions are not

---

[17] This terminology is, for example, used by Kierkegaard's pseudonym Johannes de Silentio in *Fear and Trembling*, 69.

under our control. But this is false. We cannot simply decide to have emotions and will them into existence. This is true even for reflective emotions, and it is especially true for immediate emotions. Reflective emotions, however, are the kind of thing that we can patiently work at nurturing and cultivating.

I believe this is true even within the sphere of what Kierkegaard calls natural or preferential loves. While Kierkegaard is certainly right to insist that such loves be distinguished from neighbour-love, I think he errs by failing to recognize analogies between such natural loves and neighbour-love. He is surely mistaken when he says that '[e]rotic love and friendship, as the poet understands them, contain no moral task' (pp. 50–1). Perhaps Kierkegaard's claim here can be defended if we emphasize the qualification here: 'as the poet understands them'. Kierkegaard may be thinking of the poet as someone who idealizes these loves as good fortune. In reality, however, we *can* take romantic love and friendship as presenting us with moral tasks. We can learn to love our husbands and wives, not merely in the romantic tingle of first love, but in a deep and satisfying way, as we share lives, living together against a background in which each of us can construe his or her love as one to whom a commitment has been made. A similar point can be made about such relations as that of parent and child, where the relation itself is not chosen, but the mode of its expression can still be a moral task.

Of course, Kierkegaard agrees with this in one sense, for he argues that spouses and friends can and should be loved as neighbours. If married love is not to become a form of idolatry, I must also construe my wife as my neighbour. I must love her as myself, neither making of her a god nor allowing myself to become a god for her. I shall discuss this theme in the next chapter, in which I shall consider how neighbour-love can permeate and transform such natural loves. However, even apart from such a transformation that is made possible when neighbour-love becomes part of the picture, we can see how love can become a task, and see how emotions can be cultivated in the case of natural loves. We can see even from these 'preferential loves' that not all emotions have to be understood as passions that simply sweep over us. There are emotions that we can work at developing and that we have some responsibility for.

This is true in an even stronger sense in the case of neigh-bour-love. Christian love for the neighbour as Kierkegaard understands it is a genuine emotion; it is not merely acting for the good of the other while inwardly lacking any concern for the other's good. But it is the enduring kind of emotion that must be cultivated, and it is cultivated by focusing on the neighbour as a fellow creature of God. It is no less genuine for being the kind of thing that can be cultivated and nurtured, no less authentic for not being something that simply bubbles out of our animal instincts, no less heart-felt because it is grounded in a construal of the other as a child of God.

Does the fact that we are commanded to love the other in this way mean that the love cannot be authentic? Well, it depends on what we mean by 'authentic'. If we mean 'spontaneous' in the sense of being immediate, neighbour-love is not authentic. However, this does not mean that such love cannot become part of our immediacy, something deeply felt, and it certainly does not mean that it cannot be *ours* in the deepest sense of the word. We must remember Kierkegaard's claim that freedom and happiness stem from having a love that is rooted in God's eternal command.[18] It is precisely being bound in this way by God's commands that frees us to be independent, to love un-conditionally and in a way that secures our own significance and freedom from despair. The command is one that frees our love from the accidents of our inclinations and misfortunes of our lives. Such a commanded love can be ours in a deeper sense than is possible for an emotion that is rooted in what is momentary.

In thinking about such a commanded love, the concept of 'command' is in some ways misleading, for we often associate commands with 'orders' that have some kind of sanction as their foundation. However, in Chapter 5 I argued that the motive for humans obeying God's command to love is not a fear of pun-ishment, but love and gratitude for the love and goodness of God as this is manifested in God's gift of life and offer of eternal life. One should not think of commanded love as something one does gritting one's teeth, but rather as something one works on because of one's love for God. I agree with John Hare, in fact,

[18] See Chapter 6, pp. 146–55.

who says that the language of 'God's call' is in some ways preferable to the language of command.[19]

Even if it is possible to love as a result of a command, one may still think that the requirement of Christian love is an impossible one. Kierkegaard says that the category of the neighbour includes every human being. Nevertheless, the neighbour is not an abstraction. I cannot satisfy the requirement merely by caring about some universal collective such as 'humanity'. Rather, Kierkegaard says that the very first person I see is my neighbour. In Danish the term for 'the neighbour' is *'den Næste'*, literally 'the next [one]'. Is it possible to love every single human being?

The problem is compounded by the ideal of equality. Kierkegaard says that I must not only love every human being, but love every person equally. 'To love the neighbor,' he says, is 'essentially to will to exist equally for unconditionally every human being' (pp. 82–3). Such a requirement seems utterly impossible, and even worse, inhuman. One cannot imagine human life as we know it, with friends and families and other 'special relations', if we literally treated every person in an equal manner. Would this mean that I must first think about the needs of other children before deciding to feed and clothe my own? I shall treat the question of what neighbour-love implies for such special relations in the next chapter. Here I want only to focus on the question as to whether it is possible to love people who are not linked to me in any particular way, especially people I do not even know.

I cannot of course actually focus on every human being as an individual and love all such people episodically. There are too many of us and in my finitude I can only know and care about a particular number of individuals. However, Kierkegaard says that if I truly love even one person as my neighbour, then I have in a way satisfied the requirement, for the ground of that love extends to all other persons (p. 21). For what I love in that person is a characteristic present in every person. One might say

[19] See Hare, *Why Bother Being Good?* 110–13, and *God's Call*, 53.

that I have the kind of love for that person that *would* be the ground of love to any other person with whom I might come into relationship. If love can be dispositional, as I have argued above, then there is a sense in which love for all is then possible.

This might seem to make it too easy to satisfy the requirement. All I have to do is love one person as my neighbour successfully and I have love for all people. However, Kierkegaard is not saying here that I could satisfy the requirement by simply concentrating on loving one person well and forgetting everyone else. For in such a case the hypothetical condition is clearly not fulfilled. If I love the one individual rightly as my neighbour, I must love the person by virtue of being a human being God created. If that motive is really operative in me, then I will not refuse love to others who are equally human beings created by God. If I make a distinction by loving the one person and not the other, clearly the ground of the love for the first person is not that characteristic all humans share, the quality that is the ground of neighbour-love.

Concretely, what does this mean? At one place Kierkegaard says that eternity demands that we make no distinctions and show no preferences (p. 58). However, Kierkegaard does not hold the absurd belief that I ought to have the same feelings and do precisely the same things for every human being, or even every human being I know or have contact with. It is literally impossible even to know every human being, and it is clear that institutions such as the family could not exist without treating some people differently than others. Hence, though we should not make distinctions as to which people are the objects of our moral concern, Kierkegaard insists that Christian love does not abolish all distinctions and differences (p. 73). I shall argue in the next chapter that Kierkegaard does not want to abolish such social institutions and the social relations they require. If anything he is too conservative in his view of the changes in such institutions neighbour-love requires.

Rather, I think Kierkegaard simply wishes to maintain that every human being must be viewed as possessing intrinsic value and worth, someone who deserves respect and moral consideration. Every human being must be regarded as a person, and I must not make distinctions in the sense that I count some people as having moral worth and others as having none.

What this principle requires from me in my dealings with other people is far from obvious. But this much at least is clear. I must refuse to draw boundaries about who is the object of my concern. I am not allowed to say, 'That person is different from me, by virtue of being a man, a woman, an African, an Asian, a gay or lesbian person, or whatever, and because the person is different, I can safely ignore the person's well-being.' What I owe concretely to my neighbours may not always be clear, but it is clear that I cannot exclude anyone from the category of neighbour. I must recognize that the first person I see is my neighbour, and that the people I will never see are my neighbours. I can care about the good of those whom I do not know and look for ways to expand the sphere of my actions on behalf of those others.

Suppose that I see a homeless person at a stop sign as I drive to work this morning. He is a man, holding a sign that says 'Hungry. Will work for food.' What should I do? The principle of neighbour-love does not by itself generate an answer to this question. Perhaps I should stop and give the man some money. Perhaps I should stop and refer him to a social agency I know about. Perhaps I should stop and talk with him about helping him get a job. Perhaps I must pass him by because I have a responsibility to another neighbour that I would violate by stopping to help. The one thing I cannot do is to tell myself that I have no responsibility to him because he is of a different race, or because he is 'undeserving' of my help. For he is a human being and I share a common humanity with him when I see him and myself in relation to God.

Kierkegaard insists that respect for other persons must show itself in a lack of condescension in my dealings with others. If I arrange a dinner for the poor, the gift is not truly loving unless I consider the occasion to be a 'banquet' (p. 82). Kierkegaard places great emphasis on physical proximity on the part of the educated and well-to-do with those who are poor and uneducated (pp. 77–8). It is easy enough to love people at a distance, perhaps through the intermediary of social agencies or government programmes. To argue for human equality and at the same time arrange one's life so that one is physically segregated from the poor and never has to touch or see someone in poverty is hypocrisy and a contradiction to love. Reflecting the strongly class-conscious character of Danish society in his time, Kierkegaard affirms that we all have a duty to 'have fellowship with others, with all people', even though if we are of the upper classes our social peers will consider this 'treason' (p. 73).

What about people that I do not personally know but perhaps only read about or hear about in the media? I cannot feel affection for all Palestinians. I cannot even know all Palestinians. I can, however, care about the plight of the Palestinians, feel sorrow for their sufferings, and do what I can to support a just peace in the Middle East. All of this must be done with a respect for my finite limitations; I am not God and cannot bear the weight of providentially ordering the world.

John Hare has written movingly and perceptively about the difficulties occasioned by an ethic that demands that I consider all humans as having moral worth.[20] The depth and extent of human needs far outrun our resources as individuals or even the resources of whatever communities to which we may belong. Hare recommends as a partial solution what he calls 'the principle of providential proximity'. Perhaps I have special obligations to the poor in Malawi, because I belong to a church that has a sister church there, and there is a history of mutual help and support. The selection of the group to help is not made on the basis that they have moral standing and others do not, but on the assumption that one expression of providence in our lives is the way in which our lives get connected with others, and an interpretation of those connections as part of God's calling to us. Here we must recall the individual dimension of God's call. It is indeed impossible for me (or even for my church) to offer help to everyone. But that is no excuse for a lack of concern and certainly not an excuse for doing nothing. We should not place ourselves in the situation of the baker described by Johannes Climacus in *Concluding Unscientific Postscript*, who turns away a poor woman who asks for bread by declaiming that 'he cannot give to everyone'.[21] He explains, as a justification of his failure to give her anything, that he has in fact already turned down three other people today. What I cannot do is write some individual or group off as beyond the pale of my concern

[20] Hare, *Why Bother Being Good*, 44–5.
[21] Kierkegaard, *Concluding Unscientific Postscript*, 517 n.

because they are not likeable or not like me. What I must do is continually work to construe others as creatures made in God's image, as I seek to love God with all my heart, strength, soul, and mind.

9

Neighbour-Love, Natural Loves, and Social Relations

We have seen that Kierkegaard draws a sharp contrast between love for the neighbour and such natural loves as romantic love and friendship. Other forms of human love, such as love of country or region, and the love within a family seen in parents, children, siblings, etc. would clearly fit under this concept as well, though Kierkegaard typically sticks to erotic love and friendship, since they are the kinds of love celebrated by 'the poet'. The contrast between neighbour-love and these natural loves is drawn so sharply that some commentators have thought that Kierkegaard's concept of neighbour-love is simply incompatible with these natural forms of love.[1]

Why does Kierkegaard distinguish so sharply between these different forms of love? All of the forms of natural love are forms of 'preferential love' (*Forkjærlighed*), since they require one to love some and not others. As a romantic lover, I love one person and no other; as a friend I love my friends, not others. Kierkegaard argues the ground of the selection is always a relation to the self. The lover is loved because she is the one who makes me happy. Friends are loved because they are found to be admirable and like-minded. The friend, in Aristotle's words, is 'the other I'. Hence, for Kierkegaard there is a partially hidden dimension of selfishness present in all these forms of love, present if and to the degree that these people are loved solely because of their similarity to myself or for the benefit they

---

[1] See, for example, Peter George, 'Something Anti-social about *Works of Love*,' in *Kierkegaard: The Self in Society*, ed. George Pattison and Steven Shakespeare (London: Macmillan, 1998), 70–81. Jamie Ferreira gives a nice summary of George's critique in *Love's Grateful Striving*, 6–7.

bring myself. It is only neighbour-love that discovers alterity, 'the first you' instead of 'the other I'.[2]

One might think then that extending any kind of preference to particular individuals is incompatible with neighbour-love, which 'makes no distinctions' and 'loves all equally' (pp. 60, 269–73). If neighbour-love demands that all people be treated strictly alike it is obviously incompatible with such special relations as marriage, romantic love, and friendship. I would hardly regard a man as a friend who made no special effort to think about my well-being, but treated me precisely as he would treat a perfect stranger.

Some who have noted the difficulty of reconciling neighbour-love of this type with what we might call special relations have argued that this shows Kierkegaard's ethical position is one that is inhuman and impossible.[3] Others, however, have recognized the tension and concluded that this merely shows how difficult the task of loving one's neighbour is, even though the ideal is an admirable one. Philip Quinn, for example, interprets Kierke-gaard in the following manner:

> But the point Kierkegaard is trying to make is not paradoxical at all, though it may seem shocking. I take it to be that the obligation to love imposed by the command places absolutely every human, including one's beloved, one's friend, and one's very self, at the same distance from one as one's worst enemy or millions of people with whom one has had no contact. And so it is an obligation that extends to all alike, excludes no one and does not even permit distinctions among persons rooted in differential preferences. It is, perhaps, easy to imagine God loving all his human creatures in this undiscriminating way. It is much more difficult to see how it could be either desirable or feasible for humans to respond to one another in this fashion. But if Kierke-gaard is right, this is exactly what the command to love the neighbor bids us to do.[4]

Quinn recognizes that such a view is 'an offense to common sense,' but of course knows that Kierkegaard believes that Christianity always brings with it the possibility of such an offence. However, Quinn wishes to 'concur with Kierkegaard

---

[2] Kierkegaard *Works of Love*, 57. Subsequent references to this work in this chapter are denoted by page nos. in parentheses.

[3] See Løgstrup, 'Settling Accounts with Kierkegaard's *Works of Love*'.

[4] Quinn, 'The Primacy of God's Will in Christian Ethics', 277.

in considering it important to highlight rather than downplay the stringency of the duty to love the neighbor even if in consequence some people are thrust back or offended.'[5] Quinn's account of Kierkegaard's view here is not completely clear. I do not think that he wants to maintain that neighbour-love is incompatible with special relations, but only that it is tremendously difficult to combine them. However, let us for the moment consider the stronger claim, which I am not attributing to Quinn, that Kierkegaard thinks that special relations and neighbour-love are incompatible.

Kierkegaard does sometimes say things that suggest this kind of view. Love for neighbour, he says, involves an 'eternal equality in loving' (p. 58). Such equality does appear to be incompatible with any kind of special relationships: 'Equality is simply not to make distinctions, and eternal equality is unconditionally not to make the slightest distinction, unqualifiedly not to make the slightest distinction' (p. 58). This is indeed the way God loves, and Kierkegaard affirms that it is our task to resemble God in loving (pp. 62–3). It is hard to see how one can have special relations without making 'distinctions' of some kind. Perhaps, however, Kierkegaard means only to say that a person must not make distinctions in the sense of loving some people but not others, rather than abolishing all distinctions. This is essentially what Jamie Ferreira argues that Kierkegaard means in her excellent recent book *Love's Grateful Striving*.[6] I think that Ferreira's view is completely correct on this point.

I do not think that it can possibly be Kierkegaard's intention to argue that love for the neighbour would preclude the special love inherent in special relationships. When we look at these statements about loving 'without distinctions' in context, it becomes clear that Kierkegaard is not making the absurd claim that a wife must treat her husband exactly as she would treat any other man, or that a husband should treat his wife exactly as he would treat any other woman. Rather, he means

---

[5] Ibid. 279.

[6] See Ferreira, *Love's Grateful Striving*, 53–64. I read Ferreira's book only after I had completed a draft of this chapter. But I am happy to acknowledge my agreement with her, and appreciation for the strong textual case she makes for this view. So far as I can see, the arguments and views I give here are quite similar to hers.

that we must not 'make distinctions' in the sense that we exclude some people from the scope of our moral concern. The category of the neighbour does truly include all people. But loving my neighbour in this sense does not mean that there are not also special relations that provide a basis for treating some individuals differently than others, even if I must try to love all of them.

As I said, I do not think Quinn actually believes that neighbour-love is incompatible with special relationships, with the special affections and actions they require. I think Quinn would agree that neighbour-love is compatible with special loves, for if we say that special relations are prohibited by the love commandment, then the biblical injunction to love the neighbour would appear to contradict other biblical injunctions such as those to honour one's parents and be faithful to one's spouse, and Quinn himself wants to argue that ethics can be rooted in divine commands, which are promulgated through Scripture even if not exclusively so.[7]

I agree with Quinn that the obligation to love the neighbour does indeed carry with it the possibility of offence to that form of 'common sense' which tells us that we should 'love our friends and hate our enemies'. Common sense tells us that these preferential forms of love are completely in order and raise no significant moral questions. I agree with Quinn that in reality it is quite hard to understand how neighbour-love and other kinds of love can be combined. This does not, however, give us a good reason to hold the view that I do not attribute to Quinn, that special loves and neighbour-love are simply incompatible. We must beware of endorsing a position as Kierkegaard's merely on the grounds that it is offensive. Understanding neighbour-love in such a way that it precludes all special relations would be altogether too offensive. Such a view would not merely carry with it the *possibility* of offence. It would actually be offensive to human beings as such, Christians and non-Christians, for we cannot understand human life as flourishing without the goods made possible by such special relations as friendship and family life.

---

[7] Quinn, 'The Primacy of God's Will in Christian Ethics', 261–2.

I shall therefore try to show that Kierkegaard does not see neighbour-love as supplanting natural loves but as transforming them. Special relations are not to be abolished, but purged of what Kierkegaard calls the 'selfishness' present in them. I will grant that Kierkegaard is not as clear as he could be about what this entails for actual human life. (This lack of precision on his part may be intentional since part of his view is that individuals must attempt to work out what the obligation means for them in the absence of algorithmic procedures.) This task of loving others will turn out to be a challenging one; no one should accuse Kierkegaard of holding to a lax or low standard. The obligation certainly does stand in tension with many of our natural inclinations, so we can understand why it carries with it 'the possibility of offence'. However, the command to love the neighbour turns out to be one that humans can fulfil, at least with divine assistance, and one that, were it to be fulfilled, would transform and humanize the special relations we humans have to each other rather than eliminate such relationships.

THE TRANSFORMATION OF ROMANTIC LOVE AND FRIENDSHIP

Kierkegaard is actually quite clear and explicit that romantic love and friendship (the kinds of special loves he discusses, as we have noted) are not to be abolished by neighbour-love. 'To be sure, the wife and the friend are not loved in the same way, nor the friend and the neighbor, but this is not an essential dissimilarity, because the fundamental similarity is implicit in the category "neighbor" ' (p. 141). He notes quite plainly that 'Christianity has nothing against the husband's loving his wife in particular', so long as he does not 'love her in particular in such a way that she is an exception to being the neighbor that every human being is, . . . ' (pp. 141–2). He repeats this claim several times: 'Christianity allows all this [earthly loves based on drives and inclinations] to remain in force and have its significance externally, . . . ' (p. 144).

However, the relation between these natural loves and Christian neighbour-love is not merely additive and external. That is, it is not the case that the task is merely to add neighbour-love to romantic love and friendship love. Rather, he claims that neighbour-love must in some way become the foundation of the special forms of love, and that when this occurs, these natural loves are transformed and purified. Neighbour-love, which is 'the spirit's love', can 'lie at the base of and be present in every other expression of love' (p. 146). Though people may be inclined to think that they are capable of loving their friends and beloved on their own, and that God's help is needed only to love the stranger and the enemy, Kierkegaard affirms that 'no love and no expression of love may merely humanly and in a worldly way be withdrawn from the relation to God' (p. 112). I think the core idea of this claim that neighbour-love can and should be 'foundational' to other kinds of love is the view that there must be, so to speak, a baseline of respect for others as humans and a desire for their good that is a component of the fuller, complete set of attitudes we have for each other. To say that this neighbour-love is foundational is not so much to rank it higher than other kinds, but to say that it is a necessary element of those other kinds, if they are to be truly humane.[8]

Preferential love is therefore not to be eliminated, but transformed. The goal of the transformation is not the elimination of preferential love but the elimination of 'the selfishness in preferential love' (p. 44). The natural needs and desires that form the foundation of preferential loves are not things 'that human beings gave themselves' (p. 52). They came from the Creator and thus cannot be inherently bad, and thus should not be abolished.

Just as neighbour-love is logically linked to learning to love oneself properly, so neighbour-love is linked to learning to love the friend and the beloved as one should: 'Just as this commandment will teach everyone how to love oneself, so it will teach erotic love and friendship genuine love; in loving yourself, preserve love for the neighbour; in erotic love and friendship, preserve love for the neighbour' (p. 62).

Does love for God require that one's natural loves be checked or kept within some kind of boundary, even if not eliminated? Here Kierkegaard seems to be of two minds. On the one hand he says that there is a danger that an earthly love could become 'too intense' so that the God-relationship is disturbed

---

[8] I owe this way of expressing the point to correspondence from John Hare.

(pp. 129–30). On the other hand Kierkegaard seems to deny that neighbour-love would require that one eliminate or at least dampen the passionate loves that are essential to particular relationships: 'Do not believe that the teacher who did not extinguish any smoking wick would extinguish any noble fire within a person' (p. 62). I believe the best way of resolving this tension is to say that the need to 'check' or 'dampen' a natural love is not grounded simply in the intensity of that love, but in its idolatrous character; it is only when that love (or the person loved) is deified that the love must be limited. What would it mean to make an idol of some human love? I do not think that mere intensity of love suffices to make love idolatrous. Love, like anything else, becomes idolatrous when it is valued dispro-portionately, when love for a human being becomes more im-portant than the individual's relation to God.[9] In any case Kierkegaard recognizes that these natural goods are important relative goods: 'erotic love is undeniably life's most beautiful happiness and friendship the greatest temporal good' (p. 267).

Kierkegaard makes a general argument that neighbour-love is compatible with recognizing the differences among humans in various ways. In fact, as I shall argue in the next section, if Kierkegaard is vulnerable to criticism in this area, it is not because he radically wants to abolish special relations. It is rather because he is too conservative in his estimate of the changes required when these special relations are transformed by neighbour-love. For example, he makes it clear that when you as an ordinary person love a ruler 'as a ruler' you must still bring him the homage he is owed by virtue of this relation, even though the ruler is also your equal as your neighbour (p. 88). Neighbour-love is thus consistent with a hierarchical political order, such as absolute monarchy, on Kierkegaard's view.

What exactly does it mean to allow neighbour-love to become the foundation that transforms such natural loves? What does he mean, for example, when he says that 'your wife must first and foremost be to you the neighbor; that she is your wife is then a more precise specification of your particular relationship to each other. But what is the eternal foundation must also be

[9] Robert Adams has a fine discussion of idolatry in ch. 8 of *Finite and Infinite Goods*, 199–213.

the foundation of every expression of the particular' (p. 141). Kierkegaard could be more explicit on this point, and I believe his lack of explicitness is not accidental.

Kierkegaard's lack of explicitness here seems connected to a general shyness about endorsing traditional moral rules. There is remarkably little discussion in Kierkegaard's authorship of such general moral principles as those in the decalogue. The chapter in *Works of Love* that touches on such principles is IIIA in Part I: 'Love Is the Fulfilling of the Law'. Here 'the Law' is a shorthand for the 'many provisions' of God's commands. He is clear that there are such provisions and that they have divine authority behind them. His attitude towards the Law does not seem to me to be entirely clear and consistent, however. On the one hand, he says that love affirms the Law: 'There is not a single one of the Law's provisions, not a single one, that love wants to have removed; on the contrary, love gives them all complete fullness and definiteness for the first time; . . .' (p. 106).

On the other hand, Kierkegaard affirms that the Law is something that is abolished by being fulfilled by Christ's love:

Whereas the Law with its requirement became everyone's downfall because they were not what it required and through it only learned to know sin, Christ then became the downfall of the Law; because he was what it required. Its downfall, its end—for when the requirement is fulfilled, the requirement exists only in the fulfillment, but consequently it does not exist as a requirement. (p. 99)

There is of course an 'eternal difference' between Christ as the God-man and every other person. We can only grasp his fulfilment of the Law in faith, and we are incapable of it ourselves (p. 101). Nevertheless, in some sense Kierkegaard seems to think that the love Christ exhibited can become ours, and that when this is so, we fulfil the Law, not by meticulously following its provisions, but by love. 'The relation of love to the Law is here like the relation of faith to understanding. The understanding counts and counts, calculates and calculates, but it never arrives at the certainty that faith possesses; in the same way the Law defines and defines but never arrives at the sum, which is love' (p. 105). The Law is merely that which 'demands' and 'starves' a human being with its many provisions, while love provides life. Kierkegaard here seems to reflect his Lutheran upbringing, which stresses the role of the Law as a 'schoolmaster' that shows us our sinfulness and drives us to grace. Those Christians more shaped by Catholic and Reformed traditions, which view the law as having a more positive role of guidance, will see Kierkegaard's view here as one-sided.

I think these Catholic and Reformed views make a valuable point. Kierkegaard does not pay sufficient attention to the fact that love itself seeks guidance as to how to express itself in particular and concrete ways, and that such guidance can come through moral principles. Such principles do not have to function merely as requirements that 'starve' us because we can never live up to them, but as expressions of love. Kierkegaard sees that 'calculation' can be a substitute for passion, but he fails to see that it can also be an instrument for responsibly expressing passion. He is right, I think, to affirm that the moral life is more than following a set of rules. Such rules can never account for all of the circumstances humans face. As Kierkegaard says, the Law, '*despite all its many provisions,*' is always '*still somewhat indefinite*' (p. 104).[10] And even when a moral rule is applicable, it must always be interpreted and applied and Wittgenstein has taught us that the process of interpreting a rule cannot always itself be understood as the application of another rule. Furthermore, it is quite possible to conform to a principle in terms of outward behaviour while failing to embody the loving motivation that is supposed to animate the behaviour. Nevertheless, principles have a larger role in the moral life than Kierkegaard seems to allow, and I think his view here to some degree impairs his discussion of the implications of neighbour-love for special relations. We need more guidance than Kierkegaard gives us. Nevertheless, certain points do emerge clearly from his discussion.

First of all, the special love one has for a particular person should never become the basis for excluding any other person as an object of love. This was a point that I made in the previous chapter, but here I wish to draw out its implications for social relations. When Kierkegaard says that one must love 'without distinctions' he means that we are not allowed to exclude

---

[10] Kierkegaard's italics.

anyone as an object of love on the grounds that we do not have a special relation to that person. I cannot limit my loving concern to my family, friends, neighbours, or even my fellow citizens. I am never allowed to say that what happens to other human beings is of no moral concern to me. Clearly every form of racism, sexism, or discrimination which dehumanizes other people by excluding them from the arena of moral concern is prohibited by this standard. Lots of questions remain about the extent of my responsibility to strangers, but it is at least clear that I am forbidden from excluding any individuals or groups from the category 'neighbour'. Kierkegaard puts this by saying that you are not allowed to deny kinship with the whole human race by living as if certain people did not exist for you (p. 74).

I do not think this means I do not have special responsibilities to some people that I do not have to others. As noted above, Kierkegaard says I must give a political ruler the 'homage' such a ruler is due; I do not give such homage to everyone. He says a spouse and a friend must be loved in a particular way. This is compatible with saying that I am not allowed to limit my moral responsibilities to those with whom I have special relations.

What do those responsibilities to those with whom I do not have special relations imply in concrete cases? How much should I limit my lifestyle, or sacrifice my own family's happiness, for example, in order to try to help strangers who are suffering, whether in my home town or across the world? Here Kierkegaard gives us little concrete help. Perhaps he does not believe that any clear rules can be given for struggling with such questions. Perhaps there is not one universal right answer, and what is obligatory for one individual might not be so for another. I do believe, however, that his view implies that this is a question that we must all struggle to answer. We are not allowed to preclude the question by regarding some people as beyond the pale of our moral concern.[11]

How can we show concern for people we don't know? Part of Kierkegaard's answer, seen in the previous chapter, is that such love can be dispositional in character. If I love even one person as neighbour, I love that person by virtue of a characteristic that

---

[11] On this point I would again cite John Hare, *Why Bother Being Good?* and his principle of 'providential proximity' as a partial solution. See pp. 188–93.

would elicit love from me for others in the appropriate situations. However, I think the dispositional answer alone is not enough. In the contemporary world, people are called upon to show love to people whom they do not know in a personal way. We become aware of their existence in an increasingly 'small' world. How can we show such love? The germ of the answer is given in Chapter 8.[12] Sometimes we can do so by cooperation with others. I cannot love every Afghan as an individual, but I can still care if injustice is done to the Afghan people, and seek to support government policies that attempt to rectify such injustice. I can work with others in my church or in charitable, relief, and development organizations to seek to help those who are suffering, even when I don't know who these people are. Finally, I can at least in some sense align myself with the good, symbolically expressing my concern for others and desire to help when I can.[13]

Part of what it means to love the neighbour as oneself is to be seen within the special relations themselves. When neighbour-love lies at the foundation of these loves, then we must recognize that our responsibility is to seek the good of others unselfishly. We are not allowed to view our friends and lovers simply as means to our own happiness, but must, in Kant's words, see them as 'ends in themselves'. Nor are we allowed to make them idols, where this might mean satisfying their desires even when it does not lead to their good or ours. Such 'obedience and adoration' must be offered only to God and never to another human being. So, for example, in my marriage I am not allowed to attempt to be a god for my spouse or to make her a god for me. Love always works for the good, not simply to maximize preferences, whether mine or another's.

An important element in the 'purifying' or transforming character of the neighbour-love that is supposed to be the foundation of special loves is that neighbour-love always involves a relation to God as the middle term. It is because the relation to the human other is rooted in the God-relation that no human can occupy the place of God. And the connection to God

---

[12] See above, pp. 198–202.
[13] See Adams, *Finite and Infinite Goods*, 214–28 for a good discussion of the importance of such symbolic expressions of alliance with the good.

as the 'middle term' in the special human relation also implies something about the goals of that relation. The married couple or the group of friends cannot make their special relationship an idol either. In fact, the special relations acquire a higher purpose, an outward thrust that prevents such relationships from becoming hermetically closed against the rest of the world. For insofar as I love my spouse or my friend, I must work to help them love God, just as they must help me to love God, and loving God in turn requires all of us to love other human beings. In this way, though friends love each other 'honestly and devotedly', what they learn from each other is not that their friendship is the highest good, but rather that their friendship itself requires them to learn from each other what it means to love the neighbour (p. 62). Such a love will tend to block friendship and marriage from becoming a wider form of self-ishness; the relation is not merely a 'group I' because it contains within it the goal of loving the neighbour by reaching out to others.

Does this interpretation take the sting out of the command to love the neighbour? On my reading of Kierkegaard's view, it clearly will be the case that I am permitted and even required to do things for my lover or friend that I do not do for others. I must love all people equally in the sense that I acknowledge the inherent worth of all people. I must make 'no distinctions' in the sense that no one is singled out as an object of love in such a way that others are excluded from being objects of love. However, special relations remain (p. 73). Kierkegaard explicitly says that neighbour-love does not abolish the distinctions in human relations, though the neighbour-love that ought to lie at the foundation of special relations makes it possible to begin the process of morally transforming such relationships.

Perhaps on this interpretation there is a possibility that humans will rationalize lack of love for others on the grounds of special responsibilities. However, there is no ethical theory that can prevent the possibility that humans will misuse the theory for selfish ends. In reality the task of loving the neighbour, when this means recognizing my friends and family members as neighbours and also the stranger and the 'enemy', strikes me as tremendously hard. Given the human tendency to limit our moral concerns to those who are 'like us' in some way, to treat as of no value those of other faiths, other races, other countries, etc., the task can in no way be regarded as easy. The demand to love unselfishly is still one that contains within it 'the possibility of offence'.

NEIGHBOUR-LOVE AND POLITICAL/SOCIAL RESPONSIBILITY: CONTACT WITH THE POOR

Kierkegaard's understanding of the implications of neighbour-love for social relations appears to embrace a certain tension. On the one hand, he argues that neighbour-love demands a strict commitment to equality in which people must recognize their 'kinship with the entire human race' which rules out living as if certain people did not exist for you (p. 74). However, he couples this egalitarianism with a view of the social order that appears to be conservative, at times even complacent. The Christian (and here 'Christian' can be read as Kierkegaard's shorthand for 'someone who loves the neighbor' rather than being taken as a sectarian label) recognizes the inequalities that characterize actual human societies, but does not concern himself 'in a worldly way' with the battle to eliminate such inequalities (p. 73). Rather, the Christian regards such worldly differences and distinctions as 'temptations' that a person must 'lift himself above' (p. 72).

The tension in Kierkegaard's view comes into full view when we contrast his comments about past social reforms with future-oriented proposals for further change. On the one hand, Kierkegaard praises the abolition of slavery and feudalism, and attributes their abolition to the beneficial impact of Christian neighbour-love: 'The times are past when only the powerful and the prominent were human beings—and the others were bond servants and slaves. This is due to Christianity . . .' (p. 74). The same kind of view is expressed with respect to the emancipation of women: 'What abominations has the world not seen in the relationships between man and woman, that she, almost like an animal, was a disdained being in comparison with the man, a being of another species' (p. 138).

However, in both cases this praise of past social reforms (and attribution of such to Christianity) is coupled with a tepid or even hostile attitude towards contemporary battles for social change. With respect to women, Kierkegaard's view seems especially reactionary and even offensive: 'famous people have famously been busy about making it obvious in a worldly way that the woman should be established in equal rights with the man—Christianity has never required or desired this' (p. 139). And though his endorsement of the abolition of feudalism and slavery is clear enough, Kierkegaard's general attitude towards attempts to abolish forms of social inequality is that such movements are attempts to establish a kind of 'worldly' equality that the Christian sees as insignificant. The Christian does not seek to abolish worldly dissimilarities, but seeks to view them as similar to an actor's outer garment that can 'hang loosely on the individual' (p. 88).

Ultimately I shall argue that Kierkegaard's perspective here is too one-sided and not sufficiently open to the need for structural social changes as expressions of neighbour-love. However, before developing this criticism, it is important to see that Kierkegaard has some concerns and insights that are praiseworthy and deserving of respect. One of these concerns is an emphasis on love as something that must be expressed in one's personal relations and not simply through support for social changes that would better the lot of the poor.

Kierkegaard's positive support for egalitarianism comes through strongly in his claim that the loving person must seek real personal and even physical contact with the poor and the uneducated. He has quite pointed words of criticism for the type of person we might describe today as a 'limousine liberal', someone who professes great support for the plight of the poor but is careful to arrange his own personal life in such a manner that he has minimal contact with the people he claims to care about. It is, after all, much easier to love the poor at a distance, and easier still to profess support for doctrines of equality that make no difference to the way one actually lives: 'In the company of scholars, or in a setting that secures and emphasizes his dissimilarity as such, the scholar would perhaps be willing to lecture enthusiastically on the doctrine of the similarity of all people—but that of course is to remain within the dissimilarity' (p. 77).

All of us, Kierkegaard says, have a kind of understanding of the highest ethical ideals: 'Basically we all understand the

highest. A child, the simplest person, and the wisest all understand the highest and all understand the same thing, because it
is, if I dare to say so, one lesson we are all assigned' (p. 78).
What makes the difference is our manner of understanding,
particularly whether our understanding of the ethical is present
only 'at a distance from action' or is present when we act. The
person whose commitment to the solidarity of the human race
expresses itself only in words or at best through support for
social policies of a certain kind does not really have the kind of
understanding of the principle of equality needed. Kierkegaard
imagines a gathering of those who are educated and financially
comfortable who pat themselves on the back for their support of
the less fortunate: 'At the distance of secret superiority, the
learned and the cultured understand the similarity between
human beings' (p. 79).

Kierkegaard believes that the common attitude of the upper
classes in his day is one of 'distinguished corruption'. It is no
longer possible openly to admit that the common people do not
exist as human beings, since the days of slavery and feudal
bondage are gone. However, this does not mean that class-
consciousness of an invidious kind has disappeared: 'Yes, the
world has changed—and the corruption has changed also.' In
the modern world, the proud individual can no longer openly
allow the masses to know that he does not respect them. Nevertheless, such an individual still 'exists only for the distinguished, ... he must not exist for other people, just as they must
not exist for him' (p. 75). This superiority has now become
something that must be kept secret, and the distinguished
person knows how to keep the secret 'lest it agitate people'.
In a withering passage that recalls the worst forms of class-
consciousness exhibited by an Evelyn Waugh character,
Kierkegaard describes the attitude of such 'distinguished
corruption':

He must never be seen among the more lowly people, at least never in
their company; and if this cannot be avoided then the distinguished
condescension must be apparent—yet in its subtlest form in order not
to offend and incite. He may very well use an exaggerated courtesy
toward the more lowly, but he must never associate with them as
equals, since that would express that he was—human, but he is—
distinguished. If he can do this smoothly, dexterously, tastefully,

elusively, and yet always keeping his secret (that the other people do not exist for him nor he for them), then this distinguished corruption will vouch for his having—good form. (p. 75)

It is important to recognize that not all moral theorists recognize such an attitude as morally problematic. Nietzsche, for example, seems positively to recommend such a recognition of superiority to the masses.[14]

In contrast with the condescension of the superior individual who is clever enough not to let his inferiors know of his contempt for them, Kierkegaard appeals to a New Testament saying, in which Christ urges that 'when you give a banquet, invite the poor, the crippled, the lame, the blind' (Luke 14: 13). The person who truly loves the neighbour not only associates with such people but invites them to a dinner. Kierkegaard finds it significant that such a dinner is given a festive label by Christ: 'But so scrupulous is Christian equality and its use of language that it requires not only that you shall feed the poor; it requires that you shall call it a banquet' (p. 82).

I believe that it is clear from this discussion that what we might call Kierkegaard's social conservatism is not driven by a lack of concern for the poor. Rather, he is clear that the person who really loves the neighbour must do so in concrete and costly ways, relating to actual individuals in need. The educated, upper-class person who acts in this manner will be regarded, Kierkegaard thinks, as a kind of class traitor; the true lover of the neighbour will incur the 'double danger' in that she not only runs the risks to one's own well-being involved in caring for the other, but also the risk of laughter and derision for doing so (p. 82).[15] However, if the person's true concern is to do God's will, the laughter and contempt of her peers will not matter.

I think the driving force behind Kierkegaard's lack of enthusiasm for social reform is a conviction that support for such reform can be a cheap substitute for actually loving the neighbour. Another factor is a pessimistic conviction that the world

[14] See, for example, Friedrich Nietzsche, *On the Genealogy of Morals* and *Ecce Homo*, trans. Walter Kaufmann and R. J. Hollingdale (New York: Random House, 1969), 24–56, and many other passages in Nietzsche.

[15] Tobit is here cited as an example of one who faced such a 'double danger'.

will always contain forms of inequality. 'To bring about worldly similarity perfectly is an impossibility...this will never be achieved in temporality, ... even if this struggle is continued for centuries, it will never attain the goal' (p. 72). In fact, it is all too easy to remove one form of inequality by putting another subtler form in its place (p. 73). Here Kierkegaard seems to have in mind the kind of situation seen in the days of the Soviet Union, where economic classes were supposedly abolished with the destruction of capitalism, only to see the flourishing of a 'new class' of party officials and managers. If love is to be real virtue, a character trait that expresses itself in action, it must then express itself through concrete relations with people, at least where this is possible. Support for social improvement and the abolition of some inequality can easily become a means for self-deception, in which a person convinces himself that he feels a kinship with the human race, even while he arranges his life so that he must deal only with those of his own social class.

THE NEED FOR STRUCTURAL SOCIAL CHANGE

I believe the points I have made in the last section on Kierkegaard's behalf are valid and important. Kierkegaard is right when he insists that perfect human equality cannot be achieved, and thus there will always be 'dissimilarities' that the loving person must be able to 'lift himself above'. I believe he is also right in his worries that concern for the poor, when this is expressed solely through support for abstract policies, or, even worse, simply through verbal declarations of solidarity with those less fortunate, can easily be a hypocritical mask that encourages self-deception. A crucial test as to whether a person's love of the neighbour is genuine is how the person treats concrete individuals, particularly those who are not in a position to reciprocate goodness shown to them.

Nevertheless, despite this agreement, I would argue that at this point Kierkegaard does not fully follow the logic of his own position. Let us grant that Utopia is not possible short of eternity and that perfect human equality is not possible either. It does not follow from this that the person who loves the neighbour can be indifferent to every form of social inequality, particularly forms that involve oppression or degradation. And though support for such reform can be a hypocritical substitute for genuine love, it can also be an expression of such love.

Kierkegaard's own endorsement of past social reforms really commits him to this position. He cannot consistently approve the abolition of slavery and feudal serfdom and praise society for refusing to treat women as 'an alien species', attributing such reforms to the power of the Christian ideal of equality, while refusing to consider whether the same ideal might demand new changes.[16]

One reason this is so is given by Kierkegaard himself. He affirms that worldly dissimilarities can function as 'temptations' for the one who loves the neighbour. This is why such dissimilarities are things one must 'lift oneself above'. However, what is a temptation to evil is at least sometimes itself an evil, in that it provides an occasion for my neighbour (as well as myself) to stumble.[17] It may not be possible or desirable to eliminate all such temptations. Nevertheless, there are surely some kinds of temptations that a loving person would seek to eliminate where this is possible.

A second reason is I think implied by the commitment to 'existing for others' and recognizing all other human beings as your 'kin'. In the first section of this chapter I argued that it is very difficult to discern in detail how such a commitment to love every human person can express itself in concrete action. I cannot possibly know every person, much less seek their good in practical ways. One way that I *can* affect the lives of those I do not know is through my support for social policies aimed at improving the lives of others in my society and throughout the world. It may be hypocritical to support such policies while personally ignoring the poor around one. But it is also hypocritical to declare a love for all human beings and then ignore

---

[16] It is worth noting that my argument here implies that H. Richard Niebuhr's influential treatment of Kierkegaard as a representative of the 'Christ against culture' position in his classic *Christ and Culture* (New York: Harper, 1956) is very misleading, since there are clear elements in Kierkegaard's thought that support the idea that faith must express itself in social reform, and thus Kierkegaard's thought can also be seen as embodying the 'Christ the transformer of culture' perspective.

[17] This argument was suggested to me in conversation many years ago by Merold Westphal.

concrete possibilities for cooperative action that seeks the good of those others I claim to love.

Think, for example, of the problem of AIDS in Africa today. The statistics are staggering, but the statistics summarize human suffering that is real and concrete. Suppose I have the opportunity to support a foreign policy on the part of my government that will help alleviate this suffering, by making possible inexpensive medication and perhaps facilitating the prevention of the spread of the disease. Surely, one way I should manifest a love for those people in Africa I do not know is through such support. Of course, this does not exhaust my responsibility. Perhaps I ought also to give sacrificially to a development or relief organization. Perhaps I should consider a trip in which I spend some time actually working in a clinic in Africa. Perhaps I ought to volunteer at a local clinic. My actual obligations will surely reflect in part my individual calling, as noted in Chapter 7. However, it is hard to see how a real commitment to love my neighbour which includes the whole human race could not include obligations for actions that can only be carried out collectively.

This issue also links up with the discussion earlier in this chapter about the relation of natural loves to neighbour-love. There I argued that Kierkegaard does not see neighbour-love as eliminating but as transforming or 'purifying' such natural loves. It appears to me that this process of transformation should also include a critical review of the social practices and institutions that embody our special loving relations. Kierkegaard is surely right to argue that such relations can become idolatrous and that neighbour-love demands that we seek to make our friendships and love relationships ones that help all concerned become more concerned for others and less selfish. However, if our social practices foster dehumanizing, one-sided relations in which one party is tempted to deify another party, then those practices cannot simply be complacently accepted by neighbour-love. For example, it seems hardly to be consistent with neighbour-love for a husband to allow or even require his wife to take on all or nearly all of the responsibilities required to care for a family and administer a household so that he can have plenty of free time to engage in his own hobbies.

In conclusion I would affirm that Kierkegaard is right to claim that neighbour-love is consistent both with special relations and obligations as well as consistent with a range of human social arrangements. As he puts it, a love that makes no distinctions can also be a love that loves each person in his or her 'distinctiveness' and thus takes into account the particularities of the situation. Genuine neighbour-love must express itself in concrete relations and actions where it has opportunity to do so, and a love that contents itself merely with verbal declarations or support for general policies is suspect. However, a love that shows no concern for collective, cooperative action is also suspect, though love should be well aware of the limits of such actions, and the ironical way in which history often shows that bad results can be the outcome of good intentions.

10

Contemporary Meta-Ethical Alternatives: Evolutionary Naturalism

What are the alternatives to Kierkegaard's divine command account of moral obligation? There are of course many other meta-ethical frameworks which provide accounts of moral obligations. Some are siblings, such as stronger or weaker types of divine command theories. A stronger divine command theory might, for example, attempt to ground not merely obligations, but goodness itself in divine commands or some act of divine willing. A weaker theory might, for example, hold that moral obligations are indeed divine commands, but that what God commands is determined by the natures he has given things. Others are cousins, theistic meta-ethical frameworks that agree with Kierkegaard in grounding moral obligations in God, but which give a lesser role to divine commands. I regard such accounts as friendly rivals to the one I have attributed to Kierkegaard, if they are to be construed as rivals at all. However, there are other accounts that are clearly competitors in the sense that they reject the need for any religious basis for ethics. In this chapter and the two succeeding ones I shall look at some of the major competitive options of this type. My hope is that by examining these alternatives we will not only gain a better understanding of Kierkegaard's views, but a clearer view of its strengths. For often the strengths of a philosophical position are best seen in contrast with rival theories attempting to make sense of the same phenomena.

My goal in these chapters is not to establish that a divine command theory of obligation is the only viable type of ethical account. Such a claim would be far too ambitious. It is unclear how one would go about showing such a thing. Even if a large number of alternative theories were assessed and found to be inferior to Kierkegaard's, it is always possible that there are other alternatives, and it is also possible that some of the ones considered could be revised and improved. So what I hope to show is only that the Kierkegaardian view I have developed is a serious competitor by demonstrating its power over against some leading secular alternatives.

I cannot possibly be comprehensive in selecting alternative theories as a basis for comparison. I shall try to select accounts that are both influential in contemporary western culture and which allow for helpful contrast with Kierkegaard's theory. Rather than develop a composite version myself of each of the alternatives that might be held by no one I shall pick one actual writer as a representative of a type. It is always possible, of course, that the writer I select will not be a good champion of his or her cause; some readers may think that stronger proponents of a view could and should have been used. Nevertheless, even though this outcome seems hard to avoid (no matter who is selected), I shall try to rely on authors who are widely respected and who represent in a clear way the major concerns of a distinctive way of thinking about the ethical life. It is my conviction that the problems that can be seen in these representatives are ones that will reappear in some form in other versions of this meta-ethical type, even if those other versions are superior in some respects.

I shall examine three types of secular alternatives. The first two are forms of ethical naturalism, which I shall call evolutionary naturalism and humanistic naturalism, respectively. Roughly, I understand by ethical naturalism a meta-ethical view that regards moral obligations as objective in the sense that they hold independently of what individual humans think and believe about them, but which sees these objective obligations as rooted in or to be explained by facts in the natural order. The evolutionary naturalist sees the relevant facts as rooted in biology, particularly the evolutionary history of human beings. The humanistic naturalist sees the relevant facts as rooted in human social interaction; in some sense ethical obligations are made by us humans, even though once created such obligations have an objectivity over against the individual human person. Both forms of naturalism can then be seen as forms of ethical realism, at least with respect to moral obligations, agreeing with the divine command theorist that there is a fact of the matter about what moral obligations hold, though disagreeing about the nature of those obligations. The third alternative I shall consider is ethical relativism, which rejects moral realism and denies the existence of an objective set of moral obligations. For the relativist, there is no need to explain the existence of object-ive moral obligations, for there are no such things, though there is a need to explain why there is a widespread belief in objective moral obligations.

DO WE NEED META-ETHICS?

Before undertaking this comparative meta-ethical analysis, it is worth asking about the value of a meta-ethical framework. Do we need an account of what a moral obligation is or an explan-ation of why such things exist in order to carry on our moral lives? If not, what is the value of a meta-ethical account?

It is very implausible to hold that substantive moral know-ledge depends on the possession of the correct meta-ethical theory. From childhood on, humans acquire knowledge of good and evil, right and wrong, and this knowledge, though fallible, shapes their lives in important ways. One does not need to know exactly what a moral obligation is, or how it is grounded, to know that one is in fact obligated to do something or refrain from doing something. A person can even have a kind of understanding of an obligation as a duty, something that is prescribed or proscribed, without having much by way of a theory of obligation. Certainly, people do not require a philo-sophical understanding of morality in order to make moral progress. It is rather the case that philosophical progress in making sense of morality depends on the fact that humans already know something about morality prior to philosophical reflection about morality. I agree with Robert Adams that '[t]he formation of a wide variety of evaluative beliefs, many of them quite confident beliefs, must precede any useful reflections on the epistemology of value, as also on its semantics and meta-physics.'[1]

From the point of view of a divine command theory of moral obligation, it is important that this be so. Does the fact that a

---

[1] Adams, *Finite and Infinite Goods*, 354.

divine command theory holds that moral obligations are or depend on divine commands mean that an atheist cannot know about moral obligations or rightly even believe there are such things? If that were a consequence of a divine command theory, then the theory would be immensely implausible. However, no such consequence follows from the theory. It is perfectly consistent for a divine command theorist to hold that people can believe in moral obligations and even know them without believing in God, even though moral obligations consist of divine commands according to the theory. If a divine command theory is true, then it follows that an atheist fails to understand the nature of moral obligations at the deepest level. However, the atheist can still understand that there are actions that he or she must do or must not do, and can still know what those actions are. The theist should have no interest in denying this, especially if the theist believes, as Kierkegaard does, that one way, perhaps the main way, that people come to know God is by recognizing moral obligations as divine commands. A person could not come to believe in God by this route if the person could not know about moral obligations antecedently to belief in God.

The atheist can certainly know that there are moral obligations and what they are, even if a divine command theory is correct, just as can theists. The atheist would in that case simply fail to realize something important about those obligations. This is no more mysterious than the inability of someone ignorant of chemistry to know the true nature of water as H_2O. Such a person can still recognize water and drink it.

Although meta-ethical knowledge is not necessary or essential for the moral life, it may still be useful and important. As we shall see in Chapter 12, one meta-ethical framework that is very appealing in our culture is that of moral relativism. I shall argue in that chapter that moral relativism is a view that is damaging to the moral life; it makes it more difficult to follow the dictates of morality, particularly when those dictates are strenuous. Ethical relativism makes it easier for me to rationalize a life that does not take the needs of others very seriously. One of the factors that may push an individual towards moral relativism is meta-ethical scepticism. To the degree that I believe that no intelligible account can be given of objective moral obligations, I may be tempted to believe that there are no such moral obligations.

It is also possible that meta-ethical insight may sharpen and improve our substantive moral understanding. We have seen in Kierkegaard's case, and it will be true for other meta-ethical frameworks as well, that there are important connections between a meta-ethical position and normative conclusions. The obligation to love all human beings for Kierkegaard is tied to the fact that the basis of the obligation is a divine command, and the fact that the people whom I must love are created in the image of the commander. So even though moral knowledge in general is not dependent on having a good philosophical account of morality, it is still possible that having the right philosophical account may allow us to sharpen and refine our moral knowledge.

THE APPEAL OF BIOLOGY: TWO TYPES OF SCIENTIFIC ACCOUNT

There are many different naturalistic approaches to ethics. A traditional approach, exemplified by classical utilitarians such as Jeremy Bentham and John Stuart Mill, is to identify the good with some natural property, such as pleasure, and then to define obligatory acts as those which produce more of this good property.[2] A more sophisticated contemporary version of a naturalistic realism about ethics can be found in Richard Boyd, who does not attempt to identify the good with one simple natural property, but rather with a number of properties that tend to occur together in what Boyd calls a 'homeostatic property cluster'.[3] With the exception of this more complex account of the good, Boyd follows the utilitarians in viewing moral obligations as dependent on the consequences of our actions, and he believes that scientific inquiry can establish which types of actions are in fact conducive to good outcomes.

[2] See Jeremy Bentham, *An Introduction to the Principles of Morals and Legislation* (New York: Hafner, 1948), 1–7; and John Stuart Mill, *Utilitarianism* (Oxford: Oxford University Press, 1998), 56–9.

[3] Richard Boyd, 'How to Be a Moral Realist', in Geoffrey Sayre-McCord (ed.), *Essays on Moral Realism* (Ithaca, NY: Cornell University Press, 1988), 181–228. See especially pp. 196–9.

Such consequentialist approaches to ethics continue to have both defenders and detractors, of course. Philosophically, this type of theory is vulnerable at two points. First there is the question of whether it is right to identify moral obligations with those actions that produce the best consequences. To many people this does not seem intuitively correct. Consider a standard problem case such as the following. Suppose that it is true that a tyrannical government can only be overthrown by a terrorist campaign that includes such actions as indiscriminate bombing. Even if the ultimate consequences of such acts as bombing school buses were better than any alternative, many people would claim that it is simply morally wrong to do such things. There are of course sophisticated versions of consequentialism that try to meet this kind of objection, but there remain grave questions about whether moral obligation can be understood in purely consequential terms.

The other philosophical area of difficulty is related to the issue of what is to count as a good consequence. It seems clear that the real work in such a theory in this aspect is done by the initial identification of the good with some natural property or properties. Once this identification is made, perhaps scientific inquiry is indeed relevant to discovering what actions will have the best consequences, assuming that a consequentialist framework is defensible. But what justification can be provided for the initial identification of the good? This is one of the challenges that faces attempts at a scientific ethics. Recently, there has been a resurgence of interest in the idea that biology can help answer this challenge, especially since the publication of Edward O. Wilson's *Sociobiology* in 1975.[4]

Most philosophers committed to naturalism today are scientific naturalists; that is to say, as naturalists they are committed to natural science as the means whereby we gain knowledge of the natural world. Scientific naturalists have an understandable reluctance then to admit as reality what cannot, at least in principle, be investigated and explained scientifically. We can see therefore that the ideal of a 'scientific ethics', an ethics that

[4] Edward O. Wilson, *Sociobiology* (Cambridge, Mass.: Harvard University Press, 1975). See also Wilson's *On Human Nature* (Cambridge, Mass.: Harvard University Press, 1978).

is in some way grounded in science, has a strong appeal, an appeal that is only strengthened by the general prestige of science in the broader culture.

It is no surprise then that there have been a series of attempts at a 'scientific ethics', particularly since the intellectual sea-change in the late nineteenth century brought about by the advent of Darwinian theories of natural selection. It is generally recognized that prior to Darwin, the apparent design in the natural order seemed to provide strong support for the view that an intelligent being had created the world. William Paley's *Natural Theology*, for example, first published in 1802, was enormously influential with its argument that 'the contrivances of nature ... are not less evidently mechanical, not less evidently contrivances, not less evidently accommodated to their end or suited to their office than are the most perfect productions of human ingenuity.'[5] A profound change occurred with Darwin's attempt to explain this apparent design as the result of chance variations of which the biologically most fit survive to reproduce themselves. It is not surprising that a contemporary non-religious thinker has claimed that 'Darwin made it possible to be an intellectually fulfilled atheist.'[6] It is equally unsurprising that Darwinian thinking has been utilized by a host of thinkers trying to make sense of ethics within a scientific framework.[7]

Two different types of scientific approaches to ethics must be clearly distinguished, however, and both can be seen in approaches to ethics inspired by Darwinism. One approach assumes that there are objective moral obligations and looks to evolutionary biology for an account of the origin and foundation of these obligations. This approach assumes the legitimacy of some version of our moral framework and tries to give a scientific explanation of that legitimacy. The other approach does not assume that moral obligations are in some sense objective and real, but rather attempts to explain why human beings

[5] William Paley, *Natural Theology* (originally published 1802) (Houston: St. Thomas Press, 1972), 14.

[6] Richard Dawkins, *The Blind Watchmaker* (London: Penguin, 1986), 6.

[7] For a good brief historical overview and critique of the English-language version of this tradition, see Paul Lawrence Farber, *The Temptations of Evolutionary Ethics* (Berkeley: University of California Press, 1994).

typically *believe* in such moral obligations. On this approach moral obligations are not taken at face value, but rather as sociological and psychological facts which must be explained. It is a fact that every human society has a moral code, and such codes have a strong impact on human behaviour, and science must give an explanation of such facts, but the explanation does not have to take the form of a justification that establishes the validity of morality. Objective moral obligations are things to be explained away, rather than realities to be accounted for. Alternatively, if such obligations are not simply to be explained away, they must be provided with some foundation other than biology.

In this chapter it is the first type of approach that I wish to consider. The second type of approach fits much better with the relativistic type of meta-ethical view that will be considered in Chapter 12. The approach to be considered in this chapter is that of the naturalist who agrees with the divine command theorist about the reality of moral obligations, but disagrees about the nature of that reality. Naturalistic views that deny moral realism in this sense will thus be temporarily put aside.

The task of the naturalist who is a realist about ethics is considerably harder than that of a naturalist who is simply trying to give an explanation of morality as a sociological or psychological phenomenon. It is one thing to try to show that creatures with moral inclinations, who can thus cooperate and work together to some degree, might have a survival advantage over less socially minded competitors. It is quite another thing to try to show that these facts, if they are facts, constitute a justification of morality, rather than merely an explanation of why humans believe in morality. It is harder to show that human moral convictions are in some way objective in character and thus that those who accept their reality are justified in doing so.

NATURAL DESIRES AND THE GOOD

One of the clearest and most straightforward attempts to show how ethics can be grounded in biology is that of Larry Arnhart in his book *Darwinian Natural Right: The Biological Ethics of*

Human Nature.[8] In this work Arnhart attempts to wed Darwinism to Aristotle so as to resolve the foundational questions of
ethics. Within such a framework he thinks that contemporary
biology has given us a solid basis for understanding what is good
and what is right for humans.

Arnhart's view does not seem initially promising. He begins
with a stark identification: 'The good is the desirable' (p. 17). If
we ask how we are to determine what it is that is desirable,
Arnhart says that we must look to what humans actually desire:
'I believe that natural human desires constitute the unchanging
ground of ethics throughout human history' (p. 17). Here Arnhart seems to follow in the footsteps of John Stuart Mill, who
notoriously identified the desirable with what is desired: 'The
only proof capable of being given that an object is visible, is that
people actually see it. The only proof that a sound is audible, is
that people hear it ... In like manner, I apprehend, the sole
evidence it is possible to produce that anything is desirable, is
that people do actually desire it.'[9]

This claim by Mill has been famously criticized as a form of
the 'naturalistic fallacy', which is alleged to be the mistake of
reducing moral terms to non-moral terms. Often the criticism is
put in terms derived from a famous quotation from David
Hume, in which Hume implies that it is not possible to derive
a statement about what 'ought' to be merely from premises
about what is in fact the case.[10] Someone who is convinced
that the naturalistic fallacy is a fallacy will swiftly reject an
approach to ethics such as Arnhart's.

Such a rejection would be too swift, however. Doubtless it is
correct to maintain that an argument cannot be formally valid if
it introduces a normative term into the conclusion that has not
appeared in the premises. However, such a logical fact cannot
establish the philosophical conclusion that truths about reality
can have no ethical implications. Nor is the famous argument of
G. E. Moore against the naturalistic fallacy (a term Moore

[8] Larry Arnhart, *Darwinian Natural Right: The Biological Ethics of Human
Nature* (Albany, NY: State University of New York Press, 1998). Subsequent
references to this work in this chapter are denoted by page nos. in parentheses.
[9] Mill, *Utilitarianism*, 81.
[10] David Hume, *A Treatise of Human Nature* (Oxford: Oxford University
Press, 1888), 469.

coined) decisive. Moore tried to show that no identification of
the good with a natural property could be correct because the
meaning of 'good' is not identical with the meaning of any
natural property. Moore claimed rightly that it always makes
sense to ask of any natural property whether that property is
good in a way that would be impossible if 'good' had the same
meaning as the term designating that natural property.[11] If
'pleasure' simply meant 'good' then it would make no sense to
ask whether pleasure is always good, but it clearly does make
sense to ask this. However, most philosophers now recognize
that even if Moore is right about the meaning of 'good' being
distinct from the meaning of any terms that designate natural
properties, it does not follow that what 'good' designates must
be distinct from any natural property. Two terms can differ in
meaning but still designate the same reality. 'The fastest
sprinter' and 'the most handsome athlete' might designate the
same individual, but the two expressions clearly do not have the
same meaning.

I shall not, therefore, dismiss Arnhart's proposal on the
grounds that he commits the naturalistic fallacy. Nor is it
right to reject his proposal immediately simply because 'what
is desired' and 'what is desirable' seem different. Arnhart himself recognizes there is a difference between the two; he knows
that it is possible to desire what is not desirable and that humans
mistakenly desire things that they should not desire: 'we sometimes get what we think we desire only to discover it is not
desirable' (p. 23).

How is this possible? The answer is that Arnhart, despite his
initial stark pronouncements, does not really identify the desirable with what is desired. Rather, he identifies the desirable
with what he terms natural human desires. Such desires are not
simply the sum total of all human desires, which Arnhart acknowledges are highly variable due to cultural and historical
factors. Rather, natural human desires are those desires that are
universal because they are rooted in human nature. Aristotle
developed an ethical theory that focuses on the good for humans

[11] See G. E. Moore, *Principia Ethica* (Cambridge: Cambridge University
Press, 1903), 9–10.

as what fulfils human nature and thus allows human beings to flourish.

Arnhart believes that modern biology gives us an objective basis for determining what human nature is and what kinds of actions do in fact contribute to its fulfilment, and thus allows us to give a scientific basis to an Aristotelian ethic. Moral relativism, whether it be an individual relativism that regards morality as determined by individual choices, or a cultural relativism that regards morality as determined by historical, cultural variables, is mistaken, because relativism does not recognize the objectivity of human nature. Arnhart argues that 'the human good is universal insofar as there are universal human desires rooted in human nature', and he claims to have identified at least twenty such desires (p. 17).[12] Modern evolutionary biology helps us to understand what these desires are and why we have them, by looking at their function for human beings, both in the period in which modern humans evolved and today. Despite the great differences between the hunting-gathering ancestors of humans in the Palaeolithic era and contemporary humans, Arnhart is confident that these identified natural desires, such as the desire to have and nurture children, are present in both periods and thus form a stable basis for ethics (p. 30).

The desires that Arnhart selects as natural and universal are quite different in character. Some, such as the desire for a long life, health, and the opportunity to mate sexually, seem relatively uncontroversial (pp. 31–2). Others, however, are of a different character. For example, Arnhart claims that 'war' is itself a universal human desire (p. 36). If this is correct then it seems to lead to the pessimistic conclusion that there are sharp limits to the human potential for moral improvement; one might hope that war, rather than being a natural and universal human need, might be a form of social interaction that humans might learn to live without. Of course Arnhart can point to the dismal record of human history in support of his claim; war certainly seems a pervasive feature of that record. However, even if war is endemic to human life as we know it, it does not follow that war itself is something that humans desire or should

---

[12] The desires are listed on pp. 29–36.

desire. It might, for example, be an unfortunate by-product of other human desires.

Another difficulty is raised by the differences Arnhart sees between the natural desires of men and women. After telling us that what is good is what is universally desired because it is rooted in human nature, it is something of a surprise to learn that human nature comes in two forms, male and female, and that the natural desires of men and women differ (pp. 31–2). Men, for example, have a greater need than women for dominance and this is reflected in the fact that '[h]uman politics is ... a sphere for male dominance' (p. 33). Women, on the other hand, on average have a much higher interest in nurturance that is reflected in a 'greater propensity to care for children' (p. 32).

One could obviously ask whether such judgements about what is 'natural' reflect biases. Perhaps Arnhart is projecting into the biological order his own approval of the social arrangements that have been typical of human societies. Is it really true that we must simply accept the male desire for dominance as a fact that cannot be changed, and even regard it as a positive good, part of what is 'desirable' in the sense of being a part of human nature? Arnhart seems to think so, though he recognizes that male dominance does produce problems:

Despite the harm that comes to both men and women from the male competition for dominance, it is an essential part of the moral nature of human beings. It is a mistake, therefore, to assume, as is often done, that human life would be better off if we could eliminate male competitiveness or at least subordinate it to female nurturance. The moral order of human nature rests on a rough balance between the predominantly male desire for dominance and the predominantly female desire for nurturance. (p. 143)

These are serious problems, I believe, and they are the kinds of problems that tend to occur in any attempt to develop an account of human nature from observation of actual human behavior. We shall see that the difficulties that arise from male-female differences produce difficulties for Arnhart's account of what is morally wrong. However, I do not wish to say as a matter of principle that one could not learn something about what is essential or necessary to human nature from observing human behaviour. Though it is obvious that the fact that people behave in a certain way does not establish that it is right or good for them to do so, one might still regard observations about human behaviour as at least suggestive of the claim that particular human desires are good and natural. However, what is needed in such a case is some plausible criterion for selecting the favoured desires. Any particular proposal about what is 'naturally good', such as Arnhart's, can then be criticized, both for the content of the conclusions arrived at, and the method whereby the selection was made.

If we compare Arnhart and Kierkegaard on the good, there are clearly huge differences. Kierkegaard holds, as I argued in Chapter 4, a 'soul-making' ethic in which the most important human good is the development of moral character. To this end, the most important human need is the need for love, not only to be loved, but the need to become loving and thereby satisfy one's true nature. Such a view is almost the antithesis of a view that sees war and male dominance as universal and necessary human goods.

However, I do not want to lay too much weight on this problem, or insist that it is unsolvable. Perhaps better biology might correct some of Arnhart's seemingly biased conclusions about what is natural. Recently, for example, the John Templeton Foundation has been sponsoring research into forgiveness, which suggests that humans who practise forgiveness are happier than those who do not, and that a need to receive and extend forgiveness can be seen as fitting our human nature, even at the level of biology.[13] One must here recall that Kierkegaard does try to argue that loving one's neighbour is linked to happiness, and seeks to identify human goods that even the unloving person can recognize as fundamental human needs that are fostered by neighbour-love. So although there are grave problems with the identification of the good, it is at least conceivable that those problems might be solved. I believe the most fundamental difficulty with evolutionary naturalism as

[13] See Charlotte Witvliet, Thomas E. Ludwig, and Kelly L. Vander Laan, 'Granting Forgiveness or Harboring Grudges: Implications for Emotion, Physiology, and Health', in *Psychological Science,* 121/2 (Mar. 2001), 117–23. Also see Michael McCullough, 'The Psychology of Forgiveness', in C. R. Snyder and Shane J. Lopez (eds.), *Handbook of Positive Psychology* (Oxford: Oxford University Press, 2002), 446–58.

providing a basis for normative ethics lies not in its account of the good, but in the account provided of moral obligation.

IS 'UNIVERSAL ALTRUISM' A UTOPIAN IDEAL?

One of the most significant questions to ask about a theory of moral obligation concerns the scope of moral duties. To whom must I extend moral concern? The moral egoist says my fundamental obligation is only to myself. I should help others only if I wish to do so. More commonly, the sphere of moral concern is broadened to include family and friends, those to whom I have natural ties of sympathy. Others would extend moral concern yet more broadly, to all the members of my tribe or society. In some of the great world religions, and in philosophical accounts such as those found in Stoicism and Kant, moral responsibility is extended to all human beings, and even beyond, sometimes to a lesser degree, to animals capable of pleasure and pain.

What does an evolutionary naturalistic perspective on ethics imply about the scope of moral responsibility? Arnhart notes an ambivalence on this question found in Darwin himself as well as Darwinist writers on ethics. He distinguishes what he terms 'realist' and 'utopian' strands in Darwin's thought. The realist strand comes through when Darwin considers the constant warfare present between many primitive societies: 'It is no argument against savage man being a social animal, that the tribes inhabiting adjacent districts are almost always at war with each other, for the social instincts never extend to all the individuals of the same species' (p. 144). From this perspective, Darwin acknowledges the reality of sympathy and humanitarian concerns as traits evolution has selected for, but he regards the sympathy that is naturally explicable to be one that extends primarily to friends and kin, and only secondarily, if at all, to those outside of such circles: This perspective implies that though altruism is real there are also real limits on the extent of our altruistic concerns, and these limits are set by human nature. Darwin says that a human being 'would from an inherited tendency still be willing to defend, in concert with others, his fellow-men, and would be ready to aid them', but this willingness extends only to acts that do not 'greatly interfere with his own welfare or his own strong desires' (p. 146).

This realism in Darwin is in tension with the utopian strand in his thinking, in which Darwin imagines that our moral concerns might be extended to all human beings and even to all living creatures:

As man advances in civilization, and small tribes are united into larger communities, the simplest reason would tell each individual that he ought to extend his social instincts and sympathies to all the members of the same nation, though personally unknown to him. This point being once reached, there is only an artificial barrier to prevent his sympathies extending to the men of all nations and races. (p. 144)

Darwin himself imagines this universal sympathy as an extension of a natural trait, grounded in 'maternal instincts', and he thinks that this advance in sympathy is now being extended even beyond the human race to other animals in a 'disinterested love for all living creatures' (p. 144).

Arnhart clearly sides with the realist strand in Darwin's thought. The utopian strand shows a desire on Darwin's part to find 'a transcendent moral norm to escape this harsh vision of human nature as based on the competition of groups' (p. 144). However, Arnhart claims, and I believe he is correct on this point, that it is impossible to give a naturalistic explanation of such a universal moral responsibility:

Darwin is wrong in thinking that female sympathy—as rooted in maternal care—can expand into a disinterested universal sentiment of humanity. After all, even maternal care manifests itself as a love of one's own offspring and a willingness to defend them against strangers. And although sympathy can be expanded to embrace ever-larger groups based on some sense of shared interests, this will always rest on loving one's own group as opposed to other groups. Darwin's appeal to universal humanitarianism can only be explained as a utopian yearning for an ideal moral realm that transcends nature, which contradicts Darwin's general claim that human beings are fully contained within the natural order. (146–7).

Arnhart recognizes that other Darwinian thinkers have followed the utopian strand in Darwin and looked for some kind of universal moral obligation as the highest form of ethics, citing Thomas Huxley, George Williams, Richard Dawkins, and James Q. Wilson as examples (p. 147). However, as Arnhart sees things, such views inevitably sever morality from its naturalistic roots. Even James Q. Wilson admits that 'universalism is not natural, localism is' (p. 147). From the point of view of moral realism, we must admit the possibility that not all conflict can be settled by appeal to common interests, and when this occurs, the only way of resolving a dispute is through appeal to 'force or fraud' (p. 149). A naturalistic morality of Arnhart's type has nothing to say at such a point; such conflicts could only be morally adjudicated by appeal to 'some transcendental norm of impartial justice (such as Christian charity) that is beyond the order of nature' (p. 149). That is precisely what Kierkegaard would say as well, though of course Kierkegaard thinks that such a norm has been provided by God's command to love the neighbour.

If Arnhart is right, we have then an 'either–or' of the following type: either a set of universal moral obligations rooted in a transcendent basis, or else a more limited set of moral obligations, extending primarily to friends and family and others with whom one shares common interests, that can be grounded in the natural order of things. Arnhart himself is clear that moral obligations must be identified with particular felt emotions that have naturalistically evolved: 'The fact of obligation is nothing more than the feeling of obligation' (p. 81). If obligations consist of such feelings, then it is hard to deny that they must be particular in scope and not universal.

How shall we decide whether a universalist view of obligation or the more particularist view that evolutionary naturalism suggests is correct? If we are already convinced that naturalism is true the choice will be easy. I believe Arnhart's argument that a purely natural morality rooted in biologically selected traits cannot be the ground of universal obligations is convincing. However, if we are open to the truth of theism, or some other metaphysical view in which there is something that transcends nature, then we ought to be willing to consider the universalist alternative.

Much depends on whether we believe that we know that certain moral obligations hold. If we are convinced that there are true universal moral obligations and that these cannot be explained naturalistically, this will be a powerful argument against naturalism in ethics. We must remember that there are other naturalistic alternatives, still to be considered in the next two chapters. However, given the prominence of Darwinian modes of thinking in our culture, it will be a significant result if it can be shown that a biologically grounded ethic cannot account for moral judgements of whose truth we are confident.

I believe that Arnhart's view shows just this type of weakness. In the end there are moral judgements of a universalist type that even Arnhart cannot deny and does not wish to deny. He attempts to show that these obligations can be explained naturalistically and without appeal to a universal norm that would require a transcendent basis. I believe those attempts fail. I shall look at two moral areas Arnhart discusses where this failure seems particularly evident to me: human slavery and male–female relations, particularly with respect to the issue of so-called female circumcision.

CONFLICTS OF INTEREST AND UNIVERSAL MORAL OBLIGATIONS: THE CASE OF SLAVERY

Both of the two cases that I wish to examine in Arnhart exhibit conflicting human interests because of conflicting natural desires. In the case of slavery there is a conflict between the natural desire of the master for dominance (and the economic rewards that go with such dominance) and the natural desire of the slave to be free and independent. In the case of male–female relations Arnhart maintains there are genuine differences in natural desires. Men naturally desire more promiscuous sexual relationships for themselves, allowing freer expression to their desire for sexual satisfaction as well as the possibility of fostering more offspring, while demanding faithfulness from their sexual partners, in part so as to ensure that men do not invest in providing for the offspring of others. Women, by contrast, desire a more monogamous life so as to provide a stable nurturing environment for children.

Despite these conflicting desires, Arnhart does not wish to view these areas of moral concern as ones where there are irreconcilable moral viewpoints that cannot be resolved within the context of a naturalistic ethic, with the only appeal being to 'force or fraud'. He rather wishes to claim that slavery and female circumcision, the latter being understood as an extreme attempt on the part of males to control female sexuality, are both unambiguously wrong, and that their wrongness can be shown without appeal to any norm that is transcendent of natural desires. I believe that his arguments clearly fail with respect to both issues.

Let us take the issue of slavery first. Though it would of course be highly politically incorrect of Arnhart to say that slavery might be morally permissible, his position in some ways would seem to favour such a view. One might think that if Arnhart had been writing in 1700 he might have said of slavery what he says of war: that it will never disappear because 'it is rooted in natural desires of human beings as political animals' (p. 148). The natural desires that lead to war, chiefly the desires for dominance and economic advantage, would appear to be the same desires that have led many human societies, perhaps most over the course of human history, to practise some form of slavery. The naturalness of slavery is even shown by its occurrence in the animal world, particularly among insects.[14]

However, as noted, Arnhart does not condone slavery but claims it is morally wrong. His reasons for doing so lie in the fact that

[a]ll human beings, or at least all those not suffering from some abnormal capacity in their emotional and rational capacities, are naturally inclined to assert their independence as human beings with a moral sense governed by sympathy and reciprocity. Consequently, the practice of slavery has always displayed the fundamental contradiction of treating some human beings as if they were not human. (p. 162)

We should begin by noting that the exception Arnhart notes is troubling. What if there are some human individuals who suffer 'some abnormal capacity in their emotional and rational capacities'? Would it be morally permissible to enslave just these individuals, who presumably will not be 'inclined to assert their independence as human beings'? Granted, it is unlikely that such people would all be members of one racial group, and thus one could not justify racial slavery on this basis. It may be racial slavery that Arnhart is chiefly thinking of, though he does not say this, but there have been many forms of slavery that

---

[14] See Arnhart's discussion of ant slavery in *Darwinian Natural Right*, 162–70.

were not racially based, and it is certainly troubling if Arnhart espouses a moral view that could justify any form of slavery.

It is also worth noting that the wrongness of slavery for Arnhart is a contingent fact, as it must be if it is rooted in biological instincts. It could have been that some inferior race of hominids, such as Neanderthal man, could have survived into the modern era, and such a group might have lacked the 'emotional and rational capacities' that makes it wrong to en- slave someone on Arnhart's view. This is worrying because it provides motivation for the kind of racist science that has in the past attempted to prove racial inferiority by appeal to IQ differ- entials or other factors. If such racist science were to succeed or was even thought to succeed in demonstrating inferiority, then the moral bar to exploitation and even enslavement that Arn- hart thinks present would be in danger of vanishing.

In many forms of slavery, slaveowners have, in a self- justifying and probably self-deceptive manner, argued that the slaves, because of their natural inferiority, are better off under slavery. Slaves are seen as like children, incapable of governing themselves. Such arguments can be seen from Aristotle all the way up to the antebellum white Southerners who attempted to justify the system of racial slavery practised in the Confederate states. Arnhart in effect concedes that such arguments would work if their factual premises were correct: 'Slavery would be justified if slaves were fitted by nature for slavery—if they were unable to care for themselves . . .' (p. 162) Arnhart insists, however, that those factual premises are false. All human beings have a natural desire for independence, and thus there will always be resistance on the part of slaves to slavery, a resistance that can be seen in many ways in human history.

Arnhart is undoubtedly correct in maintaining that the factual premises used to justify slavery are false. It is certainly not true that slaves are naturally inferior and that they are therefore better off being slaves. And he is right that this implies that resistance to slavery is natural and is to be expected. However, though Arnhart is right about these things, he is wrong in think- ing that the correctness of his contentions shows that slavery is always unambiguously morally wrong on his premises.

In effect Arnhart assumes that slavery is morally wrong unless the slaveowner can show that slavery as an institution is better, not only for the slaveowner himself, but for the slave. Slavery would be morally justified only if the slaveowner could come up with a justification for slavery that would be acceptable to the slaves. But why should the slaveowner assume such a position? It is natural for the slaveowner to hope that he might convince the slaves that they are better off under his paternalistic rule and care. Perhaps some masters even convinced themselves this was the case. However, this was likely to require a strong dose of self-deception on the part of the master, who surely knew at some level that if the slaves were able to do so, they would opt for freedom. Even the most benevolent slaveowner thus resorted at times to the lash, and slavery as an institution depended, not on the ability of slaveowners to convince the slaves that slavery was good for them, but on the threat and often the exercise of force and physical punishment.

The problem for Arnhart can be put bluntly. Granted that he is right in contending that slavery is not in the best interests of the slave, why should the master care about this? There are perhaps three possible answers to this question. Of the three answers the only one that is really adequate is, in my judgement, not open to Arnhart. The two that are open to him are, unfortunately, woefully inadequate.

One possible answer to the question about why the slaveowner should care about the well-being of the slaves is that the slave is a human being, and that as a human being he or she is entitled to moral respect. There are fundamental duties that humans have to all other humans. Since the slave is a human being, the master ought to treat the slave as a human being, a moral responsibility that follows from the duty to respect the value and dignity of all humans. It is clear that from this perspective slavery is morally wrong. However, it is just as clear that this perspective assumes the kind of universal moral obligation that Arnhart rejects as utopian, presupposing by his own admission a transcendent standard that cannot be naturalistically explained. It is, of course, just such a transcendent standard that is provided in Kierkegaard's view by God's command to love all human beings as our neighbours.

The second possible answer is that the master's own self-interest demands that he consider the well-being of the slave. Since the slave will never be content to be a slave, resistance to slavery is always to be expected. This is I think the answer Arnhart gives to the question, and perhaps it is the best answer he can give. '[A]ny attempt by the masters to ignore the humanity of their slaves is self-defeating. Unlike slave ants, human slaves will resist their enslavement as contrary to their moral sense' (p. 176).

I certainly believe it is true that slaves will seek to resist enslavement, particularly when this is likely to be effective, in ways both small and large. However, the fact that slavery survived successfully in many cultures for thousands of years would seem to imply that such resistance is often not very powerful. So long as the slaveowner has the superior force necessary to crush any resistance, why does the likelihood of such resistance imply that the slaveowner should reject slavery? At most, the likelihood of such resistance and the necessity of using force to put it down would seem to be factors that the slaveowner must consider as costs of 'doing business'. One could imagine that the possibility of resistance might temper the exploitation of slaves. Perhaps a wise slaveowner will be careful in some cases not to treat slaves in ways that might engender resistance that he cannot suppress or that he might prefer not to have to suppress.

The fact is that the history of slavery shows very few examples of successful slave revolts. The abolition of slavery in the United States was not accomplished primarily by the resistance of slaves that made slavery unprofitable and unreasonable for slaveowners, but by a bloody war, inspired in part by the moral dedication of abolitionists committed to the ideal that enslaving human beings was morally wrong, a moral ideal which most people saw as grounded in a transcendent ground. Arnhart is certainly right that slavery is a form of 'exploitation' and that it can only be established by 'coercion and manipulation' (p. 178). What he cannot explain is why such exploitation is morally wrong in cases where the power to coerce the other is present. He himself insists that humans (especially males) have a natural desire to dominate and control others. Why then is it morally wrong to seek to satisfy such a desire in the case where the other cannot effectively resist?

The third possible answer to the question as to why slavery is wrong is to appeal to what Arnhart calls 'reciprocal justice' (p. 149). The notion of 'reciprocal justice' is not, I think, altogether clear. If Arnhart means by this some kind of formal principle that applies to all people impartially, then this would appear to be the kind of 'utopian' principle that Arnhart has rejected. If Arnhart means by this merely that people make reciprocal agreements for their mutual benefit, then it seems that there is still no reason why the slaveowner should be constrained by reciprocal justice, in the kind of case in which the slaves have no real chance of effective resistance. For reciprocal justice extends only as far as utility, and we have already seen that there are cases in which slavery will pay for the slaveowner. Why then should the slaveowner in such a case not continue to hold slaves?

From the point of view of a universal ethic of obligation, the answer to such a question is clear. It is wrong to exploit other humans even if one has the power to do so effectively, because I owe moral respect to all humans. From the perspective of such a universal ethic, one can see the appeal of the slaveowners' desperate arguments to show that slavery is even better for the slaves. Such arguments were not merely intended to pacify the slave, but also to salve the conscience of the slaveowner, most of whom in the American South were at least nominally committed to a Christian ethic of love for all humans that made it impossible for them to acknowledge slavery for what it was: a brutal form of oppression.

In a case where we have a genuine conflict of interest between natural desires, such as the desires of the slaveowner for dominance and the desires of the slave for independence, it is hard to see what resources there are within Arnhart's naturalistic ethic to adjudicate the disputes. It would appear we have the situation he describes as a 'moral tragedy' where 'force and fraud' are the only ways of resolving the issue, precisely the kind of case that makes war inevitable (p. 149). (It is, by the way, noteworthy that enslavement has often been the outcome of war.) Unless the slaveowner has moral obligations to all human beings, it is hard to see why the master has a duty not to hold slaves in the case where he has the ability to do so. It is worth noting that this issue is not merely of theoretical interest. Slavery is still widely practised in certain areas of the world today.[15]

[15] See, for example, Marcus Mabry, 'The Price Tag of Freedom', *Newsweek*, 3 May 1999.

MALE–FEMALE RELATIONS: THE CASE OF FEMALE
CIRCUMCISION

A second area where the problematic character of Arnhart's views can be clearly seen concerns male–female relations. Arnhart believes that the evolutionary history of the human race is such that there are marked psychological as well as physiological differences in men and women. 'Typically male desires incline most men towards dominance, while typically female desires incline most women towards nurturance. Consequently, in every society, the overwhelming number of high-status positions in hierarchies are filled by men' (p. 138). There simply are no known matriarchal societies, according to Arnhart, and this fact cannot be an historical accident but must be rooted in the inherited biological properties of men and women. Because of his belief that this male desire for dominance is part of human nature, Arnhart rejects calls for the abolition of sexually based social roles. Instead he argues that male dominance and female nurturance provide 'complementary expressions of the human nature that has emerged from human evolutionary history' (p. 124). Though I do not find Arnhart's discussion at this point to be completely clear in its implications, presumably he would be inclined to accept some continued male dominance of society, but would advocate that extreme or harsh forms of exploitation be prevented.

One area of male–female relations to which Arnhart gives particular attention is that of female circumcision (clitoridectomy and infibulation), cultural practices often described by critics as female genital mutilation. Female circumcision is widely practised, particularly in the Middle East and in Muslim parts of Africa and Southeast Asia (though it is important to recognize that the practice is not taught in the Koran and is not practised by the majority of Muslims). Arnhart himself cites a researcher who estimates that 60 to 100 million women have undergone the procedure (p. 150). On the face of it, female circumcision does not seem to satisfy natural desires. For the female, the practice 'seriously interferes with sexual function and poses serious health hazards', not to mention making it impossible for the women to experience sexual pleasure (p. 150).

However, as Arnhart himself notes, though 'female circumcision seems so utterly foolish that it is hard to explain why women would submit to such unnecessary pain', some explanation must be given 'for any practice that has been accepted by many people for a long time' (p. 154). Such practices 'probably originated to satisfy some natural desires' and this requires us to 'understand how they conform to the ecological circumstances of some societies' (p. 154).

In reality, given Arnhart's own account of the different natural desires of men and women, it is not too difficult to see what natural desires are being satisfied by this practice. Female circumcision is to be explained in the same way as footbinding in traditional Chinese societies, as a way of reducing the likelihood of female sexual infidelity:

Female circumcision would seem to have a similar purpose [to footbinding]. The cutting off of a woman's clitoris and the sewing up of her vagina seem to reduce her sexual pleasure and thus suppress her inclination to any sexual contact outside of her marriage. Like many other customs that restrict the freedom of women, female circumcision is designed by women and their families to reassure men with resources that a woman's children have been conceived by her husband and not by another man. (p. 155)

I would question Arnhart's contention that this practice has been designed *by women*, but in general this account does provide at least one plausible reason why the practice may have developed.

Given that the practice does have this social function, which counts as a 'natural' one on Arnhart's scheme, why does Arnhart believe that it is morally wrong? A practice that frustrates one set of natural desires (women's desire for sexual pleasure) but realizes another set of natural desires (men's desire to be assured of the sexual fidelity of their wives) would appear to be another case of moral tragedy. In such a case of conflicting natural desires, to what standard can Arnhart appeal, other than the familiar 'force and fraud'? In particular, given that men actually control the societies in question, why should it not be the case that their desires should be satisfied, even if this satisfaction comes at the expense of women?

The actual answer Arnhart gives is that female circumcision is wrong because it not only harms women but actually fails to satisfy the interests of men as well. This is because it is 'probably not completely successful in controlling female sexuality' and, in any case, 'probably frustrates the sexual and familial desires of men as well as women' (p. 160). Arnhart appeals to the fact that 'many men in societies with female circumcision have found that sexual intercourse is more pleasurable for them if their wives have not been mutilated' (p. 160).

What must be asked at this point is for what type of man is such intercourse likely to be more pleasurable? I believe the most reasonable answer is that it will be for men who care about the happiness of their wives. In other words, Arnhart's argument will seem powerful to those men who are already committed to the happiness and well-being of their wives. Such men enjoy sex with women who are capable of pleasure because they receive pleasure from giving pleasure. However, if a man cares only or mainly about his own pleasure and happiness, it is not clear that female circumcision will necessarily reduce his pleasure. It is even likely that there are men whose pleasure is enhanced by the fact that a woman is forced to submit in a joyless way to his sexual advances. And even if the practice of female circumcision does lessen the pleasure of the male, it seems very likely that for some men the increased probability of female fidelity that the practice of female circumcision promotes may more than compensate for any loss of male pleasure. If female circumcision provides an overall benefit for men in a particular social and cultural location by satisfying natural desires, and if the men have the power to ensure that the practice is maintained, why, for Arnhart, is it morally wrong? It would seem that the most Arnhart is entitled to say in such a situation is that we have another case of moral tragedy, in which one set of natural desires conflicts with another set, and where the conflict can only be resolved by appeal to 'force or fraud'.

Arnhart himself senses this problem. He knows that 'natural self-love inclines some human beings to exploit their fellow human beings whenever they can get away with it. Some men desire to exploit women, and masters desire to exploit slaves' (p. 160). Ultimately, his answer to this is simply that, because of our natural moral sense, 'the natural desire of some to exploit others will be checked by the natural desire of their victims to resist exploitation' (p. 160). Tragically, sometimes exploitation is checked in this way and sometimes it is not. What Arnhart cannot explain is why such exploitation is wrong even when we know it will not be adequately 'checked' by the victim.

KIERKEGAARDS UNIVERSAL ETHIC OF LOVE: COMPARISON WITH EVOLUTIONARY ETHICS

If the scope of moral duty is universal, then the situation appears to be very different. If female circumcision is damaging and painful to women, then it can be condemned as morally wrong, even if it does benefit men. For it is not morally right for men to treat women simply as means to their own ends. Women are fully human, and as human beings deserving of moral respect.

From Kierkegaard's point of view, our obligation to love other human beings is an obligation to seek their good. It can hardly be good to enslave another human being to further one's own dominance, or for men to cause pain, mutilation, and frustration for women simply to further their own desires. Every human being is my neighbour, and if I love God I must obey his command to love my neighbour as myself, recognizing my neighbour as rooted in God's love just as I myself am.

Of course Arnhart and Kierkegaard are not the only moral alternatives. I will in the next two chapters examine other naturalistic meta-ethical perspectives. And one might explore other meta-ethical traditions, not only those rooted in Christianity but in the other great theistic and non-theistic religions as well. However, the kind of evolutionary ethic presented by Arnhart provides a particularly sharp contrast with Kierkegaard.

As we saw in Chapters 5–9, Kierkegaard stresses the fact that the love for the neighbour commanded by God is not reducible to those 'natural' loves found in all human societies for family and friends. The neighbour is not 'the other-I' to whom I am bound by natural ties of affection grounded in biology, but the 'first-you', to whom I am linked by the fact that we are equally human beings made in the image of God. The obligation to love the neighbour cannot then be understood simply as a broadening or extension of maternal affection or any other natural kind of sympathy. From Kierkegaard's point of view, it is something new, something that points to the fact that human beings are not merely biological creatures but spiritual beings.

Arnhart shows commendable honesty in admitting that a naturalistic ethic cannot explain such a universal obligation. He is, however, confused in thinking that he has an adequate basis for condemning exploitative practices such as slavery and female circumcision without the resources provided by such a universal obligation. And in practice he does—inconsistently—assume the standpoint of universal moral obligation and argues that slavery and female circumcision are wrong because they are not in the best interests of slaves and women.

Why should not Arnhart simply bite the bullet at this point and admit that some exploitative practices may not be morally wrong? Why should he not say with Thrasymachus that 'justice is the interest of the stronger'? I know no decisive argument that would prevent him from taking such a stance. I suspect that he would reject this option for the same reason that I think he actually rejects such practices as slavery and female circumcision. That is simply that he knows that these practices are morally wrong, and as a person with moral concerns he does not wish to endorse them. In effect, I would argue that Arnhart's own moral instincts override his moral theory at this point.

It is instructive to see that this is so. I would argue that a great many people are in the same situation as Arnhart. They recognize—rightly—moral truths that are too obvious to deny, even if their moral theories do not accommodate these truths. I do not claim that they are unreasonable to do this. One of the strengths of Arnhart's position is that he is committed to moral claims that are objectively true and he seeks to make his theory fit those moral facts. If his theory does not really fit those claims, I think it is praiseworthy that he holds stubbornly to those moral truths. This is a stance that will be particularly worth recalling when we consider in Chapter 12 the standpoint of the moral relativist, who is willing to deny those moral truths that cannot be adequately explained within a naturalistic framework.

11

Contemporary Meta-Ethical Alternatives:
Humanistic Naturalism

The evolutionary naturalism illustrated by Arnhart attempts to reduce moral obligation to natural moral feelings: 'The fact of obligation is nothing more than the feeling of obligation.'[1] If one thinks, as Kierkegaard and many other moral philosophers do, that moral obligations are universal in scope (in the sense that we have some duties that extend to all persons and thus no person is excluded from the scope of our moral concern) such a view is inadequate, for it is clear that our natural feelings of sympathy do not extend to all human persons. I don't mean, of course, that there is no connection between morality and emotion at all, but that moral obligations cannot be grounded simply in natural emotions. It is noteworthy, therefore, that the other naturalistic meta-ethical framework I wish to examine recognizes the limitations of such an appeal and attempts to ground morality primarily in reason and not in emotions that may or may not be present.

This second form of naturalism I shall call naturalistic humanism, and I will employ David Gauthier as my exemplar of the position. In *Morals By Agreement* Gauthier recognizes that duty must be distinguished from desires of any kind, including 'tuistic' desires to help other people that are grounded in empathy or sympathy.[2] Such desires may or may not be present in actual humans, and they cannot provide a firm foundation for what Gauthier calls the 'stern visage' of duty (p. 1). For Gauthier it is obviously important that moral obligations are binding on people who lack natural feelings of sympathy for others:

---

[1] Arnhart, *Darwinian Natural Right*, 81.

[2] David Gauthier, *Morals by Agreement* (Oxford: Clarendon Press, 1986). Subsequent references to this work in this chapter are denoted by page nos. in parentheses.

morality, as a system of rationally required constraints, is possible if the constraints are generated simply by the understanding that they make possible the more effective realization of one's preferences, whatever one's interests or preferences may be. One is then not able to escape morality by professing a lack of moral feeling or concern, or a lack of some other particular interest or attitude, because morality assumes no such affective basis. (pp. 102–3)

Such a view clearly differs from Arnhart's evolutionary naturalism, and is in my view superior in this respect. It is of vital importance that precisely those people who lack natural sympathy for others should fall under the authority of moral obligations to those others.

Gauthier's work falls into the distinguished tradition of social contract theories of morality, drawing on such classical modern philosophers as Thomas Hobbes and John Locke, as well as contemporary thinkers such as John Rawls, though the similarities to other philosophers should not mask the originality of Gauthier's own account.

CONTRACT VIEWS OF MORALITY AND LEARNING ABOUT LIFE IN KINDERGARTEN

The seminal insight that underlies a social contract theory of morality is simple enough for a child to understand, though when developed with the rigour of a Gauthier such a theory can be complex and difficult indeed. But let us begin with what is simple.

James and Susan are kindergarten pupils. On the playground James likes to pull Susan's pony tail. Susan likes to make fun of James and call him names. The conflict escalates. James pulls harder on the pony tail and actually pulls out hair. Susan in her pain is furious and gives James a well-deserved slap. Both James and Susan have acted on their natural desires. However, despite being able to do what each wishes to do, neither is very happy. If James and Susan have enough maturity to reflect on their situation, they may negotiate a truce. James agrees not to pull Susan's hair and Susan agrees not to make fun of James. Both Susan and James are willing to accept a constraint on their natural desires because of the consequences of not doing so.

The kindergarten classroom of Susan and James resembles in important respects the 'state of nature' postulated by Thomas Hobbes. In our account of the classroom we have ignored the role of the teacher, assuming that Susan and James are interacting on the playground without a central authority to intervene and mediate their dispute. The state of nature that Hobbes describes is a human society that lacks a state or any other authority with the power to enforce social rules. In such a state of nature Hobbes famously claimed that there would be a 'war of all against all' and that in consequence human life would be 'solitary, poor, nasty, brutish, and short'.[3] Our hypothetical kindergarten does not quite descend to such a level, perhaps because in real classrooms there are teachers and principals. Nevertheless, Susan and James illustrate how individuals who interact may each worsen his or her own situation by following natural desires, and thus why it can be reasonable in such a situation for participants to try to reach an agreement on basic rules of behaviour that will be binding on all, and which will be for the ultimate good of all.

Note that for such an agreement to be reasonable for James and Susan it is not necessary for them to have any affection for each other. Both Susan and James primarily want to satisfy their own desires. Presumably, if either had complete power to act on those desires with impunity no agreement would be advantageous for the individual with the power. But in the real world Susan and James both have to reckon with the consequences of their behaviour and those consequences include the reactions of the other to that behaviour. So although Susan and James may not care about each other or even like each other, it still may 'pay off' for them to 'be nice' to each other in ways that require them to curb their natural desires. All that is required for this is that they recognize that the agreement is in the best interest of each of them. Of course if they do have positive feelings for each other, that makes it easier to accept the constraints of morality, but such feelings are not the basis of any moral obligation.

---

[3] Thomas Hobbes, *Leviathan*, ed. Richard Tuck (Cambridge: Cambridge University Press, 1996), 88–9.

A social contract theory of morality is one in which the situation of Susan and James is taken as a miniature model of human society. Moral obligation comes into being as a result of an agreement, a rational bargain that constrains the interests of everyone but which ultimately serves the interests of everyone. We shall see that many of the features of the agreement of Susan and James are present in Gauthier's account of the social agreement that constitutes moral obligation.

VALUE AND UTILITY MAXIMIZATION

Gauthier's theory begins with a slightly modified version of the conception of human beings that dominates contemporary economic theory, the conception of 'economic man' that sees human beings as 'rational maximizers'. In this ideal conception (which Gauthier recognizes does not fully correspond with actual human nature) persons seek to maximize 'utility', which is a measure of satisfaction of their 'considered preferences', such preferences being understood as those that are 'stable under expression and reflection' and that are manifested in both choices and attitudes (pp. 32–3).

Rational maximizers aim at achieving the greatest possible amount of value that it is possible for them to achieve. Gauthier rejects the notion of 'value' as an objective quality, however, in favour of the view that value simply designates the satisfaction of a person's considered preferences, whatever those may be. 'Value is then not an inherent characteristic of things or states of affairs, not something existing as part of the ontological furniture of the universe in a manner quite independent of persons and their activities. Rather, value is created or determined through preference' (p. 47). Such preferences are both individual and temporally limited to the present. The perspective of economic man is one characterized by private goods and mutual unconcern; other people and even my own future are important to me only insofar as I presently care about them (pp. 38, 87).

Gauthier recognizes that this subjectivist perspective on value is at odds with ordinary ways of thinking, and even conflicts with ordinary language: 'Our typical evaluative terms presuppose a common standpoint which may or may not be shared by the evaluator. A good eating apple is thus one that is commonly or usually preferred for eating' (pp. 53–4). Nothing philosophically interesting follows from this fact about language, however, since a person can use such evaluative terms without personally being committed to the standpoint they seem to embody. Gauthier endorses what J. L. Mackie has called an 'error theory' of value: 'We suppose that persons objectify their preferences and so come to consider their subjective attitudes and affections as properties characterizing the objects of their preferences' (p. 58). Most people think of values as objective, but they are simply mistaken.

It seems to me that this subjectivism about value is logically independent of at least some of the elements of Gauthier's theory of moral obligation. He could, I believe, adopt an objective theory of value and use that as a basis for his view of morality as rooted in an agreement, although this would certainly change the shape of what he says about many issues. However, the subjectivism about values does, I believe, make his project more interesting in several respects. As a consistent naturalist, he sees no way of selecting some desires as 'natural' and therefore 'good' and 'desirable', as does Arnhart. Gauthier is not therefore tempted to the mistake of equating what is desired with what is desirable, and in general avoids the problem as to how values are to be generated from natural facts. All preferences are created equal, and as preferences are neither rational nor irrational. What can be rational or irrational is behaviour intended to maximize the satisfaction of preference. If successful, Gauthier would be able to show that even in a world that lacks objective value, moral obligations can still have a kind of objective reality, perhaps as an ideal on which rational agents would converge, and that would be no mean achievement.

Gauthier has great faith in the virtues of a free market; he agrees with Adam Smith that when markets operate properly individuals who seek their own utility will nevertheless act in ways that lead to the good of all. The constraints of morality are unnecessary when markets operate as they are supposed to, with free exchanges of goods and perfect competition. A perfect market would be a 'morally free zone, a zone within which the constraints of morality would have no place' (p. 84). The actual world, however, does not contain societies that realize these conditions. Economic exchanges are often not free, partly because the individuals making the exchanges do not do so from an equal basis. Force and fraud contaminate the market. Even when these conditions are absent, markets are plagued by 'externalities,' which come in two forms: 'free-riders' and 'parasites'. The free-rider is exemplified by listeners who enjoy public radio but do not subscribe; they enjoy benefits without sharing in the costs, as they should in a perfect market. The parasite is someone whose economic gain actually comes at the expense of others, such as the factory owner who cheaply disposes of toxins by dumping them in a river, saving himself money but costing those downstream clean drinking water. According to Gauthier it is externalities that make morality necessary: 'Morality arises from market failure' (p. 84).

A society characterized by morality is one in which utility maximization, with all individuals pursuing their own individual preferences, has been replaced by what Gauthier terms 'optimality maximization', in which individuals strive for an optimal outcome for all, and do not consider simply their own utilities. But why should individuals who are utility-maximizers be willing to do this?

PRISONER'S DILEMMA SITUATIONS AND THE EMERGENCE OF MORALITY

The answer to this question for Gauthier lies in the consideration of a classic problem called 'The Prisoner's Dilemma'. A prosecutor holds two individuals, Ed and Fred, who have committed a serious crime, but the prosecutor does not have enough evidence to convict the two men of this serious crime. She does have evidence to convict them of a lesser charge. She visits each of the prisoners and makes the following offer: 'Confess to the serious crime, and if your partner in crime does not confess, I will convince the Judge to sentence you to one year and your partner to ten. If, however, your partner confesses and you do not, you will get ten years while he gets only one. If neither of you confesses, you will receive two years for the lesser crime. If both of you confess to the serious crime, you will each receive five years.'

How should Ed and Fred rationally respond to this offer? If they cannot communicate, it looks as if each should confess, for confession seems rational no matter what the confederate does. Take Ed's perspective, for example. If Fred confesses and Ed does not, then Ed will get ten years. By confessing in that case he will get only five years. If, on the other hand, Fred does not confess, Ed will get only one year. So it looks like confession is a more rational strategy, regardless of what the other party does. Furthermore, since each will know that confession will seem a rational strategy, it is likely that the other will confess. In that case, if Ed does not confess he gets ten years. From the viewpoint of utility maximization, confession looks like the rational strategy. Of course if the two could reach an agreement that neither will confess, both would be better off. But such an agreement will lead to a better outcome for both only if each is assured the other party will abide by it; if Ed agrees with Fred that neither will confess, but Fred does not abide by the agreement, then Fred is better off but Ed is worse off.

In the 'state of nature', prisoner's dilemma outcomes are inevitable, Gauthier thinks. In such a world we are all condemned to 'non-optimal outcomes that, in 'Prisoner's Dilemma-type' situations, may be little better than disastrous' (p. 82). However, when we become aware of the undesirable character of these consequences, we are led to see the reasonableness of an agreement in which individuals give up the right to pursue their own utility—precisely so as to be able better to secure their own utility. Just as Susan and James limit their natural desires for the sake of satisfying their own considered preferences in light of the other's reactions to their behaviour, so individuals in the state of nature accept constraints on their own utility-maximization in light of their knowledge of how others will respond to their behaviour: 'Practical reason is linked to ... individual utility, and rational constraints on the pursuit of interest have themselves a foundation in the interest they constrain. Duty overrides advantage, but the acceptance of duty is truly advantageous' (p. 2). Rational maximizers find it rational to cooperate with each other in ways that involve limitation of preferences, thereby to secure the satisfaction of preferences.

On this view morality does not arise from the commands of a loving God or the instincts that have been selected by biological evolution. Rather, the foundation of morality is a social agreement and the foundation of the agreement lies in our own self-interest.

Many questions emerge at this point. I shall examine three of the most important ones. First, what is the content of the agreement? What exactly do rational maximizers agree upon when they opt for cooperation? Secondly, what is the nature of the agreement? Is it an actual agreement or a hypothetical agreement? If the latter, what relevance does such an agreement have to actual human beings? Finally, why should the agreement be kept? Even if we grant that it would be rational for utility maximizers to negotiate such an agreement, it does not follow that they also have reason to live up to the agreement. Consider some particular individual Jerry who is a utility maximizer. Perhaps the most beneficial outcome for Jerry is a situation in which he agrees with others to seek their mutual good, while Jerry considers himself free to violate the agreement when it is in his best interest to do so.

THE SOCIAL BARGAIN: THE PRINCIPLE OF 'MINIMAX CONCESSION'

Since Gauthier rejects any objective theory of value, his account of the social agreement that underlies morality cannot specify the pay-off in terms of some objective amount of value, either for individuals or for society as a whole. Rather, he thinks of the outcome of the rational bargain in terms of the relative concessions each must make in the satisfaction of their preferences. Since there is no common unit of objective value, I cannot compare the value of the goods I must give up for the sake of morality to those others must give up. However, I can compare the proportion of my preferences that I can satisfy and that I must limit to those that others must give up, and my 'concession' can thus be 'relative' to those others must make.

Underlying any such rational bargain is the view that cooperation will allow human persons to achieve goods they would not otherwise be able to realize. One difference between Gauthier's view of society and my kindergarten example is that in society cooperation not only limits the harms done by people to each other (as was the case for Susan and James), but makes possible new goods that would otherwise be unachievable. The 'excess' utility that cooperation makes possible constitutes a 'co-operative surplus' which is to be distributed to those who participate 'in the interaction required to provide it' (p. 143).

Presumably, even in the state of nature there are some preferences that people would be able to satisfy. There would be no reason for individuals to be willing to give up these goods for the sake of cooperation in society, since they represent what could be had even without the constraints of the agreement. There is no incentive for morality unless the acceptance of the limits of morality will make possible goods not otherwise obtainable.

Gauthier argues that a rational bargain would centre around the idea of what he calls 'minimax relative concession'. The idea is that a rational person would accept the constraints of a social bargain 'only if the greatest or *maximum* relative concession it requires, is as small as possible, or a *minimum*, that is, is no greater than the maximum relative concession required by every other outcome' (p. 137). It is this solution, he says, that allows each person who is to be a participant in the process to 'claim the co-operative surplus that affords him maximum utility' (p. 143).

When we reflect on this principle of minimax relative concession, we can see, thinks Gauthier, that it is not only a rational bargain for utility-maximizing individuals to make. It is at the same time, and for the same reasons 'a rational and impartial basis for co-operative interaction' and this is enough to establish 'its credentials as a moral principle' (p. 146). The principle can express both the demands of utility and morality: the first as the outcome of a bargain struck by utility maximizers, the second as the basis of the cooperative behaviour agreed to in the bargain. It can in that way both be grounded in utility maximization while at the same time constraining such maximizing behaviour (p. 146). 'Impartiality and rationality coincide in bargaining' (p. 155).

For Gauthier, the individual who makes such a bargain is not a 'dupe' (p. 169). She does not promise to keep the agreement no matter what other parties to the agreement do, but rather to comply only if others do so as well. In this way 'she ensures that those not disposed to fair co-operation do not enjoy the benefits of any co-operation, thus making this unfairness costly to themselves, and so irrational' (p. 179). Without this policy of 'narrow' compliance, there would be no incentive for others to comply with the social agreement and morality would break down.

To decide what portion of the cooperative surplus is due a person, it is necessary first to determine what the individual 'brings to the table', so to speak. What would a person be able to achieve by himself apart from cooperation? Gauthier speaks of this as the individual's 'base utility', which is in turn a product of the individual's 'initial factor endowment'.[4] An important part of his theory is acceptance of what he calls the 'Lockean proviso'. In Locke's account of the origin of private property, Locke claims that people have a right to appropriate natural goods by 'mixing their labor' with those goods so long as they leave 'enough, and as good' of the appropriated materials for others.[5] Without this proviso, one might think that the appropriation of natural resources would be unfair to those who do not have an opportunity so to benefit. Such a proviso is important, because if people believe that what individuals 'own' (and thus the initial factor endowments and base utilities they bring to the bargain) is the result of exploitation, then the resulting bargain will not be regarded as fair.

Gauthier illustrates this by an imaginary slave society (pp. 190–2). In this society, the masters have to use many resources to keep the slaves in line, carrying out harsh punishments, and such a situation is a drain on their resources. The situation of the slaves is of course even worse than that of the masters. If the masters proposed a bargain to the slaves in which the masters would cease to use physical force to keep the slaves in line in exchange for the slaves' willing servitude, justifying the agreement on the grounds that it would better the situation of both

---

[4] Gauthier's view here is controversial. He rejects the view of Rawls, Dworkin, and other liberal theorists that goods made possible by natural talents that one has by virtue of what might be called 'the natural lottery' are goods that society may have some claim to, in favour of a more individualistic view in which persons are entitled to what their talents enable them to achieve, though he does not go so far as Nozick. See Gauthier, *Morals By Agreement*, 272–7.

[5] John Locke, *Two Treatises of Government*, ed. Thomas I. Cook (New York: Hafner, 1947), 134.

slaves and masters, the slaves might be rational to make such an agreement. They would not, however, be rational to keep such an agreement, since it was made under a very unequal situation. If the masters are foolish enough to disarm themselves, the slaves could rationally rebel and refuse to comply with the agreement.

It is important then that the initial bargain be made in a situation that all parties will regard as fair. Gauthier attempts to secure this condition by a modified version of Locke's proviso, namely by requiring that each individual's initial endowment 'affording him a base utility not included in the co-operative surplus, must be considered to have been initially acquired by him without taking advantage of any other person, or, more precisely, any other co-operator' (pp. 200–1). In this way, the initial situation will be a fair one, in which no individual's endowment will be the result of taking advantage of others. Of course in real life what people actually possess is often the result of such exploitation. What is important is that any good possessed as a result of taking advantage of others not be considered part of the 'base utility' which an individual brings to the table as his own. It is not something to which the individual has an entitlement, and cannot be regarded as inviolable. Such a constraint on private property, Gauthier says 'is part of morals by agreement, not in being the object of an agreement among rational individuals, but in being a precondition to such agreement' (p. 192).

Gauthier rounds out his account of the social agreement by a defence of his own view of what he calls, following Rawls, the 'Archimedean point for judging the basic structure of society'. Such a point is 'that position one must occupy, if one's own decisions are to possess the moral force needed to govern the moral realm' (p. 233). For Gauthier such a point is occupied by an 'ideal actor' who is a godlike figure in being fully informed about human nature and society and completely impartial. This impartiality is secured by the device of imagining a person who knows she will occupy a particular position in society but is ignorant of what that position will be.

The ideal actor may not collapse the identities of the persons, any one of whom she may be, into a single identity, or their utilities into a single utility, which we would then endeavour to maximize. She must maintain their separate identities and utilities, and so must choose as if she were bargaining as each person. This is the essential feature of Archimedean choice. (p. 265)

Such a standpoint, he thinks, is one with which each person can identify, and yet which is independent of any particular characteristics.

When we look at society from this Archmidean point, Gauthier thinks that it is clear that the ideal actor will endorse the principle of minimax relative concession. Thus, 'a decision made in complete ignorance of one's identity proves coincident with an agreement made among persons individuated in all possible ways. The lines of rationality that lead from each individual to converge on the ideal actor are the same lines that lead from each to converge on a rational bargain' (p. 266).

HYPOTHETICAL AND ACTUAL AGREEMENTS

If morality consists in a social agreement, what kind of agreement is this? Specifically, is it an actual agreement, or a merely hypothetical one? The idealized character of the agreement Gauthier describes suggests that the latter is the case, since in the actual world people cannot be assumed to be purely rational 'utility maximizers' who negotiate freely from a position of equality, being fully informed about the costs and benefits of transactions. Gauthier appears to agree with this: 'We have not supposed that actual moral constraints represent the outcome of real agreement, but we have argued that, if they are to be justified, we must be able to consider them as objects of a hypothetical *ex ante* agreement, the rationality of which we now recognize *ex post*' (p. 339). The hypothetical character of the agreement seems clear in the following passage as well:

A rational bargain ensures the participation of each in reaching an agreed outcome. As we noted at the beginning of this chapter, not all co-operation is based on actual agreement. We may not then suppose that every joint strategy is chosen by a bargaining procedure in which all of those basing their action on the strategy participated. But for co-operation to be rational, we must suppose that the joint strategy would have been chosen through such a procedure, so that each person, recognizing this, may voluntarily accept the strategy. (pp. 128–9)

However, Gauthier at times wavers in his acceptance of the hypothetical character of the agreement, perhaps recognizing that there may be problems grounding morality in an agreement that never took place: 'This agreement, if rational, will ensure optimality. It may of course be implicit rather than explicit, an understanding or convention rather than a contract. But it is not a mere fiction, since it gives rise to a new mode of interaction, which we identify as co-operation' (p. 117). This quote does not say that the agreement is not hypothetical, but only that it is 'not a fiction'. Perhaps Gauthier means only that the cooperation the agreement inspires is actual. However, it seems to me that an agreement that inspires such cooperation must be more than hypothetical itself. So is the social agreement hypothetical or is it an actual, though only implicit, agreement?

Perhaps it is both. I suspect Gauthier wants to claim that actual moral obligations must be grounded in actual agreements, even if those agreements are embodied in implicit understandings and are not the result of an explicit contract. However, in order for us to see those agreements as binding on us, we must be able to assess them in light of a hypothetical ideal agreement, the one we would have made if we were fully rational and in the appropriate bargaining situation. We thus have an actual agreement, whose rationality is to be assessed in light of an ideal agreement.

Actual moral principles are not in general those to which we should have agreed in a fully rational bargain, but it is reasonable to adhere to them in so far as they offer a reasonable approximation to ideal principles. We may defend actual moral principles by reference to ideal co-operative arrangements, and the closer the principles fit, the stronger the defence. (p. 168)

Though Gauthier does not in *Morals by Agreement* give a detailed account of how close the approximation must be in order for moral principles to be binding, he does claim that actual moral principles can be defended as grounded in the principles that would have been chosen by ideal rational bargainers:

Let us conclude this discussion by noting that many of our actual moral principles and practices are in effect applications of the requirements of minimax relative concession to particular contexts. We may suppose that promise-keeping, truth-telling, fair dealing, are to be defended by showing that adherence to them permits persons to co-operate in ways that may be expected to equalize, at least roughly, the relative benefits afforded by interaction. These are among the core practices of the morality that we may commend to each individual by showing that it commands his rational agreement. (p. 156)

The ideal, hypothetical agreement plays a crucial role, since it is only to the degree that our actual agreements approximate it that they are rationally binding. The hypothetical ideal is what gives objectivity to morality for Gauthier. Without such an ideal we would be left with a plethora of culturally diverse agreements, none of which would be rationally binding on individuals. In the following chapter I shall examine a view of morality, defended by Gilbert Harman, that sees it as consisting of just this kind of culturally relative agreements.

MORAL COMPLIANCE: WHY SHOULD INDIVIDUALS KEEP THE BARGAIN?

Before moving to critical examination, I want to explore one final area in Gauthier's account: the compliance issue. Clearly, it is one thing to make an agreement, and another to keep the agreement. There are certainly times when it might pay off for a rational maximizer to negotiate an agreement that it will not pay the maximizer to keep. Anyone who has played a multi-person strategy game, such as Diplomacy, will recognize the truth of this observation, since the winner of such a game typically will be a person who makes various strategic alliances, but who select-ively, at a crucial moment in the game, betrays one or more allies. To take a real life example, a student at a school with an honour code that requires an explicit promise not to cheat may make such a promise, agreeing to the code in order to be admitted to the school. However, circumstances may well arise in which more of the student's preferences will be satisfied by cheating than by not cheating, particularly if the cheating is of such a nature that it is extremely unlikely that it will be detected. It is worth noting at this point that a very high percentage of Ameri-can students admit to cheating at some point in their academic careers, so it must not be uncommon for such behaviour to be perceived by students as utility-maximizing.

Gauthier is well aware of this problem and devotes a lot of attention to its solution. He appears to develop a number of different lines of thought in response to it. One response he makes is simply to concede that reason does not always require compliance with morality: 'In reconciling reason and morals, we do not claim that it is never rational for one person to take advantage of another, never rational to ignore the proviso, never rational to comply with unfair practices. Such a claim would be false' (p. 232). He admits that sometimes a rational maximizer who has no emotional bond to morality will behave in immoral ways. 'There are circumstances in which it is rational for one person to take advantage of another. Reason and justice there part company, leaving justice with no hold on the non-tuistic individual' (pp. 312–13).

Gauthier does argue, however, that the circumstances in which this will occur are not common. In doing so he develops two different lines of argument, one that appeals to self-interest and one that deserts the appeal to self-interested 'reason' in favour of an appeal to emotion. The appeal to self-interest is straightforward, and I will consider it first.

A person who is committed to morality is described by Gauthier as a 'constrained maximizer' and such an individual is contrasted with a 'straightforward maximizer' (pp. 171–2). One might think that the straightforward maximizer follows a better strategy. For either others will abide by morality or they will not. If they do, then I will get the benefit of their constraint even if I always maximize my own utility. If they do not, then I am not duped by their failure to abide by the social agreement, as I seek my own best good in the situation. Either way I am better off.

Gauthier claims that this argument (which I have paraphrased) 'would be valid only if the probability of others acting co-operatively were ... independent of one's own disposition' (p. 172). But this is not so, since others will act cooperatively only towards those whom they believe are also committed to cooperation. In effect, if I do not comply with the social agreement then others will be less likely to comply as well, particularly in their relations with me. We will all lose the benefits of cooperation, and we will all be worse off, including myself. Faced with a choice of adopting a disposition to be a rational unconstrained maximizer and a constrained maximizer, we can see the rationality of opting for the latter disposition.

It follows that a constrained maximizer is not a dupe who simply allows herself to be exploited willy-nilly. Rather, if a constrained maximizer finds herself among straightforward maximizers, she will also behave 'as a straightforward maximizer, acting on the individual strategy that maximizes her utility given the strategies she expects the others to employ' (p. 169). The implied threat in the conditionality of everyone's commitment to morality is necessary if morality is to be linked to our self-interest, for without this conditionality, it would be all too easy for free-riders and parasites to take advantage of the morally committed. It is clear that this argument for compliance does not even attempt to produce a conclusion that a person must always abide by morality, and we can now understand why Gauthier admits that it is possible for reason and morality to part company. It seems all too likely that there will be at least some times when all of us find ourselves in the company of those for whom the characterization 'straightforward maximizer' appears charitable and even euphemistic, and our own best 'rational strategy' will be to act in the same manner towards them, if we are concerned with maximizing utility.

The weakness of this first line of response to the compliance problem makes it understandable that Gauthier should look for another reason for keeping one's moral commitments. Remarkably, after developing a theory of morality wholly grounded in the 'non-tuistic' conception of human beings as self-interested rational maximizers, he argues that morality requires a link to the emotions if it is to survive. To be fully moral we must be more than economic creatures: 'Properly understood, the just man is the person who, recognizing a certain course of action to be just, finds his feelings engaged by that recognition and so finds herself moved to adhere to that course of action because of its justice' (p. 328). Such an engagement of feelings is necessary, because economic man is not truly committed to morality and cannot be trusted to comply with its dictates:

Economic man lacks the capacity to be truly the just man. He understands the arguments for moral constraint, but he regards such constraint as an evil from which he would be free. Given the opportunity to use morality as an instrument of domination, he unhesitatingly does so, because his concern with morality is purely an instrumental one, and his goals to which morality is instrumental are asocial. (p. 328)

If it turns out that if human beings are really exactly like the economic creatures assumed by rational choice theory, the prospects for morality would not be very bright. It is only because we are *not* simply economic people that morality can work: 'Because we real human beings share some of his [economic man's] characteristics, morals by agreement afford us a beneficial constraint, and because we are nevertheless not economic men and women, we can be constrained' (p. 317). Even though the constraints of morality are justified by appeal to self-interest, they are not constraints that are applicable only to people who are wholly self-interested. Rather, those people who through morality have learned to act cooperatively with each other may learn to value participation in social activities and the morality that makes such participation possible. Though morality is not initially developed on the basis of 'tuistic values', those who accept those constraints may develop the tuistic values necessary to keep the moral project alive (p. 338).

SOME PROBLEM AREAS

It is now time to take stock of Gauthier's account and compare it to Kierkegaard's theistic alternative. There are a number of areas where Gauthier's theory looks quite problematic in comparison with Kierkegaard's view that moral obligations are rooted in divine commands. None of the difficulties I shall outline are in themselves decisive; someone who is committed to metaphysical naturalism, and therefore to ethical naturalism, may regard the problems simply as a price that must be paid. However, for those who are open to non-naturalistic alternatives, I believe that these problems are significant. I shall examine just three points of difficulty, though a number of other issues could be discussed.

1. *The ground of moral obligation.* The first problematic area concerns the ground of moral obligation. Gauthier attempts to show that morality as a constraint on the satisfaction of preferences can be understood as a strategy employing an agreement that helps individuals satisfy those preferences more effectively.

We have just examined his views on the rationality of compliance with the agreement, and I do not believe that his answer to the question as to why individuals should abide by morality is adequate. I believe, along with many moral philosophers and many ordinary people, that genuine moral obligations have a kind of absolute character. Someone who feels bound to act morally simply 'most of the time' or when it appears to pay to do so, or when some other condition applies, does not really recognize the true character of moral obligation.

We saw above that Gauthier gives two different answers to the compliance question. The first is to attempt to show that compliance is in my self-interest, at least most of the time, since if I do not comply with the agreement, others are less likely to comply, particularly in their dealings with me. It is certainly correct that people are less likely to deal fairly with people whom they do not think can be trusted to deal fairly. For this reason it does seem that for the most part it would 'pay' for people to attempt to give the appearance to others that they are morally observant. A shopkeeper who wants repeat customers has a reason to appear honest to those customers. And no doubt it is impossible to appear to be moral to others unless one actually does behave in a moral manner a good deal of the time.

However, there are certainly occasions on which people can deviate from moral behaviour with only a very slight chance of being detected, or even with no chance of this occurring at all. A waitress who gets cash tips might have problems with the tax collectors if she reports no income of this kind at all. However, there are certainly times when the waitress could moderately under-report cash tips with no realistic chance whatsoever of being detected by the tax men. And there are many other occasions on which a shrewd utility maximizer could take advantage of others with no fear of detection.

Perhaps at this point Gauthier will respond that if one individual plays fast and loose with morality this will contribute to a general breakdown of moral bonds, and we will all be worse off. However, it seems unlikely that this will occur in cases where my deviation from morality is undetected. Since no one else will know about my moral defection, it will not serve as a bad example to others.

In any case deviations from moral behaviour are distressingly common in actual human societies. Gauthier argues that morality is rooted in a bargain we make with others, in which we agree to certain constraints on the condition that others will abide by the same constraints. However, we know that in reality many others will violate the agreement *regardless of what we do*. Many other students in my class will cheat whether I do so or not. Many taxpayers will cheat whether I cheat on my return or not.

The underlying issue here is the hypothetical character of the agreement that is supposed to be the basis of morality. I do not think purely hypothetical agreements can be binding on actual individuals. As I claimed in Chapter 5, if I were to visit the Vatican and hear an appeal to help support its artistic beauty, I might promise to help. But the fact that I would do this if certain conditions were fulfilled does not mean I now have such an obligation.

Recognizing this, Gauthier asserts that the agreement that is the basis of morality is not merely hypothetical, but is a kind of implicit agreement or convention. The hypothetical agreement is an ideal against which the actual agreement is to be measured. However, if the gap between the ideal and the actual situation of society is too great, the hypothetical agreement will have little relevance to us. Suppose it to be true that in a society of pure rational maximizers who are equal, completely informed, and who accept Gauthier's version of Locke's proviso, a principle of relative minimax concession would be agreed upon by all. In actual human societies it is evident that people are not purely rational, not equal in status or power, and not completely informed. Nor is their 'initial endowment' usually acquired in a fair manner that respects the Lockean proviso. Why is it relevant to actual humans what people in such an ideal situation would do?

This question is even more pressing when we consider the fact that we know that many people in reality will violate whatever implicit moral agreements are present in society when they know they can do so with impunity and without detection. Perhaps it would be rational for me to comply with morality if I had good reason to think most other people would do so as well, but if the latter condition is not fulfilled this hypothetical fact generates no obligation.

It is probably for this reason that Gauthier himself shifts horses, as we saw, and claims that human beings are not, after all, purely economic creatures. It is possible, he says, for humans to develop an emotional connection to morality, to be just because they care about justice. Furthermore, they must do so if morality is to survive. Later in this chapter I shall discuss the question as to whether this view that morality can be valued intrinsically is consistent with the subjectivist theory of value Gauthier adopts. Here I shall simply point out that such feelings cannot provide a sure basis for moral obligation. Genuine moral obligations must hold whether such feelings are present or not. I freely grant that it is a good thing for us to learn to value morality for its own sake, and perhaps it is necessary to do this if moral obligations are to be effective. However, such feelings cannot constitute obligations; the obligations must be real for me rationally to learn to appreciate and value them.

How does Gauthier's view compare with Kierkegaard's divine command ethic on this point? On Kierkegaard's view the basis of my obedience to God's commands lies in God's goodness and love, towards me and all others. From Kierkegaard's perspective, all human persons have good reason to obey the dictates of morality, because all are the recipients of God's love and all were created to enjoy a relationship with God. In obeying God a person is also seeking his or her own deepest good, because God's commands are aimed at the good, both of those to whom the commands are addressed and others. Those who obey God's commands are those who in the long run discover their true selves and true happiness. However, this does not mean, as we saw in Chapter 6, that my motive for moral action is simply a concern for my own happiness. Nor is moral obligation rooted simply in a fear of divine power, as Gauthier seems to think would be the case in a theistic ethic.[6] Rather, it is the love and gratitude that is owed and naturally

---

[6] Gauthier considers a theistic basis for ethics in *Morals By Agreement* on p. 238, but thinks that God could only provide a basis for ethics through divine power and sanctions: 'The demands of a theistic morality, in its pure form, must appear to beings who view themselves as rational and independent actors in the way expressed by Hobbes—"there is no kicking against the pricks." Only the power of the proprietor makes his demands relevant to utility-maximizers, and we, unlike Hobbes, reject might as the basis of right.' It is

given to God as the one who created me and has given me all good things that ideally motivates obedience to divine commands.

2. *The scope of moral obligation.* If morality is grounded in a self-interested bargain, then its scope would appear to extend only to those who are party to the agreement. Gauthier specifically holds that rational individuals agree to constrain their preferences because by doing so they make possible cooperation with others that produces a 'surplus of utility'. That surplus is to be shared, but only shared by those who had a hand in contributing to it. However, this leaves out all those who are unable to make such a contribution, and Gauthier recognizes this limitation: 'Animals, the unborn, the congenitally handicapped and defectives fall beyond the pale of morality tied to mutuality' (p. 268). Of course many—perhaps most—people who could be described as 'handicapped' are in fact economically productive, and so I assume that by this term Gauthier means to refer to people with physical problems of such severity that they are unable to contribute economically to society.

I would affirm, and this is surely not an eccentric view, that people who must contend with handicaps (to continue to use the term Gauthier uses even though it is now regarded by some as politically incorrect), far from being outside the pale of moral obligation, should be regarded as special objects of moral concern. From this perspective, our level of moral advancement can be measured in part precisely by how we treat those who cannot reciprocate and do us good in return. Gauthier, consistently with his own commitment to a morality based on a rational bargain, signals his disagreement with this stance early in the book, in a comment about the negative effects of new medical technology:

From a technology that makes it possible for an ever-increasing proportion of persons to increase the average level of well-being, our society is passing to a technology, best exemplified by developments

not clear why the goodness and loving character of God are not part of a theistic account in its 'pure' form. However, it is clear that Gauthier fails to see the appeal of an ethic of obligation that is grounded in a relation between a creature and a loving God. Perhaps this is due to the individualistic and self-interested character of the view of human nature with which he is working.

in medicine, that makes possible an ever-increasing transfer of benefits to persons who decrease that average. (p. 18)

A footnote to this remark makes it clear that Gauthier does
not have older people in mind, because they have already 'paid'
for their medical benefits, but is thinking of those who are
unable to make a productive economic contribution because of
their medical situation: 'Life-extending therapies do, however,
have an ominous redistributive potential. The primary problem
is care for the handicapped.' Let us grant that new medical
technologies do pose difficult questions for the justice of our
system to distribute health care. Be that as it may, I do not find
new life-extending therapies to be nearly so 'ominous' as the
attitude exemplified in Gauthier's footnote, where it appears
that moral worth is being equated with ability to make an
economic contribution.

Gauthier might of course argue at this point that the limitations of his morals by agreement require that we supplement
this kind of morality with one grounded in natural emotions,
perhaps along the lines of Arnhart's theory. If that is so, then it
is important to recognize that morals by agreement cannot do
the whole job. However, it is by no means clear that a morality
of feeling is well-suited to supply what is needed at this point,
since we saw in our examination of Arnhart that such a morality
cannot plausibly give a basis for obligations that are universal in
scope. Perhaps a morality of natural feeling can provide a basis
for care for friends and family who are unable to make a financial contribution, but with whom our natural feelings of sympathy dispose us to share. However, it is hard to see how such a
morality of feeling can provide a ground for obligations to
strangers who offer us no economic pay-off. We should also
recall that a morality based on such feelings can be no stronger
than the feelings, which seem to be lacking in some people
altogether. It was just this fact that made Gauthier's approach
initially appealing, in that he was attempting to base morality on
something that would make its authority valid even for individuals who lack sympathy for others.

We can now see, however, that the scope of such a morality is
severely limited. And of course Gauthier himself points out that
these limits do not affect simply those who are handicapped, but

animals and foetuses as well. In fact, it is arguable that there are many human beings who are not handicapped who are very unlikely to make significant economic contributions to human well-being. They are simply too poor, too uneducated, and too unskilled, and the costs of remedying these problems seems out of proportion to any potential benefit they might be able to provide. It is hard to see why such people do not fall outside the scope of morality for Gauthier as well. For example, if morality must be grounded in an actual agreement between people who can contribute towards a surplus of utility, then it is hard to see why rational maximizers in rich countries should see the people in poorer countries as necessarily part of such a bargain.

Gauthier treats this issue of obligations towards people in poorer countries through a fictional story (pp. 282–8). He imagines a planet with two islands separated by stormy seas, with each island populated by a different people called the 'purples' and the 'greens'. The purple people have developed an ideally just society and are very prosperous, while the greens 'live in totally chaotic squalor', which is caused by their own foolish actions. If the purples should discover the greens, how should they treat them? Various options present themselves. The purples could extend their cooperative society to include the greens. Such a policy does not necessarily lead to equality; it could even increase the inequality between the purples and greens, but it could be rational so long as both greens and purples benefit.

However, Gauthier recognizes that some of the purples might prefer simply to ignore the greens, and thus avoid having to deal with any resentment on the part of the greens due to the inequality, or to deal with their own natural feelings of sympathy, which might induce them to help the greens in a costly way. Or, more radically, the purples might simply opt for making what use they can of the greens' island, either in a frankly predatory and exploitative way, or in a way that does not cause the greens any harm. In such a case, Gauthier says, the purples would be treating the greens 'not as fellow human beings, not as "us", but as animals, as "them". Behaviour towards animals is quite straightforwardly utility-maximizing, although it may be affected by particular feelings for certain animals' (p. 285).

Gauthier gives three arguments why the purples might reject this policy and treat the greens as falling within the scope of moral obligation. The first is that doing so may be in the purples' self-interest. Cooperation with the greens may in the long run lead to a surplus of utility. Predation, on the other hand, may produce hostility that will in the long run be unproductive. This seems possible, but it also seems possible that a straightforward utility-maximizer making an unsentimental evaluation of the situation would conclude that predation might pay off. As evidence this could be the case, consider the treatment of Native Americans by European immigrants in the United States. From the viewpoint of the settlers, policies that were unjust and in some cases genocidal can be argued to have paid off from the viewpoint of utility.

The second argument that Gauthier gives is that 'the purples may already be disposed to such co-operation', so that they literally have no choice but to treat them morally (p. 286). In effect, when they developed their own society the purples became the kind of people who cannot help being generous towards other humans they encounter. The long record of human history does not, however, support the claim that any human society would invariably respond in this way to a group considered foreign or strange. All the evidence shows that the idea of a pluralistic society, one in which people of different races, religions, nations, areas, etc. live together in peace and cooperation, is a difficult one for humans to implement. Such an ideal is not impossible, but it is also not easy to achieve. The idea that no other option is even possible might be true for a race of angels, but it is hard to imagine it being true for actual human beings. The purples might conceivably rise above the general human record in this area, but if they are human beings it strains credulity to think that it would be *impossible* for them to be anything but generous.

The third reason Gauthier appeals to lies in the area of the emotions. '[T]he purple people may possess a certain measure of sympathy for all whom they consider human' (p. 286). Once more it looks as if when push comes to shove, the morality of social agreement must be supplemented by a morality of feeling. But once more the problem is that it is just at this point that a morality of feeling is most inadequate. Natural feelings of sympathy are most likely to be present towards those who are like ourselves, or tied to us as family and friends. It is hard to see how universal obligations could be rooted in such feelings. How do we know the purples *will* in fact see the greens as fellow humans and not use some demeaning and degrading category instead such as 'gooks'? The fact that a few very good people possess such disinterested feelings of sympathy for all other humans hardly can be the ground of a universal duty for all humans.

Gauthier anticipates that some will criticize his view for not enabling us to make the right kind of normative judgements. In effect, his response is that we must stick with a morality of rational agreement, even if it does not coincide with the moral judgements we would otherwise be inclined to make: 'If the reader is tempted to object to some part of this view, on the ground that his moral intuitions are violated, then he should ask what weight such an objection can have, if morality is to fit within the domain of rational choice' (p. 269). It seems to me that we should indeed ask this question, and that the answer is that the objection can have very great weight indeed. Perhaps if it were self-evident that morality must be grounded in rational choice we would be justified in jettisoning deep moral convictions in the interest of consistency with a moral theory. However, it does not appear obvious at all that morality must be grounded in rational choice theory. If we are seeking to determine whether such a perspective is the correct one for meta-ethics, we can hardly dismiss objections to it on the grounds that if we allow the objections, we cannot stay within the bounds of rational choice theory. Such a perspective would be rational only for one dogmatically convinced of the truth of the theory. And here it may be worthwhile to remind ourselves that rational choice theory has no monopoly on the term 'rational'. There are many alternative conceptions of reason and rational action.

The divine command theory of Kierkegaard clearly differs from the rational bargain theory at this point. From the point of view of Kierkegaard's account, my obligation to love my neighbour is in no way dependent on the ability of my neighbour to benefit me or help me produce a 'surplus utility'. Rather, I am commanded by God to love all those humans he has created in his image, and this certainly includes those who are poor, sick, handicapped, and completely unable to repay me for any help I extend to them. The obligation to the neighbour in no way depends on the ability of the neighbour to repay me, any more than it depends on the existence of natural feelings of sympathy for the neighbour.

Though Kierkegaard does not develop this line of thought in *Works of Love*, it is clear that a divine command theory of obligation can extend the range of moral duty even beyond the scope of the human race. Since God created the natural world, with its myriads of sentient creatures as well as complex ecosystems, one can easily see why a good and loving God might also issue commands to protect and care for that wider natural order. Moral duties may extend not only to unfortunate humans who cannot benefit me, but to non-human creatures and even non-sentient beings. In an extended and perhaps analogous sense, such beings may be 'neighbours', and there may be duties to value the natural world as God's good creation. This clearly differs from Gauthier's position, since on his view any duties towards the natural order we have must be shown somehow to lead to human benefit.

3. *The intrinsic value of morality*. I noted above that Gauthier, though he develops his account of morality on the basis of an idealized conception of human nature as 'economic man', does not wish to regard such a conception as a true, complete account of that nature. 'Our theory of morality, although it makes use of economic man, is not committed to that idea as a full and adequate account of human nature' (p. 317). Rather, it turns out that we are enough like economic man that a theory based on this assumption is relevant for us, but we are different enough that it is possible for us to take a different perspective on morality. The perspective Gauthier holds out as ideal is that of the 'liberal individual', who has learned to value morality, not simply as a necessary evil, but as a good in itself.

Morality takes on different colouration when viewed in relation to participation. For asocial seekers and strivers morality could be no more than a needed but unwelcome constraint. But for those who value participation, a morality of agreement, although still a source of constraint, makes this shared activity mutually welcome and so stable, ensuring the absence of coercion or deception. (p. 337)

People who value social participation can become truly just people, who do not merely accept the limitations of morality as a necessary evil, but become positively attached to morality by emotion. Such a person does not view justice merely as a necessary evil, but loves it: When she considers a just course of action she 'finds herself moved to adhere to that course of action because of its justice' (p. 328).

I completely agree with Gauthier that a morally good person is one who values morality intrinsically, and not merely as a necessary evil. However, it also seems true that when a person does so value morality, he or she does so because morality is seen as truly valuable; valuing morality is not merely a personal preference. If I am right about this, then I do not see how Gauthier's plea for valuing morality intrinsically can be consistent with the subjectivist account of value that Gauthier gives. According to this account, to think that anything has objective, intrinsic value is to make a mistake. Values are simply personal preferences, and no preference can be seen as rationally superior to another. In fact, Gauthier does not flinch from endorsing David Hume's claim that it is 'not contrary to reason to prefer the destruction of the whole world to the scratching of my finger'.[7] It is hard to see how seeing morality as intrinsically valuable can be squared with such a view. Surely if we take seriously the idea that morality and justice are things to be intrinsically valued, we cannot see them as mere 'personal preferences', none of which can be superior to others.

There are of course lots of preferences that people have that are regarded as just that: preferences with no implication of objective superiority. I happen to prefer the taste of Crest toothpaste to Colgate, but I would hardly argue on that basis that Crest has more value than Colgate. Nor would I view myself or anyone else as having any kind of obligation to use one kind of toothpaste rather than the other. However, with respect to matters we consider deep and important such an attitude seems out of place. If I truly value justice and moral goodness, I do not view them as mere 'personal preferences', but as goods that are somehow central to a human life that is worthwhile. What Charles Taylor has called 'strong evaluation'

---

[7] Gauthier is quoting Hume, *A Treatise of Human Nature*, 416.

seems incompatible with a subjectivist account of values, but without strong evaluation human life seems trivialized.[8] We are reduced to 'economic man', since ultimately there is no part of us that is not for sale, no central concerns of the self that cannot be put into an economic calculus.

The thinness of Gauthier's conception of the self is especially clear when he pronounces on the basis of personal identity. I am identical with the person I will call myself at some future time only to the degree that I now give weight to the preferences I expect my future self to have (pp. 342–3). This criterion of personal identity would entail that if I do not care what happens to myself in the future, then I will not even be that self, but someone else. Momentary preferences are too thin to sustain a notion of an enduring self.

Gauthier senses the problems with economic man, and he wants to argue that in the end we are not completely 'non-tuistic'. Each of us can become the 'liberal individual', who 'although not a natural tuist' is someone who 'comes to value those whom he encounters as fellow participants' (p. 347). Such a liberal individual 'does not lack emotional ties to other persons, but those she has are of her own volition' (p. 347). Such people are bound by moral obligations, but the ties that bind them are nonetheless ties grounded in their own free choice. 'There is no reason for persons whose affections are free, subject to their autonomous control, not to enter into enduring and binding relationships with others. What is essential to free affectivity is that the bonds be of that person's own making.' In the end, it turns out that the constraints of morality are grounded not in society, but in the individual's own commitment. Gauthier ends on a Nietzschean note: There are no essential social relationships; we humans must choose who we are to become. Through those choices we can create genuine obligations, however: 'An animal with the right to make promises must be able to commit itself, giving itself a reason for choice and action that overrides its usual concern with fulfilling its preferences' (p. 347).

---

[8] See Charles Taylor, 'Self-Interpreting Animals', *Human Agency and Human Language: Philosophical Papers* (Cambridge: Cambridge University Press, 1985), i. 65–8.

I believe that Gauthier's notion of 'free affectivity' is deeply flawed. The problem is that if the bonds of morality are solely of my own making, it is hard to see how they can really bind. For a bond that I have the power to make I also have the power to unmake. Indeed, Gauthier insists that this power is required by free affectivity. A genuine obligation is one, however, that is recognized as binding even when I do not want to be bound. Kierkegaard himself affirms that it is no more possible to create an obligation for oneself by an act of will than it was possible for Sancho Panza to spank himself in *Don Quixote*.[9] It is true that the recognition of moral obligation involves free consent. What is called for, however, is not the *creation* of an obligation, but the free *recognition* of an obligation. The individual recognizes the force of the obligation and endorses it. But what is thus endorsed must be regarded by the individual as having an authority that transcends his or her own act of choice.

It is telling, I think, that Gauthier himself admits that free affectivity may not be an adequate basis for the social institution of parenting; on his view parents are not obligated to their children merely by having had them (p. 349). This seems to mean that to incur the obligations of being a parent I must continue to choose to be parent. To think otherwise would be to admit that some social relationships might be essential after all, and not the product of voluntary choice. However, the social institution of parenting becomes unrecognizable on such a view. To be a parent one must recognize obligations that one might often prefer to avoid, and indeed which are in reality often avoided by bad parents.

It is, I think, ironical that Gauthier worries that human beings are becoming too similar to 'economic man'. If this occurs, morality may no longer be possible:

In so far as the idea of economic man is part of our way of understanding ourselves, part of our idea of what it is to be human, and in so far as this idea persists even in the face of conscious disavowal, then the rational bonds of morals by agreement may be too weak to hold us. We need exorcism in addition to argument. But that I have no power to provide. (p. 317)

---

[9] See *Søren Kierkegaard's Journals and Papers*, i. entry 188, p. 76.

The irony is that works such as Gauthier's, which root morality in the idea of economic man, can only contribute to this self-understanding that he deplores. It is worth noting that there is empirical research to show that students who take classes in introductory economic theory become more selfish.[10] When we study or think about human beings as rational maximizers, we tend to become that which we study. Gauthier is thus decrying a process that he himself has advanced. It is commendable and right that he recognizes that humans are not, and should not be, purely economic creatures. However, it is odd that he does not see that making the main foundation of morality to be economic self-interest will contribute to the problem he deplores.

Perhaps we need to take more seriously therefore the kind of perspective Kierkegaard provides. If human beings are created by God, and if God's primary aim is to create individuals who can resemble him in loving, then economic man will be seen clearly for what he is: a temptation we often succumb to but which we must resist if we are to become our true selves. We can also recognize that God may be able to provide the 'exorcism' that Gauthier acknowledges we need, but knows that he has no way of providing.

---

[10] For the debate about this research see the following: R. Frank, T. Gilovich, and D. Regan , 'Does Studying Economics Inhibit Cooperation?', *Journal of Economic Perspectives*, 7, (1993), 159–71; R. Frank, T. Gilovich, and D. Regan, 'Do Economists Make Bad Citizens?', *Journal of Economic Perspectives*, 10 (1996), 187–92; G. Maxwell, and R. Ames, 'Economists Free Ride, Does Anyone Else?', *Journal of Public Economics*, 15 (1981), 295–310; A. Yezer, R. Goldfarb, and P. Poppen, 'Does Studying Economics Discourage Cooperation? Watch What We Do, Not What We Say or How We Play', *Journal of Economic Perspectives*, 10 (1996), 177–86.

12

Contemporary Meta-Ethical Alternatives:
Relativism and Nihilism

I have examined two forms of ethical naturalism: the evolutionary naturalism of Arnhart and the humanistic naturalism of
Gauthier. We have seen that both forms have serious difficulty
in accounting for many of our ordinary moral obligations. Arnhart cannot explain the existence of serious moral obligations
that are universal in scope, and therefore denies there are any
such obligations. Gauthier cannot account for obligations to
those who are seriously handicapped or who otherwise cannot
be contributors to a 'cooperative surplus' that makes morality
beneficial to the individual. Perhaps the most honest naturalistic perspective is a bolder one that frankly denies the existence
of objective moral obligations altogether.

Gilbert Harman has been a long-time advocate of such a
position. Harman defends a position he calls moral relativism,
which holds that 'the judgment that it is wrong of someone to do
something is true or false only in relation to an agreement or
understanding.'[1] Superficially, Harman's view resembles that
of Gauthier, who also understands morality to be rooted in an
agreement. There is a substantial difference between the two,
however. Gauthier grounds morality in a hypothetical ideal
agreement that would be made by perfectly rational, fully
informed utility-maximizers. Our actual moral agreements are
rationally justified and therefore binding on us to the degree
they approximate this ideal agreement, which all of us are
supposed to have reason to consent to. For Harman, however,
though there may be such a thing as an ideal moral agreement
that would be concluded by ideal people, this does not imply
that there is a single true morality: 'A claim about ideal [moral]

---

[1] Gilbert Harman, 'Moral Relativism Defended', in *Explaining Value and
Other Essays in Moral Philosophy* (Oxford: Clarendon Press, 2000), 3.

codes has no immediate relevance to questions about what reasons people actually have to hope for certain things or to do certain things.'[2] Any actual moral obligations we have rest on actual agreements made by actual people with all of their beliefs intact. Such agreements reflect such things as differences in power among those who make the agreement. There are many such agreements that hold among various social groups and the agreements differ in fundamental ways. There is therefore no single true morality, no moral obligations that hold for all human beings.

In this chapter, I shall examine Harman's position in some detail. I will argue that Harman's view is a more consistent form of naturalism than the view of Arnhart and Gauthier. If one rejects theism or some alternative religious world view, then a position such as Harman's is an attractive option in many ways. Harman himself recognizes that there is a link between metaphysical naturalism and his ethical views, and gives an illuminating account of the way in which naturalism fits better with such a view of morality. However, I shall argue that Harman's position comes at a price. If he is correct, then we are unable to make objectively true moral judgements, even about the most heinous forms of evil. Although Harman himself attempts to distinguish his moral relativism from what he terms moral nihilism, I shall argue that the distinction collapses in the end. If this is correct, then the most consistent form of ethical naturalism turns out to be moral nihilism. If one believes that moral nihilism is false, and that some moral claims are objectively true or false, one ought to consider seriously non-naturalistic frameworks for ethics, including theistic divine command theories such as Kierkegaard's.

MORALITY AS RELATIVE TO A FRAMEWORK

What exactly does Harman's moral relativism amount to? He explains the notion by an analogy with motion. Since Einstein we have known that '[m]otion is always relative to a choice of spatio-temporal framework. Something that is moving in

---

[2] Gilbert Harman, 'Is There a Single True Morality', in *Explaining Value and Other Essays in Moral Philosophy*, 84.

relation to one spatio-temporal framework can be at rest in
relation to another.'³ Furthermore, Einstein's Theory of Relativity implies that 'no spatio-temporal framework can be
singled out as the one and only framework that captures the
truth about whether something is in motion.'⁴

Harman sees morality as analogous to motion in this respect:

> [M]oral right and wrong (good and bad, justice and injustice, virtue
> and vice, etc.) are always relative to a choice of moral framework.
> What is morally right in relation to one moral framework can be
> morally wrong in relation to a different moral framework. And no
> moral framework is objectively privileged as the one true morality.⁵

As Harman sees things, this relativistic view of morality is to
be distinguished from what he terms 'moral nihilism'. Moral
nihilism agrees with relativism that moral absolutism, defined
as the view 'that there is a single true morality', is false.⁶ However, the moral nihilist takes the falsehood of moral absolutism
to be a reason to reject morality altogether, while Harman
wishes to maintain that it is possible to reject moral absolutism
while still holding on to a relativistic morality. As we shall see, it
is critical to determine whether or not this distinction between
relativism and nihilism can be maintained.

HARMAN'S ARGUMENTS AGAINST ABSOLUTISM

Why does Harman think that moral absolutism is false? He
gives, I believe, three different types of arguments for his
view, though the first two are closely related, and I shall look
at them together in this section. The third argument is important enough to be considered by itself.

Harman first presents what we might call the argument from
the diversity of moral views. It is a striking fact that human
societies have differed greatly in their views about what is
morally wrong. Some societies have practised and prescribed
human sacrifice; other societies see such practices as the height

---

³ Gilbert Harman and Judith Jarvis Thomson, *Moral Relativism and Moral
Objectivity* (Oxford: Blackwell, 1996), 3. This book is designed in a 'debate'
format with essays by Harman and Thomson and then responses. My references will all be to Harman's portion of the book.
⁴ Ibid. 3.   ⁵ Ibid.   ⁶ Ibid. 5.

of moral evil. Some cultures believe it is morally wrong to eat meat; most cultures see nothing wrong with the practice.

However, this moral diversity is found not only between societies, but also within contemporary societies. In contemporary western societies, people disagree strongly about such things as the moral acceptability of euthanasia and abortion. Furthermore, such disagreements seem intractable, since they 'survive extensive discussion and awareness of all relevant information'.[7] Other examples of basic moral disagreements cited by Harman include such questions as whether it is 'morally wrong to purchase a new record player instead of trying to help people who cannot afford food' and about 'the relative importance of liberty versus equality in assessing the justice of social arrangements'.[8]

Harman recognizes that 'rejection of moral absolutism is not an immediate logical consequence of the existence of moral diversity'.[9] It is possible that the moral disagreements really rest on differences in situations or differences in beliefs about non-moral facts, so that people who were fully rational and fully informed and considering similar situations would make similar moral judgements. Alternatively, if basic moral disagreements cannot be explained in this way, the absolutist might claim that some people are simply in a better position than others to discern moral truth, so that some moral views are just mistaken, even if those holding them are not wrong about any non-moral facts.[10] Harman, however, claims that such explanations are much less plausible than the relativist's view, which is that the disagreements can be traced to differing moral outlooks which provide different frames of reference for moral judgements. The rejection of moral absolutism 'is a reasonable inference from the most *plausible explanation* of the range of moral diversity that actually exists'.[11] Moral diversity then, suggests, even if it does not prove, that moral absolutism is false and there is no single moral framework which is true for all humans.

The second type of argument that Harman gives stems from the nature of moral obligation. If absolutism is true, then there are moral obligations that hold for everyone. However, Harman

[7] Ibid. 11.   [8] Ibid.   [9] Ibid. 10.   [10] Ibid. 12.
[11] Ibid. 10.

argues there are no such obligations in the following manner. If a person has a moral obligation to do an action X, then that person must have a sufficient reason to do X. However, a person only has a sufficient reason to do something if there is warranted reasoning in favour of doing that thing. This means that if the person does not think he should do that thing, then he or she has made some kind of mistake. However, Harman says that there are people who are fully informed and rational and reject the conventional moral principles of our society without making any kind of mistake. He gives as an example a 'successful criminal', who rejects the alleged moral requirement 'not to harm or injure other humans'.[12] This kind of argument shows that 'different people can be subject to different moral demands "all the way down"'.[13] He imagines an assassin who is an employee of 'Murder, Incorporated', a firm in which all the workers accept as a matter of course that it is sometimes right to kill people. Harman comments 'it strikes us as a misuse of language to say of the assassin that he ought not to kill ... or that it would be wrong of him to do so.'[14] Since the assassin has no reason to refrain from killing, he has no obligation not to kill.

METAPHYSICAL NATURALISM AND ETHICAL NATURALISM

The third type of argument, and the one I find most interesting, is connected to Harman's espousal of philosophical naturalism. Harman is struck by the fact that one of the intractable disagreements about morality is the disagreement about relativism itself. Though he had known that there were 'philosophers and friends of mine who were not moral relativists', he had, somewhat uncharitably, previously 'attributed this to their perversity and love of the bizarre'.[15] Harman was chagrined to discover that those philosophers who accepted a single true morality explained his own relativism in the same manner.

---

[12] Harman, 'Is There a Single True Morality', 87. Harman gives another version of this same argument in 'What is Moral Relativism?' in the same volume, 33–4.

[13] 'Ibid.' 34.

[14] Harman, 'Moral Relativism Defended', 5.

[15] Harman, 'Is There a Single True Morality', 78.

The existence of this basic moral disagreement strikes him as itself something that cries out for an explanation:

On the one side are relativists, sceptics, nihilists, and noncognitivists. On the other side are those who believe in absolute values and a moral law that applies to everyone. Strangely, only a few people seem to be undecided. Almost everyone seems to be firmly on one side or the other, and almost everyone seems to think his or her side is obviously right, the other side representing a ridiculous folly. This is strange, since everyone knows, or ought to know, that many intelligent people are on each side of this issue.[16]

I myself do not think such a situation in philosophy is as unusual as Harman seems to think. However, I believe that his explanation of this particular disagreement contains valuable insight. The disagreement, he says, stems from two different approaches to ethics, the difference between the two approaches turning on 'a difference in attitude toward science. One side says we must concentrate on finding the place of value and obligation in the world of facts as revealed by science. The other side says we must ignore that problem and concentrate on ethics proper.'[17]

I think Harman means by this that the latter group he describes simply assumes that we have moral knowledge and that such knowledge is objective. The philosophical task is to refine this knowledge and discern the general principles that underlie it. Those who pursue this task are doing what Harman calls 'autonomous ethics'. The other side, however, is puzzled by such moral facts and wonders about their ontological status. The autonomous ethicist simply leaves these metaphysical puzzles aside, but the second side 'has come to think that the basic issue in moral philosophy is precisely how value and obligation fit into the scientific conception of the world'.[18] Harman aptly labels the second approach to moral philosophy as 'ethical naturalism'.

Though I think the account Harman gives of this dispute is on the right track, I disagree with his description of the conflict. So far as I can see, the root of the disagreement does not lie in a 'difference in attitude toward science' as Harman claims. Rather, any such difference in attitude toward science stems from a more fundamental difference. It is important to see that

[16] Ibid.   [17] Ibid. 79.   [18] Ibid.

claims such as 'all knowledge is scientific knowledge' and 'if moral facts are genuine facts, then they must be discoverable by science' are not themselves scientific claims. No chemist or biologist or physicist could possibly test such claims by experiment or make discoveries that would confirm or falsify them. Rather, such claims are philosophical claims made about science. A person who rejects such claims is not therefore being 'unscientific' in any clear way, and may have precisely the same 'attitudes' toward genuine science as Harman himself presumably does, at least if we mean by 'attitudes' such stances as accepting the conclusions of science, respecting and appreciating the value of scientific knowledge, etc.

Harman seems to mean by 'attitude toward science' something different from this. For him the relevant attitude toward science is something like a conviction that science gives us the whole and final truth about reality. There is indeed an important difference between people such as Harman and those he considers his opponents, but the ground of the difference does not lie in science itself, but in a difference in metaphysical outlook. A metaphysical naturalist is, roughly, someone who believes that the only reality that exists is the natural world that is investigated by scientists. Such an individual might reasonably believe that there are no genuine facts except for those discoverable by science. The naturalist believes this, not because it is a truth that can be scientifically established, but because it is a consequence of his naturalism.

In contrast, a metaphysical theist, who believes in God, might naturally believe that there are some truths, for example those about God's nature, which natural science cannot discover. This disagreement is not, however, a disagreement about the value of science, nor does it necessarily entail any disagreement about the results of science. The theist may accept all of the conclusions of science (in whatever manner scientists accept such conclusions) as grounded in empirical study of the natural world. Of course the theist believes that this natural world, with all of its marvellous and intricate regularities, exists because of God's creative activity, but this belief does not contradict any scientific theory.

Of course there are particular theists who disagree with particular scientific theories for religious reasons, as in the 'scientific creationist' movement. However, such disagreements with science do not stem from theism per se but from more particular religious beliefs, usually stemming from convictions about truths alleged to be revealed by God. There are no intrinsic contradictions between theistic beliefs per se and the acceptance of scientific theories.[19]

I think, therefore, that the disagreement Harman describes is better captured in the following way. Some people, those who follow the approach of 'autonomous ethics', begin by assuming that humans have some moral knowledge about moral facts and try to determine the content of that knowledge more precisely. Metaphysical naturalists, however, are puzzled by the alleged existence of such facts. Moral facts do not seem to be the kind of reality that could be discovered by any natural science, and they do not appear to be facts that we need to invoke to explain facts in science. Such a naturalist 'cannot understand how value, justice, right, and wrong might figure in explanations without having some sense of their "location" in the world'.[20] In effect the ethical naturalist tends to be sceptical about the existence of objective moral obligations because he or she does not see how they can be understood as 'natural facts', in the sense of being facts about the physical world studied by science, and the naturalist believes such physical facts are the only facts there are.

Harman of course realizes that there are many philosophical naturalists who accept objective moral obligations. What would be needed to make sense of moral values and obligations for the naturalist is a 'naturalistic reduction', definitions of ethical terms that mention only non-moral facts, by which the naturalist would be 'able to locate value, justice, right, wrong, and so forth in the world in the way that tables, colours, genes, temperatures, and so on can be located in the world'.[21] Harman is

[19] For a strong argument that theists may accept not only scientific theories in general but even evolutionary theory see Michael Ruse, *Can a Darwinian Be a Christian? The Relationship between Science and Religion* (Cambridge: Cambridge University Press, 2001). For a Christian perspective on the relation between science and religion, see Del Ratzsch, *Science and Its Limits: The Natural Sciences in Christian Perspective* (Downers Grove, Ill.: InterVarsity Press, 2000).

[20] Harman, 'Is There a Single True Morality', 83.

[21] Ibid.

doubtful that such reductions can be provided for absolute values, which would be states of affairs that are intrinsically good and which everyone would have a reason to want to be actualized.[22] 'Naturalism leads to scepticism at this point. How could we ever be aware of absolute values? How could we ever know that everyone has a reason to want a certain possible state of affairs?'[23] What underlies our judgements of value, according to Harman, are interests, and interests are relative. From the point of view of a dog that is the subject of a medical experiment, the state of affairs consisting of the experiment is bad, but from the point of view of a human being suffering from a disease the same state of affairs may be good.

Harman goes on in 'Is There a Single True Morality?' to repeat arguments similar to the first two we examined in the previous section. However, it now becomes clear that what gives those arguments their bite, so to speak, is an underlying commitment to naturalism. Take, for example, Harman's argument that an obligation presupposes a reason to perform the action one is obligated to perform. The ethicist could simply respond to this by saying that people do have a reason to follow their obligations, since the existence of the obligation itself gives the person such a reason, and the person who does not recognize this is just immoral. Such a person does not have to make a non-moral mistake in order to be in error. Harman recognizes this reply may be acceptable to the autonomous ethicist, but claims that '[i]t does not explain having a sufficient reason to do something in terms that are acceptably factual from a naturalistic perspective.'[24] The real problem is that the existence of the obligation itself cannot be explained as a natural fact.

For someone committed to metaphysical naturalism, then, if Harman is right about the difficulty of making sense of moral facts within the natural world, this provides a reason to doubt there are such facts. In effect, the argument against objective ethical truths is that they do not make sense within a naturalistic universe. We cannot understand how such facts could come to

[22] For an example of a philosopher committed to naturalism who is more sanguine about the possibility of such naturalistic reductions, see Boyd, 'How to Be a Moral Realist'.

[23] Harman, 'Is There a Single True Morality', 93.

[24] Ibid. 88.

be in such a universe. However, such an argument is a two-edged sword. As is frequently the case in philosophy, one individual's *modus ponens* is another individual's *modus tollens*. If we are convinced that there are indeed moral facts, then if Harman is right and it is not possible to make sense of such facts within the framework of metaphysical naturalism, this provides a reason to question whether metaphysical naturalism is true.[25]

MORALITY AS A CONVENTIONAL BARGAIN

Harman's relativism shares with moral nihilism a conviction that ethical absolutism is false. However, Harman himself wishes to reject the nihilist position as well. That is, he does not think that the falsity of ethical absolutism implies that morality must simply be rejected. Instead, he thinks that moral obligations can be viewed as relative in a sense analogous to the way in which motion is viewed as relative within Einsteinian physics. There is no single true moral framework for all human beings. Nevertheless, there are a plurality of moral frameworks that give rise to moral obligations, and at least most individuals are in some way bound by one or more of these frameworks.

Harman's explanation of the existence of such moral frameworks is superficially, as I have noted, similar to Gauthier's account of morality. The heart of his view is that a moral framework is grounded in a conventional agreement by a group of humans. '[A] morality is basically a group affair, depending on moral demands jointly accepted by several people after a certain amount of tacit bargaining and adjustment.'[26] The major difference with Gauthier is that Harman does not think that the obligatoriness of any such moral code depends on its approximation to some ideal agreement that would be made by completely rational agents. Harman doubts that any agreement would necessarily be reached in such a situation, and even

---

[25] For a good example of an argument for the falsity of naturalism that follows this line of reasoning, see George Mavrodes, 'Religion and the Queerness of Morality', in Robert Audi (ed.), *Rationality, Religious Belief, and Moral Commitment* (Ithaca, NY: Cornell University Press, 1986), 213–26.

[26] Gilbert Harman, 'Relativistic Ethics: Morality as Politics', in *Explaining Value and Other Essays in Moral Philosophy*, 51.

if an ideal agreement were possible it would have no applicability to actual human beings.[27] Instead Harman simply thinks there are different moral frameworks, reflecting the different situations of the people who made the underlying agreement, including differences in power and status among them. 'Moral relativism denies that there are universal basic moral demands, and says different people are subject to different basic moral demands depending on the social customs, practices, conventions, values and principles they accept.'[28]

Harman believes one particularly powerful piece of evidence in favour of his view is the differential moral status given in 'our morality' to the principle of refraining from harming others as compared to the principle of rendering aid to others. Some of our conventional moral judgements appear odd to Harman if we assume that morality is founded on a principle of sympathy for others or a desire to contribute to the general good or happiness. Most of us think, for example, that it would be wrong for a doctor to kill a healthy person and harvest that patient's organs, even if thereby the doctor were able to save the lives of many people. It might appear on utilitarian grounds, in which moral obligations are to further the greatest happiness for the greatest number, that such an act could be justified on the grounds of the overall benefit the action would produce. Harman says, however, that we can understand the higher status of the principle that we should not harm others if we view morality as grounded in a conventional agreement.

[T]he hypothesis that morality derives from an agreement among people of varying powers and resources provides a possible explanation. The rich, the poor, the strong, and the weak would all benefit if all were to try to avoid harming one another. So everyone could agree to that arrangement. But the rich and the strong would not benefit from an arrangement whereby everyone would try to do as much as possible to help those in need. The poor and the weak would get all of the benefit of this latter arrangement.... In other words, although everyone could agree to a strong principle concerning the avoidance of harm, it would not be true that everyone would favour an equally strong principle of mutual aid.... So the hypothesis that morality

---

[27] Harman, 'Is There a Single True Morality', 84; and 'Justice and Moral Bargaining', in *Explaining Value and Other Essays in Moral Philosophy*, 66–8.

[28] Harman, 'Is There a Single True Morality', 85.

derives from an understanding among people of different powers and resources can explain why in our morality avoiding harm to others is taken to be more important than helping those who need help.[29]

Why should we accept the moral conventions that do apply to us? Harman's answer is straightforward: 'There are various reasons, but the main reason why a person accepts the principles he or she does is that it is in her interest to do so if others do too.'[30] Morality is founded on such simple considerations as 'I don't push you around so that you won't push me around. You are nice to me so that I will be nice to you.'[31] Although Harman, as noted, believes these conventional agreements must be actual and not merely hypothetical, he thinks that they are, for the most part, implicit and arrived at without conscious deliberation: 'The conventions are normally arrived at tacitly, by mutual adjustment of different people's behaviour, without conscious awareness.'[32] Though moral obligations depend on the acceptance of conventions, those who are subject to morality can defend themselves against those who are not bound by morality because they do not accept the relevant conventions: 'Moral relativists need not be tolerant of harms committed by criminals who have not accepted conventional morality. There are strong self-interested reasons for us to include in our moral understanding the proviso that we can use force against those who harm others.'[33]

Since almost everyone belongs to more than one group, and different groups may accept different moral frameworks, how do we determine which moral frameworks apply to a given individual? Despite his claim that morality is 'basically a group affair', Harman gives an individualist answer to this question: 'What makes a society your society is not, say, the proximity of its members, but rather that you accept the principles of that society as principles for you and other members of that society.'[34] This is implied as well by Harman's claim that '[p]eople can always opt out of the morality they currently

[29] Harman, 'Moral Relativism Defended', 11.
[30] Harman, 'Justice and Moral Bargaining', 68.
[31] Ibid.
[32] Ibid.
[33] Ibid. 76.
[34] Harman, 'Relativistic Ethics: Morality as Politics', 56.

accept; and they can always threaten to opt out if their self-interest is not sufficiently taken into account by the current morality.'[35]

Given that we can 'opt out' of a moral agreement in this way, a problem arises for Harman. Why should people keep the agreements they have made? On his view, I commit to morality by agreeing to abide by certain principles on the condition that others do so as well. It follows that if I do not believe others are likely to do so, I am not obligated to follow the principles. Are there good reasons for people to keep their moral commitments, especially given that any moral obligation at times will require an individual to curtail what is in that individual's self-interest? (Harman acknowledges the truth of this fact.[36]) Why should not an individual be a free-rider or parasite, to use Gauthier's language, and enter into the moral agreement without any serious intention of keeping it, hoping thereby to take advantage of others?

Harman's response to this problem is that it rests on a misunderstanding of the nature of an agreement. He says that 'the apparent force of the objection derives entirely from taking an agreement to be a kind of ritual.'[37] I believe that Harman means by 'ritual' here something like a verbal promise. On his view, an agreement in the relevant sense is nothing like a promise, but rather consists solely in an intention that is formed against the background of a knowledge of others' intentions:

To agree in the relevant sense is not just to say something; it is to intend to do something—namely, to intend to carry out one's part of the agreement on the condition that others do their parts. If one agrees in this sense to do something, one intends to do it, and intending to do it is already to be motivated to do it. So there is no problem as to why one is motivated to keep one's agreements in this sense.[38]

[35] Harman, 'Justice and Moral Bargaining', 68.

[36] Harman claims that '[o]nce some moral principles and values are accepted, these restrict further appeals to self-interest.' See 'Justice and Moral Bargaining', 68.

[37] Harman, 'Moral Relativism Defended', 13.   [38] Ibid.

This will obviously not do as it stands as an analysis of agreements, since Harman uses the term 'agreement' to explain what intentions are relevant. However, he later gives an account that lacks this circularity: 'there is an agreement in the relevant sense when each of a number of people has an intention on the assumption that others have the same intention.'[39]

It is not hard, I think, to show that this is inadequate as an account of what an agreement is. Suppose I discover that a robber hid some money in a box in a forest under a particular tree, and you discover the same information at the same time. I form the intention to go and find the money as quickly as possible, with the understanding that you have formed the same intention. Both of us clearly 'have an intention on the assumption that the other has the same intention'. However, there is no agreement between us, though of course we might decide to negotiate such an agreement. Apart from such an agreement, our 'agreement in intentions' does not prevent each of us from doing whatever he wishes to undermine or sabotage the other's quest for the money.

This shows, I think, that Harman's account leaves out the heart of the notion of an agreement. Though it is true that agreements can be implicit or tacit, and do not have to be verbally expressed, an agreement in the sense of a contract still represents something *like* a promise. Promises may be conditional and usually are when they take the form of contracts. But whether conditional or unconditional, the heart of a promise is something like a commitment or pledge. For example, when I hire a painter to paint my kitchen, I promise to pay him on the condition that he does the agreed-upon work. To say that such a promise consists solely of intentions that various individuals form is precisely to leave out what makes a promise a promise, that aspect of a promise that binds the individual who made the promise.

Whether a promise be verbally explicit or merely tacit, the heart of a promise has a future-orientation. I promise at $t1$ to do something at $t2$; for example, I promise to pay the painter in full after he finishes the job. It follows that one cannot evade the question as to why an individual should keep a promise by

[39] Ibid. 16.

saying that the person intends to fulfil the promise at the time
the promise was made. Even if Harman's analysis of agreements
in terms of shared intentions were adequate (though we have
seen that it is not), and even if the individual does have the
intention to keep a promise at *t*1, the time the promise is made,
it does not follow that he or she will continue to have the
intention to keep the promise at *t*2, the time the promise must
be kept. Agreements are, after all, broken all the time. It is not
at all clear, why, on Harman's view, an individual who has made
an agreement to live by a certain set of moral principles should
keep that agreement if at a later time the agreement seems to go
against his or her self-interest. After all, Harman himself insists
that the individual can at any time 'opt out' of a moral agreement. So it looks as if the individual may very well have no
reason for keeping moral agreements at all.

   This is particularly damaging, since on Harman's view the
agreements that constitute morality are conditional on confidence that others will keep the agreements. Since I know that
there is no reason for others to keep such agreements if it is
damaging to their self-interest, I have little reason to think that
they will do so in cases, surely not infrequent, where morality
requires some personal sacrifice. If I do not believe others will
follow the rules of morality, it is hard to see why I should regard
myself as bound, even if I am committed to keeping my promises, since in this case I only promised to follow morality so long
as others do so as well. Nor are such problems purely hypothetical or contrary-to-fact. As I noted previously, cheating is fairly
common among students in the USA, and cheating on income
taxes is common among the general population. Who would
argue that lying is rare or unheard-of in today's world? Even
political advertisements are so deceptively worded that they
come perilously close to lying. If I am obligated to be moral
only on the assumption that others will be too, the ground of the
obligation is weak.

THE COLLAPSE OF RELATIVISM INTO NIHILISM

We have noted that for Harman it is important to distinguish
moral relativism from moral nihilism. Both reject moral absolutism in Harman's sense. However, the nihilist takes the falsity

of moral absolutism to be a reason to reject morality altogether. Harman believes, however, as we have seen, that the collapse of moral absolutism does not mean morality itself must be rejected. We are still left with relativistic moralities, in the sense of agreements made among various groups of people.

We must ask, however, whether such relativistic moralities are really morality at all. Or, to ask the same question in another way, does such a relativistic morality really differ significantly from the stance of the moral nihilist? To answer this question, it is crucial to recognize that at the very heart of morality is the notion of an obligation. An obligation is not reducible to a preference, a desire, or even an intention. If I am obligated in the moral sense to perform an action, it is not relevant that I do not wish to perform the action. Even a lack of intent to perform the action does not affect the status of the obligation; people often fail to act on obligations they have, even on ones they acknowledge. ('I know I ought to have told the truth, but I was afraid of the consequences if I did so.')

Harman himself acknowledges that our moral obligations constrain us in some way. Even though basically founded on self-interest, once morality is present it must have some binding character: 'Once some moral principles and values are accepted, these restrict further appeals to self-interest.'[40] The point is recognized even more clearly by Gauthier, who understands that the essence of morality is that it makes us 'constrained maximizers', rather than 'straightforward maximizers'.[41] Harman's account of morality, however, is almost ludicrously inadequate in explaining this binding character.

I have noted that Harman says that an individual can at any time 'opt out' of a moral agreement, if the individual judges that the agreement is not in his or her interest. All that is necessary to eliminate moral obligations is a simple decision that one no longer wants to be party to the relevant agreement. Furthermore, we have seen that Harman provides little reason why individuals should keep their agreements in any case. Since the relevant moral agreements are conditional on other people

---

[40] Harman, 'Justice and Moral Bargaining', 68.
[41] Note, however, my argument in Chapter 11 that Gauthier ultimately cannot account for the binding force of moral obligations either.

abiding by them, in many cases an agreement will not be regarded as binding. But even if other people do keep the agreement, it is hard to see why a self-interested individual should not simply decide to break the agreement when it appears that this would 'pay'. People who do not have the relevant moral intentions simply are not bound by morality: 'Someone refuses to agree to the extent that he or she does not share these intentions. Those who do not agree are outside the agreement.'[42] So a person who does not intend to live morally is free from the obligation to live morally. It is hard to see how such a stance differs, except verbally, from that of the moral nihilist, who may for pragmatic reasons conform some of the time to conventional moral obligations but does not regard them as truly binding.

The moral nihilism at the bottom of Harman's view is easy to see when he discusses the situation of individuals who do reject what he calls 'conventional morality'. He admits, that a 'successful criminal may well have no reason at all not to harm his or her victims'.[43] Harman does not flinch from the consequences of this perspective, even when considering cases of monstrous evil such as Hitler's genocide. A moral relativist such as himself believes that 'for Hitler, there might have been no reason at all not to order the extermination of the Jews.'[44] We might, of course, say that Hitler's actions were wrong from our own moral perspective, but we cannot make the 'inner judgement' that they were wrong *for him*, or claim that our own moral condemnation of him is objectively correct or superior to the Nazi's own moral understanding.

Harman might respond to this that his view must be different from the nihilist's, because on his view it is possible to truly say 'Hitler violated his obligations to the Jews' and the nihilist's view does not allow this. It is true that Harman says that the proposition is indexed such that it is only relative to Harman's framework that it is true, but the difference remains. The problem with this reply is that the indexing removes the bindingness of obligations. If I am only bound by an obligation that

---

[42] Harman, 'Moral Relativism Defended', 16.
[43] Harman, 'Is There a Single True Morality', 86.
[44] Harman, 'Moral Relativism Defended', 9.

I have not chosen to 'opt out of', it is hard to see why Hitler could be said to have any obligation to the Jews, since if someone can simply decide to 'opt out' of such an obligation, presumably Hitler would have done so. It is precisely to preclude this possibility that my initial characterization of morality in Chapter 1 stressed the idea that moral obligations are overriding; they take precedence over such things as individual preferences and desires.

The contrast with Kierkegaard's divine command theory of obligation could not be sharper. On Kierkegaard's view, our duties to love all human beings are grounded in the objective reality of God's command. Harman says that what clinches moral relativism is that people can reject the demands of morality without being irrational, stupid, or uninformed.[45] However, if Kierkegaard's view is correct, a person who rejects moral obligations is at least uninformed. Such a person does not realize that he or she was created by God for a relationship of love with God, and that such a relationship leads, at least in the very long run (the perspective of eternity) to his or her own deepest happiness. He or she does not recognize that such a relation to God requires obedience to his commands, the primary command God has issued being to love all human beings, including myself, as neighbours, those close to or next to me. My obligations are universal in scope and they in no way depend on what others do or do not do, on any agreements I make or unmake, or on my attitudes and desires.

Of course we argued that it is possible for people to know about their moral obligations without realizing that they are in fact divine commands. However, we can now see one of the reasons why meta-ethics is important. An individual such as Harman who is committed to metaphysical naturalism may be tempted to reject moral obligations, because he cannot see how to explain the existence of such obligations within his naturalistic framework. I do not wish to argue that such a person would be correct to reject morality, but I do acknowledge that the pressure of consistency with naturalism pushes him in that direction. Within a theistic framework the existence of moral obligations makes sense in a way that is not the case in Harman's

---

[45] Harman 'Relativistic Ethics: Morality as Politics', 43.

framework. The recognition of moral obligations as divine commands, when combined with faith in the reality of God, removes a grave temptation to doubt the reality of such commands.

13

Conclusions: Divine Command Morality in a Pluralistic Society

I wish to begin this concluding chapter with a summary of the argument given up to this point. I have developed the outlines of an account of moral obligation found in Kierkegaard's writings, an account I believe represents Kierkegaard's own best thoughts about the issues. The account is a version of a divine command theory of moral obligation that claims, following Robert Adams, that moral obligations are grounded in the commands of a good and loving God. Humans have good reasons to obey God's commands, on this account, because God has created them, graciously showering them with many goods, including the capacity for love that mirrors God's own love. God's creation of humans is shaped by his intention that humans enjoy a relationship with himself. As his creatures we cannot help being metaphysically related to him, but we have the capacity for a conscious, free relation that is genuinely fulfilling. Since we have been created by God in this way, we can only actualize our true selves by coming to know God and relate properly to God.

This particular social relation, like other social relations, gives rise to obligations. The particular obligations our relation to God grounds are excellent candidates for being *moral* obligations because they possess the characteristics I identified in Chapter 1 as essential to morality: they are objective, overriding and, at least for some of them, universal in at least two senses: (1) all persons are subject to God's commands; and (2) God's command to love our neighbour requires us to care about all persons. God's commands hold unconditionally, and are not rooted simply in self-interest, taken in its normal sense of the satisfaction of natural egoistic and even sympathetic desires. Contrary to Gauthier and Arnhart, moral obligations on this view are not the result of a bargain or social contract, whether hypothetical or actual. Nor can such obligations be viewed simply as rooted in biologically based universal desires, as Arnhart thinks.

I reviewed in Chapter 6 Kierkegaard's arguments that such a divine command theory of moral obligation is humanistic in the sense that it views moral obligations as successfully directed towards human flourishing. Though our human motivation for following our moral obligations is not self-interest, but rather love and gratitude towards the God who has created us, we can understand God's commands as directed towards human good and happiness rather than being arbitrary. My obligation to love my neighbour as myself helps make love constant, gives human individuals a desirable independence that protects against exploitation and victimization, and protects against despair by showing that any human life can have meaning and worth if it is characterized by loving others.

The most fundamental of God's commands is the great command to love one's neighbour as oneself. For Kierkegaard, this command is not merely a formal demand for equality in how one treats the self and others, but an obligation to respect the worth and value of all humans, including oneself, as creatures made by God and endowed by God with that love which is God's own supreme characteristic, so that humans are literally made in God's image. To love my neighbour (or myself) is to recognize and esteem the worth of persons as creatures capable of love and to assist them in realizing their potential for love. The obligation is not merely to act in a certain way towards others but actually to love them, an emotion that can be cultivated when I learn to construe others as my neighbours. This in turn is unpacked by understanding the concept 'neighbour' in terms of a person's relation to God. God becomes the 'middle term' in every genuine case of neighbour-love, because in such a relation I construe the other as like myself, a child of God, in which love has been placed 'in the foundation'.

Although Kierkegaard himself does not develop the account in this direction, I suggested that it would be relatively easy to develop this account of moral obligations towards humans into a broader account that recognizes moral obligations to other animals and to the natural world generally.[1] If God exists, he is the maker of animals and that natural order; they too possess value and worth as the result of God's creative activity. It is not surprising that God might give human creatures made in his image special responsibility to value and care for that creation.

The first person I see and people I never will meet are equally my neighbour. This means that it is always wrong to draw boundaries for moral concern, to regard the 'Other' who differs from me in family, sex, race, religion, ethnic group, or geographical region as outside the scope of my moral obligation. Such neighbour-love is not reducible to any natural affection, but requires a fundamental transformation of every natural relation and affection, while not leading to their abolition. Kierkegaard himself stresses that these obligations cannot be fulfilled merely by support of general social policies, but must express themselves in concrete relations with others, particularly the poor. While agreeing with the positive message here, I argued that consistency demands that Kierkegaard recognize that neighbour-love may also require support for structural social change that reduces or minimizes oppression and inequality.

Kierkegaard holds, I claimed, that these divine commands are promulgated by both general and special revelation. In our human moral conscience, all humans encounter the call of God to love the neighbour. However, in our sinfulness we humans evade and suppress this call, a condition that requires the revelation of God's love for us, and God's demand for love in us, in the Old and New Testaments. Committed Christians (and those committed to Judaism as well, since the love command is common to Christians and Jews, at least according to Kierkegaard) should recognize the authoritativeness of these revealed commands, and recognize how sharply they diverge from our sinfully shaped understanding of our duties. Nevertheless, when revealed, such a divine command view can commend itself even to humans who do not accept such a revelation,

[1] For an attempt to explore how a Christian vision might shape an ethic that focuses concern on animals and the natural order as an ecological whole, see Steven Bouma-Prediger, *For the Beauty of the Earth: A Christian Vision for Creation Care* (Grand Rapids, Mich.: Baker Books, 2001).

as it points to the love that is rooted in the creation order within every person.

It is easy, I think, to show how our most widely recognized moral duties towards humans can be seen as flowing from the command to love the neighbour as oneself. Violent and oppressive actions are obviously violations of such a duty; one cannot love the neighbour if one intentionally kills the innocent neighbour, rapes, enslaves, or degrades the neighbour, and since all persons are my neighbour, such acts cannot be excused even if they are directed towards those who are 'Other'. However, mere lack of compassion for others is also inconsistent with loving those others as my neighbours. It seems unloving indeed to enjoy luxuries when my neighbour is starving or has no place to sleep. An ethic of neighbour-love is demanding and disquieting, especially to those of us with material wealth.

One can also see how love for the neighbour demands that a person should meet the ordinary demands of morality for our daily relationships: keeping my promises, telling the truth, showing gratitude where someone has graciously helped me. Though Kierkegaard is anything but a casuist, and I have argued that more attention to the role of what we might call intermediate principles would strengthen his account, we can certainly see how breaking a promise, deceiving a person for one's own benefit, and refusing to acknowledge the ways others have helped us can be seen as incompatible with love for the neighbour.

I have argued that such a divine command theory of moral obligation is defensible. It does not imply that divine commands are arbitrary, as many have alleged, since on this view God's commands are directed towards human flourishing. Even though the commands cannot for the most part be derived simply from reflection on human nature and human happiness, once promulgated we can see how well they fit with that nature and advance that happiness. The strengths of such a view can be clearly seen when contrasted with naturalistic alternatives: An evolutionary naturalist such as Arnhart has no convincing account of why our natural desires for dominance should not legitimize such things as slavery and sexual oppression. Gauthier has no convincing account of why human persons should be obligated to all other persons, particularly persons who cannot conceivably contribute to the benefit of others, and indeed no convincing account of why a person should not become a 'free-rider' or even 'parasite' in human society. Harman sees the problems with other naturalistic perspectives and boldly says that objective moral obligations do not exist, but this implies we cannot seriously maintain that committed racists and successful criminals are morally mistaken. The strengths of the Kierkegaardian account stand out clearly when contrasted with these leading secular alternatives. There are of course other secular alternatives, but I hope that my argument at least shows that a view such as Kierkegaard's deserves serious consideration.

Despite this, however, I fear that many will still regard a divine command theory of obligation as one that does not rise to the level of a serious competitor. Why should this be so? Doubtless there are many reasons. I shall discuss three possible reasons, one briefly and two at greater length.

The first reason to be sceptical of a divine command theory, to which I shall give only brief attention, is that many see a divine command theory as incompatible with genuine moral autonomy. According to this criticism, a divine command theory infantilizes human beings and makes responsible moral decision-making impossible. I think that I have already shown how Kierkegaard responds to this criticism. In Chapter 6, I reviewed Kierkegaard's argument that human autonomy is actually fostered and not diminished by an account of obligations as rooted in the loving commands of God.[2] On this view, the God who commands us to love is a God who values human freedom and wants us as free beings to be responsible decision-makers. God does not desire humans to relate to him as infants but as friends who can cooperatively with him work for the good. God not only gives us the freedom to accept or reject his commands, but also requires us to think for ourselves about how to apply his commands to love to concrete moral problems. Such creative, responsible thinking is necessary both for God's universal and individual commands. Universal commands have to be interpreted and applied to particular situations. Individual commands have to be discerned in and through the particular

---

[2] See pp. 151–3 above.

circumstances of the individual's life. A respect and reverence for transcendent divine commands in fact fosters genuine autonomy; an individual who hears the call of God is an individual who may break with established social norms for the sake of the good.

There is doubtless more to be said about a divine command theory and autonomy. However, in this final chapter I have decided to focus on two other common criticisms of a divine command theory which I think are particularly influential. The first is the claim that a divine command account of obligation has unacceptable consequences, namely that if God were to command us to kill or hate our neighbours, then such actions would become our moral duties. The second is the claim that viewing moral commands as divine commands is an unacceptable view in a pluralistic society, because it grounds morality in a sectarian set of beliefs.

ABRAHAM AND ISAAC: WHAT IF GOD COMMANDED HUMAN SACRIFICE?

Robert Adams has rightly said that a 'convincing defence of a divine command theory of the nature of obligation must address our darkest fear about God's commands—the fear that God may command something evil.'[3] A divine command theory of moral obligation, as I characterized it in Chapter 5, is committed to the claim that whatever God commands humans to do is morally obligatory for them. This would seem to imply that if God commanded humans to kill, rape, lie, and steal, then such evil actions would become morally right. Many would say that such a consequence is absolutely unacceptable in a theory of moral obligation, even if the possibility that God might command such things is purely hypothetical. Surely, the critic may argue, it is false that such actions would be right if God commanded them, even if it is true that God never actually commands them.

Kierkegaard has perhaps done more than any other thinker to make this issue central to our thinking about the relation between God and moral obligation because of his treatment of the

---

[3] Adams, *Finite and Infinite Goods*, 277.

'binding of Isaac' story from Genesis in *Fear and Trembling*. In the treatment of Johannes de Silentio Abraham's willingness to obey God's command to sacrifice his son is held up as a model of faith, and the fact that Abraham is not actually called upon to do it at the last minute is held to be irrelevant, since in the story the Abraham who is being praised cannot have known ahead of time that this is how things would turn out.

One might try to save Kierkegaard here from this view by noting the pseudonymous character of *Fear and Trembling*. I have made the case for the non-identity of Kierkegaard and his pseudonym in Chapter 3. I also argued in that chapter that *Fear and Trembling* is not primarily a book about ethics at all, but rather one that focuses on the nature of faith. Ethics comes into the picture only as Hegelian *Sittlichkeit*, with the thrust of the argument being that one cannot identify genuine faith with the conventional morality of Christendom.

All of this is perfectly correct, but unfortunately does not get Kierkegaard, or a divine command theory of moral obligation, off the hook. Insofar as Abraham is praised as a model of faith, then his unquestioning obedience to God is implicitly recognized in the book as a praiseworthy ideal to emulate. In any case, we do not have to rely on *Fear and Trembling* to know Kierkegaard's view of this issue, for, as we saw in Chapter 5, he explicitly and unambiguously commits himself in *Works of Love* to the view that a person must obey any commands God gives:

But you shall love God in unconditional obedience, even if what he requires of you might seem to you to be to your own harm, indeed, harmful to his cause; for God's wisdom is beyond all comparison with yours, and God's governance has no obligation of responsibility in relation to your sagacity. All you have to do is obey in love.[4]

In my treatment of this issue I shall defend three claims as consistent with each other and correct: (1) It is indeed the case that a person ought to perform any action God commanded, and this implies that *if* God commanded someone to take the life of a child, that action would be right. (2) It is not possible

[4] Kierkegaard, *Works of Love*, 20. Subsequent references to this work in this chapter denoted by page nos. in parentheses.

for God to command an act that is unloving; if a being whom we thought to be God made such a command, that being would no longer warrant being thought of as divine, and its commands would not be moral obligations. (3) In our current epistemological situation, a person could not rationally believe that God has commanded an act of child sacrifice unless God supernaturally took control of the person's beliefs. I shall discuss these claims in reverse order, beginning with (3).

COULD A PERSON RATIONALLY BELIEVE GOD HAS COMMANDED AN ACT OF CHILD SACRIFICE?

As Robert Adams rightly notes, and as Kant had already argued, there is an important epistemological dimension to this issue. Suppose we assume for the sake of the argument that *if* we knew with certainty that God had actually commanded an act of human sacrifice that it would be right to perform it. Could we actually come to know that the antecedent condition is fulfilled? Kant argues that we can know with certainty that killing a child is wrong, but we could not know with certainty that a voice or vision commanding such an action is truly from God. If Kant is right about this, then this would seem to imply that we could affirm that if God truly commanded such an act of sacrifice, it would be morally right, but at the same time affirm that we would never actually be in a situation in which we would be right to believe that God was asking us to do such a thing.

Is Kant right about this? To answer this question we must relativize it to a particular epistemic situation. I believe, for reasons that I will soon spell out, that something like Kant's view is correct for someone in a contemporary cultural context, though it was not right for Abraham. At least the claim is correct for someone living in the contemporary period who is committed to Christianity or Judaism. To be more precise, I want to claim that no such person could reasonably believe that God has today issued such a command. This is not the same thing as a claim that God could never have issued such a command. Perhaps God did indeed command Abraham to kill his son, although never actually intending for Abraham to perform the action. God might have done this for any number of reasons. Some Jewish commentators have suggested that the command was given for the sake of teaching the ancient Israelites that God would not require human sacrifices, as was the case for some other Canaanite religions. Even if God did in fact command Abraham to perform such an act, it does not imply that it would be reasonable to believe that he might make a similar request today. If I saw a neighbour building an altar in his back yard, and he announced that God had commanded him to sacrifice one of his children on that altar, I would not for a moment hesitate to call the police to stop him; I would not linger very long with the worry that God might actually have asked him to do it.

Why would I take this view? One might think that I have thereby deserted a divine command theory of obligation in favour of a view that holds that some acts are wrong regardless of what God commands us to do. However, this is not necessarily the case. I may firmly believe that if God had actually commanded him to do the act it would be morally right for him, but believe even more strongly that God has not made any such command and would not do so. Nor is it the case that in believing this I am necessarily holding God accountable to a standard of moral obligation that is independent of his commands. Rather, I may simply believe that God has commanded us to refrain from child sacrifice and therefore believe that he will not command such actions to be performed. If I believe this firmly, any visions or voices urging a person to engage in child sacrifice may rightly be rejected as divine commands. Such commands might come from natural or demonic supernatural sources, but do not come from God.

Why should a person believe that God would not issue such a command? I think the best answer is that we know that God has commanded us *not* to perform such an act. If I believe that God has commanded all humans never to perform an act of type A, then an alleged command to perform an act of type A cannot come from God. How could we know that God has commanded us never to perform such an act? Presumably, in the usual way, through general and special revelation, as explained in Chapter 7. In particular, Christians and Jews have good reason to believe that God has forbidden human sacrifice, since the practice not only conflicts with the general biblical injunction not to murder or kill the innocent, but is specifically denounced in several passages.[5]

One might object to this argument on the grounds that many Christians, such as Augustine and Aquinas, who are aware of the Decalogue and the prophets, as Abraham was not, have nevertheless believed that God can indeed command such an act, since he did in fact command Abraham to perform it, and have continued to hold that if God commanded such an act it would be morally right.[6] However, I do not wish to contest either of these claims. It is indeed possible that God actually commanded Abraham to perform the act, and we can imagine reasons why God might have done so. This does not entail, however, that we might be justified in believing God has issued a similar command today. My epistemic claim does not imply that God could not generate such an obligation if he did issue such a command or even that it would not be possible for God to do so. It does imply, I think, that to do this God would simply have to causally determine an individual to believe accordingly. Such a belief could not be formed through rational processes.

I think the case that a person should now believe that God will not give such a command is strongest for those committed to biblical revelation. However, even without the biblical teachings, it might be possible for someone to reach the same conclusions because of a knowledge of God's commands through general revelation. We must remember that we are not starting with a divine command theory of moral obligation and then asking what those divine commands might be. Rather, we begin by assuming that we know something about what our moral obligations are, even if this knowledge is imperfect and defective in various ways, and then go on to try to show that those obligations are in fact divine commands that we have learned about through general and special revelation.

Any alleged divine command must be tested for its consistency with what a person already takes to be the commands of God. We can certainly envision that as we gain more insight

---

[5] See Jeremiah 7: 31 and Ezekiel 20: 25–6.

[6] My thanks to Philip Quinn and an anonymous reader for Oxford University Press, for forcefully posing this problem.

into God's commands, and thus the nature of moral obligations, our initial understanding of what is commanded by God might be modified and corrected over time. However, we cannot imagine that through such a process our understanding of right and wrong should be completely reversed, so that everything we previously thought to be forbidden is now regarded as obligatory and everything we previously thought to be obligatory is now regarded as forbidden. It is not conceivable that rape and murder should suddenly become obligatory, while kindness and love would become forbidden.

One might think that God should be able to revoke a command he has given, and thus the fact that he has previously forbidden child sacrifice would not preclude his commanding an instance of it for some special reason. I think we can certainly understand that God could give some commands that are in some way limited: applicable only to a particular time, people, or even individuals. Such commands could indeed be revoked. However, a God who revoked commands that were given as universal and absolute in character would be a God so inconsistent and unpredictable in character that it is questionable whether or not such a God would merit our obedience. We must remember that the ground of our obligation to obey God is our relation to God, a relation that makes possible our own true happiness. A God who gave contradictory commands could hardly be a God who could be counted on to fulfil his promises, and such a God would not seem to be a being to whom a relationship would necessarily be the highest human good. Another way to arrive at the same point would be to say that such inconsistency would cast the very identity of God into doubt. If God is identified as a good and loving being, the faithful and trustworthy one who has revealed himself in the Old and New Testaments as well as our general moral consciousness, then a being who contradicted the central message of these revelations could not be regarded as the same being.

One might object here that my claim that a person could not today rationally believe that God had commanded child sacrifice limits the power of God. Surely, one might think, an omnipotent God could reveal to a human being that the human being was commanded to carry out an act of child sacrifice in such a way that the human being would be rational to believe it. God's omnipotence does require me to qualify the claim I have made in one respect. I agree that God could create a belief that a sacrifice is required for a person today by causally taking control of the person's beliefs in such a way that the person cannot help but believe he has been commanded to perform the act. In this case the person would surely be reasonable to believe that God has commanded the act, since no other belief is possible for that person. But in such a case it is questionable whether the person would really be morally responsible for the belief and any acts stemming from it.

In any case, if God were to do this, *ex hypothesi* the person could do nothing about it. Perhaps in such a case the person would be right to have the belief and even to attempt to act upon it, if the person believes that whatever God commands is morally right. However, this does not mean that others of us, in whom God has not instilled the belief that this act is commanded by God, should not do all in our power to stop the individual. Unless God miraculously determines my thought processes, I will steadfastly disbelieve any alleged vision or voice that delivers such a command, and disbelieve any other person who claims to have received such a message from God. It is noteworthy that *Fear and Trembling* does not discuss the question as to how Abraham came to know that God had asked him to perform the act. The book simply assumes that Abraham knows this and knows it with certainty. Given that assumption, then Abraham's act may indeed be praiseworthy. To say that is not to say that we could imagine ourselves today knowing what Abraham is represented as knowing.

One might think that I have in this argument demonstrated too much, at least if someone believes that the Genesis account is historical (which would, of course, be denied by many). Does my argument imply that Abraham should not have believed that God had asked him to sacrifice his son? Not at all. I take it that Abraham is not in the same epistemic situation as contemporary Christians and Jews (and other people of goodwill as well). He lived in a culture in which child sacrifice was common and regarded as morally acceptable. God had not yet spoken through Moses or given the Ten Commandments, and the prohibitions of child sacrifice given by various prophets had not yet been given. Given the cultural milieu, it is also not obvious at all that Abraham could have known through general revelation that child sacrifice was wrong. So far as we can tell Abraham would have had no good reason to think that God would not ask him to perform such an act. Thus, the historical truth of the Genesis story is quite consistent with my argument, though of course my argument does not mean that the story must be taken as historical.

Let us continue to suppose for a moment that the story is historically true. Why would God make such a request of Abraham? Obviously since we are not God, we cannot say, but we can speculate. Perhaps, as I suggested above and as a long Jewish tradition holds, God put Abraham to this test precisely to teach the Jewish people that he would not require human sacrifices from them, unlike the pagan gods of surrounding cultures. In this way the people could come to see that their total devotion to God was not less than the devotion of surrounding groups which did practise child sacrifice, since their father Abraham was willing to do this, while coming to know that this devotion would not need to be expressed in this way. On this interpretation, it seems an important feature of the story that God never actually intends Abraham to carry through on the act. Even though this feature of the story, as Kierkegaard rightly notes, is not a factor in determining the rightness of Abraham's behaviour, since Abraham did not know in advance that God would in fact not require the action, and so his faith and trust in God was not based on such knowledge, it can rightly be a factor in our understanding why God would put Abraham to such a test.

It is true that it might have occurred to Abraham that God would in the end not require the sacrifice. However, his willingness to obey is surely not premised on such a possibility. In fact, it seems likely that Abraham could make no sense of the situation at all. God had promised Abraham that he would become a father of many nations through Isaac. How could this promise be fulfilled if Isaac were sacrificed? Presumably Abraham does not know, but his confidence in God led him to trust that God knew what he was doing. Perhaps, as the writer of Hebrews suggests, Abraham believed that if he were required to sacrifice Isaac, God would raise him from the dead.

This line of thought is particularly attractive to Christians, since many Christians hold that the story is partly a prefiguring of the story of Jesus, in which God the Father 'sacrifices' his son, and Isaac serves as a 'type' of Christ, who is indeed raised from the dead. This kind of 'prefigurement' gives another reason why God might have required the test of Abraham, as well as a reason why God might have ensured that the story was included in a divine revelation, though this is obviously a reason that Abraham would know nothing about. This second interpretation is completely consistent with the first; there is no reason God could not have had multiple reasons for testing Abraham in this way. Whatever God's reasons might be, we can understand how such an action might be an appropriate test of Abraham's character without assuming that such a test would be an appropriate one for God to impose today.

One might think that my argument here is most un-Kierkegaardian, since Kierkegaard (actually Johannes de Silentio) insists in *Fear and Trembling* that one must become a 'contemporary' of Abraham, and not allow learned exegesis to rob the case of its power. However, exactly where does the contemporary relevance of the story lie? Is it in the particular historical details? I doubt that this is so, since the book gives as examples of 'ethical' actions, doings that we are supposed to approve uncontroversially, such acts as Agamemnon's sacrifice of Iphigenia. This, however, is an act that, if performed today, would be regarded as morally questionable at best.[7] *Fear and Trembling* argues vigorously, as we saw in Chapter 3, that religious faith cannot be reduced to *Sittlichkeit*, the conventional morality of a particular society. One cannot assume that God's commands are mediated through society or the State. God can command an act that will go against such conventional moral standards, just as he did in the case of Abraham (on the assumption that the story is historical). We do not have to imagine that the actions God commands would be identical to what was asked of Abraham. The parallel with Abraham lies in the possibility of a conflict with prevailing moral standards, even though the prevailing moral standards of our culture are quite different from those of Abraham.

---

[7] See my discussion in Chapter 3, pp. 69–71.

When Johannes de Silentio discusses the teleological suspension of the ethical, he immediately relates Abraham's action to New Testament passages, such as Luke 14: 26, in which Jesus says that anyone who wishes to be his disciple must 'hate his father and mother'.[8] Silentio clearly does not think that a Christian must literally hate his parents, any more than he thinks that Abraham hated Isaac. Rather, his interpretation seems to be that to be a Christian disciple, the higher loyalty to God required may make it necessary for the individual to behave towards the parents in a way that will appear to the secular world as 'hate'. If the parents are not Christians, even the decision to be a Christian may appear to the parents to be an act of rejection, a 'hateful' action, though in reality the individual in question may love the parents deeply. Even if the parents are nominal Christians, they may not understand the calling of the individual. Suppose the Christian is called to leave his or her home country to work among the poor in some distant land? The parents could well see such behaviour as 'hateful indifference' if they do not share the faith of their adult child. Faith in God can still today, as was the case for Abraham, require actions that will appear to many to be immoral, even shockingly so. God's commands to the individual can be strikingly opposed to *Sittlichkeit*, even in a case where the culture in question is not committed to flagrantly immoral practices, such as racist discrimination.

I think that this claim that divine commands can conflict with accepted moral convictions is fully consistent with my argument that we could not today rationally believe God has commanded child sacrifice. For my argument that today we could not believe God would do such a thing is not based on *Sittlichkeit*. It is rooted, for responsible, committed Jews and Christians, in convictions about what God has actually commanded humans to do. It is indeed important to allow for the possibility that God's commands could modify and even overturn aspects of the conventional morality of any society, including our own. God could indeed command something that goes against what I believe to be morally right. Of course it is easier to see this for other societies than our own, particularly societies that we see as

---

[8] Kierkegaard, *Fear and Trembling*, 72–4, 81.

holding deeply flawed moral beliefs. A person brought up in a slave-holding society might be taught that it is morally right to enforce the rules of slavery and wrong to help a slave to freedom. In such a society God might help the person whom Kierkegaard calls 'the individual' to see that slavery is actually wrong and forbidden by God. Such a person will come into conflict with *Sittlichkeit* and, depending on how deeply depraved the moral consciousness of the society is, may be unable to argue convincingly that his view is correct to his or her contemporaries. However, we must accept the possibility that such a conflict could occur with respect to our own society too. Obviously, in such a case by definition the individual will be perceived by most of us as immoral, even though the person is courageously following the call of conscience.

So we can continue to affirm the central message of *Fear and Trembling*: so far from its being the case that genuine faith is exhausted by conventional morality, obedience to God may require the individual to oppose conventional moral views, and even suffer as a consequence of this nonconformity. A divine command morality must not be simply a 'baptism' of conventional morality; the possibility that a divine command may challenge and even correct our understanding of moral duties must be preserved.

Of course if we believe we know something about God's commands already, since they have been promulgated through general revelation and some special revelation accepted as authentic, this limits the possibility of a challenge. It is impossible for responsible, believing Jews and Christians today to think that God might command humans to hate their neighbours. However, this limitation is quite consistent with the claim that a divine command morality may challenge conventional morality, especially since for most (perhaps all) human societies, the obligation to love the neighbour, when the neighbour includes all people, is indeed challenging, to say the least. When we recognize the possibility that there is an individual dimension to God's requirements—that God may call me to do what my neighbour is not expected to do—then we can easily see how a divine command morality may lead to actions that conventional morality would never regard as obligatory or even exemplary. I might be called by God to forsake a lucrative career to work for the poor in a difficult region of the world. Such an act would be regarded by most people as foolishness. Yet perhaps it is an act that is required if I am to become the person God wants me to become.

WHY GOD CANNOT COMMAND EVIL

The argument in the preceding section was primarily for the epistemological claim that in the contemporary situation no one, or at least no responsible believing Jew or Christian, could rationally be justified in believing God has made a demand for something like a child sacrifice.[9] We can, however, go further, I believe, and claim that God could not command any act that is truly evil in the sense of being fundamentally bad. Of course, given that our understanding of good and evil is fallible, this is compatible with the possibility that God might command an action that appeared to be evil, at least initially. The claim that God could not command what is genuinely evil does not make it impossible for a divine command to surprise us, perhaps even shock us initially, since our knowledge of what is evil is fallible. As I argued in the last section, divine commands may certainly come into conflict with *Sittlichkeit*. However, this is consistent with saying that such commands cannot be directed against what is truly good.

One might think that the claim that God cannot command evil follows trivially from a divine command theory of moral obligation. If we identify evil with the violation of moral obligation, and identify moral obligations with divine commands, then it will be tautologous to say that acts that are divinely commanded will be obligatory and therefore not evil. However, I do not merely want to affirm such a weak, tautologous claim, but something more substantive. Here it must be recalled that not any alleged divine being is an adequate candidate for the role of being the foundation of moral obligation. Moral obligations are to be identified with the commands of a loving God; and thus the account given of moral obligation is rooted in a

---

[9] The one exception I allowed is the case where God miraculously intervenes to causally determine an individual to believe this is what God requires. But in that case the belief is one that the person has no responsibility for.

Conclusions

broader theory of value that sees value as objective. To view moral obligations as divine commands is to believe that those commands are directed towards good and loving ends, and not at bad ends, though of course this does not mean that such commands would never to us be puzzling and strange. However, even if we do not fully understand some of God's commands, it is important that we be able to believe that they are in fact directed towards good and loving ends.

I think this means that commands that are actually directed against what is good and loving could not come from God. We must indeed allow that God's ways are higher than ours, and that what appears to be bad and unloving to us might not in fact be that way to God. However, a believer in a divine command theory of morality of the type I am defending cannot be completely ignorant about what is good and loving, because such a theory assumes that we have some knowledge of God himself as a good and loving person. Without such knowledge we would have no reason to obey God's commands. Hence, if confronted by commands apparently from God that are deeply and squarely antithetical to what is known to be good and loving, the believer in a divine command theory will be thrown into a quandary. Such a person might conclude that such commands do not really come from God, the being we have identified as the source of moral obligation. A second alternative, which may be compelling if the person is convinced that the command is from God, and firmly convinced that God is trustworthy, is to rethink what is good and loving. Perhaps God has a plan that will lead to a good end that we humans cannot understand. Something like this could have been true for Abraham, if we assume the biblical story really happened. Yet another alternative, if a person is convinced that a command which is fundamentally unloving did come from the being the individual had been calling 'God', would be to say that there is no such being as God; the being previously regarded as God is not a being worthy of our total devotion.

ARE ALL GOD'S COMMANDS OBLIGATORY?

Once more it may appear that my argument has succeeded too well. Is it consistent for me to argue both that (1) contemporary

Christians, Jews, and other morally informed people could not rationally believe God has commanded an act of child sacrifice; and that (2) God as a loving being would not command an act that is cruel or evil; and yet hold (3) any act God commands is morally obligatory? The last claim implies that if God commanded an act of child sacrifice, it would be morally obligatory. Can one consistently believe that and also hold claims (1) and (2)? Certainly (1) is consistent with (3). There is no logical contradiction in believing that if God commanded an act it would be right, while holding that I could never in the contemporary situation be justified in believing that God has in fact issued such a command (unless God has miraculously controlled my beliefs). Since God is the author of life and death, it may indeed be true that if God were to command that an innocent's life be taken, the act would not be wrong. However, one can affirm this without believing that God would ever make such a request. (An individual who holds such a view could of course say that God could have made such a request of Abraham, though never intending for Abraham to obey it, precisely to teach Abraham and Abraham's descendants that God would not require such actions.)

One might think, however, that (2) limits the authority of God and thus at least contradicts the spirit of a divine command theory of moral obligation. What force does the claim that anything God commands is obligatory have if there are a priori limits on what God can command? The first point to be made here is that the limits are not imposed by *Sittlichkeit*. It is indeed possible for God to issue commands that surprise us and go contrary to what we thought was morally right. The second point is that the limits are present from the start in the kind of divine command theory being proposed. In saying that it is only the commands of a loving God that would constitute moral obligations, we are saying from the start that a God who issued cruel and hateful commands would not be a being whom we were obligated to obey. This is not to say that our understanding of what is loving and what is hateful could not be in error at points. This does not mean, then, that God could not issue a command that would surprise us, perhaps even shock us, at least initially. But it does mean that God could not issue a command that would have the force of moral obligation if that command were really evil in intent. To the degree that we really do understand love and goodness (and their antitheses) we can be confident that we know something about the general character of God's commands.

Neither of the restrictive claims I have made (that people in our situation could not reasonably believe God has commanded an act of child sacrifice and that God could not command an act that is genuinely unloving) is the imposition of an alien and external standard of morality on God. Those committed to a theory of moral obligations as divine commands must rather see these claims as grounded in God's successful revelation of his commands and character. Those who believe God would not issue such a command do so because they believe they know something about what God actually commands us to do.

A DIVINE COMMAND THEORY OF OBLIGATION IN A PLURALISTIC DEMOCRACY?

Suppose that I am right in my argument that on the kind of divine command theory of obligation developed by Kierkegaard that God could not command what is truly evil, and that we could never be justified in believing God has commanded such an act as one of child sacrifice. Many will think that even if such a divine command theory is free of horrible consequences, it is still a non-starter in a pluralistic democracy. In such a pluralistic society, moral justification must appeal to 'public reasons', reasons that are not grounded in sectarian religious beliefs.[10] Contemporary nations such as the United States, Canada, and many European countries have citizens of many different religious persuasions and many with no overt religious commitments at all. That God has commanded a particular type of act is a reason that can only be compelling for those who believe in God, and perhaps in a particular type of God. And if the

---

[10] See, for example, James Rachels, whose 'minimum conception of morality' affirms that moral beliefs must be based on reasons or arguments, and also that divine commands cannot provide such a basis for morality, in *The Elements of Moral Philosophy*, 9–14, 44–50. The only religious ethic that Rachels is willing to entertain is a natural law ethic, which entails that moral knowledge is independent of religious knowledge, and thus implies that believers and unbelievers 'inhabit the same moral universe'. See ibid. 50–5.

command is one that is promulgated through a special revelation, then it will be recognized as binding only by those already committed to that revelation. A divine command theory of moral obligation then appears to be intrinsically sectarian in character, not the kind of account that could be usefully employed in the context of a pluralistic society.

Adding to the problem is the fact that religious sectarianism seems to many to be what generates many of our moral problems, rather than constituting a possible solution. The contemporary world is wracked by violence, and much of the violence is at least partially grounded in religious divisions. The division between Catholics and Protestants bedevils Northern Ireland. Christians and Muslims have fought in several regions of the former Yugoslavia. In the Middle East Jews and Muslims quarrel violently over the status of Jerusalem, a city holy to three religions. It is hardly surprising that John Lennon, in singing about Utopia, asked us to 'imagine' a world with 'no country, and no religion too'. Can a religiously grounded theory of moral obligation be taken seriously in such a world?

Let me begin by dealing with the question of whether a religiously grounded ethic will lead to divisiveness or even violence. The first thing to be said in response to such a charge is that Kierkegaard's version of a divine command theory of moral obligation absolutely rules out any kind of violence towards or oppression of 'the other', whoever the other might be. Since every human being is my neighbour, my moral duty is to love every human being. Whether or not human beings are like me in religion, race, gender, ethnicity, or ideology has no bearing on my obligation to love those human beings. Unlike ethical systems that root obligations in friendship, kinship, or reciprocal benefit, there is no possible way to limit the scope of moral obligations. If I am a Christian white male heterosexual from North America (as I am), I must recognize that Hindus and Muslims, gays and lesbians, Africans and Asians, men and women are all equally my neighbours. Loving my neighbour means seeking the good for my neighbour, especially helping my neighbour become more loving, and is incompatible with oppressing my neighbour in any way. It is certainly true that sectarian violence pervades the contemporary world, but such violence can in no way be justified by an ethic of neighbour-love. That those who identify themselves as Christians (or Muslims or Hindus or whatever) have frequently failed to live in accordance with this normative ideal in no way undermines its validity as a moral ideal.

Not only is Kierkegaard's ethic of neighbour-love incompatible with violence, it is arguable that Kierkegaard's account provides the basis for a powerful account of the origins of violence, an account that implicitly contains a prescription for social healing as well. To explore this theme in detail would require another book, but a good start along these lines has been made by Charles Bellinger, in *The Genealogy of Violence: Reflections on Creation, Freedom, and Evil*.[11]

Most of what I have to say in response to this charge that a religiously grounded ethic is divisive or undermines the character of a pluralistic society has actually been said along the way already in this book. Hence I mostly will assemble some reminders about points already made. However, I will begin by asking what is to count as a 'public reason' for moral action? Must a public reason be a conviction shared by everyone or almost everyone in a society? If so, then I am afraid that public reasons for moral action will be extremely scarce or even non-existent. If, on the other hand, a public reason is simply a conviction that can be defended by argument, there is no reason in principle why a moral theory grounded in religious convictions cannot count as a public reason.[12] For, as the example of this book shows, a religiously grounded ethic can make a case that it preserves and captures what is important about morality,

---

[11] Charles Bellinger, *The Genealogy of Violence: Reflections on Creation, Freedom, and Evil* (Oxford: Oxford University Press, 2001).

[12] Of course there are other possible concepts of what might count as a 'public reason'. One might, for example, think that Rawls' notion of a reason that a person could appeal to in the original position 'behind the veil of ignorance' is neither a generally shared belief or a belief that could be defended by reasons in an actual society. A full treatment of this issue would thereby be considerably more complicated. For fuller discussions, see Nicholas Wolterstorff, 'Why We Should Reject What Liberalism Tells Us about Speaking and Acting for Religious Reasons', in *Religion and Contemporary Liberalism*, ed. Paul J. Weithman (Notre Dame, Ind.: University of Notre Dame Press, 1997), 162–81, and also 'Audi on Religion, Politics, and Liberal Democracy', in Nicholas Wolterstorff and Robert Audi, *Religion and the Public Square* (Lanham, Md.: Rowman and Littlefield, 1997).

and even does so better than secular alternatives. In any case, I think it is important to distinguish between meta-ethical and normative moral discussions. To claim that the best ultimate meta-ethical account of moral obligation is religious in character is not to claim that every normative claim must be immediately backed by religious claims. Rather, a religiously grounded account of moral obligation can recognize that there can be moral common ground between believer and non-believer.

This point is really one made frequently in the course of this work; the account of moral obligation I have given is not sectarian in the sense that it claims that a person must be explicitly religious to recognize the moral ideal or attempt conscientiously to follow it. I argued in Chapter 7 that the command of God to love the neighbour is one that has been promulgated through general as well as special revelation. In creating human beings God has placed love 'in the foundation' of every human self. This implies both the worth of every human being and the capacity of human beings to recognize that worth. So the theory is not committed to the claim that one can recognize our moral duties only if one first accepts some special revelation, such as the Bible or the Koran, as authentic. In fact, the theory does not even claim that a person must be a theist in order to see moral truths; it is quite possible for someone to recognize the commands of God, that is, recognize a moral duty as a moral duty, without realizing that these duties are in fact divine commands, just as a person can recognize water—and drink it—without knowing that water is chemically composed of oxygen and hydrogen. Hence, the theory is not committed to the implausible claim that a person must be religious to recognize the ideals of morality and attempt to ground one's life around those ideals.

It is true that Kierkegaard thinks that because of human sinfulness our capacity to recognize God's commands has been severely damaged. Most of us do not really want to know that all human beings are our neighbours and that we are obligated to love them. We would rather live in accordance with the principle of Polemarchus: Love your friends and hate your enemies. It is quite possible that we humans would be ignorant of the demands of morality were it not for exceptional individuals who are rightly regarded as prophets. The ancient Hebrew prophets, Socrates, Confucius, the Buddha: all seem to have at least some understanding of the same truth that Jesus proclaims in the New Testament. Such individuals either can be viewed as those granted a special revelation or as individuals who made exceptional use of the capacities given by God through general revelation. If someone believes that the words of the Buddha, or Muhammad, or Jesus have special authority because of the special status of the messenger understood as a prophet, then for that individual moral knowledge may rest on a commitment to that special revelation.

However, even if moral knowledge is introduced to humans through a special revelation, this does not mean that once these insights are available they cannot be recognized and defended by appeal to general revelation. We saw in Chapter 5 that Kierkegaard himself follows this procedure. Though he thinks the morality of neighbour-love is derived from the New Testament, he claims that the soundness of this ethic can be defended on the basis of criteria recognized by all, even opponents of religion: such an ethic allows human beings to flourish by preserving the constancy of love, enhancing human freedom and autonomy, and protecting human life against despair.[13]

One might wonder at this point what the value of a religiously grounded moral theory might be. If human persons can recognize their moral duties without belief in God (or acceptance of any authoritative special revelation), then why do we need a divine command theory of obligation? The answer to this question essentially will be an answer to the question as to what value a philosophical account of the nature of moral obligation has. Of course one answer is that if the theory is true, or close to the truth, then its recognition will have whatever intrinsic value any genuine philosophical insight will have. Even if one does not believe the theory is true, it might still contribute to philosophy by provoking and stimulating discussion, prodding alternative views to focus on problems that need to be addressed, and contributing to the quest for truth in that way. If someone believes that philosophy does not discover truth, and thinks of the value of philosophy in some other way, as contributing to a conversation or as the development of alternative perspectives, this philosophical account would

---

[13] See Chapter 5, pp. 146–55.

seem to have the same kind of value other philosophical theories would have.

Besides the intrinsic philosophical value of the view, however, I do believe that an account of the moral life that clarifies the ontological status of moral obligations can have practical value as well; it can be a positive contribution to the moral life. Though I have argued that through conscience human beings can be and often are aware of their moral obligations, regardless of their religious beliefs, this does not mean that this awareness is not subject to doubts and scepticism. It is, I think, possible for a person to be aware of moral obligations without holding any views as to the nature of those obligations or why those obligations are binding. I would even argue that a person who has no idea as to what moral obligations are or why they hold is still more rational to continue to believe in their validity than to reject them. However, it is surely easier to deal with the kinds of doubts about objective moral obligations that we saw exemplified in Gilbert Harman if a person has a convincing account of the status of moral obligations.[14] Especially when morality pinches us, when we would strongly like to believe that we are free of our moral responsibilities, it is a good thing for a person to have an understanding of what moral obligations are and why they are binding. This is exactly what the kind of divine command theory of moral obligation developed by Kierkegaard offers us. Kierkegaard's account offers the added benefit that the theory gives us a convincing reason to be moral; it explains why morality connects with our own long-term deepest happiness without reducing morality to self-interest.[15]

My claim that an account of the nature of morality that offers a justification for moral obligations is itself helpful to morality is one that makes good sense to us as reflective beings who seek to understand ourselves and what we do. However, more than this can be said. There is actually strong empirical evidence that a plausible meta-ethical story is an aid to moral education. Research into the moral education of adolescents shows that young people are much more likely to believe in the objectivity of morality and attempt to live according to its standards when their moral education includes an attempt to explain why moral

[14] See Chapter 12, pp. 294–8.   [15] See Chapter 6, pp. 140–6.

obligations hold.[16] Children naturally want to know why moral obligations hold, and they are more likely to believe in morality when they are given an answer to the question as to why they hold rather than simply being told that they ought to be moral and that is the end of the story.

DIVINE COMMAND THEORY AND THE 'ESTABLISHMENT OF RELIGION'

However, one might still object that the particular justification being offered in this case is one that cannot be appealed to in a liberal democracy committed to the separation of Church and State. Many people believe that religion is something that in a liberal democracy must be a private affair. Religion is a 'conversation-stopper' and can play no significant role in the 'public square'.[17] Obviously large issues are raised here, issues that have been extensively discussed.[18] My own argument will merely be a sketch of what needs to be said. However, the issues raised are too important to ignore.

It is, I am convinced, impossible to think hard about the nature and status of morality without thinking about the nature of human beings and the kind of universe we humans find

[16] See James Hunter, *The Death of Character: Moral Education in an Age Without Good or Evil* (New York: Perseus, 2000), 13, 193–8.

[17] See Richard Rorty, *Philosophy and Social Hope* (New York: Penguin, 1999), 168–74. Rorty has subsequently modified his position slightly. He now admits that there is no principled reason why citizens in a democracy cannot appeal to religious reasons to justify their position. However, he still thinks that this appeal to religion should be limited to the level of 'the parish and the individual', since the overall effect of larger ecclesiastical structures he believes to be pernicious. So far as I can see, Rorty gives no principled reason why the influence of religion should be limited in this way; Rorty's conviction that religion overall has negative effects appears to be based on his personal convictions and attitudes rather than hard evidence. See his 'Religion in the Public Square: A Reconsideration', in the *Journal of Religious Ethics*, 31/1, 141–9.

[18] I would particularly recommend arguments advanced by Robert M. Adams, 'Religious Ethics in a Pluralistic Society', in Gene Outka and John P. Reeder, Jr. (eds.) *Prospects for a Common Morality* (Princeton: Princeton University Press, 1993), and by Nicholas Wolterstorff in 'Why We Should Reject What Liberalism Tells Us about Speaking and Acting for Religious Reasons'.

ourselves in. In other words, no account of the nature of morality can plausibly claim to be metaphysically neutral. Indeed, an account of the status of moral obligations is manifestly itself metaphysical; it is an attempt to become clear about the ontological status of such obligations. If any account one gives about such matters will be metaphysically charged, it is hard to justify excluding a religiously based metaphysic from consideration.

What exactly does it mean to be a liberal democracy? Is a society really liberal if it excludes the deepest beliefs and convictions of the majority of its citizens from discussion in the public arena? I believe there are two ways of understanding a liberal society. On one view such a society is committed to a free and open debate, a debate in which everyone committed to the principles of a free society is welcome to participate, including religiously committed individuals. On the second view religious convictions may not be appealed to or debated in the public arena because they are supposed to be among the concerns of the private individual. I would argue that only the first view really embodies the aims of a liberal society. The second view amounts to the exclusion of the convictions of some citizens, and the implicit adoption of a secular world view, under the guise of 'neutrality'. For suppose that, when people think about the good life and the good society, they are not allowed to consider the implications of such beliefs as that humans were created in God's image for the sake of becoming loving individuals. This would mean in effect that the world view of naturalism, which says that the natural physical world is all that exists, has been adopted as a working framework from which to address moral questions. Such a stance is hardly religiously neutral.

To say that religious convictions should be allowed into the debate is not to say that they are likely to be convincing to everyone or even a majority. And it is certainly not to say that religious people are committed to some kind of theocratic society, whether that takes the form of an established religion or a civil religion. In fact, it is just at this point that Kierkegaard is most helpful, I believe.

Kierkegaard of course lived in a country, nineteenth-century Denmark, which did have an established Church, with the priests being civil servants. At the end of his life Kierkegaard launched a sharp attack on this official Church, an attack waged in the newspapers and in a popular magazine he himself founded and published.[19] Many scholars would agree with Bruce Kirmmse that this open attack on the State Church was the logical culmination of themes deeply embedded in Kierkegaard's whole authorship.[20] Kierkegaard's fundamental objection is not simply to the idea that the Church should be an arm of the State (though he does indeed object to that). His objection is not motivated primarily by a desire to see people freed from authoritarian ecclesiastical control; he in fact refused to cooperate with sectarians who wished to enlist him in their fights. His motivation is simply opposition to the very idea of Christendom, the whole idea that the ideals of true Christianity can be identified with the concrete norms of an actual human society.

The genius of a divine command theory, according to Kierkegaard, lies precisely in the transcendence it gives to our moral obligations. Since our duties stem from God, and God is indeed transcendent, the commands of God can never be identified with the *vox populi*. Every society is rooted in a set of concrete norms, a *Sittlichkeit* that must be passed down to new generations if that society is to survive. The dominant groups in a society are the groups that maintain and transmit these norms, and Kierkegaard characterizes these groups, in language that strikingly anticipates the language of the radicals of the 1960s and 1970s, as 'the establishment' or 'the established order'.[21]

An established order is necessary, and Kierkegaard rejects anarchic rebellion, rejection of established norms simply in the name of individual freedom. However, he insists just as strongly that the established order must not be deified. The authentic ethical individual must always receive the established norms 'with fear and trembling', because such a person has a higher loyalty. We cannot rule out the possibility that God may require us to take a stand that will bring down the wrath of the

[19] Kierkegaard, *The Moment and Late Writings*.

[20] See Bruce Kirmmse, *Kierkegaard in Golden Age Denmark* (Bloomington, Ind.: Indiana University Press, 1990).

[21] See, for example, Kierkegaard, *Practice in Christianity*, 47–8, 83, 85–94, 87–92, 169–70, and many other passages from the late works and late journal entries.

establishment on us. When any human society forgets this, then it is in effect in rebellion against God's authority and it seeks to deify itself. When Christians identify their faith with the *Sittlichkeit* of a particular society they have betrayed their faith and become complicit in such a rebellion.

Kierkegaard's own position is actually stronger than the one I have sketched. Because of his strong belief in human sinfulness, he thinks that a genuine commitment to God's command to love the neighbour will not merely bring with it the possibility of opposition from the establishment. He thinks that such opposition is virtually guaranteed. The truly loving individual always faces the 'double danger'. Such individuals do not merely have to contend with their own temptations to lower the standard. If they successfully conquer this temptation they will face a second danger; namely that as a reward for their loving efforts they will incur opposition, resentment, and outright persecution.[22]

The truly loving person does not expect to usher in the New Jerusalem by his or her efforts. Rather, the genuine lover is merely a 'witness to the truth', a term with intentional connections to the New Testament term for 'martyr', a person whose witness to the truth was sealed by a willingness to die. Kierkegaard is careful to say that the witness to the truth does not seek persecution, much less martyrdom.[23] Such a stance would be genuinely unloving. However, Kierkegaard believes firmly that the genuine lover must be willing to accept such persecution when it is demanded by a person's calling. His own understanding of the Christian life implies that the faithful follower of Jesus must always be part of what might be called, borrowing another term from the 1960s, a counterculture. The identification of Christianity with a State or nation thus constitutes for him almost the greatest possible perversion of the faith. His divine command theory of moral obligation is therefore in no way a step along the road towards privileging Christianity or any other religion in the political sphere.

[22] There are many passages in Kierkegaard, *Works of Love* that discuss this 'double danger'. Some of the more characteristic can be found on pp. 81–2 and 194–204.

[23] See Kierkegaard, *Without Authority*, ed. and trans. Howard V. Hong and Edna H. Hong (Princeton: Princeton University Press, 1997), 51–89.

I think it is clear that Kierkegaard's own sympathies lie with the Anabaptist strains of Christian faith, as Vernard Eller argued nearly forty years ago.[24] In many ways he is close to such Christian groups as the Mennonites, Quakers, and Church of the Brethren. This can be seen in his advocacy of specific Anabaptist themes: pacifism, rejection of oath-taking, suspicion of infant baptism, and opposition to the State Church, among others.[25] But it comes through most clearly in his basic understanding of Christian discipleship as a form of witness to the wider community, with no hope that the wider community will fundamentally be transformed by that witness. Any form of Christian triumphalism is anathema to Kierkegaard, and the Constantinian fusion of Church and State is seen by him as a kind of 'fall' that the Church is still suffering from.[26]

I am far from underestimating the tremendous value this kind of countercultural witness can have for a society. Nevertheless, I think that Kierkegaard's divine command account of moral obligation can be usefully employed by Christians, Jews, and other people of goodwill who have a different perspective on the relation between religious communities and the civic polity. Both Catholics and Reformed Protestants, for example, see the State and other social organizations as divinely ordained institutions. On such a view, the follower of Jesus' commands should not merely form a countercultural community, but should seek to participate in and transform these God-given institutions, striving for justice and the good of all. We saw in Chapter 9 that Kierkegaard himself applauds the abolition of slavery and (at least up to a point) the emancipation of women as social transformations that have been made possible by the teaching that humans are to love their neighbours as themselves. (Though we also saw in that chapter that Kierkegaard unjustifiably and inconsistently seems to resist the idea of further social reforms in the service of love.)

---

[24] See Vernard Eller, *Kierkegaard and Radical Discipleship: A New Perspective* (Princeton: Princeton University Press, 1968).

[25] See ibid., 232 ff, 264 ff, 309 ff.

[26] For a fine discussion of this Constantinian fall, and the application of Kierkegaard's thought to the problem of violence, see Bellinger, *The Genealogy of Violence*, 98–133.

Can one engage in the quest for social transformation if one's basic moral stance is one that sees moral obligations as rooted in divine commands? I see no reason why not so long as the person is willing to admit, as Kierkegaard does, that the moral knowledge he or she uses as a foundation for such efforts is knowledge that is viewed as rooted in God's work in creation available through general revelation. Such a view still makes possible an appeal to common ground. To transform society it is not necessary to privilege one particular Church or revelation as an authority, even if many individuals and communities find nourishment and encouragement in particular Churches and revelations for the social tasks.

It is in fact such a 'transformer of culture' perspective that most needs to hear Kierkegaard's warnings about Christendom. It is only when such warnings are properly heeded that the deification of *Sittlichkeit* can be clearly avoided. Human efforts to transform human society can never be equated with the Kingdom of God itself, and any triumphalist gloating over whatever partial successes in social institutions have been achieved only blurs the line between what is truly transcendent and the temporal order. This is why even the 'transformer of culture' position must reject the idea of a Christian state, or any kind of privileging of a religion. It is not because an individual has doubts about the truth of his or her religious convictions that the person should oppose the establishing of his or her faith. It is precisely when the individual is convinced of religious truth that the person should be most opposed to such privileging. For what is genuinely divine and transcendent cannot be identified with the temporal order without being fatally compromised and falsified.

Kierkegaard affirms that love always acts to bring love out of the other by presupposing that love is already present in the other. Love presupposes love. I believe this principle implies, as I argued in Chapter 7, that Kierkegaard should not be quite so pessimistic as he is about the possibilities for embodying and expressing love in broader social practices and communities. It is hard to see how I can presuppose love as present in others and still see human societies as so thoroughly incapable of goodness that the genuine lover can only serve as a persecuted witness to the truth. Nevertheless, it is all the more important that the one who wishes to serve God and love the neighbour by faithfully working to transform his or her society understand that we humans are not God. Our victories are at best partial and incomplete and fundamentally they are not our victories at all, but victories for the Good.

One of the most powerful sections of *Works of Love* is entitled 'The Victory of the Conciliatory Spirit in Love, Which Wins the One Overcome' (pp. 331–49). This chapter of the book deals with some of the perils that attend the struggle of good with evil, the danger of self-righteousness and superiority that so easily creeps into even the noblest moral struggle. Kierkegaard does not have in mind here the hypocrite or the self-deceived person who merely baptizes self-interest by adding a moral veneer that disguises fundamentally selfish actions, but the individual who truly does stand for the good, who truly loves the good and the other, but who must battle someone devoted to evil. He imagines that the loving person has 'overcome' the evil person, not by any force or violence, but purely by lovingly repaying evil with good (p. 334). Kierkegaard says that the good individual in this situation is in moral peril:

The more good the one who loves has done for the unloving person, the longer he has persevered in repaying evil with good, the closer in a certain sense the danger comes that finally the evil overcomes the one who loves, ... (p. 334)

It is easy to understand this danger. It is only too easy for the person who has fought for the good in such a situation to feel superior; it is very hard indeed for the person on the side of the right to perceive his or her own need of reconciliation with the other. But that is precisely what love demands. The same God who commands us to love our neighbours as ourselves commands us to 'be reconciled' (p. 335). The achievement of reconciliation is particularly difficult; not only is there the temptation of the one who is loving to feel superior, but a natural tendency on the part of the one who has now repented to feel ashamed and humiliated (p. 338).

These problems cannot be resolved by relativistically pretending that evil was not evil. 'It would be a weakness, not love, to make the unloving one believe that he was right in the evil he did' (p. 338). To see the wisdom in this remark, one has only to think of genuine, monstrous evil. One cannot rightly trivialize the seriousness of rape, murder, and torture by assuring the perpetrator, even a repentant perpetrator, that the acts were really not so bad.

What is necessary in this situation is not to deny the seriousness of evil. Rather, Kierkegaard says that to be reconciled the two people need to bring between them 'a third party'. 'This third party, what thinkers would call the idea, is the true, the good, or more accurately, the God-relationship' (p. 339). Here we must recall Kierkegaard's claim that God is the 'middle-term' in every genuine love relation. The good person who is victorious over evil must become conscious of this third or middle term. What is essential is that the loving person acknowledge the transcendence of the Good. In relation to this transcendent power, even his or her own efforts on behalf of the Good are relativized.

The one who loves humbles himself before the good, whose lowly servant he is, and, as he himself admits, in frailty; and the one overcome does not humble himself before the loving one but before the good. But when in a relationship between two people both are humbled, then there of course is nothing humiliating for either one of them. (p. 340)

This common humility makes true reconciliation possible without eliminating the need for repentance:

Expressions of grief over the past, sorrow over his wrong, pleas for forgiveness—in a certain sense the loving one accepts all this, but in a holy abhorrence he promptly lays it aside, just as one lays aside something that is not one's due—that is, he intimates that this is not his due: he assigns it all to a higher category, and gives it to God as the one to whom it is due. This is the way love always conducts itself. (p. 341)

This is for Kierkegaard the essence of 'fear and trembling', living in the awareness that we humans are responsible to a higher power. It is just because this higher power must be a truly transcendent one that no human society may rightly be identified with God or God's concerns. It is only a God who is truly transcendent that can humanize and equalize human relationships in this way.

I believe that the person who believes in and is committed to a life devoted to serving such a God of love is indeed one who can make a vital contribution to civic and social life in a pluralistic society. It is true that such a person will not see human social life in time as the final destiny and highest end of human persons. Our ultimate destiny and highest end is life with God and others who love God in the heavenly banquet. However, Kierkegaard, like C. S. Lewis, was convinced that the person who believes in heaven is precisely the person who best understands earth.

If you read history you will find that the Christians who did most for the present world were just those who thought most of the next. The Apostles themselves, who set on foot the conversion of the Roman Empire, the great men who built up the Middle Ages, the English Evangelicals who abolished the Slave Trade, all left their mark on Earth, precisely because their minds were occupied with Heaven.... Aim at Heaven and you will get earth 'thrown in'; aim at earth and you will get neither.[27]

A divine command theory can thus be defended, not only as philosophically true, but as a theory whose widespread acceptance would have a humanizing, beneficial effect in a pluralistic, democratic society.

[27] C. S. Lewis, *Mere Christianity* (New York: Simon and Schuster, 1996), 119.

BIBLIOGRAPHY

ADAMS, ROBERT, 'Kierkegaard's Arguments Against Objective Reasoning in Religion', in *The Virtue of Faith and Other Essays* (Oxford: Oxford University Press, 1987).

—— 'The Leap of Faith', in *The Virtue of Faith and Other Essays* (Oxford: Oxford University Press, 1987).

—— 'A Modified Divine Command Theory of Ethical Wrongness', in *The Virtue of Faith and Other Essays* (Oxford: Oxford University Press, 1987).

—— 'Divine Commands and the Social Nature of Obligation', in Michael Beaty, Carlton Fisher, and Mark Nelson (eds.), *Christian Theism and Moral Philosophy* (Macon, Ga.: Mercer University Press, 1998).

—— *Finite and Infinite Goods* (Oxford: Oxford University Press, 1999).

—— 'Religious Ethics in a Pluralistic Society', in Gene Outka and John P. Reeder, Jr. (eds.), *Prospects for a Common Morality* (Princeton: Princeton University Press, 1993).

ADORNO, THEODORE, 'On Kierkegaard's Doctrine of Love', *Studies in Philosophy and Social Science*, 8 (1939–40).

ALSTON, WILLIAM, 'Some Suggestions for Divine Command Theorists', in *Divine Nature and Human Language: Essays in Philosophical Theology* (Ithaca, NY: Cornell University Press, 1989).

ANNAS, JULIA, *The Morality of Happiness* (Oxford: Oxford University Press, 1993).

ANSCOMBE, G. E. M., 'Modern Philosophy', *Philosophy*, 33/124 (Jan. 1958), repr. in Steven Cahn and Joram G. Haber (eds.), *Twentieth Century Ethical Theory* (Englewood Cliffs, NJ: Prentice-Hall, 1995).

AQUINAS, THOMAS, *Summa Theologica of St. Thomas Aquinas*, ii, trans. Fathers of the English Dominican Province (Westminster, Md.: Christian Classics, 1948).

ARISTOTLE, 'Nicomachean Ethics', *The Basic Works of Aristotle*, trans. W. D. Ross (New York: Random House, 1941).

ARNHART, LARRY, *Darwinian Natural Right: The Biological Ethics of Human Nature* (Albany, NY: State University of New York Press, 1998).

AUGUSTINE, *Confessions*, trans. F. J. Sheed (Cambridge, Mass.: Hackett Publishing Co., 1993).

BELLINGER, CHARLES, *The Genealogy of Violence: Reflections on Creation, Freedom, and Evil* (Oxford: Oxford University Press, 2001).

BENTHAM, JEREMY, *An Introduction to the Principles of Morals and Legislation* (New York: Hafner, 1948).

BOUMA-PREDIGER, STEVEN, *For the Beauty of the Earth: A Christian Vision for Creation Care* (Grand Rapids, Mich.: Baker Books, 2001).

BOYD, RICHARD, 'How to Be a Moral Realist', in Geoffrey Sayre-McCord (ed.), *Essays on Moral Realism* (Ithaca, NY: Cornell University Press, 1988).

BRADLEY, F. H., *Ethical Studies* (London: Oxford University Press, 1876).

CAPUTO, JOHN, *Radical Hermeneutics* (Bloomington, Ind.: Indiana University Press, 1987).

CUPITT, DON, *Taking Leave of God* (New York: Crossroad, 1981).

DAVENPORT, JOHN J., 'Towards an Existential Virtue Ethics: Kierkegaard and MacIntyre', in John J. Davenport and Anthony Rudd (eds.), *Kierkegaard After MacIntyre* (Chicago: Open Court, 2001).

DAVENPORT, JOHN J. and RUDD, ANTHONY (eds.), *Kierkegaard After MacIntyre* (Chicago: Open Court, 2001).

DAWKINS, RICHARD, *The Blind Watchmaker* (London: Penguin, 1986).

DEWEY, JOHN, *The Quest for Certainty* (New York: G. P. Putnam's Sons, 1929).

DOOLEY, MARK, *The Politics of Exodus: Kierkegaard's Ethics of Responsibility* (New York: Fordham University Press, 2001).

ELLER, VERNARD, *Kierkegaard and Radical Discipleship: A New Perspective* (Princeton: Princeton University Press, 1968).

EVANS, C. STEPHEN, *Subjectivity and Religious Belief* (Grand Rapids, Mich.: Wm. B. Eerdmans Publishing Co., 1978).

——*Kierkegaard's Fragments and Postscript: The Religious Philosophy of Johannes Climacus* (Atlantic Highlands, NJ: Humanities Press, 1983).

——'Kierkegaard and Plantinga on Belief in God: Subjectivity as the Ground of Properly Basic Beliefs', *Faith and Philosophy*, 5/1 (1988).

——'The Epistemological Significance of Transformative Religious Experience', *Faith and Philosophy*, 8/2 (1991).

——*Passionate Reason: Making Sense of Kierkegaard's* Philosophical Fragments (Bloomington, Ind.: Indiana University Press, 1992).

——'Faith as the Telos of Morality', in Robert L. Perkins (ed.), *Fear and Trembling and Repetition: International Kierkegaard Commentary* (Macon, Ga.: Mercer University Press, 1993), 9–27.

——'Who is the Other in *Sickness Unto Death*? God and Human Relations in the Constitution of the Self', in Niels Jørgen Cappelørn (ed.), *Kierkegaard Studies: Yearbook 1997* (Berlin: Walter de Gruyter, 1997).

—— 'A Kierkegaardian View of the Foundations of Morality', in Michael Beaty, Carlton Fisher, and Mark Nelson (eds.), *Christian Theism and Moral Philosophy* (Macon, Ga.: Mercer University Press, 1998).

—— 'Authority and Transcendence in *Works of Love*', in Niels Jørgen Cappelørn (ed.), *The Kierkegaard Studies: Yearbook 1998* (Berlin: Walter de Gruyter, 1998).

—— 'Kierkegaard on Religious Authority: The Problem of the Criterion', *Faith and Philosophy*, 17/1 (Jan. 2000).

FARBER, PAUL LAWRENCE, *The Temptations of Evolutionary Ethics* (Berkeley: University of California Press, 1994).

FENGER, HENNING, *Kierkegaard: The Myths and Their Origins: Studies in the Kierkegaardian Papers and Letters*, trans. George Schoolfield (New Haven: Yale University Press, 1980).

FERREIRA, JAMIE, *Love's Grateful Striving* (New York: Oxford University Press, 2001).

FINNIS, JOHN, *Natural Law and Natural Rights* (Oxford: Oxford University Press, 1980).

FLETCHER, JOSEPH, *Situation Ethics: The New Morality* (Philadelphia: Westminster Press, 1966).

FRANK, R., GILOVICH, T., and REGAN, D., 'Does Studying Economics Inhibit Cooperation?', *Journal of Economic Perspectives*, 7 (1993).

—— —— —— , "Do Economists Make Bad Citizens", *Journal of Economic Perspectives*, 10 (1996).

GAUTHIER, DAVID, *Morals by Agreement* (Oxford: Clarendon Press, 1986).

GEORGE, PETER, 'Something Anti-social about *Works of Love*', in George Pattison and Steven Shakespeare (eds.), *Kierkegaard: The Self in Society* (London: Macmillan, 1998).

GOOCH, PAUL, *Reflections on Jesus and Socrates: Word and Silence* (New Haven: Yale University Press, 1996).

HABERMAS, JURGEN, *Moral Consciousness and Communicative Action*, trans. Christian Lenhardt and Shierry Weber Nicholsen (Cambridge, Mass.: MIT Press, 1992).

HARE, JOHN, *The Moral Gap: Kantian Ethics and God's Assistance* (Oxford: Oxford University Press, 1996).

—— *God's Call: Moral Realism, God's Commands, and Human Autonomy* (Grand Rapids, Mich.: Wm. B. Eerdmans, 2001).

—— *Why Bother Being Good?* (Downers Grove, Ill.: InterVarsity Press, 2002).

HARMAN, GILBERT, 'Is There a Single True Morality?', in *Explaining Value and Other Essays in Moral Philosophy* (Oxford: Clarendon Press, 2000).

—— 'Justice and Moral Bargaining', in *Explaining Value and Other Essays in Moral Philosophy* (Oxford: Clarendon Press, 2000).

—— 'Moral Relativism Defended', in *Explaining Value and Other Essays in Moral Philosophy* (Oxford: Clarendon Press, 2000).

—— 'Relativistic Ethics: Morality as Politics', in *Explaining Value and Other Essays in Moral Philosophy* (Oxford: Clarendon Press, 2000).

—— 'What is Moral Relativism?', in *Explaining Value and Other Essays in Moral Philosophy* (Oxford: Clarendon Press, 2000).

HARMAN, GILBERT and THOMSON, JUDITH JARVIS, *Moral Relativism and Moral Objectivity* (Oxford: Blackwell, 1996).

HEIDEGGER, MARTIN, 'The Origin of the Work of Art', in David Krell (ed.), *Martin Heidegger: Basic Writings* (New York: Harper and Row, 1977).

HOBBES, THOMAS, *Leviathan*, ed. Richard Tuck (Cambridge: Cambridge University Press, 1996).

HUME, DAVID, *A Treatise of Human Nature* (Oxford: Oxford University Press, 1888).

HUNTER, JAMES, *The Death of Character: Moral Education in an Age Without Good or Evil* (New York: Perseus, 2000).

JACOBS, LOUIS, 'The Problem of the *Akedah* in Jewish Thought', in Robert L. Perkins (ed.), *Kierkegaard's* Fear and Trembling: *A Critical Appraisal* (Tuscaloosa, Ala.: University of Alabama Press, 1981).

KANT, IMMANUEL, *Critique of Practical Reason and Other Writings in Moral Philosophy*, trans. Lewis White Beck (Chicago: University of Chicago Press, 1949).

—— *Religion Within the Limits of Reason Alone*, trans. Theodore M. Greene and Hoyt H. Hudson (New York: Harper and Row, 1960).

—— *Groundwork of the Metaphysic of Morals*, trans. H. J. Paton (New York: Harper and Row, 1964).

—— *The Conflict of the Faculties*, trans. Mary J. Gregor (Lincoln, Nebr.: University of Nebraska Press, 1992).

KIERKEGAARD, SØREN, *Purity of Heart is to Will One Thing*, trans. Douglas V. Steere (New York: Harper and Brothers, 1956).

—— *Søren Kierkegaard's Journals and Papers*, ed. and trans. Howard V. Hong and Edna H. Hong (Bloomington, Ind.: Indiana University Press, 1967), i.

—— *Søren Kierkegaard's Journals and Papers*, ed. and trans. Howard V. Hong and Edna H. Hong (Bloomington, Ind.: Indiana University Press, 1975), iv.

—— *The Concept of Anxiety*, trans. Reidar Thomte (Princeton: Princeton University Press, 1980).
—— *The Sickness Unto Death*, ed. and trans. Howard V. Hong and Edna H. Hong (Princeton: Princeton University Press, 1980).
—— *Fear and Trembling*, ed. and trans. Howard V. Hong and Edna H. Hong (Princeton: Princeton University Press, 1983).
—— *Either/Or (2 vols.)* ed. and trans. Howard V. Hong and Edna H. Hong (Princeton: Princeton University Press, 1987).
—— *The Concept of Irony with Continual Reference to Socrates*, ed. and trans. Howard V. Hong and Edna H. Hong (Princeton: Princeton University Press, 1989).
—— *Practice in Christianity*, ed. and trans. Howard V. Hong and Edna H. Hong (Princeton: Princeton University Press, 1991).
—— *Concluding Unscientific Postscript*, ed. and trans. Howard V. Hong and Edna H. Hong (Princeton: Princeton University Press, 1992).
—— *Upbuilding Discourses in Various Spirits*, ed. and trans. Howard V. Hong and Edna H. Hong (Princeton: Princeton University Press, 1993).
—— *Works of Love*, ed. and trans. Howard V. Hong and Edna H. Hong (Princeton: Princeton University Press, 1995).
—— *Without Authority*, ed. and trans. Howard V. Hong and Edna H. Hong (Princeton: Princeton University Press, 1997).
—— *The Moment and Late Writings*, ed. and trans. Howard V. Hong and Edna H. Hong (Princeton: Princeton University Press, 1998).
—— *The Book on Adler*, ed. and trans. Howard V. Hong and Edna H. Hong (Princeton: Princeton University Press, 1998).
—— *The Point of View*, ed. and trans. Howard V. Hong and Edna H. Hong (Princeton: Princeton University Press, 1998).
KIRMMSE, BRUCE, *Kierkegaard in Golden Age Denmark* (Bloomington, Ind.: Indiana University Press, 1990).
—— 'On Authority and Revolution: Kierkegaard's Road to Politics', in Niels Jørgen Cappelørn and Jon Stewart (eds.), *Kierkegaard Revisited* (New York: Walter de Gruyter, 1997), 254–73.
KUYPER, ABRAHAM, *Lectures on Calvinism* (Grand Rapids, Mich.: Eerdmans, 1931).
LEON, CELINE and WALSH, SYLVIA (eds.), *Feminist Interpretations of Søren Kierkegaard* (University Park, Pa.: Pennsylvania State University Press, 1997).
LEWIS, C. S., *Mere Christianity* (New York: Simon and Schuster, 1996).
LIPPITT, JOHN, *Humor and Irony in Kierkegaard's Thought* (New York: St. Martin's Press, 2000).

LISSKA, ANTHONY, *Aquinas's Theory of Natural Law* (Oxford: Oxford University Press, 1996).

LOCKE, JOHN, *Two Treatises of Government*, ed. Thomas I. Cook (New York: Hafner, 1947).

LØGSTRUP, KNUD E., 'Opgør med Kierkegaards *Kaerlighedens Gerninger*', *Den Ethiske Fordring* (Copenhagen: Gyldendal, 1956), trans. as 'Settling Accounts with Kierkegaard's *Works of Love*', in Hans Fink and Alasdair MacIntyre (eds.), *The Ethical Demand* (Notre Dame, Ind.: University of Notre Dame Press, 1997).

MABRY, MARCUS, 'The Price Tag of Freedom', *Newsweek* (3 May 1999).

MCCULLOUGH, MICHAEL, 'The Psychology of Forgiveness', in C. R. Snyder and Shane J. Lopez (eds.), *Handbook of Positive Psychology* (Oxford: Oxford University Press, 2002).

MACINTYRE, ALASDAIR, *After Virtue*, 2nd edn. (Notre Dame, Ind.: University of Notre Dame Press, 1984).

MCKINNON, ALASTAIR, 'Kierkegaard and His Pseudonyms: a Preliminary Report', *Kierkegaardiana* (Copenhagen: Munksgard, 1968).

MACKEY, LOUIS, *Points of View: Readings of Kierkegaard* (Tallahassee, Fla.: Florida State University Press, 1986).

MALANTSCHUK, GREGOR, *Kierkegaard's Thought*, ed. and trans. Howard V. Hong and Edna H. Hong (Princeton: Princeton University Press, 1971).

MAVRODES, GEORGE, 'Religion and the Queerness of Morality', in Robert Audi (ed.), *Rationality, Religious Belief, and Moral Commitment* (Ithaca, NY: Cornell University Press, 1986).

MAXWELL, G. and AMES, R., 'Economists Free Ride, Does Anyone Else?', *Journal of Public Economics*, 15 (1981).

MILL, JOHN STUART, *Utilitarianism* (Oxford: Oxford University Press, 1998).

MOONEY, EDWARD, *Knights of Faith and Resignation: Reading Kierkegaard's* Fear and Trembling (Albany NY: SUNY Press, 1991).

——'Getting Isaac Back: Ordeals and Reconciliations in *Fear and Trembling*', in George Connell and C. Stephen Evans (eds.), *Foundations of Kierkegaard's Vision of Community: Religion, Ethics, and Politics in Kierkegaard* (Atlantic Highlands, NJ: Humanities Press, 1992), 71–95.

MOORE, G. E., *Principia Ethica* (Cambridge: Cambridge University Press, 1903).

MURDOCH, IRIS, *The Sovereignty of Good* (New York: Shocken Books, 1971).

NIEBUHR, H. RICHARD, *Christ and Culture* (New York: Harper, 1956).

NIETZSCHE, FRIEDRICH, *On the Genealogy of Morals* and *Ecco Homo*, trans. Walter Kaufmann and R. J. Hollingdale (New York: Random House, 1969).

NOWELL-SMITH, PATRICK, *Ethics* (Baltimore: Penguin, 1961).

NUSSBAUM, MARTHA, 'Aristotle on Human Nature and the Foundation of Ethics', in J. E. J. Altham and Ross Harrison (eds.), *World, Mind, and Ethics: Essays on the Ethical Philosophy of Bernard Williams* (New York: Cambridge University Press, 1995), 86–131.

OUTKA, GENE, 'Religious and Moral Duty: Notes on *Fear and Trembling*', in Gene Outka and John P. Reeder, Jr. (eds.), *Religion and Morality* (Garden City, NY: Anchor Books, 1973).

PALEY, WILLIAM, *Natural Theology* (originally published 1802), (Houston: St. Thomas Press, 1972)

PLANTINGA, ALVIN, 'Reason and Belief in God', in Alvin Plantinga and Nicholas Wolterstorff (eds.), *Faith and Rationality* (Notre Dame, Ind.: University of Notre Dame Press, 1983).

PLATO, *Apology* in *The Collected Dialogues of Plato*, eds. Edith Hamilton and Huntington Cairns, trans.Hugh Tredennick (Princeton: Princeton University Press, 1963).

POOLE, ROGER, *Kierkegaard: The Indirect Communication* (Charlottesville, Va.: University Press of Virginia, 1993).

—— 'The Unknown Kierkegaard: Twentieth Century Receptions', in Alastair Hannay and Gordon D. Marino (eds.) *The Cambridge Companion to Kierkegaard* (Cambridge: Cambridge University Press, 1998), 18–75.

QUINN, PHILIP, *Divine Commands and Moral Requirements* (Oxford: Oxford University Press, 1979).

—— 'Divine Command Ethics: A Causal Theory', in Janine M. Idziak (ed.), *Divine Command Morality: Historical and Contemporary Readings* (New York: Edwin Mellem Press, 1979).

—— 'Moral Obligation, Religious Demand, and Practical Conflict', in Robert Audi and William Wainwright (eds.), *Rationality, Religious Belief, and Moral Commitment* (Ithaca, NY: Cornell University Press, 1986).

—— 'The Recent Revival of Divine Command Ethics', *Philosophy and Phenomenological Research*, 50, suppl. (Fall 1990), 345–65.

—— 'The Divine Command Ethics in Kierkegaard's *Works of Love*', in Jeff Jordan and Daniel Howard-Snyder (eds.), *Faith, Freedom and Rationality* (Lanham, Md.: Rowman and Littlefield, 1996).

—— 'Kierkegaard's Christian Ethics', in Alastair Hannay and Gordon Marino (eds.), *The Cambridge Companion to Kierkegaard* (Cambridge: Cambridge University Press, 1998).

—— 'The Primacy of God's Will in Christian Ethics', in Michael Beaty, Carlton Fisher, and Mark Nelson (eds.), *Christian Theism and Moral Philosophy* (Macon, Ga.: Mercer University Press, 1998).

—— 'Divine Command Theory', in Hugh La Follette (ed.), *The Blackwell Guide to Ethical Theory* (Oxford: Blackwell, 2000), 53–73.

—— 'Unity and Disunity, Harmony and Discord: A Response to Lillegard and Davenport', in John J. Davenport and Anthony Rudd (eds.), *Kierkegaard after MacIntyre* (Chicago: Open Court Publishing Co., 2001).

RACHELS, JAMES, *The Elements of Moral Philosophy*, 2nd edn. (New York: McGraw Hill, 1993).

RATZSCH, DEL, *Science and Its Limits: The Natural Sciences in Christian Perspective* (Downers Grove, Ill.: InterVarsity Press, 2000).

RAWLS, JOHN, *A Theory of Justice* (Cambridge, Mass.: Harvard University Press, 1971).

ROBERTS, ROBERT C., 'What is an Emotion: A Sketch', *Philosophical Review*, 97 (1988), 183–209.

—— 'Feeling One's Emotions and Knowing One's Self', *Philosophical Studies*, 77 (1995), 319–38.

—— 'Existence, Emotion, and Virtue: Classical Themes in Kierkegaard', in Alastair Hannay and Gordon Marino (eds.), *The Cambridge Companion to Kierkegaard* (Cambridge: Cambridge University Press, 1998).

RORTY, RICHARD, 'The Contingency of Language', *Contingency, Irony, and Solidarity* (New York: Cambridge University Press, 1989).

—— *Philosophy and Social Hope* (New York: Penguin, 1999).

—— 'Religion in the Public Square: A Reconsideration', *Journal of Religious Ethics*, 31/1: 141–9.

RUDD, ANTHONY, *Kierkegaard and the Limits of the Ethical* (Oxford: Oxford University Press, 1993).

RUSE, MICHAEL, *Can a Darwinian Be a Christian? The Relationship between Science and Religion* (Cambridge: Cambridge University Press, 2001).

SARTRE, JEAN-PAUL, *Being and Nothingness*, trans. Hazel E. Barnes (New York: Washington Square Press, 1966).

SCHLEIERMACHER, FRIEDRICH, *On Religion: Speeches to its Cultured Despisers*, ed. Richard Crouter (Cambridge: Cambridge University Press, 1988).

Scotus, John Duns, 'Individuation, Universals, and Common Nature', *Ordinatio*, II, in William A. Frank and Allan Wolter (eds.), *Duns Scotus, Metaphysician* (West Lafayette, Ind.: Purdue University Press, 1995).

Summers, Richard M., ' "Controlled Irony" and the Emergence of the Self in Kierkegaard's Dissertation', in Robert L. Perkins (ed.), *The Concept of Irony: International Kierkegaard Commentary* (Macon, Ga.: Mercer University Press, 2001).

Taylor, Charles, 'Self-Interpreting Animals', *Human Agency and Human Language: Philosophical Papers*, I (Cambridge: Cambridge University Press, 1985).

Taylor, Mark Lloyd, 'Practice in Authority: The Apostolic Women of Søren Kierkegaard's Writings', in Poul Houe (ed.), *Anthropology and Authority: Essays on Søren Kierkegaard* (Atlanta, Ga.: Rodopi, 2000).

Veatch, Henry, *Aristotle: A Contemporary Appreciation* (Bloomington, Ind.: Indiana University Press, 1974).

Westphal, Merold, 'Abraham and Hegel', in *Kierkegaard's Critique of Reason and Society* (Macon, Ga.: Mercer University Press, 1987).

—— *Becoming a Self: A Reading of Kierkegaard's* Concluding Unscientific Postscript (West Lafayette, Ind.: Purdue University Press, 1996).

Wierenga, Edward, 'A Defensible Divine Command Theory', *Nous*, 17 (Jan. 1983).

—— *The Nature of God* (Ithaca, NY: Cornell University Press, 1989).

Williams, Bernard, *Moral Luck: Philosophical Papers* (New York: Cambridge University Press, 1981).

Wilson, Edward O., *Sociobiology* (Cambridge, Mass.: Harvard University Press, 1975).

—— *On Human Nature* (Cambridge, Mass.: Harvard University Press, 1978).

Wittgenstein, Ludwig, *Philosophical Investigations*, 3rd edn., trans. G. E. M. Anscombe (New York: the Macmillan co., 1968).

Witvliet, Charlotte, Ludwig, Thomas E., and Vander Laan, Kelly L., 'Granting Forgiveness or Harboring Grudges: Implications for Emotion, Physiology, and Health', *Psychological Science*, 121/2 (Mar. 2001).

Wolterstorff, Nicholas, 'Audi on Religion, Politics, and Liberal Democracy', in Robert Audi and Nicholas Wolterstorff, *Religion in the Public Square*, (Lanham, Md.: Rowman and Littlefield, 1997).

—— 'Why We Should Reject What Liberalism Tells Us about Speaking and Acting for Religious Reasons', in *Religion and Contemporary*

Liberalism, ed. Paul J. Weithman (Notre Dame, Ind.: University of Notre Dame Press, 1997).

YEZER, A., GOLDFARB, R., and POPPEN, P., 'Does Studying Economics Discourage Cooperation? Watch What We Do, Not What We Say or How We Play?', *Journal of Economic Perspectives*, 10 (1996).

INDEX